Praise for *The Good Girls Revolt*:

"Povich's account of the case unspools with a cinematic energy.... But *The Good Girls Revolt* is powerful in part because it doesn't seek to tie up the messy, imperfect, real-life events with a neat bow of made-for-TV, proto-you-go-girl closure.... In delving into a piece of women's history and exploring its legacy for women today, *The Good Girls Revolt* is both a compelling case study and a reminder that we shouldn't be too quick to append the prefix 'post' to the word 'feminism.'"
　　—*Los Angeles Review of Books*

"A powerful chronicle of how—in the context of wider social ferment—institutions can be forced to evolve.... [Povich] does not shy away from the emotional and political complexity of feminist struggle."　　—*Ms. Magazine*

"*The Good Girls Revolt* is as compelling as any novel, and also an accurate, intimate history of new women journalists invading the male journalistic world of the 1970s. Lynn Povich turns this epic revolt into a lesson on why and how we've just begun."
　　—**Gloria Steinem**

"The personal and the political are deftly interwoven in the fast-moving narrative.... *The Good Girls Revolt* has many timely lessons for working women who are concerned about discrimination today.... [T]his sparkling, informative book may help move these goals a tiny bit closer."
　　—*New York Times*

"A meticulously reported and highly readable account of a pivotal time in the women's movement."　　—**Jeannette Walls**

"Feminist history at its best. Povich evokes, with clear-eyed affection and a keen sense of history the heady atmosphere of 'Swinging Sixties'-era *Newsweek*: a real-life Mad Men with a social

conscience and sense of mission. . . . The transformation of Povich—who subsequently became *Newsweek*'s first female senior editor—and her colleagues from polite, deferential girls to women of courage forms the heart of this lively, engaging book."
        —*Publishers Weekly*

"Solidly researched and should interest readers who care about feminist history and how gender issues play out in the culture."
        —*Boston Globe*

"Povich's memoir of the tortuous, landmark battle that paved the way for a generation of female writers and editors is illuminating in its details [and] casts valuable perspective on a trailblazing case that shouldn't be forgotten."   —*Macleans*

"[Povich] strikes a fair tone, neither naïve nor sanctimonious. . . . Among her achievements is a complex portrait of *Newsweek* editor Osborn Elliott and his path from defensive adversary to understanding ally."   —*American Journalism Review*

"Crisp, revealing. . . . [A] taut, firsthand account of how a group of razor-sharp, courageous women successfully fought back against institutional sexism at one of the country's most esteemed publications."   —*Washingtonian*

"Women still have a long way to go, the journalist Lynn Povich rousingly reminds readers in *The Good Girls Revolt*, her fascinating (and long overdue) history of the class-action lawsuit undertaken by four dozen female researchers and underlings at *Newsweek* magazine four decades ago. . . . If ever a book could remind women to keep their white gloves off and to keep fighting the good fight, this is the one."
        —Liesl Schillinger, *New York Times*

"Povich's in-depth research, narrative skills, and eyewitness observations provide an entertaining and edifying look at a pivotal event in women's history." —*Kirkus Reviews*

"With vivid recollections of the author and major and minor participants, Povich, a party to the suit, succeeds in making recent history enraging, poignant, and even sexy."
—*Philadelphia Inquirer*

"[H]er storytelling is compelling and she ably makes the case for the debt still owed to all forty-six *Newsweek* women for their willingness to 'take off the white gloves.' Quickly-paced social history for media, feminism, and history buffs."
—*Library Journal*

"A painstakingly researched story of one of the seminal events affecting the rights of women in the American work place in the early years of the women's movement. . . . I would recommend this volume especially to young women who were born long after the struggles fought by their mothers and grandmothers."
—Rabbi John Rosove, JewishJournal.com

"*The Good Girls Revolt* . . . is a book that needed to be written. Those of us who came of age during those years can relate to the courage it took to fight for equality. . . . This story is not just a Who's Who of feminist achievement, but an honest portrayal of the battles of a few meant to benefit not only themselves but those who came after them. Young women of today will benefit from being reminded about what it took to secure their places in today's workplace and far beyond."
—*New York Journal of Books*

THE
GOOD GIRLS REVOLT

How the Women of *Newsweek*
Sued their Bosses and Changed the Workplace

Lynn Povich

PublicAffairs
New York

Published in the United States by PublicAffairs™, an imprint of Perseus Books,
a division of PBG Publishing, LLC, a subsidiary of Hachette Book Group, Inc.
First paperback edition published in 2016 by PublicAffairs

Printed in the United States of America.

PublicAffairs books are available at special discounts for bulk purchases in the U.S.
by corporations, institutions, and other organizations. For more information, please
contact the Special Markets Department at Perseus Books, 2300 Chestnut Street,
Suite 200, Philadelphia, PA 19103, call (800) 810-4145, ext. 5000, or e-mail
special.markets@perseusbooks.com.

Book Design by Pauline Brown
Typeset in 11.75 point Adobe Garamond Pro by the Perseus Books Group

The Library of Congress has cataloged the printed edition as follows:
Library of Congress Cataloging-in-Publication Data

Povich, Lynn.
    The good girls revolt : how the women of Newsweek sued their bosses and changed the
workplace / Lynn Povich.—1st ed.
        p.   cm.
    Includes bibliographical references and index.
    ISBN 978-1-61039-173-3 (hardcover)—ISBN 978-1-61039-326-3 (paperback)—
ISBN 978-1-61039-174-0 (electronic)
    1. Sex role in the work environment—United States. 2. Sex discrimination in
employment—United States. 3. Women journalists—United States. 4. Newsweek.
I. Title.
HD6060.5.U5P65   2012
331.4'81070572—dc23

ISBN 978-1-61039-746-9 (2016 paperback)

For Steve, Sarah, and Ned
and for the *Newsweek* women

CONTENTS

Photo insert between pages 124–125

PROLOGUE

WHAT WAS THE PROBLEM?

JESSICA BENNETT GREW UP in the era of Girl Power. It was the 1980s, when young women were told there was no limit to what they could accomplish. The daughter of a Seattle attorney, Jessica regularly attended Take Your Daughter to Work Day with her dad and was the academic star in her family, excelling over her younger brothers and male peers. In high school, she was a member of Junior Statesmen of America, a principal in the school orchestra, and a varsity soccer player. Jessica was accepted to the University of Southern California, her first choice, but transferred after freshman year to Boston University because it had a stronger journalism program. When the *Boston Globe* offered a single internship to a BU student, she was the recipient.

Then Jessica got a job at *Newsweek* and suddenly encountered obstacles she couldn't explain. She had started as an intern on the magazine in January 2006 and was about to be hired when three guys showed up for summer internships. At the end of the summer, the men were offered jobs but Jessica wasn't, even though she was given one of their stories to rewrite. Despite the fact that she was writing three times a week on *Newsweek*'s website, her internship kept getting extended. Even after she was hired in January 2007, Jessica had to battle to get her articles published, while guys with the same or less experience were getting better assignments and faster promotions. "Initially I didn't identify it as a gender issue," she recalled. "But several of us women had been feeling like we weren't doing a good job or accomplishing what we wanted to. We didn't feel like we were being heard."

Being female was not something that ever held Jessica back. "I was used to getting everything I wanted and working hard for it," said the twenty-eight-year-old writer at Newsweek.com, "so my feeling was, why do I need feminism? Why do I need to take a women's studies course? And, of course, there was the stereotype of the feminist—the angry, man-hating, granola-crunching, combat-boot-wearing woman. I don't know that I consciously thought that, but I think a lot of young women do. I went to public school in the inner city, so issues of racial justice were more interesting to me than gender because, frankly, gender wasn't really an issue."

Her best friend at *Newsweek*, Jesse Ellison, was also frustrated. She had recently discovered that the guy who replaced her in her previous job was given a significantly higher salary. She was doing well as the number two to the editor of Scope, the opening section of the magazine that featured inside scoops and breaking news. But that summer, a half-dozen college-age "dudes" had come in as summer interns and suddenly the department turned into a frat house. Guys were high-fiving, turning the TV from CNN to ESPN, constantly invading her cubicle, and asking her, as if she were their mother, whether they should microwave their lunches. They were also getting assigned stories while she had to pitch all her ideas. Since a new boss had taken over, Jesse felt as if she had been demoted. She didn't know what to do.

Jesse, thirty, sought the advice of a trusted editor who had been a mentor to her. He told her, "You're senior to them—shame them." Then he said, "The problem is that you're so pretty you need to figure out a way to use your sexuality to your advantage," she recalled, still incredulous about the remark. "Even though I think he was just being an idiot for saying this—because he had really fought for me—hearing that changed my perception of the previous six months. I was like, 'Wait a minute! Were you being an advocate for me because you think I'm pretty and you want me in your office? And, more important, is this what other people in the office think? Not that I'm actually talented, but this is about something else?' It really screwed with my head."

Jesse had grown up in a conservative town outside Portland, Maine. Her mother, a former hippie who was divorced, had started a small baby-accessories business. During the Clarence Thomas Supreme Court hearings, Jesse was the only one in her eighth-grade class to support Anita Hill. She went to a coed boarding school, where she was valedictorian of her class, and then to Barnard, an all-women's college, where she graduated cum laude. She, too, never took a women's studies course. "I just felt like I didn't need it," she said. "Feminism was a given—it was Barnard!" After a brief job at a nonprofit, she enrolled part-time in Columbia University's Graduate School of Journalism. She also got an internship on the foreign language editions of *Newsweek* and was hired full-time when she graduated with her master's degree in June 2008. But now, a year later, she, too, was struggling to move ahead at *Newsweek*. What was the problem?

"It wasn't like I believed that sexism *didn't* exist," said Jesse. "It was just that it didn't occur to me that what was happening at work was sexism. Maybe it's because we are a highly individualized culture now and I had always done really well. So I just assumed that everything that was happening was on the basis of merit. I grew up reading *Newsweek* and I had tremendous respect for it. I felt like, I'm in this world of real thinkers and writers and I have to prove myself. The fact that I wasn't being given assignments was simply an indication that they didn't think I was good enough yet. It didn't occur to me that it was about anything else. For the first time in my life, I was feeling inadequate and insecure."

Jessica Bennett felt the same way. "Maybe it's a female tendency to turn inward and blame yourself, but I never thought about sexism," she said. "We had gotten to the workforce and then something suddenly changed and we didn't know what it was. After all, we had always accomplished everything we had set out to do, so naturally we would think *we* were doing something wrong—not that there *was* something wrong. It was us, not it."

What *was* the problem? After all, women composed nearly 40 percent of the *Newsweek* masthead in 2009. It wasn't like the old days, when there was a ghetto of women in the research department from which they couldn't get promoted. In fact, there were no longer researchers on the magazine, except in the library. Young editorial employees now started as researcher-reporters. There were women writers at *Newsweek*, several female columnists and senior editors, and at least two women in top management. Ann McDaniel, a former *Newsweek* reporter and top editor, was now the managing director of the magazine in charge of both the business and editorial sides—a first. So it couldn't be that old thing called discrimination that was inhibiting their progress. The fight for equality had been won. Women could do anything now at *Newsweek* and elsewhere. Hadn't Maria Shriver's report on American women just come out in October 2009, declaring, "The battle of the sexes is over"?

Jesse and Jessica stewed about the situation, discussing it with other *Newsweek* women and friends outside the magazine, who, it turned out, were also feeling discouraged in their careers. "It felt so good just talking to each other," recalled Jesse. "It was like, 'Oh my God, I'm so sick of feeling silent and scared. It's not fair and we should say something.' That impulse was great; knowing that 'I'm not alone' was empowering."

One day Jen Molina, a *Newsweek* video producer, was talking about the magazine's "old boys club" to Tony Skaggs, a veteran researcher in the library. Tony informed her that many years before, the women at *Newsweek* had sued the magazine's management on the grounds of sex discrimination. Jen was shocked. She had no idea this had happened—and at her own magazine. She told Jessica, who told Jesse, and the two friends began investigating. Jessica immediately Googled "*Newsweek* lawsuit" and "women sue *Newsweek*" but she couldn't find any reference online. "Funny," she remarked, "we're trained in digital journalism, so we think if it's not on Google, it doesn't exist."

A few weeks later, Tony walked into Jessica's office with a worn copy of Susan Brownmiller's vivid chronicle of the women's movement, *In Our Time: Memoir of a Revolution*. A crumpled Post-it note marked the chapter mentioning a lawsuit at *Newsweek* in 1970, almost forty years earlier. "I just remember sitting at my desk reading it," she said, "and every two sentences saying, 'Holy shit,' because I couldn't believe this had happened and I didn't know about it! So I instant-messaged Jesse and said, 'You have to get over here and read this.' Why didn't we know this? Why has this died? And why was there only one person in the research department who had to get this book for us to let us know about it?"

When they read about the case, it all seemed so familiar. "We realized we were far from the first to feel discrimination," said Jesse. "So much of the language and culture was still the same. It helped drive home the fact that it was still the same place, the same institutional knowledge, the same *Newsweek*."

This happened in the fall of 2009, just as a scandal at CBS's *Late Show with David Letterman* was making headlines. Joe

Halderman, a CBS News producer who was living with one of Letterman's assistants, had found her diary revealing her on-going affair with her boss. Halderman threatened to expose the relationship if Letterman didn't give him $2 million. On October 1, Letterman confessed—on air—that yes, "I have had sex with women who work for me on this show." That same month, ESPN analyst Steve Phillips, a former general manager for the New York Mets baseball team, was fired from the sports network after admitting that he had an affair with a twenty-two-year-old production assistant. In November, editor Sandra Guzman, who was fired from the *New York Post,* filed a complaint against the newspaper and its editor-in-chief alleging "unlawful employment practices and retaliation" as well as sexual harassment and a hostile work environment. (The case is pending in Manhattan federal court.)

The Letterman scandal infuriated Sarah Ball, a twenty-three-year-old Culture reporter at *Newsweek,* particularly after she read an article by a former Letterman writer. "I was galvanized by Nell Scovell's story on VanityFair.com," recalled Sarah, who cited the beginning of the piece by heart: "At this moment, there are more females serving on the United States Supreme Court than there are writing for *Late Show with David Letterman, The Jay Leno Show,* and *The Tonight Show with Conan O'Brien* combined. Out of the fifty or so comedy writers working on these programs, exactly zero are women. It would be funny if it weren't true." Sarah told her editor, Marc Peyser, about the piece and in the course of the conversation, Peyser suggested a story on young women in the workforce, pegged to the scandals. "He was really into it," Sarah recalled. "He kept saying, 'This could be a cover, this could be a cover.'" Sarah, who had seen the Brownmiller book, immediately told Jessica and Jesse about Peyser's interest. The three women went back into his office and pitched a story combining the old and new elements. "It was perfect," said Jesse. "It was bigger than us, we had our own narrative that we felt was important, and there was the forthcoming fortieth anniversary of the lawsuit in March."

Peyser had heard about the lawsuit and told them that it had gone all the way to the US Supreme Court. That night, Jesse started searching online through all the 1970 Supreme Court cases but found nothing mentioning *Newsweek*. "We knew there was something about a lawsuit," she said, "but we didn't know what it meant." Jessica finally paid to search the *New York Times* archives, where several articles on the lawsuit turned up. "I was bouncing out of my chair I was so excited," she said. "We knew we had to do something but it still wasn't clear from those clips whether the suit had been settled or whether it actually went to court."

The three women spent the next few weeks digging deeper and calling various sources, including Susan Brownmiller and some former *Newsweek* women whose names were mentioned in the book. I was one of the women. Jessica and Jesse contacted me when they learned that I was writing about the case. They wanted to find out what had happened and why. They were determined to write a piece for *Newsweek* questioning how much had actually changed for women at the magazine, in the media, and in the workplace in general.

When I met the two young women for lunch, they reminded me so much of my friends and myself forty years earlier. We, too, had been bright young things, full of energy and expectations. We also had been thrilled to be working at an important magazine and we, too, had begun to realize that something wasn't right at *Newsweek*. But if they were post-feminists, we were pre-feminists. Unlike these young women, many of us were far more conflicted about our ambitions and clueless about having a career. My only desire after college was to go to Paris, and I was lucky enough to get a job there as a secretary in the *Newsweek* bureau. I never imagined that five years later, I would be suing the magazine for sex discrimination.

As I listened to Jessica and Jesse struggle to understand what they were feeling—their marginalization, the sexual banter and innuendo, the career cakewalk for men their age—it reminded me of "the problem that had no name" that Betty Friedan had defined in her 1963 groundbreaking book, *The Feminine Mystique*: that "strange stirring, a sense of dissatisfaction" of the American housewife who, "as she made the beds, shopped for groceries, matched slipcover material, ate peanut butter sandwiches with her children, chauffeured Cub Scouts and Brownies, lay beside her husband at night—she was afraid to ask even of herself the silent question—'Is this all?'"

Friedan's "problem" did not apply to working-class women, who had to earn a living but were confined mainly to low-paying jobs. It described the condition of the postwar suburban house-wife. Although many middle-class women had been recruited to work during World War II, they were forced to go home when the soldiers returned. For educated women, whose husbands could support them, *not* having to work was seen as a status symbol until, as Betty Friedan pointed out, many of them realized they wanted—needed—something more than a husband and children.

Finding meaningful work, however, was not easy. In just about every industry, "office work" for women meant secretarial jobs and typing pools. Even in creative fields, such as book publishing, advertising, and journalism, where there was a pool of educated females, women were given menial jobs. In the 1950s, full-time working women earned on average between fifty-nine and sixty-four cents for every dollar men earned in the same job. (It wasn't until the passage of the Equal Pay Act in June 1963 that it became illegal to pay women a lower rate for the same job.) And there were very few professional women. Until around 1970, women comprised fewer than 10 percent of students in medical school, 4 percent of law school students, and only 3 percent of business school students.

At *Newsweek,* our "problem that had no name" in the mid-1960s was sexism, pure and simple. At both *Time* and *Newsweek,* only men were hired as writers. Women were almost always hired on the mail desk or as fact checkers and rarely promoted to reporter or writer. Even with similar credentials, women ended up in lesser positions than men. One year, two Columbia Journalism School graduates were hired—

Paul Zimmerman as a writer and Ann Ray Martin as a researcher/reporter. That's just the way it was, and we all accepted it.

Until we didn't. Just as young women today are discovering that post-feminism isn't really "post," we were discovering that civil rights didn't include women's rights. Just like Jesse, Jessica, and Sarah, we began to realize that something was very wrong with the *Newsweek* system. With great trepidation, we decided to take on what we saw as a massive injustice: a segregated system of journalism that divided research, reporting, writing, and editing roles solely on the basis of gender. We began organizing in secret, terrified that we would be found out—and fired—at any moment. For most of us middle-class ladies, standing up for our rights marked the first time we had done anything political or feminist. It would be the radicalizing act that gave us the confidence and the courage to find ourselves and stake our claim.

***

THIS BOOK IS THE FIRST full account of that landmark *Newsweek* case, the story of how and why we became the first women in the media to sue for sex discrimination. Like *Mad Men*, the popular TV series on life at an advertising agency in the 1960s, not only does our tale reflect the legal and cultural limits for women at the time, but it also is a coming-of-age story about a generation of "good girls" who found ourselves in the revolutionary '60s. But if our pioneering lawsuit has been forgotten by many people, even at *Newsweek*, our fight for women's rights still reverberates with the younger generation.

There have been many victories. Women today have more opportunities and solid legal support. They are more confident, more career-oriented, and more aggressive in getting what they want than most of us were. But many of the injustices that young women face today are the same ones we fought against forty years ago. The discrimination may be subtler, but sexist attitudes still exist.

Jessica, Jesse, and Sarah, and many young women like them, are beginning to understand that legal principles are not the only impediment to power. They see that the rhetoric they were taught—and believed—does not fully exist in the real world; that women still don't have equal rights and equal opportunities; that cultural transformation is harder than legal reform; and that feminism isn't finished. The struggle for social change is still evolving, and now they realize that they are part of it, too.

Here is our story.

CHAPTER 1

"Editors File Story;
Girls File Complaint"

ON MARCH 16, 1970, *Newsweek* magazine hit the news-stands with a cover story on the fledgling feminist movement titled "Women in Revolt." The bright yellow cover pictured a naked woman in red silhouette, her head thrown back, provocatively thrusting her fist through a broken blue female-sex symbol. As the first copies went on sale that Monday morning, forty-six female employees of *Newsweek* announced that we, too, were in revolt. We had just filed a complaint with the Equal Employment Opportunity Commission charging that we had been "systematically discriminated against in both hiring and promotion and forced to assume a subsidiary role" simply because we were women. It was the first time women in the media had sued on the grounds of sex discrimination and the story, irresistibly timed to the *Newsweek* cover, was picked up around the world.

"'Discriminate,' le redattrici di *Newsweek?*" (*La Stampa*)
"Newsweek's Sex Revolt" (*London Times*)
"Editors File Story; Girls File Complaint" (*Newsday*)
"Women Get Set for Battle" (*London Daily Express*)
"As Newsweek Says, Women Are in Revolt, Even on Newsweek" (*New York Times*)

The story in the *New York Daily News,* titled "Newshens Sue Newsweek for 'Equal Rights,'" began, "Forty-six women on the staff of *Newsweek* magazine, most of them young and most of them pretty, announced today they were suing the magazine."

The UPI photograph capturing the announcement shows three young white women sitting alongside our attorney, a serious black woman with an imposing Afro. Behind them are pictured several rows of women in their twenties; I am shown standing in the corner with long dark hair. At 10 A.M. our lawyer, Eleanor Holmes Norton, the assistant legal director of the American Civil Liberties Union, began reading a statement to a packed press conference at the ACLU's office at 156 Fifth Avenue. "It is ironic," she said, waving a copy of the magazine, "that while *Newsweek* considers women's grievances newsworthy enough for such major coverage, it continues to maintain a policy of discrimination against the women on its own staff. . . . The statistics speak for themselves—there are more than fifty men writing at *Newsweek,* but only one woman." She pointed out that although the women were graduates of top colleges, held advanced degrees, and had published in major news journals, "*Newsweek*'s caste system relegates women with such credentials to research jobs almost exclusively and interminably."

Eleanor noted that a copy of the complaint had gone to Katharine Graham, publisher of the *Washington Post* and president of the Washington Post Company, which owned *Newsweek*. "The *Newsweek* women believe that as a woman, Mrs. Graham has a particular responsibility to end discrimination against women at her magazine," she said. She called on Mrs. Graham and the editors to negotiate and asked for "the immediate integration of the research staff and the opening of correspondence, writing, and editing positions to women."

Then she opened the floor to questions for the three *Newsweek* women at the table. One reporter asked who was the top woman at the magazine. Lucy Howard, a researcher in the National Affairs department, replied that it was Olga Barbi, who was head of the researchers and had been at *Newsweek* for forty years—which got a big laugh. Then Gabe Pressman, the veteran investigative reporter for local WNBC-TV, pushed his microphone in front of Mary Pleshette, the Movies researcher, and asked whether the discrimination was overt. "Yes," she answered. "There seems to be a gentleman's agreement at *Newsweek* that men are writers and women are researchers and the exceptions are few and far between."

It was an exhilarating moment for us, and a shocking one for *Newsweek*'s editors, who couldn't have been more surprised if their own daughters had risen up in revolt. We had been secretly strategizing for months, whispering behind closed doors, congregating in the *Newsweek* ladies' room, and meeting in our apartments at night. As our numbers increased, we had hired a lawyer and were just reviewing our options when we were suddenly presented with a truly lucky break. In early 1970, *Newsweek's* editors decided that the new women's liberation movement deserved a cover story. There was one problem, however: there were no women to write the piece.

I was the only female writer on the magazine at the time, but I was very junior. As a researcher at *Newsweek*, I had also done a lot of reporting, and my editor in the Life & Leisure department, Harry Waters, had liked my work and encouraged me. He recommended to our senior editor that I be promoted to a junior writer, and in March 1969, I was. In addition to fashion, I wrote about social trends, including the gay-rights and women's movements. But things weren't going well. The senior editor who promoted me had moved to another department and the new editor thought my stories were too sympathetic to the activists. My copy was often rewritten.

When the idea of doing a women's lib cover was proposed in early 1970, the editors were savvy enough to realize they couldn't have a man write the story. Though I was not experienced enough to tackle a cover story, another woman on the magazine could have written it: Liz Peer, a gifted reporter in *Newsweek's* Washington bureau. But the editors never reached out to her. (When I asked my editor why they hadn't asked Liz, he told me that although she had been a writer in New York and a foreign correspondent for five years, he "wasn't sure" she could write a *Newsweek* cover.)

Instead, for the first time in the history of the magazine, the editors went outside the staff and hired Helen Dudar, a star writer at the *New York Post,* to do the piece. (Helen's husband, Peter Goldman, was a top writer for *Newsweek.*) That galvanized us. Our case might take years to wind its way through the EEOC backlog, but announcing our lawsuit the morning the "Women in Revolt" cover came out would get us prominent press coverage. We knew that worse than being sued, the publicity would mortify the magazine's editors, who prided themselves on the progressive views and pro–civil rights coverage that put *Newsweek* on the map in the 1960s.

The Sunday night before the press conference, we gathered at Holly Camp's West Eighty-Third Street apartment to prepare for the historic day ahead. We were nervous, excited, and resolute. I felt especially happy for my close friend Judy Gingold, the conscience of our collective. Judy had been the first one to see our situation at *Newsweek* as a moral issue, and against the grain of her good-girl up-bringing, she had pushed us to file a lawsuit. First on our agenda was deciding who would speak at the press conference. Silence. No one wanted to do it. Pat Lynden, a reporter in the New York bureau who never shied from confrontation, finally said, "I'll do it with someone else." Lucy Howard, a good friend of Pat's, stepped up. "I thought if I don't do this, the whole lawsuit will go down the drain," she recalled. "It never occurred to me that I would have to answer a question. I just assumed I would be a warm body and that Eleanor would speak." Then Mary Pleshette proposed that I join them, but I demurred. "As someone who has become a writer, I don't think I should represent the class," I said, throwing it back to her. "Mary, why don't you do it?" Mary, always the first to raise her hand in class, said she would be willing to do it as long as everyone agreed, which they did.

The three spokeswomen moved to a corner to practice answers and to discuss what they would wear (Lucy decided on a pink John Kloss dress, Pat a rose-colored T Jones dress, and Mary a burnt-orange shift). Another group formed to write a release about the Monday press conference, which Susan Agrest's husband would drop off later that night at various news organizations to get the event on their daybooks. The rest of us, with our lawyer's help, drafted a letter to Katharine Graham informing her that we were about to file the suit. "We are writing to you," the letter said, "because we cannot believe that you are fully aware of the extent to which we are discriminated against at *Newsweek*." Then we all chipped in to fly Sunde Smith, a twenty-three-year-old Business researcher, to Washington the next day because she still qualified for the $17 student fare on the Eastern Airlines shuttle. Sunde, who had to get back to work Monday morning, was to hand the letter to a friend of Lucy's, who would deliver it to Kay Graham at her stately Georgetown home.

The top editors were off on Mondays, having put the magazine to bed Saturday night, so we had to find someone to deliver a similar notice to *Newsweek*'s editor-in-chief, Osborn "Oz" Elliott. None of us wanted to confront our fearsome leader at the door of his East Seventy-Second Street town house. I volunteered my husband, who relished the task. As we carefully choreographed our insurrection, several women were still arguing that we should first go to management with our grievances. Others were filled with dread. "When I got home that night," recalled Lucy Howard, "I sat sobbing in the bathtub and thinking my eyes were going to be all puffy tomorrow. I was feeling I have to do this—but I can't."

We were hardly radical women. Nine days earlier, on March 6, five members of the Weatherman Underground had accidentally blown up a town house on West Eleventh Street as they were assembling bombs in the basement, killing two men and a woman—all in their twenties. Even in the media, there were far more outrageous actions than ours. Several weeks before our suit, freelance writer Susan Brownmiller convinced the newly formed Women's Media Group to hold a sit-in at one of the major women's magazines. Except for Helen Gurley Brown's *Cosmopolitan*, which promoted sexual liberation (mostly to please men), the other leading women's publications, all edited by men, were still preaching *Kinder, Küche, Kirche*, the German maxim for "children, kitchen, and church." The protestors decided to target the *Ladies' Home Journal*, whose slogan, "Never underestimate the power of a woman," took on new meaning two days after we filed our complaint. On March 18, more than one hundred members of various women's lib groups gathered at the *Journal* building at 9:15 A.M. and filed up to the fifth-floor corner office of John Mack Carter.

In his career, Carter had edited the big three women's magazines: *Good Housekeeping, McCall's,* and *Ladies' Home Journal.* A small, Southern, courtly gentleman, Carter was stunned as the brigade of women barged into his office. The protestors immediately began reading a list of demands, including hiring only female staffers—and a female editor-in-chief—providing free on-site day care, ceasing to publish advertisements that degraded women, and turning over the editorial content of one issue to the women, to be named the *Women's Liberated Journal.* Cornered at his desk for more than eleven hours, Carter was silent while various women spoke to him about their lives, their aspirations, and their frustrations. Elsewhere on the floor, protestors engaged secretaries and editorial assistants in earnest conversations. Only Lenore Hershey, Carter's deputy editor, spoke up. "She was a tiger at the gate, a bear guarding her cub, a magpie passing judgment on our clothes, our hair, our extremely rude manners," wrote Brownmiller in her memoir. "Sisterhood failed us badly with Lenore Hershey. I got the feeling that even Carter wished she'd just shut up and listen."

At one point, Shulamith Firestone, leader of the New York Radical Feminists, jumped onto Carter's desk screaming, "I've had enough of this," and lunged at him. One of the radicals who had taken judo grabbed Firestone's arm and flipped her into the crowd. After that, according to Brownmiller, Carter started negotiating with the women. In the end, the *Journal* agreed "to explore" opening a day-care center and to turn over eight pages in the August issue to the protestors, paying them $10,000.

Compared to that kind of guerrilla action, we were models of propriety. We didn't want to overthrow the system. We were proud to be part of a powerful and liberal institution like *Newsweek*; we just wanted to transform it to make it better for women. In the 1960s, feminists had scored several important legal victories, including the 1963 Equal Pay Act, the 1964 Civil Rights Act, and in 1967, an executive order that prohibited sex discrimination in hiring and promotion by federal contractors. In the 1970s, female journalists would declare war on their newsrooms and protest how women were covered in the media—and we were the first to challenge the industry's sexist policies. "The *Newsweek* case was pathbreaking in terms of impact on the law and on society," Eleanor Holmes Norton told me. "It encouraged other women to come forward, it had an effect on journalism, and it had a wide-ranging effect on women. Journalists had to write about it, and because the women were so extraordinary, because the case was so clearly one of blatant, unmitigated discrimination, it made people understand discrimination against women in an important way."

Two months after we filed our complaint, ninety-six women at Time Inc. would file a sex discrimination complaint against *Time, Life, Fortune,* and *Sports Illustrated.* In the next few years, women sued their employers at the *Reader's Digest, Newsday,* the *Washington Post,* the *Detroit News,* the *Baltimore Sun,* the *New Haven Register,* and the Associated Press. In 1974, six women at the *New York Times*—represented by one of our lawyers—filed sex discrimination charges on behalf of 550 women and in 1975, sixteen women at NBC initiated a class action lawsuit covering 2,600 present and past employees. "When women with staff jobs in the media began to rise up, feminism moved into another dimension," said Brownmiller. "Their courageous actions were to change the face of journalism forever."

In the end, it turned out that our extraordinary efforts to reach Katharine Graham that Monday in March were for naught. She was on vacation in the Bahamas. When Oz Elliott and *Newsweek* chairman Frederick "Fritz" Beebe telephoned her later that morning to tell her about the women's lawsuit, she was flummoxed. "Which side am I supposed to be on?" she asked them.

***

LIKE KATHARINE GRAHAM, we all were confused. We were women in transition, raised in one era and coming of age in another, very different time. It is hard for people today, even many women, to comprehend the social order that prevailed in the roughly two decades after World War II. The 1940s and 1950s were a period of growing prosperity, incipient suburban sprawl, and a baby boom that kept our mothers fully occupied. Jim Crow was nearly everywhere, gays were strictly closeted, and a woman's place was in the home, at least after marriage and children. In those rare instances when women were hired for jobs usually held by men, they generally earned a lot less and often were treated as sexual fodder.

"We were the tail end of the old generation," explained personal finance columnist Jane Bryant Quinn, who worked briefly at *Newsweek* in the early 1960s. "We wore hats and gloves. We couldn't go to proms and parties without dates—and the men had to do the asking. We also didn't have many role models in the working world." Most of us had graduated from college in the '60s, when half of our classmates earned their "M-R-S" and got married when they graduated in June. "Our generation was raised to be attractive and smart—but not too smart," said Pat Lynden. "We were to be deferential to men, to get married, raise children, and be ornamental wives dedicated to our husbands' careers."

Yet here we were, entering the workplace in the 1960s questioning—and often rejecting—many of the values we had been taught. We were the polite, perfectionist "good girls," who never showed our drive or our desires around men. Now we were becoming mad women, discovering and confronting our own ambitions, a quality praised in men but stigmatized—still—in women. In her insightful book, *Necessary Dreams: Ambition in Women's Changing Lives,* psychiatrist Anna Fels described the two emotional engines of ambition: the mastery of specific skills and the necessary recognition of that mastery by others. Even today, she told me, as women have developed skills and expertise, they are "subtly discouraged from pursuing their goals by a pervasive lack of recognition for their accomplishments." Women fear that seeking recognition will expose them to attacks on everything from their popularity to their femininity. But recognition in all its forms—admiration from peers, mentoring, institutional rewards, and societal approval—is something that makes us better at what we do,

Fels explained, and without it "people get demoralized and ambitions erode."

In January 2012, Sheryl Sandberg, chief operating officer of Facebook, spoke about an "ambition gap" at the World Economic Forum in Davos, Switzerland. She noted that ever since the 1980s, women have progressed at every level except at the top, where, in the past ten years, they've leveled off at 15 percent to 16 percent of executive jobs and board representation. "We don't raise our daughters to be as ambitious as our sons," she said. One reason, she noted, was that "success and likeability are positively correlated for men and negatively correlated for women. As a man gets more powerful and successful, he is better liked. As a woman gets more powerful and successful, she is less liked."

What led to our revolt? Why did our generation suddenly realize that our place in society was changing—and had to change? In part, we were carried by the social and political currents of our time. The civil rights movement was forcing a national conversation about equality and providing a model for all the protest movements of the 1960s. The music revolution was empowering a new "youth generation," which in turn was creating a "youthquake" in art and fashion. And over it all, like an ominous shadow, the war in Vietnam was fostering a deep skepticism—and cynicism—toward authority.

For women, especially young, white, middle-class, college-educated women, the booming postwar economy provided new opportunities and jobs far more interesting than the tedious suburban lives of our mothers. The birth-control pill, which went on sale in 1960, allowed us to control our destinies while the sexual revolution gave us permission to explore our desires. All that fueled a women's movement that questioned how we wanted to live our lives. As Gail Collins wrote in *When Everything Changed,* her 2009 history of American women from 1960 to the present, "It was, all in all, a benevolent version of the perfect storm."

But even with the social winds in our sails and the women's movement behind us, each of us had to overcome deeply held values and traditional social strictures. The struggle was personally painful and professionally scary. What would happen to us? Would we win our case? Would we change the magazine? Or would we be punished? Who would succeed and who would not? And if our revolt failed, were our careers over—or were they over anyway? We knew that filing the suit legally protected us from being fired, but we didn't trust the editors not to find some way to do us in.

Whatever happened, the immediate result is that it put us all on the line. "The night after the press conference I realized there was no turning back," said Lucy Howard. "Once I stepped up and said I wanted to be a writer, it was over. I wanted to change *Newsweek,* but *everything* was going to change."

CHAPTER 2

"A Newsmagazine Tradition"

WHEN *NEWSWEEK'S* EDITOR-IN-CHIEF, Osborn "Oz" Elliott, responded to our lawsuit that Monday in March, he released a statement that served only to confirm the institutional sexism of the magazine. "The fact that most researchers at *Newsweek* are women and that virtually all writers are men," it said, "stems from a newsmagazine tradition going back almost fifty years."

That was true—and most of us never questioned it. Although we held impressive degrees from top colleges, we were just happy to land a job—even a menial one—at an interesting place. Saying you worked at *Newsweek* was glamorous compared to most jobs available to college-educated women. Classified ads were still segregated by gender and the listings under "Help Wanted—Female" were mainly for secretaries, nurses, and teachers or for training programs at banks and department stores such as Bloomingdale's (that wouldn't change until 1973, when the US Supreme Court ruled sex-segregated ads were illegal). But compared to jobs at newspapers, where women were reporters and editors—even if they were ghettoized in the "women's pages"—the situation for women at the newsmagazines was uniquely injurious. We were confined to a category created especially for us and from which we rarely got promoted. Not only was research and fact-checking considered women's work, but it was assumed that we didn't have the talent or capability to go beyond it.

That infamous "tradition" began in 1923, when Henry Luce and Brit Hadden founded *Time, The Weekly News-Magazine.* Positioning their publication between the daily newspapers, which printed everything, and the weekly reviews, which were filled with lengthy commentary, these two young Yalies decided to create a conservative, compartmentalized digest of the week's news that could be consumed in less than an hour. But although *Time* would give both sides of the issues, it would, they said in their prospective, clearly indicate "which side it believes to have the stronger position." In the beginning, the magazine was written by a small group of their Ivy League friends, who distilled stories from newspapers and wrote them, echoing Hadden's beloved *Iliad,* in a hyphenated news-speak ("fleet-footed Achilles") and a backward-running sentence structure ("Up to the White House portico rolled a borrowed automobile"). *Time* didn't hire "stringer correspondents" until the 1930s, when the magazine decided to add original reporting.

But from the very beginning, the editorial staff included "girls" known as "checkers," who verified names, dates, and facts. Thus was created a unique group-journalism model, which, unlike newspapers, separated all the editorial functions: the reporters sent in long, colorful files from the field; the writers compiled the information and wrote the story in the omniscient, Lucean Voice of God; and the researchers checked the facts. Only "lady assistants" were hired as fact checkers, which, according to Oz Elliott, who worked at *Time* for six and a half years, was a "liberating thing for young fledgling women out of college because they could get into publishing without being stenographers or secretaries."

Years later, the honorific of "checker" was upgraded to "researcher." At *Time*'s twentieth anniversary dinner in 1943, Luce explained that although "the word 'researcher' is now a nation-wide symbol of serious endeavor," the title was originally conceived when he and Hadden were doing some "research" for a drinking club called the Yale Professors. "Little did we realize," he said, "that in our private jest we were inaugurating a modern female priesthood, the veritable vestal virgins whom levitous writers cajole in vain, and managing editors learn humbly to appease."

When *News-Week* began in 1933, it copied *Time*'s "tradition" of separating editorial functions. But at *Newsweek* (which joined its name in 1937 when it merged with the weekly journal *Today*), women didn't even start as researchers; we were hired two rungs below that—on the mail desk. At *Time*, office boys delivered the mail and relevant newspaper clippings. But at *Newsweek* only girls with college degrees—and we were called "girls" then—were hired to sort and deliver the mail, humbly pushing our carts from door to door in our ladylike frocks and proper high-heeled shoes. If we could manage that, we graduated to "clippers," another female ghetto. Dressed in drab khaki smocks so that ink wouldn't smudge our clothes, we sat at the clip desk, marked up newspapers, tore out relevant articles with razor-edged "rip sticks," and routed the clips to the appropriate departments. "Being a clipper was a horrible job," said writer and director Nora Ephron, who got a job at *Newsweek* after she graduated from Wellesley in 1962, "and to make matters worse, I was good at it."

We were all good at it—that was our mind-set. We were willing to start at the bottom if it led to something better, and in most cases, it did: to the glorified position of researcher. Working side by side with the writers, we were now part of the news process, patrolling the AP and UPI telexes for breaking news, researching background material in the library, chatting with the guys about their stories, and on closing nights, fact-checking the articles. The wires were clacking, the phones were ringing, and we were engaged in lively conversations about *things that mattered.* It was thrilling to feel the pulse of the news and to have that special pipeline to the truth that civilians couldn't possibly have. "It was everything you wouldn't think of growing up in Merion, Pennsylvania," said Franny Heller Zorn, who still remembered the thrill of finding the first wire report about a breaking news event, in her case when Adlai Stevenson collapsed on a sidewalk in London and died later that day. "The guys were great, the women were terrific, and everyone was smart. It was a privilege to be part of the *Newsweek* culture and to have that job, even with all the crap we had to do."

Our primary job was to fact-check the stories and that meant checking nearly every word in a sentence except "and" and "the." We underlined what we confirmed and in the margin, we noted the source—the reporter's file, a newspaper story, or a reference book. All proper names had to be checked against telephone books or directories. If the only source was the reporter, we grilled him on the correct name, title, and spelling. If we had any questions about the accuracy, we would underline the suspicious word or sentence with a red pencil. A fact was not to be checked against a newspaper story unless it was the only source we had. The *New York Times* was considered the best newspaper, but even that wasn't to be relied on for spellings or history unless it was a last resort. "If there was a difference of opinion between your research and the reporter, you had to call him up and gingerly say something like, 'I'm really sorry and I'm sure you're right, but the *New York Times* said it happened on Monday and you said Tuesday in your file,'" recalled Lucy Howard. "And the reporter would inevitably say, 'Goddamn it, what is the point of sending me out here if you're using the *New York Times*?'"

Unlike our counterparts at *Time,* we also ran interference between the bureau correspondents and the writers and editors. If a *Time* researcher had a problem or question on a story, she wasn't allowed to call the reporter in the field; she could only tell the editor. We were constantly on the phone with the correspondents. "I saw myself as an advocate for the reporter, to keep them out of trouble," said Lucy. "I wanted to make sure the writer didn't screw up and spell anything wrong. But I thought it was more important for the reporters to file what they saw and heard rather than worrying that they got the name wrong." Even Peter Goldman, who had the reputation of being an accurate writer, said, "I don't think I wrote anything longer than eighty lines where one of the researchers didn't catch something."

The modern, green-glassed Time-Life tower on Sixth Avenue and Forty-Ninth Street was only two blocks away from our modest, Art Deco building on Madison Avenue and Forty-Ninth, but the *Newsweek* culture was a world away from Henry Luce's empire. *Time* was WASPier, classier, and better resourced than us younger, scrappier upstarts at *Newsweek*. At *Newsweek*, we spent hours in the thirteenth-floor library, rummaging for relevant information in the "morgue," which housed valuable old (hence, "dead") newspaper and magazine clippings and reporter's files. At *Time*, the researchers would call up the library for sources, and carts would appear at their doors filled with files and books carrying the appropriate place marks.

On Friday nights at *Newsweek*, the writers and researchers went out to the local bars or ordered greasy food from Harman's or Beefburger on Forty-Ninth Street. At *Time*, the editorial staffers were treated to a buffet dinner of lobster or filet mignon on a table set with silver and china, all catered by the ritzy Tower Suite restaurant on the forty-eighth floor of the Time-Life building. While the men at *Newsweek* drank their Scotch and bourbon from bottles hidden in their bottom desk drawers on Friday nights (and many other nights as well), the senior editors at *Time* set up a full bar for their staffers in their offices or antechambers.

Still, working at *Newsweek* was a dream job and I felt lucky to have landed there. Like many of my colleagues, I was a graduate of one of the Seven Sisters schools, which in the early '60s were still mired in the '50s. Vassar College, when I arrived in 1961, was politically apathetic and boy-obsessed. Student clubs had been abolished and even the campus newspaper, the *Misc.* (short for *Miscellaneous*), had ceased publication my freshman year. Every weekend the campus emptied out as girls boarded buses to Yale, Princeton, Columbia, and other nearby men's schools. Other than having female professors and a safe environment where women could be the first to raise their hands— and be heard—there was little left of the founder's feminist legacy when I got there. Women were praised for their intelligence and commended for their capabilities but certainly not encouraged to have careers.

I majored in modern European history but became enthralled by my French professor, Olga Bernal. She would invite her favorite students to her apartment, where we would drink white wine and talk about life, love, and French literature (I was taking her course on avant-garde French writers). It was what I had pictured life at a small college would be like and by junior year, I had a passion if not yet an ambition: I would go to Paris. Since my history degree wouldn't get me a job, my only hope for employment was to be hired as a secretary. I was a fast typist, earning extra money by typing college papers, but I didn't know shorthand. I scoured the local ads and found a course at a nearby high school. My last semester at Vassar, as I was writing my thesis on France between the wars, I spent my evenings walking to Dutchess County Community College to learn Stenoscript.

Although I had taken French through high school and college, I applied only to US companies in Paris, including Pan Am, TWA, the USIA (the government information agency), *Time,* and *Newsweek.* At *Newsweek,* the chief of correspondents offered me a job in New York but I turned it down, determined to go abroad. At his suggestion, I wrote to *Newsweek's* Paris bureau chief, Joel Blocker, who, unfortunately, had no vacancies. So I planned to go to Paris anyway and find a job when, just before my final exams in May, Blocker sent a telegram to my father, a celebrated sports columnist at the *Washington Post*: UNFORESEEN OPENING STAFF, NOW ALMOST CERTAIN JOB POSSIBILITY FOR LYNN IN PARIS BUREAU. . . . PLEASE ONPASS TO LYNN AND ADVISE SOONEST WHEN SHE ARRIVING AND ABLE BEGIN WORK. It turned out that Blocker's secretary had suddenly quit. Thank God for Stenoscript.

In June 1965, I packed two suitcases and left for Paris. For over a year, I worked in the *Newsweek* bureau as a secretary, photo researcher, occasional reporter, and telex operator. After the correspondents had written their stories, I would stay at night to type them—on a French keyboard—into the telex machine, which transmitted them to New York. Typing the files was a good lesson on how to report and write, even if it was a lonely one. Each night as he was leaving the bureau, the staff photographer would look at me, alone in the office, and say with a smile, "Good luck in your chosen profession."

Newsweek's Paris bureau was on the third floor of the *International Herald Tribune* building at 21 Rue de Berri, just off the Champs-Elysée. In addition to the bureau chief and his French secretary, Jacqueline Duhau, who befriended me, the office housed three correspondents and the magazine's senior foreign correspondent, Arnaud de Borchgrave, a perennially tan Belgian nobleman known around *Newsweek* as "the short count." I was closest to Liz Peer, the only female correspondent. A tall, sharp-featured woman with piercing brown eyes accentuated by layers of mascara, the twenty-nine-year-old Liz was *Newsweek's* Brenda Starr. She could match the toughest foreign correspondent with her cigarettes, her swagger, and her fluent French. She was also a gifted writer and versatile reporter who covered everything from politics and the arts to fashion and food. (She loved tromping after the boars on the annual truffle hunts.) As I typed Liz's files into the telex, I admired her ability to find just the right anecdote or quote and weave it into a lively, compelling report.

The daughter of a prominent surgeon who was a pioneer of plastic surgery, Liz had graduated from Connecticut College and joined *Newsweek* on the mail desk in 1958. She showed so much talent that in 1962, she was the only woman on staff to be promoted to writer. Two years later, she was assigned to the Paris bureau. But as recounted by Oz in his

THE GOOD GIRLS REVOLT

memoir, *The World of Oz,* Liz later told him, with some bitterness, that she never felt she was treated fairly. After Oz announced her posting, proudly telling her that *Newsweek* had never sent a woman abroad, Liz hesitantly asked whether the job would mean a raise—it was after all, a promotion. According to Liz, Oz responded indignantly, "What do you mean? Think of the honor we are paying you!"

As a single woman in a highly visible job, Liz led a busy social life in Paris and flaunted it. Returning to the office at night to type her files, she would often end her telexes to New York with "You guys are ruining my sex life." From time to time, she would bring me along on assignments, including a memorable Balenciaga fashion show, or ask me to report a "Newsmaker," the gossipy items about international celebrities that New York regularly requested. But Liz was also status conscious and didn't want to diminish her star in any way. She once asked me to join her one evening because her date was bringing along a male friend. I was surprised at this bit of camaraderie but I was flattered and quickly agreed. Before we left the office, she turned to me and said, "Just say you are a reporter in the bureau, not the secretary."

In Paris, I began to have glimmerings of ambition, of finding something to do for the rest of my life. Surrounded by reporters and writers, I naturally began to think about journalism. But that was complicated for me. My father, Shirley Povich, was a famous sports journalist and a very stylish writer. Afraid of measuring up to him—or with what his success represented— I had purposely avoided anything having to do with journalism in school. Then there was the terror of just putting oneself out in the world, to be judged by others. As I wrote to my best friend back home, becoming a writer would be "my first exposure to a real challenge, something which will prove whether I'm really intelligent and disciplined and eager to do something. This is it, baby, either you start to do something good now or forget it—kinda scary, huh?"

After more than a year in Paris, I returned to the States to be with my boyfriend. I had met Jeffrey Young on Christmas vacation during my senior year at Vassar. He was a first-year student at Harvard Law School and also a Washingtonian (his father owned the famous Paul Young's restaurant). With his dark brown hair and dreamy brown eyes, Jeff was bright, handsome, and charismatic, charming everyone in his path, including me. We got serious quite quickly, but with Jeff having two more years in law school, I decided that I would not give up my plan to go to Paris. After a year and a half abroad, I returned to New York in November 1966 to plan for our wedding the following June, when Jeff graduated. But in the spring of 1967, he suffered a serious depression and took to his bed. He managed to go to classes and finish his degree, but the depression lasted several months. I was very worried about him and visited him every weekend in Cambridge. But I wasn't willing—or able—to look deeper into what this might tell me about him or mean for our marriage. At twenty-three, I was in love.

When I returned to *Newsweek* in New York, I requested a position in the back of the book since Liz Peer told me there was more reporting in those sections. The magazine was informally divided into two parts: the front of the book, which comprised three sections—National Affairs (which we called Nation), International (referred to as Foreign), and Business—and the back of the book, which included Life & Leisure, Press, TV-Radio, Sports, Religion, Education, Medicine, Science & Space, and the Arts. I was put in the Life & Leisure section, which appealed to me. A Vassar course on Victorian England had gotten me interested in social behavior after studying the hypocrisy of the Victorians' strict moral code with the prevalence of prostitution. Life & Leisure covered social trends as well as fashion, which in the '60s was a vivid reflection of how men and women were changing and why. I loved reporting on *Newsweek*'s many fashion covers and interviewed every designer from Betsey Johnson and Mary Quant to Yves Saint Laurent and Halston.

The tedium of fact-checking on Fridays was the price I paid for spending the early part of the week doing interviews. Most of the researchers in the back of the book reported for their sections. But unlike many of my colleagues, my boss in Life & Leisure, Harry Waters, encouraged and mentored me. A graduate of Columbia Journalism School (on scholarship), Harry was a gifted writer who was raised in a working-class Catholic family by two older sisters and a strong mother. His politics were to the right of most of us, and he bristled at the Ivy League snobbery on the magazine, but he wasn't afraid of smart women. In fact, he admired them. He gave me opportunities to report and tutored me on getting good quotes. When he sent me to cover the funeral of Robert F. Kennedy at St. Patrick's

Cathedral, across the street from *Newsweek,* I nervously asked him whom I should interview. "Anyone who's crying," he said. He also edited my files so that I could sharpen my writing.

Since we had to provide colorful commentary, quotes, and background material, our files were often very long compared to what ended up in the magazine. When Harry assigned me to cover a traditional singles weekend at Grossinger's, the famous Jewish resort in the Catskills, my report started on an upbeat note: "They came 1600 strong in search of 'the One' or just a good telephone number." For pages, I described the typical Catskill "get acquainted" activities ("Simon says all the single fellows stand up—Simon says all the girls look them over quickly"), the compulsive mingling at the skating rink and on the ski slopes, and the false identities that everyone used to find a partner. "No one tells the truth," said one woman. "We say we're stewardesses one minute and the next minute we're in television." I ended with the scene at the buses back to the city on Sunday—"the last judgment" when everyone desperately exchanged information. "The girls practically have their phone numbers pasted on their foreheads," one guy said. But as a woman bitterly told me, "The boys are up here to have fun and accumulate phone numbers while we're here to get a husband." And with that, my thirty-one-page file was boiled down to a two-page Life & Leisure feature titled "The Last Resort," written by Harry.

The Business researchers also did a lot of reporting, since New York was the financial capital of the world. Because most of the material for Nation and Foreign stories came from the bureaus, the Nation researchers were sent out of the office mainly during political campaigns and crises, such as the riots. Those in Foreign spent their time in the library or on the phone, providing historical context for their stories and cultivating important sources in academia or foreign affairs. Some women, such as Fay Willey, the chief researcher in Foreign, loved that work. With a master's degree in international relations and American constitutional law, Fay had more depth of knowledge of her subjects than most of the writers she was checking. She was promoted three times before she was twenty-four, and found the work intellectually challenging.

Fact-checking might be a decent entry-level job in journalism, but many of us chafed at the work once we realized it was a dead end. Occasionally a researcher was promoted to reporter. Pat Lynden had started on the magazine as a researcher in Nation, took a leave to do reporting, and came back as a reporter in the New York bureau. But most of the eleven female correspondents working in the bureaus in 1970 had been hired from outside. *Newsweek* never hired women as writers and only one or two female staffers were promoted to that rank no matter how talented they were. During and after World War II, there had been several women writers on the magazine, but they had all mysteriously disappeared by the early 1960s. Any aspiring journalist who was interviewed for a job was told, "If you want to be a writer, go somewhere else—women don't write at *Newsweek*."

Some of the more ambitious young women saw the lay of the land right away. Nora Ephron, Ellen Goodman, Jane

Bryant Quinn, and Susan Brownmiller all started at *Newsweek* in the early 1960s, but left fairly quickly and developed very successful writing careers elsewhere. "I thought I'd work my way up—to the clip desk, to research, and eventually to writer—once I proved my worth," said Jane Bryant Quinn. "But I discovered that I'd never become a writer, just an older and older researcher, making my younger and younger male writers look good."

Ellen Goodman, the Pulitzer Prize–winning columnist for the *Boston Globe*, said that for researchers, "the turnover was expected to be great because women didn't stay in these jobs, either because they got married or because they left, but never because they were promoted. We're talking 1963, before the Civil Rights Act of 1964, so sex discrimination was legal." When an opening came up for a researcher in the Television department, Goodman, who graduated from Radcliffe (and never had a woman teacher), ended up working for her Harvard classmate Peter Benchley. "The only difference between Peter and me was gender," she said. "I mean, there were other differences. His grandfather was Robert Benchley. But, you know, it wouldn't have mattered if my grandfather had been Robert Benchley."

Some young women knew they wanted to be writers from the get-go. At fourteen, Jane Bryant Quinn discovered the comic strip *Brenda Starr, Reporter*. "She had glorious hair, impossible eyelashes, mysterious boyfriends—remember the patch?—and an internationally glamorous life," she recalled. "I don't remember that she reported on much, but wherever she was, something thrilling was going on. I wanted to be a reporter, too."

Nora Ephron's father *and* mother worked in Hollywood and Nora had written for both her high school and college newspapers. "My mother was a screenwriter, so of course we were all going to work and we were all going to be writers," she said. "And all four of her daughters are writers—that's a sign of her terrifying strength." When Nora was a researcher in Nation, *Newsweek* did a cover story on McGeorge Bundy, President John F. Kennedy's top advisor on national security. Ambitious and a self-starter, Nora volunteered to report on Bundy's early years at Yale, where he went to college. "Her file was absolutely spectacular," recalled Peter Goldman. "Everyone was passing it around like samizdat, it was so brilliant." But within a year Nora left *Newsweek* for the *New York Post*. "I knew I was going to be a writer and if they weren't going to make me one, I was going to a place that would," she explained. "Had they said to me when I said I was leaving, 'How would you like to be a writer?' I don't think I would have been any good at it. It's a kind of formulaic writing that requires quite a lot of craft and quite the opposite of the kind of writing I was doing."

Even now, I don't know why the rest of us didn't "get it," why we just didn't leave and try our luck elsewhere. Maybe because we were simply happy to have jobs in a comfortable, civilized workplace that dealt with the important issues of the day. Maybe it was because we, too, were elitists, thrilled to be at least a minor part of the media establishment. "Nora was eager to be a writer, so she was quite disgusted by the place," noted Trish Reilly, a researcher in the Arts sections. "I was thrilled to be a handmaiden to the writer gods and thought it was all quite wonderful." Or maybe we just weren't ambitious enough—or angry enough—at that point in our lives to buck an inherently sexist system. "I certainly saw what was going on," Ellen Goodman later said, "but I don't think I was angry about it for years."

For many of us, *Newsweek* was just a way to earn pin money before getting hitched. "At Radcliffe, the expectations were that you would leave college, work for a couple of years, get married, and then write the great American novel while your children were napping," said Ellen Goodman. At least working at a place like *Newsweek* might increase your chances of meeting a more interesting Mr. Right—or even a Mr. Rich and Famous. That fantasy was fueled by Karen Gunderson, a reporter in *Newsweek*'s Arts sections. In 1965, Karen was sent out to interview Alan Jay Lerner, the lyricist and librettist of *My Fair Lady* and *Camelot*, among many other musicals. They fell in love and the following year, Karen left *Newsweek* to become the fifth Mrs. Alan Jay Lerner (he married eight times).

Whatever our destinies, *Newsweek* was an exciting place to work. It mattered what the newsmagazines put on their covers in those days. Every Monday morning, *Time* and *Newsweek* set the news agenda for the week and in the 1960s, that agenda was filled with cataclysmic events. In the beginning of the decade, *Newsweek* was a pale also-ran to *Brand X*, which is what we called *Time* magazine. But that would change rather spectacularly under the brilliant hand of Osborn Elliott.

CHAPTER 3

The "Hot Book"

ON THE SURFACE, it seemed unlikely that Oz would be a transformative editor. A balding man with a beak nose, Oz was the quintessential WASP: his Dutch ancestor, Stephen Coerte van Voorhees, had come to New Amsterdam early in the seventeenth century; he was raised on the posh East Side; he graduated from St. Paul's prep school and Harvard; and like everyone in his family except his mother, he was a Republican (he switched to Independent when he became a journalist). But Oz had a rebellious streak that he credited, ironically, to the strong women in his life. His mother's mother, Josefa Neilson Osborn, started a successful dress-designing business in 1898, after her wine-merchant husband lost his money. She held salons at the Waldorf, supplied costumes to the fashionable ladies on Park Avenue, and wrote a monthly column for the *Delineator*, the *Vogue* of its day. When Oz's father lost his money and his partnership at Kidder, Peabody in the Crash of 1929, his mother went to work in real estate, where she became a top broker and the first female vice president of her firm.

During the Depression, Oz's father had to arrange for scholarships to Harvard for Oz and his older brother, Jock, who later became chairman of the Ogilvy & Mather advertising agency. (When Oz's father finally got a job as an investment advisor, he paid Harvard back in full.) After college, which he finished on an accelerated program, Oz served with the navy in the Pacific in World War II. When he returned, he landed a job as a cub reporter on the *New York Journal of Commerce* and two years later went to *Time* magazine, where he became a business writer (he also met his first wife, Deirdre, there). In 1955, Oz moved to *Newsweek* as Business editor and became friends with Ben Bradlee, then a reporter in the magazine's Washington bureau. Five years later, when rumors started that the Vincent Astor Foundation was putting *Newsweek* up for sale, Bradlee called Oz, then the magazine's managing editor, and said, "Ozzie baby, I know where the smart money is. It's in Phil Graham's pocket."

Philip L. Graham was the publisher of the *Washington Post*. His father-in-law, Eugene Meyer, had bought the *Post* in a bankruptcy auction in 1933. His wife, Katharine Meyer, had worked as a newspaper reporter before they married but had retreated home to raise their four children. In 1954, Graham bought the rival morning paper, the *Washington Times-Herald*, and merged it with the *Post*, propelling the *Post* into first place over the afternoon *Washington Star* and doubling its circulation. Phil Graham was a dazzling figure around Washington. A former president of the Harvard Law Review and law clerk to Justice Felix Frankfurter, he was a friend of both John F. Kennedy's and Lyndon B. Johnson's (he helped persuade Kennedy to offer the vice presidency to LBJ) and he was high on Ben Bradlee's radar.

To get Phil Graham interested in *Newsweek,* Bradlee called him at eleven one night and said he wanted to talk. "Why don't you come over?" Graham said. "Now." According to Bradlee, "It was the best telephone call I ever made—the luckiest, most productive, most exciting, most rewarding, totally rewarding." Bradlee enlisted Oz in his crusade and together they convinced Graham to buy *Newsweek* in 1961 for $15 million. In a fifty-page memo to the new owner, Bradlee recommended that the thirty-six-year-old Oz become the new editor.

It was the magazine's salvation. Phil Graham immersed himself in *Newsweek,* setting up shop in New York, visiting reporters in the bureaus and traveling abroad to wave the flag. With his financial support, the magazine grew to sixteen bureaus and some forty correspondents by 1963. When Phil Graham visited *Newsweek's* London correspondents in April 1963, he forever set the mission of the magazine with these now famous words: "So let us today drudge on about our inescapably impossible task of providing every week a first rough draft of history that will never really be completed about a world we can never really understand."

But it was Oz who invigorated the magazine with late-breaking covers, national polling, well-known columnists

(Walter Lippmann and Stewart Alsop), and big "acts" (*Newsweek*'s twenty-five pages on JFK's assassination versus *Time*'s thirteen). He also instituted in-depth coverage of the incendiary social issues of the 1960s: from student unrest (at Berkeley, Columbia, and Harvard) to sex (Jane Fonda in *Barbarella*), drugs (LSD), and rock 'n' roll. Although the magazine was the first to feature the Beatles on the cover in 1964, it hilariously missed the point. "Visually they are a nightmare: tight, dandified, Edwardian-Beatnik suits and great pudding bowls of hair," *Newsweek* said. "Musically they are a near-disaster: guitars and drums slamming out a merciless beat that does away with secondary rhythms, harmony, and melody. Their lyrics (punctuated by nutty shouts of 'yeah, yeah, yeah!') are a catastrophe, a preposterous farrago of Valentine-card romantic sentiments."

Oz also hired talented deputies in Gordon Manning, a former editor at *Collier's*, and Kermit Lansner from *Art News*, and together they built a staff of better writers and stronger editors. "With Kermit, we had a Jewish intellectual from New York," Oz told the *New York Times*, "and with Gordon, an Irish Catholic sportswriter from Boston, and in my case, a WASP from the Upper East Side. It made for a wonderful balance." Perhaps it was because Oz was so good balancing competing interests and ideas that the top editors of *Newsweek* were called the Wallendas, after the famous circus family and their "death-defying" aerial stunts; their executive offices were dubbed "the Wallendatorium."

It was Oz's commitment to covering the paramount issues of race, poverty, and the war in Vietnam that not only distinguished *Newsweek* in the '60s and '70s, but made it, finally, the equal of *Time*. In 1963, Oz assigned Lou Harris to do a poll of black Americans, which resulted in a July cover story titled "The Negro in America: The first definitive national survey—who he is, what he wants, what he fears, what he hates, how he votes, why he is fighting . . . and why now?" The eighteen-page report found that the black revolution extended to every community and aimed to establish equality in every field. Suddenly everyone was talking about *Newsweek* and the magazine became the place to turn to for full and fair coverage of the civil rights movement. Three months later, the magazine published a cover on "What the White Man Thinks of the Negro Revolt." In 1967, Oz decided that the time for advocacy had come. Departing from the newsmagazine tradition of never editorializing, *Newsweek* appeared on the stands in November 1967 with a special issue titled "The Negro in America: What Must Be Done," a landmark cover that offered a twelve-point program on how to accelerate progress for black Americans.

"Oz was the godfather of our civil rights coverage," explained Peter Goldman, who was the chief writer on civil rights and author of the book *The Death and Life of Malcolm X.* "I don't think he knew very many black people, damn few. But he had a profound WASP social conscience, which led us to jump on the civil rights story and become the voice of the movement in a way. And it also helped on our coverage of Vietnam and our advocacy issues on both race and the war. We were a moderate voice for progressive America and that was Oz's conscience setting the compass." Oz was simply following in the tradition of his WASP forebears, Teddy Roosevelt and his cousin Franklin, those upper-class Episcopalians who, noted Goldman, "starting in the late nineteenth century and early twentieth century, thought, 'Oh my God, our system is broken. It's our duty to intervene and fix it. We have to get political even though we don't want to, because politics has fallen into the wrong hands.'"

In early 1968, Oz decided the magazine should again take a stand, this time against the war in Vietnam. *Newsweek*'s first cover on Vietnam appeared in 1961, when the magazine took a skeptical view of America's strategy even though, as Oz later wrote, "we—I—rarely questioned the basic wisdom of America's commitment to 'holding Southeast Asia.'" But after the Tet Offensive in March 1968, when the North Vietnamese forces surprised the US and South Vietnamese armies, Oz ordered up a special section titled "More of the Same Won't Do," which argued in favor of de-escalation and ultimate withdrawal. "The war cannot be won by military means without tearing apart the whole fabric of national life and international relations," *Newsweek* said. "Unless it is prepared to indulge in the ultimate, horrifying escalation—the use of nuclear weapons—it now appears that the U.S. must accept the fact that it will never be able to achieve decisive military superiority in Vietnam."

We were proud of our leader and of our magazine. Even though we were professional observers, many of us were sympathetic to the antiwar movement. During one antiwar march on Madison Avenue, a group of editorial staffers stood in a silent vigil outside the *Newsweek* building. In 1970, we held an open forum on the war in the *Newsweek* offices, much to the dismay of the reporters in the field as well as a few writers and editors. "No doubt the war has become a tremendously emotional issue in the United States," cabled Saigon bureau chief Maynard Parker, "but if the *Newsweek* staff cannot keep some objectivity and coolness on the subject, then who can?" The Tokyo bureau chief, Bernie Krisher, worried that "once identified with a cause, those who oppose that cause will hesitate to confide in us."

That concerned Oz as well, but as he wrote to the correspondents, "the divisions and passions among the *Newsweek* employees would have been exacerbated had we denied the turf for this purpose." Oz felt better about the staff's ability to keep their feelings in check when Dick Boeth, one of the senior writers and moderator of the mass meeting, wrote to him privately. Boeth said that although a poll of the editorial employees showed that a majority of the staff opposed the war, it also showed that "a majority of them hold exactly the same opinion about company activism as Parker and Krisher do." In other words, they were journalists first.

Under Oz, *Newsweek* became the "hot book" in the media and on Madison Avenue. Coinciding with the 1960s, life at the magazine not only was fascinating, it was a fun and even wild place to be. Since most of the writers were in their thirties and nearly all the researchers in their twenties, the culture inside the office mirrored the "Swinging Sixties" on the street. Everyone, including Oz, was on a first-name basis, which gave a feeling of equality even to us utterly powerless. After work we went out drinking either to the Berkshire Bar, a front-of-the-book favorite, or to The Cowboy, where Pete Axthelm, the Sports department's wunderkind writer and champion drinker, held forth every night.

Waiting for the files to roll in at the beginning of the week, or for the edits on Friday nights and Saturdays, we spent hours joking around in the office. "I loved the intense but nutty, free-wheeling atmosphere on Saturday afternoons," recalled Pat Lynden, "drinking wine, strumming guitars, playing baseball in the hallways." Peter Goldman and Ed Kosner used their downtime in Nation to cowrite a never-finished parody of a dirty novel. Dwight Martin, a senior editor in the back of the book, moved an old Steinway upright into his office so he could practice piano in the afternoons; at cocktail time he poured sherry for his staff.

One Friday night, Betsy Carter, the media researcher, was so bored waiting for her story to be edited that at 2 A.M., she decided to make a copy of herself. "I just lay on the Xerox machine and copied my body piece by piece," she recalled. "I stapled them all together and mailed it to my parents with a note that said, 'Here I am at work and I thought you would like to know.' I think my mother said something like, 'Do you think you're working too hard?'"

The back-of-the-book researchers had a classic "office wife" relationship with their bosses. While the front-of-the-book researchers sat in an open bullpen and checked stories by different writers every week, each of us sat in a twenty-five-foot-by-twenty-five-foot office with our section writer. The men's desks were by the window, of course; we perched by the door. To add some personality to our steel-gray work spaces, we pinned up pictures of our idols or celebrities we had interviewed. I put up photographs of nearly naked models Veruschka and Marisa Berenson from *Vogue,* prompting several writers to ask me if I was a lesbian. Sitting only six feet from our writers, we were on intimate terms with them, sharing more than we ever wanted to know about their personal grooming habits, their intimate medical issues, and their heated arguments with the ex-wife or girlfriend.

The back-of-the-book and the Business sections worked Monday through Friday, but the official week didn't begin until Tuesday morning, when Oz held a 10 A.M. story conference in his eleventh-floor office. After the story line-up was set, the writers sent queries to the bureaus asking for on-the-ground reporting. The color-coded files arrived on Thursday and Friday: blue from the international bureaus, green from Washington, and pink from the domestic correspondents. Then the creative rituals and angst would kick in. Pacing the halls in their socks or rocking in their chairs, the writers would cull the information from our reports and the rainbow-colored files and weave it all into a smart, colorful analysis or description of the week's events. Harry Waters, my boss, would pepper me for the right word or phrase, nervously asking, "How does this sound?" or "Listen to this." Paul Zimmerman, a movie critic, was called "the talking blue" because he proudly read aloud to any passerby the blue-inked mimeographs of his latest review. The entire magazine was written and edited in forty-eight hours, culminating in Friday nights that lasted until one or two in the morning because the Wallendas would take a two-hour, martini-soaked dinner break at Giambelli's across the street.

Describing the weekly routine, Carole Wicker, a researcher at *Time*, wrote a typically sexualized, over-the-top piece for *Cosmopolitan* magazine titled "Limousine to Nowhere . . . if You're a Girl at a News Magazine." In it she quoted an unnamed *Newsweek* staffer on what it was like to be a researcher: "It's a mini-marriage, between researcher and writer, with the orgasm coming at the end of the week. Monday, Tuesday and Wednesday, everything goes easy. By Thursday, the pitch is higher. Friday afternoon you're flying, and by Friday midnight you go over the top." "What she's saying," explained Wicker in the piece, "is that the researcher is drawn into the writer's pattern, inch by inch, pressure by pressure, until she's lost her own being and becomes an extension of her boss."

That didn't describe most of us but there was definitely a caste system at *Newsweek*. "For every man there was an inferior woman, for every writer there was a checker," said Nora Ephron. "They were the artists and we were the drones. But what is interesting is how institutionally sexist it was without necessarily being personally sexist. To me, it wasn't oppressive. They were just going to try to sleep with you—and if you wanted to, you could. But no one was going to fire you for not sleeping with them."

By the mid-'60s when the sexual revolution was in full swing, the magazine was a cauldron of hormonal activity. Protected by the Pill, women felt as sexually entitled as the men, and our short skirts and sometimes braless tops only added to the boil. Mix in a schedule culminating in long days and nights, and it ignited countless affairs between the writers and editors and the researchers. For the most part, the office flings were friendly and consensual, and a few turned into marriages. "The way we related to men was through sexual bantering," recalled Trish Reilly, a former researcher in the back of the book. "It was the way a compliment was made at *Newsweek*." "Flirting was part of the game," said Lucy Howard, "and you knew how to handle it. You had to be charming and witty and not cringe at their dirty jokes. It was a *Mad Men* kind of atmosphere."

There were elements of *Mad Men* at *Newsweek,* except that unlike the natty advertising types, journalists were notorious slobs and our two- and three-martini lunches were out of the office, not in. When she was visiting one time in New York, Liz Peer sat in on a story meeting. "The dialogue was eighth grade boys' locker room," she told a reporter at the *Village Voice.* "To see the powerful decision-makers of a national magazine talking about tits and asses and farts! I thought, *I'm working for these clowns.*" Kevin Buckley, who was hired in 1963, described the *Newsweek* of the early 1960s as similar to an old movie, with the wisecracking private eye and his Girl Friday. "The 'hubba-hubba' climate was tolerated," he recalled. "I was told the editors would ask girls to do handstands on their desk. Was there rancor? Yes. But in this climate, a laugh would follow."

Many guys looked at us as people they wanted to cheat on their wives with—and many women were happy to accommodate them. It was easy with suburban-based writers who stayed at hotels in the city on late Friday nights, but there was also sex in the office, literally. The infirmary, two tiny rooms with single beds, was the assignation of choice. Often a writer would go there to "take a nap" for an hour or two, albeit with a female staffer. The offices in the back of the book also served as action central. "You would open the door sometimes and there were these two heavy bodies against the door," recalled Betsy Carter, "and they would both be on the floor drinking Jack Daniel's or having sex under the desk." The outrageous behavior often spilled out into the corridors. Pete A. and Pete B. (Axthelm and Bonventre), the bawdy Sports writers, would stand outside their twelfth-floor office and audibly rate the women on their physical attributes as they walked by. "It was loose and fraternizing and I thought it was a lot of fun," remembered Maureen Orth, a former back-of-the-book writer, who hung out with the Sports guys. "But women were clearly subordinate."

I, too, was caught up in the sexual energy of the place. In January 1968, Jeff and I married and moved to Greenwich Village to be closer to New York University, where he had enrolled in film school. After graduation, Jeff won an internship with Arthur Penn on *Alice's Restaurant* and lived in Stockbridge, Massachusetts, for several months; I visited on weekends. It looked as if his career was taking off. He made a short film with Viveca Lindfors and in 1969 was hired by Paramount—in the post-*Easy Rider* days—to make a movie based on

Richard Fariña's popular counterculture novel, *Been Down So Long It Looks Like Up to Me.*

But there was something missing in our marriage and I felt emotionally abandoned. I didn't realize just how unhappy I was until I found myself getting involved with a colleague at work. I wasn't the only married researcher who was having an affair, but it scared me. One night I told Jeff about it because I knew the affair had more to do with problems in our marriage than with the guy. Jeff was furious, but then confessed that he, too, had been sleeping with someone. Maybe I had sensed it, I'm not sure. But I certainly wasn't feeling loved. After several long, tearful conversations, we decided to stay together and each of us began psychotherapy.

Looking back, there was a lot of inappropriate behavior at *Newsweek,* the kind of "sexual favoritism" and "hostile work environment" that today might be considered illegal. The Nation researchers were referred to condescendingly as "the Dollies." When a back-of-the-book researcher handed her senior editor some copy, he told her she had "perfectly pointed breasts." One Saturday afternoon, as Betsy Carter was fitting her story into the allotted space at the makeup desk, a writer she barely knew walked by, leaned over, and planted a soft kiss on her neck. Jane Bryant Quinn remembered that when she was on the mail desk, "randy writers and editors would cruise the newcomers, letting them know that their so-called careers would be helped if they joined the guy for drinks."

The short, gray-haired sixty-year-old man who ran the mail room was particularly sleazy. "After a while he would say, 'I want to take you out for a soda at the ice cream parlor around the corner,'" recalled Lucy Howard. "I went with him once. He would tell you his life story, including his war stories and that he had a war wound on his back. Then he would say, 'You have lovely hands,' and would ask you to go to his apartment to massage his back. Nobody did, but nobody said anything and no one turned him in. We just tried to avoid him. Finally somebody thought it was revolting and reported him and he was fired. He was just a creepy little guy."

One Monday my senior editor, Shew Hagerty, assigned me a story on a trendy new club in New York. It was a lascivious lounge where everyone disrobed, tied sheet-like togas around their bodies, and reposed on mattresses floating on pools of water as they were served cocktails. Shew was a gentleman and a good boss, but I was stunned when later that week he asked if he could come along with me. What could I say? To assure me that he was on the up-and-up, he invited Elisabeth Coleman, another of his researchers and a good friend of mine, to join us. I was never more humiliated than when I was lying on a large white cushion in a toga, with nothing underneath, across from my mustached, pipe-smoking boss, who sat there smiling, so pleased to be taking in the scene.

Nation researcher Kate Coleman (not related to Elisabeth), a proud member of Berkeley's Free Speech Movement, described reporting a *Newsweek* cover story in 1967 on the rising use of marijuana. Her senior editor, Ed Diamond, asked if he could come to her apartment and smoke some pot—to better understand the phenomenon. Not wanting her to think he meant just the two of them, he asked her to invite some of her friends as well so he could witness the whole experience. Then, at the last minute, Ed asked Kate if she would mind if he brought along his wife, Adelina. According to Kate, who left *Newsweek* in 1968, both Ed and Adelina came to her pot party and they both took more than a few tokes. Ed later claimed that he never got high; he said he only got a "slight buzz."

A few guys had a habit of hitting on women in ways that would qualify today as sexual harassment. One Thursday afternoon in Nation, Dick Boeth, a talented but temperamental writer, kept harassing Margaret Montagno, who tried to ignore him. He hovered over her desk, speaking quietly but clearly hammering at her. When she didn't respond, he said, very audibly, "Well, if you want to continue playing the thirty-year-old virgin from Columbus, Ohio, you go right ahead and do that." Everyone in the bullpen heard it and Margaret, in tears, fled into Peter Goldman's office. She closed the door and pleaded, "Can't you do anything about him?" "I didn't know what to do," Peter later confessed. "When Dick was in one of his crazies you couldn't deal with him. All the women were kind of scared of him. I should have nonviolently punched him out but I couldn't. After Meg calmed down, she went back to work. I had work to do and I couldn't do it in the eye of that storm, so I packed up and went home."

Several editors and writers were known for having affairs with women who reported to them directly, most likely a firing offense—or at least a reassignment—today. One writer told me that his editor was sleeping with his researcher, putting him in an awkward position, to say the least. A married senior editor, who regularly used the infirmary for his trysts, had a liaison with a researcher in his section and then lobbied for her promotion, which she received. Several editors and writers, married and single, had flings with their researchers. One writer dated both his researcher and his reporter at the same time.

Jack Kroll, the Arts senior editor, was a notorious flirt and played favorites with his young researchers. When Mary Pleshette first started working as the Movies researcher, Jack, who was divorced, asked her out to dinner and then a second time. It was collegial at first, talking about movies and actors and Zero Mostel, a friend of Mary's family. But when Jack asked her to dinner the third time, she told him she didn't feel comfortable accepting his invitation. "In those days," she recalled, "everyone knew that the third date meant you had to put out."

Jack was a Falstaffian character. His belly seemed to inflate and deflate with the seasons. Hidden behind a desk stacked with books in an office piled high with dirty shirts (he couldn't be bothered with sending them to the laundry), Jack was a polymath who could write brilliantly on just about anything. When Lee Harvey Oswald was gunned down by Jack Ruby in a Dallas police station basement, the editors called him in to write the story. The lead was classic Kroll: "It was," he wrote, "as if Damon Runyon had written the last line of a tragedy by Sophocles."

But Jack could also be volatile and vindictive. One evening after a cultural event, a good friend of mine who was one of his researchers asked me to come home with her because Jack was following her. She said he had been stalking her for weeks, sometimes waiting outside her building until two in the morning. When we got into her apartment, we doused the lights and looked out the window. There was Jack, walking up and down the sidewalk looking up at her window. She was terrified and didn't know what to do.

When she started dating the guy she would eventually marry, Jack became crazed. He asked her to lunch one day at a nearby Irish pub. "We started talking and he took out a box," she recalled. "He opened it up and there was a diamond ring. Then he took out an envelope with two tickets to the Iranian film festival, which was to be our honeymoon. I almost threw up. Thank God I was in therapy and had a man in my life. I said, 'You know, Jack, I love you but I'm not in love with you. This is overwhelming, this is incredible, you're such a close friend.' And he said, 'If you don't marry me, you'll have to leave *Newsweek*.'"

She refused his offer and he turned nasty. In the weeks that followed, she told me, "He would walk up and down the hall and yell, 'Where's that c—?' No one said anything, no one did anything." Finally, one of the male writers offered to help her find another job. She left shortly thereafter.

My boss, Harry Waters, told me that when he came to the magazine in 1962, "it was a discreet orgy. When I interviewed

49

for the job, my editor said to me, 'The best part of the job is that you get to screw the researchers.' That," he went on, "reflected the position of women at the newsmagazines, both literally and figuratively. It reinforced in young women that that's their position—it's underneath. That's as far as they can get."

CHAPTER 4

Ring Leaders

J UDY GINGOLD WAS SITTING at her weekly consciousness-
raising meeting in Judy Levin's tiny Greenwich Village
apartment when it struck her. Levin, a friend from Judy's college days, was working at Ogilvy & Mather and heavily involved in the downtown political scene. The group consisted
of eight women, among them a married architect, a social
worker, and a woman who worked for the Clergy Consultation
Service, a network of twenty-six Christian and Jewish clergy
that helped women find safe abortion services.

A precocious New Yorker with a hearty laugh, Judy was
intrigued by the new sense of power that women were exploring in their CR groups. Developed by the New York Radical
Women, consciousness-raising was a process of using women's
feelings and experiences to analyze their lives and society's

assumptions about women. A member of that group, Kathie Amatniek Sarachild, who had changed her last name to reflect her mother's lineage—a common move for radical women in those days—had popularized the practice of consciousness-raising in a paper in 1968, which was widely disseminated. Judy's group followed the rules of the Redstockings, another group of radical feminists, which took its name from the seventeenth-century term for intellectual women, "Blue Stockings," and substituted "Red" for revolution. The rules required going around the room so that each woman was forced to contribute to the conversation. By airing their intimate feelings, women were to discover that what seemed like isolated, individual problems actually reflected common conditions all women faced. In other words, the personal was political.

The consciousness-raising session at Levin's Waverly Street apartment was a particularly memorable one for Judy. "Betsy Steuart, who was an assistant at NBC and very beautiful and capable, was saying, 'If I were Barbara Walters I would get ahead,'" she recalled, "and everyone was saying the same thing—'if I were better I would get ahead.' All of us in that room felt inadequate. And that's when I thought, wait a minute, that's not right. It's not because we're undeserving or not talented enough that we aren't getting ahead, it's how the world is run. It made me see that the problem wasn't our fault—it was systemic. That was my first 'click!' moment."

The famous "click!"—that moment of recognizing the sexual politics of a situation. Jane O'Reilly would later coin the term in the 1971 preview issue of *Ms.* magazine. O'Reilly was writing on "The Housewife's Moment of Truth," such as watching one's husband step over a pile of toys that needed to be put away. But in fact, she was writing about every woman's moment of truth. "The click! of recognition," she wrote, "that parenthesis of truth around a little thing that completes the puzzle of reality in women's minds—the moment that brings a gleam to our eyes and means the revolution has begun."

***

JUDY'S "CLICK!" MOMENT was the spark of our rebellion. It might have happened eventually but in the fall of 1969, that moment of insight at her consciousness-raising group got Judy thinking—and Judy was a thinker. Raised on the liberal Upper West Side of New York City, Judy was from a smart but humble family. Her father owned an electrical supply company and doted on his daughter, but from the beginning her parents' marriage was troubled and the household was tense. "I don't recall very many pleasant moments with them," recalled Judy. "They either fought or there was silence." Judy's younger brother Alfred, who became an actor and humor writer, filled the void at the dinner table with jokes and funny stories. Judy agonized. "My mother's favorite color was red and my father's favorite color was green, and when people would ask me, 'What's your favorite color?' I would chose orange," she said. "To me, orange looked like red but tasted like green. I saw myself as someone who couldn't take sides. I loved my parents equally but if I sided with my father, my mother would call me disloyal."

In seventh grade, Judy was admitted to Hunter High School, the elite public school for intellectually gifted girls, but four years later she transferred to Dalton, a top private school. She was attracted by Dalton's progressive curriculum and by its superior record of college acceptances. Judy chose to go to Smith College, where she graduated summa cum laude and Phi Beta Kappa, but she was still filled with insecurities and self-doubt. Her senior thesis at Smith, "Some Metaphysical Views of Logical Necessity," was submitted for a prize that came with the honor of publishing it as a book. Judy won the prize but wouldn't let Smith publish her thesis because she didn't think it was good enough.

After graduation, Judy went to Oxford University in England on a prestigious Marshall Scholarship. At that time, the Marshall was awarded to only twenty-four students and, unlike the Rhodes Scholarships, accepted women as well as men (the Rhodes wasn't extended to women until 1977). At Oxford, she did the typical three-year course in PPE (philosophy, politics, and economics) and wrote her thesis, "Freud's Use of the Concept of 'Meaning' in the Theory of Dreams." She was planning to stay in England, where she was happy and away from family strife, when she received a phone call from her mother in 1967. After twenty-seven years, her father had finally walked out. Her mother was so hysterical that Judy, ever the "good girl," came home.

Back in New York, this brilliant Marshall Scholar couldn't find a job for six months. She thought about going to graduate school in psychology, but "I didn't have a real goal," Judy said.

"I didn't have a goal of getting married, but I didn't have a career goal either. I thought about law school but I needed money." She also needed a home. While living with her mother, Judy continued to see her father, which infuriated her mother even more. Judy finally left, sleeping on friends' couches until, with the help of her father, she rented an apartment at 14 East Ninety-Second Street.

Later that year, Judy got an interview at *Newsweek* with Rod Gander, the chief of correspondents, who told her up front, "If you want to write, go someplace else." Short of money, she took a job as the "Elliott girl," the young woman—always a woman—who ran copy from Oz Elliott to the editors on Thursday and Friday nights until two in the morning, and all day Saturday. It was a terrifying job because when Oz would call "copy," he would eye you like a cop waiting to nab a perp, sternly looking over his glasses to make sure you took the story from the correct wooden out-box. But it was a good schedule for Judy because it allowed her to continue to search for a job where she wouldn't have to type. After six months of looking for work, Judy reluctantly took a research position in early 1968 in the Nation department. The other Marshall Scholar at *Newsweek* was her boss, Nation editor John Jay Iselin, a direct descendant of one of the founding fathers, John Jay.

In the fall of 1969, Judy got a call from Gladys Kessler, a friend of a friend who had just moved to New York. Over lunch Gladys, a lawyer, asked Judy about her job at *Newsweek*. When Judy explained what she did at the magazine and how all the women were researchers, Gladys said, "You know that's illegal?"

Judy was incredulous. Gladys explained that Title VII of the Civil Rights Act of 1964 prohibited employment discrimination based on sex, among other things, and told her to call the Equal Employment Opportunity Commission, which had been set up in 1965 to handle such cases. The next day, Judy went to work and, on the magazine's free tie-line to Washington, dialed the EEOC office. Hesitantly, she explained the situation to the woman on the other end of the line. "I don't think these men know that it's illegal," she said. "They're very liberal and they have daughters and I think we should talk to them." The gruff-voiced woman barked back, "Don't be a naive little girl. People who have power don't like to give up that power. What's so wonderful about your case is that it couldn't be more clear-cut and that's going to change if you let on. You have to organize and keep it secret and file a complaint. If you ask them about it, they will hire two token women and that will be the end of it."

Click!

Judy was shaken by the call. Now there was a moral issue. "I thought if this is illegal and it's going on here, then I should do something to correct it," she later explained. "That was really hard." She also knew that what she was going to do would change her life. "I saw myself as a nice person but I was starting to behave in a way that I never had before," she said. It was tearing her apart. As she weighed her thoughts, Judy struggled, with great inner courage, to overcome a deep-seated code of conduct. "Part of what is involved in participating in cultural change is violating what you were raised to believe was sacrosanct," she said. "It is getting yourself to accept a different set of values and relinquish old ones. That is one of the hardest things I've ever done, but I felt I had to sue." She scheduled a lunch with her two pals in the Nation department, Margaret Montagno and Lucy Howard.

Margaret and Lucy were close friends and later shared a weekend house in the Hamptons, but they were from different worlds. Margaret had grown up in Columbus, Ohio, the daughter of an engineer and a housewife—"standard issue 1950s Republican conservatives," as she described them. More liberal than her parents, she had always been interested in history and avidly read the newspapers. After public school, Margaret went to St. Mary's College, the sister school of Notre Dame, and earned a master's in medieval history from Fordham University. She was working on her PhD in Russian history at New York University when she landed a job at *Newsweek,* which she found far more interesting than a previous teaching job.

A petite brunette with a sardonic sense of humor, Margaret became a Nation researcher just as the 1968 campaign season was heating up. "I loved being plugged into the political scene," she said. She was sent out on the Eugene McCarthy campaign and covered the assassinations of Martin Luther King and Bobby Kennedy. Margaret quickly gave up the idea of teaching and became a political junkie, keeping meticulous track of the ever-changing convention delegate counts on a giant chart in Nation. "We were all obsessed with politics," she recalled. "That's all we talked about, especially in the early part of the week before the files came in. I think that's what brought us all together."

Lucy Anne Calhoun Howard was descended from John Eager Howard, a member of the Continental Congress, a senator from Maryland and former governor for whom Howard County, Maryland, is named. On her mother's side, she was related to the famous American painter Charles Willson Peale. Her father's family had lost everything in the Civil War and, at the age of fourteen, her grandfather went into the investment banking/brokerage business and bought a seat on the stock exchange. After he lost money in the Depression, he wanted his son to become a minister. Instead, Lucy's father became a doctor at Johns Hopkins Hospital.

Lucy's mother, also named Lucy, didn't work outside the home but she was very competitive. She excelled in fox hunting, and after she had children, continued to play tennis—"club tennis," her husband disparagingly called it. She hated to lose and she also hated to give up her maiden name. "Everyone knew her as Lucy Iglehart," said Lucy. "Late in life she said things like, 'If I had been a young woman in the 1980s and 1990s, I would have been a jockey and ridden in the Hunt Cup.' She was a very good rider but women weren't allowed to do that."

Lucy grew up on a small farm outside Baltimore, Maryland. She had a horse, which she showed in competitions and rode to hounds. She was far more competitive in school and sports than her two older brothers. At Garrison Forest, a boarding school, Lucy played field hockey and was a member of the riding team. "I was conditioned to want to do well in school—and I did," she said. "But I didn't do it to get into college. I did it to get more points for my [intramural] team. I was a very competitive person, that's why I wanted to be at the top of the class—you got more points for that. Part of me didn't want to lose that status. But part of me hated it and wanted to disappear from it because it put so much pressure on me and I was always anxious."

A pretty girl who hid her strong opinions beneath a pleasing demeanor, Lucy was also a debutante like her mother. "All my friends were debutantes," she explained. "That's what we were thinking about—parties, dancing, boys, and martinis." Although her parents didn't care whether she went to college, Lucy chose to go to Radcliffe because a cousin went there. "Something was driving me to get out of how I grew up," she said, and indeed, she found life on campus liberating. "I had a good time at Radcliffe. You could goof off. I got contact lenses—I wasn't 'froggy four-eyes' anymore—and I got honors. I didn't take advantage of all the academic things, but I became much more adventuresome in terms of meeting all kinds of people, which is why I came to New York."

In New York, Lucy found herself totally unprepared for the work world. "The word 'résumé' was completely foreign to me," she recalled. "I didn't have a goal. I thought I was going to get married." Determined not to be a secretary—"at Radcliffe, they fill your head with the 'best and brightest,'" she said—she scoured the "Help Wanted—Female" ads for something other than menial jobs and two weeks later, ended up at the Career Blazers employment agency. "They told me there was a training program at *Newsweek*," she recalled. "Did I ask what was involved? Did I have any idea what it was?" In her best dress and gloves, she went off to the interview at *Newsweek,* where an editor asked her if she knew George Trow, another Harvard graduate who later became a writer for the *New Yorker.* Worried that she might say the wrong thing, Lucy cautiously answered that she knew George had written the Hasty Pudding show at Harvard. The editor said, "His father's my best friend—when can you come to work?"

Lucy joined *Newsweek* on the mail desk in September 1963. She got hooked on news when, in November, the first wires came across that President Kennedy had just been shot and *Newsweek* scrambled to cover the story. In March, she moved to Nation as a researcher. During the 1968 primary, when Hubert Humphrey, Eugene McCarthy, and later, Bobby Kennedy were running for the Democratic nomination, Lucy and Margaret did a fair share of reporting. "Jay [Iselin] sent us all out because there were so many candidates in 1968 and not enough guys to cover them," said Lucy, "and we suddenly realized we could be reporters."

In the fall of 1969, Judy Gingold invited Margaret and Lucy to lunch at the New York Women's Exchange, a cheery consignment shop and restaurant on Madison Avenue whose aim was to help "gentlewomen in reduced circumstances"—the perfect description for our little group. Founded in 1878 so that Civil War widows could earn a living by selling their wares, the Women's Exchange was overflowing with knitted baby clothes, hand-made rag dolls, and beautifully embroidered linens hanging on the walls. In the back, down a few stairs, was a small restaurant filled with wooden tables and chairs. Over the next six months, the Women's Exchange became "Command Central" for the *Newsweek* crew as we plotted our homegrown revolution over home-baked crab cakes and claret lemonade.

When Judy approached her, Lucy had just returned from a month in San Francisco, California, where women's lib was in the air. She had brought back tie-dye shirts from the Haight-Ashbury district and buttons that read UPPITY WOMEN UNITE. Over lunch with Lucy and Margaret, Judy explained about Title VII and they discussed writing an anonymous letter to the EEOC describing the *Newsweek* situation and asking the commission to investigate. After endless meetings, they gathered one night at Margaret's apartment on Eighty-Ninth and York, where the three women finally drafted the letter. "Judy was the philosopher and theoretician—super smart and could talk every angle," explained Lucy. "Margaret could cut right to the heart of the matter and say this was wrong, this is what it should be. My role, as I saw it, was to make sure everything was nailed down, that there were no holes or openings for mistakes. On the way home I was supposed to drop the letter in the mailbox but like a good researcher, I wanted to reread it once more, so I didn't mail it after all."

Lucy was particularly offended by the treatment of her friend Pat Lynden, a fellow researcher in the Nation section. Pat had been reporting on New York Mayor John Lindsay, who was hoping for a slot on the Republican presidential ticket in 1968. But just before the Republican convention in Miami that summer, Pat was told that she wasn't going. Instead, a young male reporter would take her place—and by the way, would she please turn over her notes to him? "That made me really angry," said Lucy. "The summer in Berkeley had really changed my view of *Newsweek*. I don't think I was capable of initiating the suit, but when I saw what happened to Pat, that galvanized me." Margaret also felt aggrieved on behalf of both Judy and Pat. "For Judy to come back from a Marshall and be offered a job running copy—that was mind-boggling," she recalled. "Judy was very angry at that point. Pat was someone who did want to be a journalist and had done a lot of reporting work in New York, and then to have to turn over everything to a guy—that was unfair."

Lucy and Margaret suggested that they bring in Pat, who was everything they weren't—ambitious and combative. Pat had graduated from the University of California at Berkeley, where she had worked on the *Daily Cal* and won awards for her reporting. In January 1962, on her way to Europe, she fell in love with New York and landed a job on the *Newsweek* mail desk. After she became a Nation researcher, she wrote several freelance pieces, including cover stories for the *New York Times Magazine* and for the *Atlantic*.

A fearless reporter—the kind who was assigned to cover the riots in Newark—Pat had an unusual background. She was a "red-diaper baby," the epithet given to children of American Communists or Communist sympathizers. Her uncle was Archie Brown, the trade union director of the Communist Party in California. Her father, an official of the International

Longshoreman's and Warehouseman's Union, had been called before the House Un-American Activities Committee, where he invoked his Fifth Amendment protection against self-incrimination. There was a profile relief, in hammered copper, of Joseph Stalin over her grandmother's china cabinet. "I wasn't sure whether it portrayed the Soviet leader or my Russian-born Jewish grandfather as a young man," Pat wrote in an article for *New York Woman* magazine. "I never asked, I suppose, because to me my grandfather and the USSR were one and the same." During the 1950s, Pat and her family became untouchables, she wrote, "partly through our own choice—we had been raised to reject much that capitalism had wrought—but in large measure it was because during the depressing postwar decade of the blacklists . . . doors were closed to us as well as our parents."

That left a powerful impression on Pat. "On the positive side of this Leftist heritage," she wrote in *New York Woman,* "is the pride in a political tradition that stands for egalitarianism, the rights of minorities, economic justice . . . and civil liberties. But ours is also a subculture that will always feel vulnerable to the powers that be; we will always believe that we are irrevocably outsiders. We often wonder when the government will, once again, need political scapegoats and choose us. As a consequence, we have very little faith in, or regard for, duly constituted authority. We also know that friends are often friends only to a point." Still, Pat was no fan of the Communist Party either—giving her a healthy skepticism about everything. "I was aware of a lot of the bullshit on the Left—the hypocrisy and the philandering and the mistreatment of wives," she later told me. "I kept myself on the sidelines."

In 1965, Pat met Allen Gore, a lieutenant of detectives in the police department's Pickpocket and Confidence Division (they would later marry). Two years later, Allen got Pat entrée to the Gypsy subculture for a cover story in *The Atlantic*. But when she showed a draft of the story to Ed Kosner, a friend in Nation, he said, "'You're a good reporter but you're not such a good writer,'" she recalled. "I was devastated." After the Lindsay assignment was taken away from her in the summer of 1968, she said, "my confidence began to flag and I left." She worked for a columnist for a while and went back to San Francisco to do some reporting. She returned in late 1969 when *Newsweek* offered her a job in the New York bureau. Shortly after that, Lucy and Margaret approached Pat in the *Newsweek* ladies' room. "I thought about it for two hours and said, 'Yes, I'll join you,'" Pat recalled. "Then a week or two went by and we didn't know what to do. Who else do we know? Who can we trust? Women just didn't trust each other. We didn't talk about our salaries. We fought over the bones like crazy. We competed with each other instead of saying, 'We're not the enemy.'"

It was around that time, in October 1969, that Judy suggested I join the group. She had transferred from Nation to the Education section the year before and had just been promoted to head researcher in the back of the book. We were sharing a small inside office on the twelfth floor and had become best friends, but approaching me was tricky. My father was a good friend of Kay Graham's and he was working at the *Post* when her father, Eugene Meyer, bought the paper in 1933. In the spring of 1965, as I was finishing up at Vassar, he had asked Kay Graham to set up a job interview for me at *Newsweek,* which she had graciously arranged. But there were no job openings in Paris at the time.

My father was a well-known journalist in Washington and the sports world, widely admired for his integrity, his fairness, and his graceful writing. He was also an Orthodox Jew from Bar Harbor, Maine, the summer playground of the wealthy "rusticators"—the Astors, the Rockefellers, the Vanderbilts, the Carnegies. Every June, they journeyed to Mt. Desert Island on their private railroad cars to spend three months at their "cottages," more often fifty-room mansions with stables and servants' quarters. Dad's father had come from Lithuania to Boston in 1878 at age twelve with his father. They had peddled north, with packs on their back, to Bar Harbor, where they opened a furniture shop on Main Street and lived above the store. The seventh of nine children, Dad caddied at the tony Kebo Valley Golf Club, where one of his clients was Edward B. McLean, owner of the *Washington Post* (his wife, Evalyn, was the owner of the Hope Diamond). Mr. McLean offered Dad a job at his paper if he would continue to caddy for him at his private golf course off Wisconsin Avenue in Washington. So in 1922, at seventeen, Shirley (not an unusual male name in Maine) started as a police reporter at the *Washington Post* before he went to cover sports for $5 more a week.

My mother, Ethyl Friedman Povich, was born in Radom, Poland. Her father, a tailor, had emigrated to Washington with fellow landsmen in the early twentieth century. In 1912, he brought his wife and children—my three-year-old mother and her six brothers and sisters—to live with him (another son would be born in the United States). After meeting on a blind date and marrying two years later, my parents lived the high life, traveling to New York and Florida and clubbing with the other sportswriters and their wives (their honeymoon was at the Washington Senators' spring training camp in Biloxi, Mississippi). But after they had children, and with Dad constantly on the road, Mom became our anchor at home, providing a sweet, warm presence for us.

Sports was the lingua franca at home, especially with two older brothers. Every February, we moved to Orlando, Florida, where the Washington Senators held spring training and where we went to school when we were young. While my brothers were living out their dreams as batboys, I rooted from the bleachers. Since girls weren't allowed in the clubhouse, Dad always arranged for Mickey Vernon or Eddie Yost to play catch with me after the game. Needless to say, I became a big sports fan and understood the finer points of baseball. One of my proudest achievements was when my father used my scorecard at a Senators game to write his column.

Although I played team sports, I didn't want to compete in that arena, so I chose to become a dancer. I was a serious ballet student until, at thirteen, my teacher recommended that I go to the School of American Ballet in New York City. The idea of moving to New York, and not going to college, was out of the question for my family and me—a bridge too far. I switched to modern dance and became part of a performance troupe founded by Erika Thimey, a German émigré who, along with Ruth St. Denis, brought a spiritual dimension to modern dance.

Given the strong personalities of my father and brothers, our house was infused with testosterone. The good part was that I felt comfortable around men and sports, something that helped me later in my career. But at the same time, our house revolved around the guys. I know it bothered my mother (she used to call us "motherless children," since everyone referred to us as "Shirley's kids"), and she took out her frustrations on me, often by being critical. I chafed under her, but I, too, was annoyed that many people didn't even know that Shirley Povich also had a daughter.

At home, the boys ruled. My parents sent my brothers to summer camp each year and, after elementary school, to Landon, an all-boys private school. I went to camp just one summer and continued in public school. Three years after the 1954 US Supreme Court decision in *Brown v. Board of Education*, which declared that separate but equal schools for whites and blacks was unconstitutional, my all-white junior high school suddenly had an influx of black students. The problem was not the kids, as I remember it. In fact, the gangs in my school were mostly white and my best friend was black. The administration just couldn't deal with the racial tensions or the influx of new students. After graduating from the ninth grade at Paul Junior High School in 1958, I went to Sidwell Friends, a private, coed Quaker school across town.

At Friends, I was one of three new students in a class of fifty-three, most of whom had been there since kindergarten. Friends wasn't a fancy school then—the most famous students were children of diplomats, not media stars—and it instilled in us the Quaker values of peace, simplicity, and social justice. I appreciated the silent contemplation of the weekly meetings for worship as well as Friends' first-class education, which helped me get into Vassar.

Still, I shied away from writing. I admired my father's talent and read his column eagerly (he wrote six days a week), but how could I measure up? I once gave an eighth-grade paper to my father to look over. He was a witty and elegant writer and cared deeply about his craft. With the best intentions and wanting me to be a good writer, he criticized my story in what he thought was a constructive way. But to me, it was devastating. I had failed the test; I couldn't play in his league. I never again showed him anything I had written.

I was expected to do well in school, but it was never explained to me that I might have to earn a living. Nor did I realize that I would have to develop my own professional skills and talents. My family's expectation—and mine—was that I would work until I married and had children, like my mother had. But seeing my father out in the world and meeting interesting people certainly appealed to me more than being a housewife. And although it hadn't occurred to me to follow in his footsteps, here I was doing just that.

When Judy confided in me in the fall of 1969, it was complicated for another reason: I was no longer a researcher. My boss, Harry Waters, had suggested that I be promoted to junior writer, and I was in March 1969. "You never voiced much ambition and I don't remember your pushing to get ahead," Harry recalled. "But I thought from your files that you should be a reporter and writer." Still, Judy knew I would be sympathetic to the idea of a lawsuit. In 1969, I had begun covering the gay-rights and the women's lib movements, which was expanding my worldview. I interviewed the radical Redstockings, who insisted on talking only to female reporters, and covered the first Congress to Unite Women, where the Daughters of Bilitis were dropped as a sponsor because Betty Friedan feared that lesbian associations would threaten the new women's movement. I would return to the office fired up by these encounters and Judy and I would talk excitedly about them. That fall, I had suggested a six-column story on women's lib. I was sent to Chicago and Boston to do the reporting because there were no women in the bureaus. My senior editor had moved to another department and Dwight Martin, the fill-in editor, thought I was "too close to the material." He asked a guy to rewrite the piece but the story kept getting delayed and never ran. Then Judy told me about the EEOC.

I must admit I wasn't the first woman to "get it," nor was I particularly angry, although I came to value those who were.

People like Judy and Pat who were angry pushed the rest of us to make it happen. But my consciousness was getting raised and the blinders were beginning to fall. We *were* competing against one another and now I, too, began to question why there was just one slot for a woman and, more important, why we were willing to go along with the system. I had been lucky enough to break through the ranks, but even if I hadn't personally been held back, I knew too many women who had. I signed on.

CHAPTER 5

"You Gotta Take Off
Your White Gloves, Ladies"

F OR THE NEXT FEW WEEKS, we were skulking around the office like spies, waiting for the right opportunity to pounce
on our next recruit. Our strategy was to bring in women one
by one, keeping things as secret as possible until we knew what
we were going to do. The *Newsweek* ladies' room was a favorite
ambush spot. Peering under the stalls to make sure no one else
was there, we would start a casual conversation at the sink
about how bad things were. "I would say, 'Oh God, I have to
research a story by some male writer and I'm sure I could write
it better myself,'" recalled Lucy Howard. "If the woman agreed,
then I would tell her some of us had been thinking about what
we could do to change this—and slowly bring her in."

Lucy, Margaret, and Pat approached the researchers in the
Nation, Foreign, and Business sections while Judy and I took

those in the back of the book. "To get into the inner circle you had to be vouched for," explained Lucy. "Given how we were raised, we didn't trust women, we didn't want to talk to women, we didn't even want to sit next to women. It was all about catering to men. You really had to trust someone to make sure she wouldn't see it as an advantage to rat you out. Judy knew Lynn and Lynn knew Mary."

Mary Pleshette and I were becoming good friends. Mary was the Movies researcher and we often double-dated. I first met her boyfriend, Jack Willis, in the fall of 1969, when we went to see *Bob & Carol & Ted & Alice* at the Lincoln Center Film Festival. To me, Mary was the consummate New Yorker. The daughter of a prominent East Side ob/gyn, she had grown up on Madison Avenue, graduated from Sarah Lawrence, and was an aficionado of art, theater, food, and French, which she spoke fluently. Mary was a wonderful storyteller and wanted to be a writer. She had begun to freelance for the counterculture *Village Voice* and other publications when I invited her into our office one evening and closed the door. Explaining that the situation for researchers at *Newsweek* was illegal, I said, "We're beginning to organize—would you be interested in joining us?" "Absolutely," Mary said without hesitation. We ended the conversation by swearing her to secrecy.

Judy and I then approached Phyllis Malamud, who had the office next to ours. Phyllis, whose father was the cantor at the Actors Temple in Times Square, was hired at *Newsweek* in 1960, after graduating from the City College of New York, and had worked her way up to a reporter position in the New York bureau. "Like most women those days, I thought I would meet a guy and get married," she later said, "but I never met the guy, and after working at *Newsweek*, all of a sudden I had a career." Judy and I stood in her doorway, not wanting to look too conspiratorial, and made our usual pitch: "We're thinking about doing something—do you want to join?" Phyllis was surprised by our proposal but readily accepted. "It was the first time I even thought about the injustice," she recalled.

I also enlisted Elisabeth Coleman, the Press researcher, whose nickname was Lala. With long golden-red hair and green eyes, Lala was, hands down, the most beautiful woman at the magazine. Guys lusted after her and many at the magazine tried to date her. After graduating from Vassar, she had come to New York City wanting to work in journalism "as an assistant to a smart man," she recalled. "My parents asked, 'Have you ever thought about being a journalist yourself?' and I replied, 'Oh my gosh, no—I couldn't do that. That's for men.'" Luckily Lala's boss, Bruce Porter, was a generous mentor, taking her along on assignments and training her to become a good reporter. When Bruce was away one day, I walked into the Press office and closed the door. In a hushed voice, I told Lala about our plans and asked if she would be interested in joining our group. She was so excited by the offer she immediately said yes. "I had this tightly wound feeling that we were changing history," she recalled, "that something was going to explode!"

What we didn't know was that for the past year Lala had been asking Rod Gander if she could go to a bureau for a summer internship. Rod, the chief of correspondents, reminded her that the summer positions were reserved as a training program for young black men. When Lala pointed out that white guys from the *Harvard Crimson* and the *Columbia Spectator* were also being recruited for summer internships, Rod told her it was simply too expensive to send her as well. One day over drinks, Lala said, "Rod, there's something you're not telling me. What is it?" After a few more drinks, Rod confessed, "I don't want to say this but—men don't want to work with women."

I also talked to my friend Mimi Sheils (now Merrill McLoughlin), who worked across the hall in the Religion department. Tall, curly-haired, and super smart, Mimi was a proper girl on the outside, but a wild child underneath. She had majored in religion at Smith College, a decision her father, an advertising salesman at *Time,* ridiculed, saying it would get her a job as a telephone operator at Dial-A-Prayer. Instead, it got her a job as the Religion researcher at *Newsweek.* At her 1966 interview, the chief of research, Olga Barbi, asked Mimi what she was interested in. When she told her she had majored in religion, "Olga jumped out of her chair and said, 'No one has ever said they were interested in Religion,'" Mimi recalled, laughing. Mimi wanted to be a doctor and finished her premed requirements in college, but she spent the summer after graduation at Radcliffe taking secretarial courses—just in case. "I got married in '68 and I thought I was going to med school," she recalled, "which is why I never expected to be a journalist or magazine person."

When I approached Mimi, "I wasn't offended that my path was being cut off," she recalled, "because I didn't think my path was there." But she was angry about other talented women being blocked. "I'd always been a little rebellious—I was a bad teenager," she said. "So to some extent rebelling wasn't all that new to me. I was always running afoul of my father, who set very strict rules, and I set my life to break them." As the Religion researcher, Mimi did a lot of reporting and was upset that her work wasn't recognized. "I did a lot of reporting, which was heavily used in stories, and I rarely got credit or mention in Top of the Week [where staffers were acknowledged before there were bylines]. That annoyed me no end."

Another early recruit was Trish Reilly, a tall, impeccably dressed researcher in the Arts sections. Trish's seeming sophistication belied the fact that she was the first in her family to go to college, at UC Berkeley. Born in Alameda, California, Trish was raised with the expectations of becoming a schoolteacher, getting married, and having kids, and she never aspired to rise beyond that. "I knew what was being done to women at *Newsweek* was as wrong as slavery and I was happy to be part of the lawsuit," she recalled. "But I saw myself as someone whose own life wouldn't be changed by it." Trish had qualms about joining the women and talked it over with Mary Pleshette. "I don't know about this whole business of women being in men's jobs," she confessed to Mary. "I like the differences between men and women and I think we should keep them." Mary asked her which differences she was afraid of losing. Trish didn't answer for a long time. "Oh well," she finally said, "we'll still be women—we'll just have better jobs."

As the circle widened in the winter of 1970, we asked the five black researchers on the staff to join us. "I had divided emotions," recalled Leandra Hennemann Abbott, a researcher in the back of the book. "Here was the women's lib movement and while I certainly could identify with that, it seemed to me that women's liberation wasn't out front in support of black liberation and never reached out to black women. I believed the difficulties we felt were because of being black and that a lot of the issues for white women didn't apply to us because we didn't have a choice. They were talking about work and we were working all the time. Our issues were larger than the work world. We had to be strong for the family, too."

Diane Camper, a Syracuse graduate who was a Nation researcher, said that although the black women never caucused, they informally discussed what to do. "There was a feeling that there had been all these conversations going on among the white women about agitating for more women to be reporters and we were an afterthought," she later explained. "At the time, there was more identity with race than gender. People just didn't see the strategic advantage of joining in." In the end, much to our disappointment, the black women decided not to join us.

There were several women we didn't approach. One was Rita Goldstein, the Newsmakers researcher, who was dating a Wallenda, *Newsweek*'s executive editor, Bob Christopher (they would marry in May 1970). We were so paranoid about being discovered that we felt we couldn't risk any pillow talk. We also were worried about approaching Madlyn Millimet, who had married Angus Deming, a writer in Foreign, in January 1970, two months before we filed the lawsuit. But in the end Maddy signed the complaint.

A critical convert to our cause was Fay Willey, the head researcher in the Foreign section. Almost a decade older than most of us, Fay had joined *Newsweek* in 1955, when Vincent Astor and other wealthy stockholders owned the magazine. On election nights, the Astors would invite British nobility in to watch the proceedings, as if the staff were animals in a zoo. Fay was well respected by the top editors, who appreciated her maturity and experience. She had established a solid reputation in the world of foreign affairs and provided important context to *Newsweek* stories with authoritative commentary from "the domes," the scholars and government sources she carefully cultivated. We weren't sure she would join us but we knew our position would be greatly enhanced if she did.

Judy and Pat nervously paid a visit to Fay at her immaculate Upper East Side apartment, the parlor floor of a brownstone filled with antique furniture. Little did they know that Fay had been seething for years about the condescending way research was regarded at the newsmagazines. In October 1964, Otto Friedrich, a *Time* editor, wrote a famous piece in *Harper's* magazine titled "There are 00 Trees in Russia: The Function of Facts in Newsmagazines," which infuriated Fay. Friedrich's article argued that the newsmagazine fetish for "the facts" did not necessarily represent the truth. He explained that *Time* and *Newsweek* had evolved "a unique system which makes it theoretically possible to write an entire news story without any facts at all." By putting in "TK" for "to kum" ("kum" being a deliberate misspelling of "come" to warn copy editors and proofreaders not to let the word get into print)—or, in the case of statistics, "00," to be filled in later—it enabled the writer, he said, "to ignore all the facts and concentrate on the drama."

To guard this fact "fetish" at newsmagazines, Friedrich wrote,

> There came into existence an institution unknown to newspapers: the checker. The checker is usually a girl in her twenties, usually from some Eastern college, pleasant-looking but not a femme fatale. She came from college unqualified for anything but looking for an "interesting" job. After a few years, she usually feels, bitterly and rightly, that nobody appreciates her work. The beginning of the week is lackadaisical and so is the research, but toward the end, when typewriters clack behind closed doors and editors snap at intruders, there are midnight hamburgers and tears in the ladies' room. For the checker gets no credit if the story is right, but she gets the blame if it is wrong. It doesn't matter if the story is slanted or meretricious, if it misinterprets or misses the point of the week's news. That is the responsibility of the editors. What matters—and what seems to attract most of the hostile letters to the editors—is whether a championship poodle stands thirty-six or forty inches high, whether the eyes of Prince Juan

Carlos of Spain are blue or brown, whether the population of some city in Kansas is 15,000 or 18,000.

Fay wrote a scathing letter to the editor of *Harper's* that was published in the December 1964 issue. "As the researcher (not checker, please) who arrived at the number of trees in Russia, permit me to say that Otto Friedrich's article is enough to send any researcher to the ladies' room for a few tears," it read. "Aside from his insulting remarks about what we do to earn a living and how we do it, Mr. Friedrich says we are not *femmes fatales,* which is most ungallant, and 'unqualified for anything,' which is untrue. We can be quite *fatale* in circumstances other than telling a writer that his story is all wrong (perhaps none of us ever trained her guns on Mr. Friedrich), and as for our training, researchers by and large have the same education as the writers they are working for, if not a better one." She ended the letter by citing four facts in Friedrich's article in need of correcting. At the bottom of her letter was his reply: "I am mortified at the accusation of ungallantry and, if guilty, deeply apologetic. As for the rest of Miss Willey's 'corrections,' I say, '*Qui s'excuse, s'accuse.*'" (He who excuses himself accuses himself.)

When Judy and Pat discussed our plans with Fay, she was cool to the idea of taking legal action. She herself didn't want to become a writer, but she did feel women should be allowed to write. What she wanted was for research to be more valued and for researchers to be considered as important to the magazine as the correspondents in the field. She was particularly unhappy that the editors entertained her sources at *Newsweek* lunches and didn't include her. Fay had been horribly embarrassed when a China scholar she had cultivated was asked to *Newsweek* one day and she hadn't been invited. The next time someone asked her to call the man for a quote, she was overheard saying, "Call him up your bloody self—you just had him to lunch!" Fay felt strongly that we should first air our grievances with the editors. She wanted to make sure we had given them a fair chance. The more she thought about the lack of respect given the researchers and their work, however, the more upset she got. She decided to join our band of sisters.

Meanwhile, we had been shopping for a lawyer of the female persuasion. The first attorney we approached was Harriet Pilpel, a senior partner in the law firm of Greenbaum, Wolff & Ernst, which specialized in First Amendment issues. With no experience in the new field of employment rights law, she declined to represent us. Even so, recalled Margaret, "she was thrilled we weren't lesbians. I don't know if she used those words, but she was delighted that we were nice, soft-spoken, decently dressed young women and not part of the lunatic fringe." We then approached the lunatic fringe—Florynce Kennedy, the flamboyant black civil rights lawyer and fiery feminist who had defended Valerie Solanas, the woman who shot Andy Warhol in 1968. Greeting us in her apartment in the East Forties wearing her signature cowboy hat, Flo had lots of ideas of what we could do, including sit-ins and guerrilla theater, but most of them were too outrageous for us. She also discussed how much money she would need, which made us realize we should think about a pro bono lawyer.

That led us to the American Civil Liberties Union, where we met with the assistant legal director, Eleanor Holmes Norton. Five feet, seven inches and five months pregnant, Eleanor was an impressive figure with an Afro to match. As we sat in her office explaining our case, she grabbed a copy of *Newsweek* and opened it to the masthead. She looked at it—then looked at us—and said, "The fact that there are all men from the top category to the second from the bottom and virtually all women in the last category proves *prima facie* that there's a pattern of discrimination at *Newsweek*. I'll take your case." (There was one male researcher on the masthead, a political refugee from Greece whom the editors had hired as a favor.)

Eleanor was perfect for us. A veteran civil rights activist and self-avowed feminist, she was smart, shrewd, and sharp-tongued—"indignant" was her middle name. The great-granddaughter of a slave who walked off a Virginia plantation, Eleanor was from an aspiring and ambitious family. Her grandfather Richard Holmes was one of Washington, D.C.'s few black firefighters and successfully petitioned the department to create the first all-black company in 1921. Her father, Coleman Holmes, a charming and dapper man, went to Syracuse University on a scholarship. In Syracuse, he met Vela Lynch, a shy woman who had grown up on a farm in North Carolina but was sent north after her mother died. They married in 1935 and came back to Washington, where Coleman worked as a public health inspector and Vela took a job in the Bureau of Engraving and Printing. More industrious—and more practical—than her husband, Vela went back to school to earn a teaching degree. In the late 1940s, she also joined the National Association for the Advancement of Colored People and paid $1 annual dues toward its "Struggle for Full Emancipation for the American Negro."

As the oldest of three girls, Eleanor easily assumed the role of the first-born, scoring top grades and leading school organizations from elementary through high school. Washington was still a Southern, segregated city, where white-owned stores in black neighborhoods wouldn't even hire "colored people" to work for them. In 1951, at age twelve, Eleanor had what she describes as her first consciousness-raising moment. The educator Mary Church Terrell threw up a picket line around Hecht's department store, creating one of the biggest civil rights campaigns at the time (even entertainer Josephine Baker dropped by). "You could go in there and use your charge-a-plate [a predecessor to credit cards], but you couldn't use the bathrooms," Eleanor explained in her biography, *Fire in My Soul* by Joan Steinau Lester. Terrell sued the store, citing the District's 1872 and 1873 open accommodation laws, which made segregation in public accommodations illegal. In January 1952, after six months of protests, Hecht's opened its cafeteria to blacks but without stools, forcing people to eat standing up. On June 8, 1953, the US Supreme Court affirmed the District's laws and Hecht's was forced to integrate.

A proud member of Washington's black bourgeoisie—and a debutante—Eleanor went to Antioch College in Yellow Springs, Ohio, where she could earn money in a work-study program. In December 1955, just months after Eleanor arrived on campus, Rosa Parks refused to move to the back of a bus in Montgomery, Alabama, sparking a city boycott led by the twenty-six-year-old Reverend Martin Luther King Jr. Only a freshman but already head of Antioch's NAACP chapter, Eleanor raised money and conducted local sit-ins for nearly a year. In November 1956, the Supreme Court upheld the Fifth Circuit Court ruling that Montgomery's segregated-bus law violated the Fourteenth Amendment's due process and equal protection clauses. "It was," Eleanor later said, "the defining experience of my life."

After Antioch, Eleanor went to Yale University, where she earned two degrees: a master's degree in American studies in 1963 and a law degree in 1964. The only other black student at the law school was Marian Wright (Edelman). Mentored by Pauli Murray, a black feminist lawyer who was getting an advanced legal degree, Eleanor started a New Haven chapter of CORE (Congress on Racial Equality). In the summer of 1963, she joined the Student Nonviolent Coordinating Committee's voter registration drive in Mississippi, where Medgar Evers drove her to meet key civil rights workers, and later helped organize the 1963 March on Washington. "I grew up black and female at the moment in time in America when barriers would fall if you'd push them," she told Lester. "I pushed . . . and then just walked on through."

When we met her, Eleanor was only thirty-two years old but she was already an extraordinarily accomplished lawyer. After clerking for Judge A. Leon Higginbotham Jr., the first black judge on the US District Court for Pennsylvania's eastern district, she joined the ACLU in 1965, where she made her mark. She wrote amicus briefs for Julian Bond (who was refused his elected seat in Georgia's House of Representatives), Muhammad Ali (who refused military conscription based on his Muslim faith), and Adam Clayton Powell (who was expelled from Congress for alleged abuses). Eleanor also represented some prominent racists. In 1968, she successfully defended presidential candidate George Wallace when New York City Mayor John Lindsay initially barred him from speaking at Shea Stadium. But her most famous case was in October 1969, when she represented the National States' Rights Party before the US Supreme Court. A white supremacist group, the States' Rights Party had been kept from rallying in Maryland on a prior restraint ruling. "I jumped at the opportunity," she recalled, "because if there is a constitutional or civil liberties point to be made, you make it most convincingly when you stand up for the right of somebody who disagrees with you. You must obviously be serving a higher cause—and I love that idea." She won that case.

Next to those high-profile clients, we felt inconsequential, but according to Eleanor, "no case I handled was more important than *Newsweek*. Defending George Wallace was an old-fashion First Amendment case. Same with the white supremacists, who were kept from speaking because of their use of defamatory language against blacks and others." *Newsweek* intrigued her for two reasons. She was one of the few prominent black women who, along with Dorothy Height and Shirley Chisholm, declared herself a feminist. "I said to black women,

'Yes, you must be part of the women's movement,'" she later said. "I remember being so frustrated that when we had one of those feminist parades down Fifth Avenue, I—who never wore dashiki-type garb—put a beautiful African turban around my Afro to make the point that if you're black, you should be marching here." But she understood why black women were hesitant to join. "There was great confusion in the black movement at that time," she said. "We were in the throes of the civil rights movement. For black women to make that transition— to make a partnership with white women, who were among the most privileged in society—was uncomfortable for them."

Another reason Eleanor took our case was that we were the first women in the media to sue and the first professional women to file a class action suit. "At that time, there were almost no classes involving women—certainly none involving white women," she recalled. "If there had been a women's class action suit, I hadn't heard of it." Most of the cases, she said, had involved black factory workers discriminated against via seniority systems or biased testing. We were professional women in a field where advancement depended on subjective judgments. "You essentially had to make a case of deliberate discrimination on where women were placed in the corporation," she explained. "I thought this was so clear that it was an offer that couldn't be refused."

Eleanor believed our case was a perfect fit for the new Civil Rights Act of 1964. The most controversial section of the act was Title VII, which in its original form prohibited only racial discrimination in employment. The provision protecting women was added only at the last minute, as a joke to scuttle the bill. The chairman of the powerful Rules Committee, Howard Smith (D-VA), was a staunch segregationist and opposed to granting federal civil rights to anybody. "Congressman Smith would joyfully disembowel the Civil Rights Bill if he could," said a 1964 article in the *New York Times Magazine*. "Lacking the votes to do so, he will obstruct it as long as the situation allows." That February, Smith laughingly moved to add "sex" to the Title VII protections, thinking it would make the bill impossible to pass. But with lobbying from the National Women's Party and Representative Martha Griffiths (D-MI), who had been laboring to get votes, the amendment passed by a vote of 290–130. In the Senate, Everett Dirksen (R-IL), whose support was key to getting it passed, wanted to remove the amendment. But Senator Margaret Chase Smith (R-ME) persuaded the Republican Conference to vote against him. On June 19, the legislation passed the Senate by a vote of 73–27. President Lyndon Johnson signed the Civil Rights Act of 1964 into law on July 2.

When we approached Eleanor in the winter of 1970, the regulations were new and the precedents few. "To me, as a discrimination lawyer, this was an easy case," Eleanor recalled. "Most cases have much of the discrimination hidden. Usually you got cases where all the women are in one place and all the men are on top—that's the way it is throughout the workplace. But women don't always have the same background as men. You all had the same background! Here you had women who were not only well educated, you had women who excelled at some of the best schools. What more could *Newsweek* want?"

Eleanor agreed to take our case in the winter of 1970, and shortly thereafter *Newsweek* decided to run the women's lib cover. Since I had been reporting on the movement, they thought that asking me to work on Helen Dudar's story would be offensive—and they were right. I was relieved not to be involved. Instead, however, they asked Judy Gingold to be the magazine's liaison to Helen on the story—needless to say, an uncomfortable position for the mastermind of *Newsweek*'s own women's movement. "I felt like Mata Hari," recalled Judy. "I felt I was betraying Helen, whom I respected and admired—and that was hard."

When we heard that the editors went outside the magazine to hire a woman writer, we were furious and exhilarated. Now we had a deadline and, more important, a news peg; we could see the headlines already. We quickly stepped up our recruiting, bringing in concentric circles of five, ten, and twenty women. One beloved addition was Ruth Werthman, the respected head of the copy desk, who was in her sixties and delighted to be part of the gang. We also invited the women in the Letters department, since they were often promoted into research jobs. That provided us with our one black signatory, Karla Spurlock, who was working part-time in the Letters department. Karla's Barnard roommate, Alison Kilgour, also worked in Letters and had gotten her the job. "Madeleine [Edmonson, the head of Letters] just rounded all of us up one day and told us we were to sign this, so I did," recalled Karla. We did not approach the female reporters in the bureaus since most of them had been hired from outside the magazine. Nor did we include the editorial secretaries whose skills were different from those of the researchers.

One of the strong points of our suit was that most of the researchers had the same or very similar qualifications as the men who held higher positions. To prove it, we came up with a list of nineteen men who had been hired at *Newsweek* as reporters and writers with no prior professional journalistic experience, including several—such as Rod Gander and Kevin Buckley—who had started as researchers in the early 1960s. (The practice of hiring male researchers ended shortly after that.) The editors always insisted they recruited writers randomly—"over the transom," as they used to say—but their standard procedure, at least in the back of the book, was to hire guys who had worked on the *Yale Daily News* or the *Harvard Crimson*. Several young men from Harvard had been hired right after they graduated, including Jake Brackman (who later became a songwriter with Carly Simon), Rick Hertzberg (now a writer at the *New Yorker*), and as a graduate student, Ray Sokolov (a former writer and editor at the *Wall Street Journal*).

We also suspected that we had been discriminated against in pay as well as position. At one meeting, we decided to divulge our salaries. Phyllis Malamud, one of two New York bureau reporters, had been told she was the highest-paid woman in New York at $15,000. But it turned out that Lucy Howard and Pat Lynden were each making $18,000. "The suit was a sea change," Pat recalled. "Until then, coming from privileged backgrounds, we all felt we were special and therefore we were better than the other women. But while we were organizing, we started to like and trust each other. We figured we're all in this together and the risk is worth taking." Organizing became an unexpected bonding experience and, like D-Day, you never forgot who fought with you in the trenches.

Now that we had a deadline with the women's lib cover, we had to quickly convince everyone to take legal action. As budding feminists, we knew that the decision had to be made by consensus, so we invited about twenty women to meet Eleanor and hear her recommendations. We met on February 25, at Mary Pleshette's apartment, where women were sprawled over her colorful Moroccan carpet. "It was really exciting," remembered Mariana Gosnell, a reporter in the Medicine and Science sections who was a decade older than most of us. "Eleanor laid out our options, but we were a little timid by her standards. Some women thought it would affect their jobs. I felt good that we had some more radical, recent college graduates who were more confident than I was. I thought, this is the way it is and it wouldn't change. Still, I don't think it occurred to many of us that we could actually change the system."

There was a discussion about whether we should work through the Newspaper Guild, which represented *Newsweek* employees in contract negotiations with management. But the Guild, dominated by blue-collar men, had not been in the forefront of civil rights, let alone women's rights, so we nixed that. Then someone raised the possibility of sending a delegation to visit Kay Graham, thinking that as a woman she might be sympathetic. Others thought we should first go to the editors and give them one more chance. "Even I found it hard to stick it to them," remembered Judy Gingold. "I respected a lot of those people. Oz had three daughters and he was so proud that one of them had gotten eight hundred on her college boards. But all I could think of was, a lot of good that will do her! It was very difficult sustaining the belief that I was right, because how could I be right and Oz Elliott wrong?" Fay was reluctant to file any legal action. She kept asking, "Why can't we just talk to them?" and we kept saying, "It won't work, they won't listen."

There was one obvious reason it wouldn't work. Six months before we started to organize, ten of the senior writers on the magazine organized what became known as "the Colonels' Revolt." They were bitching about the usual issues of newsmagazine writers: their ideas weren't listened to and they wanted a more personal voice in their stories. The writers held a meeting and drew up a list of "nonnegotiable demands," which is what all movements presented to the power structure in those days. They drew a map of the Wallendatorium on a chalkboard with arrows pointing to each office—wanting them to think they were plotting a sit-in—and purposely left it there, hoping it would be found. It was, and the Wallendas immediately met with the Colonels, not as a group but individually. "Every Wallenda was assigned to someone and I got Oz," recalled Peter Goldman. "They picked us off one by one. Some people got raises, some promotions, and we all got to recite our demands. But essentially nothing happened."

If the editors co-opted their most valued employees, we thought, why would they listen to their lowliest staffers? That's why many of us were willing to go to court. But Eleanor still had to convince us. We began meeting with Eleanor in the evenings, in what became a six-week boot camp in power politics. "It wasn't a case of me convincing you," she later said. "We met so many times precisely because the women had to convince themselves. You knew you were on the frontier and you all had to discuss what was happening. But I had to keep telling you the truth. You're the crème de la crème—what the hell are you afraid of? You're smarter than these guys, they're taking advantage of you, and when the court sees your credentials, their eyes will pop out."

Sitting in her apartment at 245 West 104th Street, Eleanor would cut and devour slices of raw onion—one of her pregnancy cravings—as she harangued us to screw up our courage. When we explained the researcher job and how all the decisions were made by men, she was shocked. "This is one of the great dictatorships in the history of magazines!" she exclaimed. She was also surprised by our naïveté. "You gotta take off your white gloves, ladies, you gotta take off your white gloves," she would say. At one point, fed up with us all, she yelled, "You God damn middle-class women—you think you can just go to Daddy and ask for what you want?"

We all were terrified of Eleanor but there was a method to her madness. She had to shape us into a tough, solid group. "Only one or two plaintiffs would have been very vulnerable at that early stage in a sex discrimination investigation," she later explained. "They could lose their jobs, even though there is a separate cause of action against retaliation. Or if they didn't lose their jobs, they're the ones who would be fingered, and everyone else would get the benefit of what a couple of people did." Even though she thought we had a strong case, Eleanor was worried about the fight. "If enough women would come forward, then there would be protection against you all becoming fodder," she recalled. "I didn't know if you would be fodder. I realized *Newsweek* was a liberal publication, so to speak. But when you go up against management—you go up against management."

CHAPTER 6

Round One

A S HARD AS WE TRIED to keep our plans secret, they began to leak out. The Friday before we were to announce our lawsuit, Rod Gander invited Lala Coleman to lunch. They were friends—she was dating one of his reporters at the time—and the two would often go out for a few mint-flavored grasshoppers. At lunch, Rod asked her what was going on with the women. Suppressing her surprise, Lala coolly replied, "I don't know what you're talking about." "You can't even look me in the eye when you say that," he immediately shot back.

The next evening, after closing the Foreign section, Fay Willey was returning home with her groceries when the phone started ringing. She picked it up and was stunned to hear Oz Elliott on the other end. It turned out that one of the researchers in the Business section, who had been checking changes with writer Rich Thomas Friday night, had let it slip that the women were going to put out some sort of press release Sunday evening. Rich called Oz on Saturday and tipped him off. That evening, Oz told me years later, "I called Fay and said that I heard something big was going to happen with the women at *Newsweek* and that it would surface the following week." Oz pressed Fay to tell him what it was, saying the women should first come to management with their grievances. Fay was shaking. She greatly admired and respected Oz but she was scared of giving anything away. "In a very cold voice," Oz recalled, "Fay said she couldn't say anything, that the train was too far down the track." He made several attempts to convince her to tell him, appealing to her as a longtime, senior employee and a levelheaded one. Bravely holding her ground, she said simply that she would pass his message on to the women. "When I was told that Fay was involved, I felt it gave the whole thing gravitas," Oz told me. "She was no miniskirted recent grad from Radcliffe. She was part of the old guard."

Clearly worried about what was going to happen, Oz called Fay again Sunday morning, this time with a more serious concern. He reminded her that the press was under attack from the government and warned her that whatever the women were planning might have political repercussions for the magazine. In late 1969, the Nixon administration had begun its war on the "Eastern establishment elitist press." At one point Vice President Spiro Agnew declared that the *Washington Post* was part of "a trend toward monopolization of the great public information vehicles," saying that the *Post* and *Newsweek*, along with the Post Company's radio and television stations, "hearken to the same master." Oz appealed to Fay not to get the government involved and offered to meet with the women anytime. Fay again held her ground and promised to relay his concerns to the women.

There was one person we felt we should call: Helen Dudar. Pat Lynden offered to call her at home after we announced our suit. "That was incredibly helpful," recalled Peter Goldman, Helen's husband, "because Pat assured Helen that the suit wasn't personal—it was about going outside for someone to write the cover." Helen was part of the generation of women who had to make it on their own against great odds and she succeeded in every respect. "I idolized her," wrote Nora Ephron in a foreword to Helen's collected works, *The Attentive Eye: Selected Journalism*, edited by Peter. Nora, who worked with Helen at the *New York Post*, said, "Helen could do anything. She could write a lyrical feature piece, she could write hard news, and she was—in a city room full of world-class rewrite men—the greatest rewrite man of all."

Like many professional women of her generation, Helen hadn't embraced the women's liberation movement; she took the *Newsweek* assignment because she thought it was interesting. "She was in pre-feminist mode then," said Peter of his wife, who died in 2002. "I don't think she thought about the political context of the cover story. If I had been smarter I would have said this assignment has hair on it. But I wasn't smart then. You all woke me up and the assignment woke Helen up." For Helen, reporting on the new feminism was a voyage of self-discovery. "It was her consciousness-heightening period but I don't think she connected it with the *Newsweek* system," said Peter. "We used to talk about how one of the fringe benefits of *Newsweek* was that I had women pals for the first time in my adult life. But I wasn't bringing home that it was a caste system and that it wasn't fair."

When the couple discussed the assignment at home, "Helen was just communicating bits to me because she was assimilating it in bits," Peter recalled, "not in the sense of becoming an activist. She was like me on the civil rights movement—we were chroniclers. When Pat Lynden called, it was the first bell, an 'Oh my God' moment for both of us. Why didn't we get it? How could we—particularly me—not have figured this out? When the story of the legal action unfolded, it was like a revelatory experience."

The final irony of hiring Helen to write the *Newsweek* cover is that she ended up being a convert to the women's cause. Although *Newsweek*'s contents page, written by the editors, introduced the "Women in Revolt" cover in ominous tones, "A new specter is haunting America—the specter of militant feminism," Helen's report on the new feminism ended with the following thoughts:

I have spent years rejecting feminists without bothering to look too closely at their charges. . . . It has always been easy to dismiss substance out of dislike for style. About the time I came to this project, I had heard just enough to peel away the hostility, leaving me in a state of ambivalence. . . . Superiority

is precisely what I had felt and enjoyed, and it was going to
be hard to give it up. That was an important discovery. . . .
Women's lib questions everything; and while intellectually I
approve of that, emotionally I am unstrung by a lot of it.
Never mind. The ambivalence is gone; the distance is gone.
What is left is a sense of pride and kinship with all those
women who have been asking all the hard questions. I thank
them and so, I think, will a lot of other women.

The Sunday evening before we filed the suit, when we gathered at Holly Camp's apartment to work out the final details,
Fay told us about Oz's calling her at home. She relayed how
he reminded her of the Nixon administration's hostility toward
the press and asked for another chance. Fay felt that Oz had
made a good case, and once again she pleaded with us to go to
the editors first with our grievances. We were shocked that Oz
had found out about our plans but we were also impressed—
and grateful—that Fay had fended off the boss and kept our
secret. Still, we were convinced that filing a legal action was
our best chance for change and protection. Our final act that
evening was to sign the EEOC complaint, which had to be in
the mail before midnight. As we solemnly lined up, I felt the
thrill and the terror of what we were about to do. There was no
turning back. One by one, we recorded our names on the historic document.

The next morning, thirty of us arrived at the ACLU an hour
before the 10 A.M. press conference. We nervously started setting up the wooden chairs in the makeshift boardroom and

then we waited—and waited. By 9:30, no one from the press corps had arrived. We started to panic. Our entire strategy hung on getting publicity. What if no one came? Finally some cameramen and reporters started filing in, including Susan Brownmiller, who had been invited by her former *Newsweek* colleagues to bear witness. When Gabe Pressman, the popular NBC reporter arrived, recalled Margaret Montagno, "I thought, 'Aha—this really is an event!'"

After the press conference, most of us in the back of the book and Business went back to the office. Judy, Margaret, and Lucy went to lunch at a small restaurant near the ACLU to celebrate. As they toasted the women's movement and each other, Judy kept yelling, "We did it, we did it!" The next morning, the women met again at the Palm Court in the Plaza Hotel with Pat and, over croissants and champagne, they read the newspaper accounts of the press conference out loud. "I was annoyed that I was called a respectable young woman," remembered Pat, "and amused that the *Daily News* called us 'Newshens'!"

When Lucy and Pat went into the office later that Tuesday morning, they ran into Oz on the eleventh floor. "How do you feel about what happened?" Pat asked him. Oz immediately invited them into his office, where they talked for forty-five minutes. "First Oz said how hurt he was," recalled Pat. "Then he asked, 'Why didn't you come to me?' Lucy said we had—we came many times in many ways. He listened to us but didn't concede anything." Lucy was insulted because Oz said, "I can understand you, Pat, but Lucy—you are such a nice girl."

Kermit Lansner, the magazine's editor, seemed to dismiss the whole thing. Whenever there was ever a ripple in the pond of tranquility at *Newsweek,* Kermit would typically say, "Madness . . . It's all mad." We thought managing editor Lester Bernstein felt betrayed, furious that these lowly employees had soiled his magazine's reputation. One editor, we were told, simply said, "Let's just fire them all." Only Oz took the lawsuit seriously. As the father of three girls, he was particularly chastened by the charges of discrimination against women. "My consciousness at the time was zero," he admitted to me before he died in 2008. "Here we were busily carving out a new spot as a liberal magazine and right under our own noses was this oppressive regime—and no one had a second thought! It was pretty clear to me on that Monday that the women were right."

That was one of the chilling contradictions of the culture: advocating civil rights for all while tolerating—or overlooking—the subjugation of women. "My theory is that we were all blind to the fact that we were sitting on top of a caste system," said Peter Goldman. "It was this '50s mentality and the fact that *Newsweek* was copying *Time*. It seemed natural that women were in servile roles and as you keep hiring, the overcaste and the undercaste become self-sustaining. By the time I got there in 1962, the men just accepted this as the way things were and I think the women accepted it the same way."

But after that Monday in March, it was a whole new story. Some of the correspondents in the field sent congratulatory cables. "The all male San Francisco bureau (and chief stringer Karen McDonald) say right on sisters," read a telex from bureau chief Jerry Lubenow and reporters Bill Cook and Min Yee. The female correspondents immediately signaled their support, especially Liz Peer in the Washington bureau. "Liz was a cheerleader," recalled Mimi McLoughlin, the Religion researcher. "She thought of herself as a woman who had succeeded on her own and somewhat distanced herself from it. But she'd always say, 'You guys are great.'"

Most of the writers supported their female colleagues. "My attitude was 'Go for it,'" recalled Peter Goldman. "We were in a 'movement' frame of mind and as soon as the women lit the match, it was obvious. I also thought doing it through a lawsuit was the right way. I had been covering the civil rights movement and Vietnam and I thought, 'Okay, here's one more revolution—this is inevitable and it had to happen.'" Harry Waters remembered viewing the women's plight less as a gender issue than as one of injustice. "I was a young guy who started as a fact checker," he said, "but I always knew—and was told—that I would get a shot at reporting, writing, and editing. For a young, ambitious, talented woman, that elevator was out of order."

Not everyone was espousing a new order, however. As in many organizations, it was middle management that was most resistant to change—in our case, some of the senior editors who ran the six editorial sections of the magazine. With the exception of my boss, Shew Hagerty, and Ed Diamond, none of the other senior editors had promoted a researcher to writer, nor had they hired a woman as a writer. In her memoir, Susan Brownmiller described being called into *Newsweek* several weeks after the press conference to meet with the Wallendas. They inquired whether she would be interested in coming back to the magazine as a writer, but she declined. "My idea of a cold-sweat nightmare was eighty-five lines for Nation on a Friday night—it still is," she wrote. Afterward, she was pulled aside by Lester Bernstein, her former boss when he was the senior editor of Nation. "When you worked here, Susan, did you have ambition?" he asked. As she noted in her book, "For two years not a week had gone by without my asking if I could 'do more.' He hadn't noticed."

After we announced our lawsuit, Oz sent a memo to the women Monday afternoon. Saying that he was "naturally dismayed at your evident unhappiness," he called for a meeting the next day at Top of the Week, the elegant penthouse of the *Newsweek* building where visiting dignitaries were entertained. Designed by I. M. Pei, Top of the Week had a sumptuous beige salon with luxurious couches and chairs, large and small dining rooms, and a kitchen. Before our Tuesday meeting with Oz, Eleanor had instructed us not to say a word until she got there, because she didn't want us to incriminate ourselves.

Oz had arranged rows of folding chairs for the women facing one of the soft suede couches where he had placed himself and Kermit. "Big mistake," Oz later told me. "The sofa was about a foot and a half lower than the chairs and now Kermit and I are looking up at forty-seven women—our knees under our chins. I said, 'I'd like to say a few words before we start,' and this cold voice from the back of the room says, 'Sorry, Oz, we're not going to do anything until our lawyer gets here.'

Oops, I thought, this is going to be a heavy session." We sat there awkwardly for a few minutes until Eleanor finally arrived. "In comes this very angry, very articulate, very smart, very pregnant, very black Eleanor Holmes Norton," Oz said. "I welcomed her and said, 'Please take a seat. I just want to say a few words to the women before we get started,' and she said, 'I'm sorry, Mr. Elliott, but this is *our* meeting—*we* will do the talking.' She had me splattered on the wall. Boy, she was tough. How much of that explosive nature was affected and how much was just sheer anger I don't know. I think a lot of it was playacting, but she was sharp."

The editors, who had supported the struggle for civil rights, were completely baffled by this pregnant black woman who questioned their commitment to equality. But they were also horrified that the women had, as they said, "hung out their dirty laundry in public." Eleanor had warned us that Oz would immediately ask why we hadn't come to him first with our dissatisfactions. Right on cue, that was his first question and we could barely stifle our giggles. "I was surprised by the anger of the women," Oz later told me. "But when I look back I'm only surprised that the women didn't wake up earlier."

Shamed and chagrined, Oz immediately agreed to enter into negotiations. He and Kermit, along with Grant Tompkins, *Newsweek*'s head of personnel, and Rod Gander, the chief of correspondents, represented management; Eleanor and ten representatives selected by the women composed the negotiating team (I was one of them). For several weeks we met in Oz's eleventh floor office, a den-like room with bookshelves, a large wooden desk, a green patterned sofa, and matching green drapes. We had asked that as the proprietor of the magazine and one of the few female media owners Kay Graham attend the negotiations. But she declined, saying that the editors who ran the magazine would deal with the matter. "Kay was concerned, obviously," Oz told me, "but she never said, 'You've got to settle this Goddamn thing' or 'Screw them.' She never got involved."

As she wrote in her remarkably candid, 1997 Pulitzer Prize–winning autobiography, *Personal History,* Katharine Graham said that when she first took over the Washington Post Company, she felt inadequate as a company boss and a "pretender to the throne." A smart, talented young woman who had been a reporter for the *San Francisco News,* Kay had stopped working after she married Phil Graham. But after he committed suicide in 1963, she courageously stepped in to keep the paper in the family. Kay was immediately elected president of the Washington Post Company. Assuming she would be a silent partner, she was terrified. "I didn't understand the immensity of what lay before me," she later wrote, "how frightened I would be by much of it, how tough it was going to be and how many anxious hours and days I would spend for a long, long time." Six years later, she became publisher of the *Post,* a title both her father and her husband had held, but she was still riddled with feelings of inadequacy. "In the world today, men are more able than women at executive work and in certain situations," she told *Women's Wear Daily* in 1969. "I think a man would be better at this job I'm in than a woman."

Although Kay never commented publicly on our lawsuit, it was clear that she wasn't happy about it. A week after we filed charges in March 1970, in another interview with *Women's Wear Daily*, she was asked about the feminists at *Newsweek*. Kay replied that she encouraged her employees to speak their minds because people perform best when they have their say. Then she added, "Sometimes when I go home at the end of the day, I think they all have too damn much freedom to speak up."

One day in April, as we were meeting with management, Kay was spotted in her *Newsweek* office at the other end of the eleventh floor. When Eleanor heard this, she stopped the proceedings. "I understand Mrs. Graham is in the building," she said, "and I want her to come to this meeting. We will not continue these discussions until she comes." Kermit dutifully wandered off to find her and came back dragging a clearly uncomfortable Kay Graham, who sat down, tightly wrapping her legs around each other like a pretzel.

The topic that day was how women were excluded from meeting visiting dignitaries who came to the magazine. We were talking about Val Gerry, a researcher in the Foreign section who also reported on the United Nations. When a UN official came to *Newsweek* for lunch, Val had not been invited. Kay offered a response and to this day, nearly every woman remembers her words. "Well," she said, "I don't know why anyone would want to go to those lunches anyway. You know they're really very boring, and by the time you invite the four Wallendas, the Foreign editor, and the head of the UN and his entourage, there's really no place left at the table." We were flabbergasted. Clearly Kay was not a "sister." "When Kay said those lunches were so boring," said one researcher later, "it might have been boring to her because she had been involved in these kind of events her whole life!" After the meeting, Eleanor remarked that it was a good thing that Kay hadn't been in the negotiations after all.

Before the next meeting, Eleanor asked us whether there was anything in particular we wanted to ask for in the negotiations. We said that since the chief of correspondents was a senior editor, we felt that the longtime head of researchers, Olga Barbi, should also be promoted to that title. Positive that the men would go for it since they liked Olga and she had the power to hire and fire, Eleanor confidently made her pitch. The men rejected it outright, saying we were trying to elevate research and that Olga didn't do senior-editor kind of work. Afterward, Eleanor was furious that we had been so tactically stupid and excoriated us to never again ask for something when we weren't sure of the outcome.

But Eleanor held the editors' feet to the fire. At one meeting, Oz was explaining that hiring women writers was difficult because there were only so many slots open when he said, "You know, we've made a commitment on this magazine to get black writers, too." Eleanor immediately fired back, "All you're telling me, Mr. Elliott, is that now you've got *two* problems!"

Our negotiations moved rapidly, partly because Eleanor was pregnant and partly, although we didn't know it, because she had been approached by Mayor John Lindsay to be chair of New York City's Commission on Human Rights. The job was to begin April 15, a month after we filed our suit. (Many of us attended her swearing-in at the Blue Room of City Hall.) Luckily, most of the terms had been hammered out by mid-April. We had negotiated a memorandum of understanding, which stated that *Newsweek* was committed to "substantial rather than token changes." In the memorandum, the women agreed to accept management's "good faith" to "affirmatively seek out women"—including employees—for reporting and writing tryouts and positions; to integrate the research category with men; and to "identify women employees who are qualified" as possible senior editors. The agreement also stipulated that *Newsweek* would invite women to join editorial lunches, panels, campus speaker programs, and other public functions. To monitor the magazine's progress, management agreed to meet with our representatives every two months.

The language we settled for in the memorandum was vague. Quotas were illegal and although "goals and timetables" had been established as a method of relief in some legal cases, we didn't use them. Before he died in 2007, Rod Gander told me that Eleanor hadn't pushed for numbers because, "being pregnant, I think she was happy to get the thing done." Eleanor later admitted that she had to "turn this case around—I didn't get into depositions because I was trying to settle the case without going further." But she insisted that as far as setting goals and timetables, "it was not at all clear that the precedents had developed. All of the cases at that time had come out of the Deep South, where working-class black men were deliberately put into situations where they couldn't use the facilities but they could do the work. So the use of numbers had come out of harshly negative discrimination. I don't think we would have opened up numbers in this case."

We picked a historic date for signing the memorandum: August 26, 1970, the fiftieth anniversary of the passage of the Nineteenth Amendment. To celebrate women's right to vote— and to launch a new crusade for women's rights—Betty Friedan had called for a nationwide "Women's Strike for Equality" that day. Designed to appeal to both the older, liberal branch of the movement and the younger, more radical factions, the demonstrations were organized around three demands: equal opportunity in education and employment, free abortion on demand, and a network of twenty-four-hour, free child-care services. Women in more than forty cities and around the world participated.

The event was scheduled for 5 P.M. in New York, so that working women could attend, and many of us did. Reports said that between 25,000 and 50,000 women marched down Fifth Avenue, spilling over from the police-approved single lane to fill the street curb to curb. Carrying hand-lettered signs that read FIGHT SEXISM, WHISTLE AT TRUCK DRIVERS, and EVE WAS FRAMED, the women gathered for a rally in Bryant Park, behind the New York Public Library. Betty Friedan was joined on the platform by congressional candidate Bella Abzug, writers Gloria Steinem and Kate Millett, and our own Eleanor Holmes Norton. "Sex, like color, is a meaningless criterion and an oppression criterion when it is made a condition for a job," Eleanor told the crowd. Friedan ended the rally with a plea for unity. "We have learned that the enemy is us—our own lack of self-confidence," she said. "We know that the enemy is not men. Man as a class is not the enemy. Man is the fellow victim of the kind of inequality between the sexes that is part of this country's current torment and that is perpetrating violence all over the world."

But some men still didn't get it. Describing the event on the ABC evening news that night, anchor Howard K. Smith introduced his report by saying, "Three things have been difficult to tame: the ocean, fools, and women. We may soon be able to tame the ocean, but fools and women will take a little longer." In fact, it was the largest protest for women's rights since the Suffragettes, and it solidified Friedan's nascent National Organization for Women (NOW) and a scattering of women's lib groups into a national political movement.

When sixteen of us gathered in Kay Graham's eleventh-floor office on that Wednesday morning to sign the agreement, our spirits were high. We now numbered sixty plaintiffs, as more women from research, Letters, and Photo had joined the suit. Sitting at her conference table, the *Newsweek* managers—Osborn Elliott, Kermit Lansner, Rod Gander, and personnel chief Roger Borgeson—signed the 1,500-word document. Then they circulated it around the table to the women from the negotiating committee: Judy Gingold, Merrill Sheils (McLoughlin), Fay Willey, Madeleine Edmonson, Lucy Howard, Pat Lynden, Phyllis Malamud, Mariana Gosnell, Mary Pleshette, and me. Eleanor returned for the signing to join Mel Wulf, from the ACLU, and Kay Graham at the table. Kay said she was pleased that the signing had taken place on such a historic day and Oz congratulated everyone, adding, "I am sure that this agreement will contribute significantly to our editorial excellence."

As we toasted one another with wine afterward, we tried not to lord it over the editors but we couldn't conceal our triumph. We'd done it! We had forced management to at least acknowledge their prejudices and to promise to change their ways. We were still worried about what would happen to us and whether the editors would actually carry out Oz's orders, but we were hoping for the best. In a *New York Times* story about the agreement, titled "*Newsweek* Agrees to Speed Promotion of Women," I am quoted as saying, "We are very pleased with the progress so far," adding, "We feel a lot better now about things at *Newsweek*."

CHAPTER 7

Mad Men: The Boys Fight Back

THE FIRST SIGN OF TROUBLE came only weeks after the agreement was signed. Oz Elliott moved over to the business side as president of Newsweek Inc., leaving Kermit Lansner in charge of the magazine's day-to-day operations. Kermit was an intellectual and a creative man but he often was oblivious to what was going on around him. A paunchy man with the waddle of a duck, he would wander around the eleventh floor staring vaguely at the ceiling. Once, when he was walking through the copy area, a visitor saw him and said, a little too loudly, "What does that float represent?"

Kermit couldn't be bothered with enforcing our agreement, so the editors made the easiest changes first. They invited more women to Top of the Week lunches, panels, and public events and sent out several researchers to the bureaus on reporting internships. But when it came to giving women the chance to write, they were recalcitrant. Since we felt that most of the senior editors were biased, we had devoted five paragraphs in the memorandum to how reporting and writing tryouts were to be conducted. Each step—from requesting and evaluating the tryout to deciding whether she had made it as a writer—was to be done with the approval of top management.

The first researcher to ask for a writing tryout was Mary Pleshette, who had been freelancing for small publications. Jack Kroll, her senior editor, was immediately defensive, saying that he disagreed with her quote at the news conference—that discrimination was a "gentleman's agreement" at *Newsweek*. He agreed to give Mary a tryout but then gave her only a few pieces to write. There was no formal assignment schedule or evaluation of her writing. In fact, none of the pieces she wrote for him ever made it through the complete editing process; they just stalled on his desk. First Mary was annoyed and then she was angry. "I felt he gave me the tryout because he had to," she recalled. "At a certain point it was clear he was just going through the motions." At one point, Jack told Mary that he really liked a piece she wrote on Patsy Kelly, who played a sidekick in the old movies, but he never ran it. Instead, she sold it to *Newsweek's* syndication unit for publication in newspapers around the country. "Nobody wanted you to succeed," she later said. "I didn't feel the editors were doing hatchet jobs, but I felt it was an exercise in futility. There weren't many teeth to our agreement."

Lester Bernstein offered Pat Lynden a tryout in "Where Are They Now?," a section in the front of the book recapping what had become of once-famous people. Pat accepted but was wary. At the time, she confided to friends that "no matter how well I did, I thought I might fail so that the editors could point to me as evidence that women didn't have the right stuff to write for *Newsweek*." She later said, however, that "it was also clear that declining the offer was not an option. I had been one of the most outspoken women in our suit, I had the so-called track record, and "Where Are They Now?" was probably the easiest section in the magazine to write." Pat decided if she didn't make it, she could live with it. "I intended to leave *Newsweek* in a year or so," she recalled. "I was newly married, working on starting a family, and planning to move out west. I could afford to fail and if I did, it would show the editors' bad faith."

Pat's pieces ran for several weeks but she didn't get any feedback. "I didn't have a 'rabbi' among the top male writers or editors like the men who tried out always had," she said. Then *Newsweek* decided to do a feature on child care. Pat was given the assignment because she had written a cover story on the subject for the *New York Times Magazine* in February 1970. The senior editor on the story, Joel Blocker, told Pat to come to him with any problems or questions about the assignment and that he would be glad to help. She took him at his word and gave him her first draft. "The next thing I knew, he called me in to his office to say he'd turned over the assignment to Jerry Footlick," she recalled. "I asked what the problem was and said I wanted to fix it. But Joel shook his head and said

Jerry was doing the story. That was the end of my tryout and I returned to the New York bureau."

This was the problem we had anticipated in arguing for more women writers: the judgment of what is good reporting and good writing is purely subjective. "The senior editors are idiosyncratic," admitted Rod Gander in the negotiations, defending the editors. "Their views of what constitutes good *Newsweek* writing differ." Maybe so, but the editors were united in believing that no woman could do it. One was either "born" with the *Newsweek* style or not, they said, and it seemed that only men were born with it—whatever "it" was. According to Rod, it was "nearly impossible to make any kind of empirical set of credentials as to what makes a good *Newsweek* writer. We have had many writers who cannot do it although they produce beautiful stuff in other media. We have found people of no experience who can do it."

There were *Newsweek* writers who seemed to be born with the gift: Dick Boeth, Jack Kroll, Harry Waters, Pete Axthelm, and Liz Peer. The best was Peter Goldman. "Some of the top writers could go 180 degrees wrong, but Peter never went wrong," said Steve Shepard, the former head of the Nation section who edited him for four years. "I never saw any writer do as much work before actually writing the story. Peter spent hours reading the files from the reporters and background material, underlining everything in different color pens and pinning the files on his wall. When he sat down to write, he had so absorbed the reporting he was able to integrate it and compress it into a poetic style that was brilliant." But that was rare.

Most writers had to learn the newsmagazine formula, which differs significantly from the newspaper style. Newspapers use the "inverted pyramid" construction: the lead sentence or paragraph consists of the most important facts—who, what, where, when, why—and subsequent paragraphs contain information of decreasing importance, which allows editors to cut from the bottom for space. The newsmagazine story, at that time, was written in an authoritative voice that told the reader, "Here's what you have to know." Unlike newspapers, magazines put a premium on stylish writing with a beginning, middle, and end, and compressed as many details and as much color as possible onto the page. Mike Ruby, a writer in the magazine's Business section, used to call *Newsweek* writing f—k-style journalism: Flash (the lead), Understanding (the billboard—why is this story important), Clarification (tell the details of the story), and Kicker (bringing it all together with a clever ending). Dwight Martin, a senior editor at *Newsweek* and a former editor at *Time*, described it simply as "literary bricklaying—you're not born with it, it's a skill to be learned."

"It's such a constipated writing style and yet they elevated it to some mystical form," remembered Margaret Montagno. "Some guy who graduated from Harvard and came to *Newsweek* over the transom had it—he was a writer—while some woman who graduated from Radcliffe was only a researcher." Even women who had journalism experience, such as Mary Pleshette, Pat Lynden, and Susan Brownmiller—or who had worked on their college publications, as Nora Ephron, Jane Bryant Quinn, and Betsy Carter had—were still hired as researchers. When

Kermit Lansner was asked once why women such as Nora Ephron had to leave the magazine to write, he snapped, "*Newsweek* isn't a training ground, you know." But it clearly was for men.

Some men questioned whether forcing management to promote women from within was a good idea. One was Ray Sokolov, a *Harvard Crimson* alum who was writing in the Arts sections. "The researchers were problematic as a category," he recalled. "Almost none of them had a background in journalism." It is curious that none of the *Newsweek* editors had hired—or considered hiring—experienced women journalists from other publications. "There really was sexism at work in some way that made no sense," said Ray. "They could have found six women reporters in any of the daily journalism publications and not have had to wait for their potentially capable researchers to make it as writers."

In the mid-1960s, there were a few women writing at *Time,* where *Newsweek* editors often looked for talent. Some magazines, such as *Business Week,* hired women as writers right out of college and all the major newspapers carried female by-lines. When Katharine Graham suggested in the early 1960s that former *New York Times* art critic Aline Saarinen be hired as an editor at *Newsweek,* the editors dismissed her out of hand, she wrote, "condescendingly explaining that it would be out of the question to have a woman. Their arguments were that the closing nights were too late, the end-of-the-week pressure too great, the physical demands of the job too tough. I am embarrassed to admit that I simply accepted their line of reasoning passively."

After the agreement, however, the editors began pursuing female writers from outside the magazine as fast as they were scuttling the tryouts of women inside. The first woman they hired was Barbara Bright, who had been a stringer for *Newsweek* in Germany. She had returned to the United States and became a writer in Foreign. Then they approached Susan Braudy, an experienced freelancer for the *New York Times Magazine*, who went on to become a writer and editor at *Ms.* magazine and the author of several best-selling books. I had met Susan when we were reporting on the first Congress to Unite Women in August 1969, and we had become good friends. In December 1969, Susan wrote a freelance piece for *Playboy* on women's lib, but it never ran—Hugh Hefner spiked it. Hef's memo as to why he didn't like the piece was later leaked to the press by a *Playboy* secretary (who was promptly fired) and it became a cause célèbre. "What I want," Hef said, "is a devastating piece that takes militants apart. . . . What I'm interested in is the highly irrational, kooky trend that feminism has taken. These chicks are our natural enemy. . . . It is time to do battle with them. . . . All of the most basic premises of the extreme form of the new feminism [are] unalterably opposed to the romantic boy-girl society that *Playboy* promotes."

Joel Blocker, by now a senior editor in the back of the book, first contacted Susan because, he told her, *Newsweek* wanted to do a "sympathetic" story on the contretemps, which ran in

May 1970 (her own piece eventually ran in *Glamour* in May 1971). The following year, he offered her a tryout. Susan wrote in the back-of-the-book sections but struggled with writing *Newsweek* style. She and I talked often about this, but I was having my own problems with Blocker and wasn't much help. After a year, she left in the summer of 1972. "They wouldn't let me do my own reporting," she recalled, "and I didn't understand the condensation, the formulaic writing, and the kickers at *Newsweek*. But I learned a lot. I learned to write when I didn't like what I was writing."

Diane Zimmerman, a star reporter in the back of the book, had been writing occasional stories for the Medicine section and others. After we filed the complaint, she asked her editor, Ed Diamond, for a tryout. "With all his peculiarities, Ed was very fair and pushed for me," she remembered. "The Wallendas said they would do it but that they weren't ready yet. I tried to get a tryout for at least eight or nine months and I couldn't get one. The Wallendas didn't approve it." Diane left in 1971, when Shew Hagerty moved to the *New York Daily News* and hired her there.

There were also pockets of resistance by some writers and reporters. In February 1971, I received the following story suggestion via telex from Jim Jones, the crusty Detroit bureau chief: "A group of women's lib sows here, who are members of the Detroit Press Club, are demanding that they be admitted to the club's annual 'Stag Steakout,' a gridiron-type affair where the insults and language are a deep blue. . . . Now it appears the club's board of governors may bend and admit the broads at the do in March (partly this is because a governor or two has a mistress or two among the libbies and are afraid that they'll get cancelled out if they don't vote favorably). This is a teapot tempest, but I'm advised the *NY Times* is working up a story involving the hassle, and maybe you'd want to take the edge off that."

Infuriated, I telexed Jones back ordering a fifty-liner, with a zinger at the end. "Allowing for your clearly sexist item, appreciate as objective an account as possible." For that, I was called into Rod Gander's office and, with Jones on the phone, told we had to settle our differences amicably. We grudgingly did but the story never ran.

By March 1971, the women's panel realized that management wasn't living up to even the spirit—much less the letter—of the agreement in recruiting women writers, inside or out. Once again, we contacted Mel Wulf at the ACLU, who wrote to the editors requesting a meeting "since there are failures involving the pace of implementation" of the agreement. He also noted that "it is unethical and a breach of the agreement to set up your obligation to seek out blacks as in some way mitigating your obligation to rectify the imbalances effecting [*sic*]women." Eleanor Holmes Norton, now chair of the New York City Human Rights Commission, also sent a letter recommending that the women's representatives no longer meet with management unless accompanied by an attorney. The editors immediately promised that the meetings would be more productive without a lawyer present. We reluctantly agreed, continuing to meet over the summer and into the fall.

One of the major problems in recruiting women writers was that vacancies were not posted. The editors simply continued to recruit through the old-boy network. At one meeting, Oz admitted that the editors didn't have any "resources" for finding writers; they just asked friends and colleagues in the business, obviously all male. Nor did editors honor their commitment to report what efforts had been made to find a woman when a man had been hired. Asked whether the Nation editor would show the panel some proof that he had searched for a woman in filling a recent opening, Oz simply said no, adding that if a good writer "came down the pike," he would not want to go searching for a female just to show us they had looked for one.

In July, Lester Bernstein promised to come up with some suggestions for better recruitment but when we met again in September, he said that after talking it over with some of his colleagues, he had thought better of it. At the same meeting, executive editor Bob Christopher said that if *Newsweek* were forced by law to set up a recruitment program, the editors would simply make up a list of resources and then ignore it. Kermit Lansner, clearly exasperated with the whole process, insisted that *Newsweek* didn't need to change its recruitment policies. "Writers come to the magazine over the transom," he said, "and women aren't coming. We can't do anything if they're not interested." We told him to go out and look for them. Then, for a good ten minutes, he lamented that actually nobody wanted to come to write for *Newsweek* anymore. In the end, management never gave us an explanation of what efforts, if any, they had made to find a woman for the last five writing slots filled by men.

We did have some success getting women into the reporting ranks. After a summer internship in Chicago, Lala Coleman became a correspondent in San Francisco in the fall of 1970. Sunde Smith was promoted from Business researcher to reporter in the Atlanta bureau and Mary Alice Kellogg went to the Chicago bureau. Ruth Ross, an experienced black reporter who had left *Newsweek* to start *Essence* magazine, returned to the New York bureau in 1971. We also got our first female foreign bureau chief when Jane Whitmore, a reporter in Washington, was given that position in Rome in 1971. Management also started hiring men as researchers and finally, after ten years as head researcher in the Foreign department, assistant editor Fay Willey was promoted to associate editor.

But there were casualties. When Trish Reilly, one of the most talented young women on staff, was sent to the Atlanta bureau for a summer internship in 1970, the move terrified her. "I was such a depressive, anxiety case," she recalled. "I was horrified at the thought of being shipped off someplace but I couldn't say anything because the women were being set free." The most helpful person was the bureau's Girl Friday, Eleanor Roeloffs Clift. Eleanor, whose parents ran a deli in Queens, New York, had dropped out of college and gotten a job at *Newsweek* in 1963 as a secretary to the Nation editor. She was later promoted to researcher and transferred to Atlanta in 1965, when her husband found work there. "Eleanor was the office manager but she ran the bureau," said Trish. "She gave out the assignments, she did everything, including some reporting." Indeed, when some of the New York women called Eleanor to say she should stop doing reporting until the editors gave her a raise and a promotion, Eleanor refused and continued her dual roles.

One night Trish was in Birmingham, Alabama, covering a school desegregation story. "I was staying in a crummy Holiday Inn all alone with the Coke machine running outside my door," she recalled. "I thought, 'If I have to do this the rest of my life, I will slit my wrist.' To another woman this would have been a shining moment—covering desegregation in Birmingham! But it totally threatened who I was, being given this adult responsibility, and I was miserable and I couldn't tell anyone."

Trish returned to New York after the summer and was offered a permanent spot as a reporter in the Los Angeles bureau. This sent her into a tailspin. "It was announced that I was going to LA and I couldn't face it," she remembered. "I told Rod [Gander] I couldn't go. I knew if you turned down a promotion it was the end of your career, but that was fine. I just wanted to be a researcher." The only person she confided in was Ray Sokolov, a close friend. Ray told her the editors were bewildered by the fact that Trish had turned down the offer, and they didn't like it. "Apparently the editors were surprised that a lot of women hadn't come forward to be reporters and writers," she later said. "But I understood that because I was one of those women. The women's movement helped me accept the fact that women were equal to men as intellectuals, but it didn't change who I was inside. A lot of women were prepared socially and emotionally for it, but for those of us who were traditional women, you couldn't switch off overnight just because we won a lawsuit." In fact, Trish thought many of us were too abrasive and too ambitious. "I just didn't think girls should behave like that—take a man's job," she later said. "I found it a little improper."

Little did she know that some of us "ambitious" types were as conflicted about pushing ourselves forward as she was. I constantly struggled with confidence issues. In 1970, Shew Hagerty, who had promoted me, moved to another department and the new editor was my old boss, Joel Blocker. Since working for Blocker as a secretary in the Paris bureau, I had been writing for nearly a year in New York. But Blocker still saw me as a secretary and told me quite clearly that I would have to prove to him that I could write. Week after week over the next eighteen months, nearly every story I handed in was heavily edited or rewritten. I was so miserable I started looking for another job and thought about leaving journalism. Though I didn't think the lawsuit was the reason he was punishing me, it didn't help. I was barely holding on to my job.

By the fall of 1971, a year after the editors committed to "actively seek" women writers, *Newsweek* had hired three women— Barbara Bright, Susan Braudy, and Ann Scott (Crittenden), a researcher at *Fortune*—and nine men. Three *Newsweek* staffers, Pat Lynden, Mary Pleshette, and Barbara Davidson, a Business researcher, had failed their writing tests. The women's panel was fed up. In October, we reported our frustrations to our colleagues. Furious at management's intransigence, we once again decided to hire a lawyer. Since Eleanor Holmes Norton could no longer represent us, we were directed to a new clinic on employment rights law at Columbia Law School. One of the teachers was twenty-seven-year-old Harriet Rabb, who agreed to represent us.

Good girls revolt: When *Newsweek* published a cover on the new women's movement on March 16, 1970 (above), forty-six staffers announced we were suing the magazine for sex discrimination (seated from left: Pat Lynden, Mary Pleshette, our lawyer, Eleanor Holmes Norton, and Lucy Howard. I am standing in the back, to the left of Eleanor Holmes Norton).

Newsweek—Tony Rollo

Newsweek—Bernard Gotfryd

The Ring Leaders: When Judy Gingold (top left, in 1969) learned that the all-female research department was illegal, she enlisted her friends Margaret Montagno (top right) and Lucy Howard (bottom, with Peter Goldman in 1968) to file a legal complaint.

Newsweek

On the job: Reporter Pat Lynden had written cover stories for other major publications (with writer David Alpern in 1966).

Covering fashion: I was the only woman writer at the time of the suit (with designer Halston and Liza Minnelli in 1972).

The "Hot Book:" Editor-in-chief Osborn Elliott transformed *Newsweek* in the Sixties. He called the gender divide a "tradition," but became a convert to our cause (1974).

At the top: When *Newsweek* owner Katharine Graham (with husband, Philip Graham, in 1962) heard about our lawsuit, she asked, "Which side am I supposed to be on?"

The Editors: We called them "the Wallendas" a joking reference to the high-wire circus act (clockwise from top left, in 1969: Oz Elliott, Lester Bernstein, Robert Christopher, and Kermit Lansner).

A key recruit: Fay Willey wanted research—and researchers—to be more valued at *Newsweek* (1967).

Newsweek—Bernard Gotfryd

Self doubt: Trish Reilly was afraid to say she didn't want to be promoted (1970).

Newsweek—Robert R. McElroy

Success stories: Religion researcher Merrill McLoughlin (left) went on to co-edit *US News & World Report* and reporter Phyllis Malamud became *Newsweek*'s Boston bureau chief (right, with writer Ken Woodward in 1971).

Newsweek—Tony Rollo

On the move: Elisabeth Coleman was given the first bureau internship in Chicago in the summer of 1970 (below) and became a reporter in San Francisco later that year.

Jeff Lowenthal

No chance: Mary Pleshette was given one of the first writing tryouts but her pieces just sat on her editor's desk (1967).

Newsweek

Historic moment: We signed our agreement on August 26, 1970, the fiftieth anniversary of the suffrage amendment (seated clockwise from top left: Eleanor Holmes Norton, Oz Elliott, Kay Graham, Kermit Lansner, Roger Borgeson, Rod Gander, me, Mariana Gosnell, Lucy Howard, Madeleine Edmondson, Fay Willey, Judy Gingold, and Mel Wulf from the ACLU).

Smiles all around: After the signing everyone was hopeful, but the optimism didn't last long (seated clockwise from left: Mel Wulf, Eleanor Holmes Norton, Oz Elliott, Kay Graham, Kermit Lansner, Roger Borgeson, and me; standing from left: Jeanne Voltz, Lauren Katzowitz, Sylvia Robinson, Harriet Huber, Abby Kuflik, Judy Harvey, Mary Alice Kellogg, Joyce Fenmore, and Lorraine Kisley).

Our Brenda Starr: Reporter Liz Peer was a gifted journalist but the editors wouldn't send her to Vietnam (1971).

My mentor: Writer Harry Waters said that for women at *Newsweek* the elevator up "was out-of-order" (1978).

Newsweek—Wally McNamee

Newsweek—Bernard Gotfryd

Civil rights: "My attitude was, 'Go for it,'" said star writer Peter Goldman (1968).

Newsweek—Bernard Gotfryd

The Famous Writers School: Dick Boeth taught the first writer training program for women with Peter Goldman (1972).

"Female Writer Seligmann": Jeanie Seligmann was the first researcher to become a writer after the lawsuit (1973).

Newsweek—David Alpern

Newsweek—Robert R. McElroy

Victory at last: Our second lawyer, Harriet Rabb, prevailed and later represented the women who sued the *Reader's Digest* and the *New York Times* (1972).

Courtesy of Columbia Law School

Liberated: Reporter Mariana Gosnell (here in 1967) wrote her first book at age 62.

The Critic: Writer and editor Jack Kroll was brilliant, but recalcitrant (1976).

Newsweek—Robert R. McElroy

Newsweek—Bernard Gotfryd

The boss and me: Looking back, Oz was the first to say, "God, weren't we awful?" (1975)

Newsweek—Bernard Gotfryd

Learning the ropes: Media reporter Betsy Carter went on to start *New York Woman* magazine and write novels (here with striking printers in 1974).

Tough call: Diane Camper was one of the black researchers who decided not to join our suit (1977).

A star is born: Eleanor Clift rose from Girl Friday to *Newsweek*'s White House correspondent (in 1976, with Vern Smith, left, and Joe Cumming, Jr., in the Atlanta bureau).

The boys' club: Integrating the story conference (clockwise from left, editor Ed Kosner, Larry Martz, Peter Kilborn, Russ Watson, Dwight Martin, and me, 1977).

Breaking the barrier: My official photo as *Newsweek*'s first female senior editor, September 1, 1975.

Forty years later: In March 2010, three young women (from left) Sarah Ball, Jesse Ellison, and Jessica Bennett wrote their story in *Newsweek*—and kept ours alive.

CHAPTER 8

The Steel Magnolia

HARRIET SCHAFFER RABB was the opposite of Eleanor—a petite Texan with a soft Southern accent and a steel-trap intellect. She was also four months pregnant. Harriet had grown up in Houston, the daughter of two physicians. Her parents practiced in the same building: her father, a general practitioner, at one end; her mother, a pediatrician, at the other. Her father's practice and examining room were integrated, but he kept his waiting room segregated because he thought people would feel more comfortable that way. Her mother's practice was mostly white. When her father was serving in World War II, Harriet's mother took her on her nightly rounds or to the Jefferson Davis charity hospital where she trained nurses. "I admired her beyond description," said Harriet. "When the phone rang at home and a patient would ask,

'May I speak to Dr. Schaffer,' I would always have to say, 'Which one?' She was Doc Helen and he was Doctor Jimmy. I thought they were amazing and wanted to be a doctor until I took biology in college and couldn't stand the labs."

Harriet's family was active in the Jewish community, and she was president of her Jewish sorority, but she felt the sting of anti-Semitism in high school. "The Jewish kids did very well in honor society, drama, and debate," she explained. "We went to the nationals on the debate team and won a lot of prizes. But when the head of the school would announce the prizes for debate, he would never pronounce our names correctly. He would say 'Schaffner' or something like that. They were unhappy with us. We could not be cheerleaders because nobody would have ever voted for us."

Knowing what it felt like to be an outsider, Harriet got involved in the voting-rights movement and other civil rights issues when she went to Barnard College in New York City. She was elected president of her freshman class and became chair of the Honor Board senior year. "I liked the process of listening to the evidence and thinking about it," she recalled, "and at some point realized I wanted to be a lawyer." She went on to Columbia Law School and got a summer internship with Kunstler, Kunstler and Kinoy, founded by the well-known civil rights lawyers Bill Kunstler and Arthur Kinoy (Michael Kunstler, Bill's brother and partner, was not involved in their civil rights work). That summer, in 1964, two white civil rights workers, Michael Schwerner and Andrew Goodman, and their black colleague, James Chaney, disappeared in Mississippi. The

Schwerner family was a client of the law firm, so Kunstler and Kinoy tried to get the FBI involved, saying that the kids had been kidnapped. The FBI declined, saying there was no evidence of a crime, and certainly not of a federal crime, so they had no jurisdiction. "There were about five interns at the law firm," Harriet remembered, "and Arthur [Kinoy] said, 'Here's the library, there's the wall of US statutes. Divide it up any way you want to. I want every single one of those books read by the end of this week and I want you to use your imagination to find any potential statute that could be a basis of the FBI getting into this investigation.' And we did. We found a document to persuade the FBI that they needed to get into it. Of course by then, the kids were long dead."

After law school and a brief marriage, Harriet got a job at the Center for Constitutional Rights, which Bill Kunstler and Arthur Kinoy had set up in Newark, New Jersey. The center represented members of Students for a Democratic Society and the Student Nonviolent Coordinating Committee, several of the Weathermen who blew up the West Eleventh Street town house, and the black militant H. Rap Brown. "The first time I ever appeared in a court by myself it was with Rap," Harriet recalled. "He was there for taking a gun on an airplane." At the time, Harriet was dating a law school classmate, Bruce Rabb, who was working on civil rights in the Nixon White House and whose father, Maxwell Rabb, later became President Ronald Reagan's ambassador to Italy. Kinoy was worried about the relationship. He told Harriet that his clients wouldn't trust her because of her close relationship with a Republican working in the White House. He said she would have to get another job. She was disappointed but understood. She quit the law firm and worked for a year for Bess Myerson, then New York City's commissioner for consumer affairs.

In 1970, Harriet and Bruce married and moved to Washington. She tried to get a job in civil rights but she was rejected, she said, either because she was white or because her husband worked in the Nixon administration. Then she found out about an opening as clerk to the US Court of Appeals for the District of Columbia, where David Bazelon was the chief judge. But two of the judges on the panel had checked Harriet's extensive FBI record and objected to her appointment. They also threatened to call the White House to get Bruce fired because his wife had worked with Kinoy and Kunstler.

Judge Bazelon called her in and told her that her FBI file troubled the people on this court; then he asked her to withdraw her application. "Bruce and I talked about it," she recalled. "I said, 'I don't want to run away. I'm not ashamed of what I've done.'" She told Judge Bazelon that she wasn't going to withdraw her application. With tears in his eyes, she remembered, he said, "You're making me ashamed because these judges have told me they won't work with me on the court if I hire you, and I don't have the courage to resist because I feel responsible and the court has to work well. You have the courage not to do this. So I'm not going to give you a job but I'll find you a job." He found her a position at Stern Community Law Firm, which handled public interest cases.

Bruce and Harriet moved back to New York in 1971, and she began teaching a clinic on employment-rights law at Columbia Law School with George Cooper. George, an expert in Title VII, had won a grant from the EEOC to train lawyers on enforcing the new antidiscrimination laws. Harriet spent the summer learning the syllabus on employment rights law. When we approached her in October 1971, she had just started teaching, and she and George began to educate us on building a better, stronger case. "The *Newsweek* case was challenging because it wasn't an assembly-line job," recalled George. "It was a subjective test [of talent], so the challenge for the lawyers is to take the subjectivity and say that on a group basis it turns out to be biased."

Harriet mobilized her law school class to start taking histories of all the women involved, which could serve as statistical evidence of discrimination and as depositions if necessary. She and George also prepared a detailed chart of prior discriminatory practices, violations of the agreement, and continuing discrimination in every category, outlining the charges and then the methods of proof. "You say, here are the credentials of all the men—where they went to school, what their grades were, what their experience was—and you compare the members of the aggrieved class with the people who got what they wanted," George later explained. "You show there's no difference in any measurable things—everybody went to an Ivy League school—and you force them to come back and respond to them using class data." It was a far different approach from that of the fiery

Eleanor Holmes Norton. "Harriet was just right for us," recalled Mimi McLoughlin. "Different talents for different times."

Just before her first encounter with the editors, George took Harriet to lunch at the Columbia Faculty Club to discuss the case. When they got there he said, "I'm not going with you to the *Newsweek* meeting." Harriet was stunned. "The bottom dropped out for me," she recalled. "While I was objecting, he said, 'You don't need me, it'll be fine.' It was my lack of confidence. I had done a lot of things but I was new to Title VII." George continued his involvement with our case, but Harriet was out front. "I knew her background," he later said. "I thought she was great. I knew she could do it."

At Harriet's first meeting with management on December 7, 1971, she proceeded to point out how the magazine was violating the memorandum of understanding by not affirmatively seeking out women to try out as reporters and writers. Only 23 percent of the newly hired writers were female, but 39 percent of the newly hired researchers were male. Of the four *Newsweek* women who had tryouts, three had failed. In November 1971, Jeanie Seligmann, the Medicine researcher, became a writer in the back of the book, the first woman staffer to be promoted. (From that point on, her boss, Dwight Martin, teasingly called her "Female Writer Seligmann.") Kermit Lansner had asked Phyllis Malamud to try out as writer but she declined, citing management's hostile attitude toward the women trying out. In a follow-up meeting on January 5, Rod Gander said that "most of the women on the staff haven't enough experience in writing to show to their proper advantage under a systemized approach in a tryout." But management refused to define what a tryout actually involved. Rod noted that in the case of men on the staff who came in as researchers or junior writers and got promoted, "the ones who have succeeded best have succeeded under . . . a flexible lack of ground rules."

In one meeting Grant Tompkins, the head of personnel, asked if, since the magazine was in the midst of "very difficult" Newspaper Guild negotiations, we would postpone our meetings until those were finished—which we declined to do. The Guild, which was voluntary, had become a pet project for the women. It was dominated by men from Makeup and Photo, and very few editorial employees were members. Two Nation researchers, Noel Ragsdale and Nancy Stadtman (whom we feminists called Stadtperson), encouraged us to join the Guild to make it more responsive to women's needs, which we did. In 1970, we elected Nancy an officer of the Guild and two years later, she became chair, the first female in that position. "Some of the union men had daggers out for me until the first contract," Nancy recalled. "We got a good maternity policy but we also got a paternity leave clause, the first one for a news publication."

Management still seemed stumped about how to move forward, and at the December and January meetings, they asked *us* for constructive solutions. Harriet sent a detailed document suggesting a program for training women writers and specifying goals and timetables for the complete integration of women into the magazine. When we met again on March 8, 1972, the editors refused to make any commitments to changing their policies. Harriet replied that if they wanted us to continue talking, management should come up with suggestions for progress within two weeks. Two weeks and two days later—and only after the women's panel had called an urgent meeting of the women—Harriet received a hand-delivered note from Grant Tompkins ignoring our request and again "welcomed" Harriet's thoughts on how to increase the number of women writers and reporters while improving the representation of the other groups.

On March 28, the women's panel called an emergency meeting, at which we summarized the history of our negotiations and presented a list of grievances. There were now five new women writers on the magazine (Sandra Salmans, a graduate of Columbia Journalism School, had been hired in Business), but since the lawsuit, at least fourteen men had been hired as writers, almost three times as many men as women. In the research category, twelve people were hired from the outside, eight of whom were men. Rod Gander told us that four other women from outside were asked to try out at *Newsweek*, but they had declined. "After one and a half years, we feel that there is no further purpose to be served by meeting with management," we said in our report. "The continuing consultation has become, finally, a means for management to present apologia for every breach of the memorandum and thereby to get away with doing nothing at all for *Newsweek* women. . . . In our opinion, the women should either go ahead and take legal action or else resign themselves to the present situation and discontinue all attempts to right it through mass movement."

Then Harriet spoke. She said that if we wanted to take action, she recommended we do two things: file a new complaint of discrimination with the EEOC and simultaneously sue for breach of contract with the New York State Division of Human Rights. Should we lose the breach-of-contract suit, our federal case would not be prejudiced. Should we win it, we would gain immediate court-ordered relief. After a few questions we decided to take a straw vote. Of the thirty-one women present, twenty-nine voted to file complaints in both jurisdictions, one voted to file only in state court, and one voted to use the legal machinery of the Guild. We sent a memo to the absent women asking for their opinions as well.

I was amazed by the vote. I couldn't believe that two years after our lawsuit—after several women had been trained, promoted, and co-opted with titles—the group was still willing to go through another legal action, with all the recriminations and unpleasantness that would inevitably ensue. We "good girls" had become radicalized. "The first time, I was very nervous," recalled Mimi McLoughlin. "Were we right? Could I defend what we were doing? The second time around I was angrier because I thought they were just stringing us along." Even Harriet was impressed. "I thought the *Newsweek* women were incredible—all of you," she said. "You were committed to *Newsweek* but you wanted opportunities."

For Harriet, we were probably her first clients who wanted to change the system from within. "I learned a great lesson from you," she told me. "After we started meeting with management, I was concerned that management would try to speak to you all individually. So I remember saying to you, 'Lynn, if Oz calls you and asks you to come to his office, you tell him everybody needs to go through your lawyer.' And you said, 'I work for this man and if he asks me to go to his office, I need to go there.' It was really evidence of how young I was to take this on. I wasn't thinking how life was for my clients, partly because I was a teacher. For me, it was breaching the barriers while you all were working there with men who were superiors or jealous. Eleanor and I were litigators. We came in wanting to win. It was so much more complicated for you."

We continued negotiating with management in the spring of 1972 while we planned our next action. During the increasingly difficult discussions about how to increase the number of female writers, we realized that the women needed a writer training program to combat the subjective—and, we thought, biased—tryout system. To teach the course, we recruited two of the best writers on the magazine, who immediately agreed. After proposing the course to the editors, one of them snidely asked, "Well, who would you get to teach this course?" When we said, "Peter Goldman and Dick Boeth," they were silenced.

The Famous Writers School, as it was called, was an eight-week seminar that began in the summer of 1972 and lasted for three semesters, training more than twenty-five women. As Peter Goldman taught it, the opening conversation was about demystifying *Newsweek* writing. He would start his writers with a short seventy-line story from a single reporter's file. Then he moved on to longer stories incorporating files from multiple bureaus. One week, everyone had to write a "Newsmaker," the gossipy items in the most popular section of the magazine. "It was distilling down a story to its essence, a reduction in cooking," Peter recalled. "It had a beginning, middle, and end and it had structural demands. Lucy did a perfect Newsmaker." Each week, Peter did a one-page critique of the women's copy but we were so terrified that the results would be transmitted to management that the women decided to use pseudonyms. "In the beginning, there were several pieces by 'Jane Eyre' and 'Emily Bronte,'" Peter said, "but within two weeks everyone knew who it was."

Dick Boeth, one of the most creative writers on the magazine, had his own method of teaching and in his course he wrote a hilarious spoof of the *Newsweek* style. To explain the various ways one could start a *Newsweek* story, he enshrined "The Wonderful World of Ledes" (purposely misspelled to distinguish it from other pronunciations of "lead"). Some of the best were:

- Action—little picture: "Henry Kissinger had not even finished shaving the stubble from his girlfriend's chin early one morning last week when his tubside hotline to the White House began beeping insistently. At the other end was President Richard Nixon himself and his voice was grim. 'Hank,' the President said, 'hold onto your Barbasol. We're moving seven divisions into the Dominican Republic before lunchtime.'"

- Historical: "Not since the Roman proconsul Fabian Cunctator marched steadily backwards for two years before invading elephants of Hannibal has a commander-in-chief sought victory in retreat with the stubborn insistence of President Richard Nixon. But last week the harassed President tired of the waiting game. Without informing anyone but the White House telephone operator, who had to make the necessary calls, Mr. Nixon dispatched seven crack divisions of Marines in a dramatic amphibious invasion—aimed not at enemy strongholds in Vietnam but at the undefended beaches of the Dominican Republic."

- Anecdotal: "One February afternoon early in his Administration, Richard Nixon was bobbing around on a rubber duck in the lagoon fronting on his house in Key Biscayne, Fla. 'You know,' the President said reflectively to C.R. (Bebe) Rebozo, who was paddling nearby, 'they all think I came down here to make points for the Southern strategy. What all those pundits don't realize is that a guy will do almost anything to get away from those Washington winters.' Last week the President's search for sun took on new and potentially explosive international dimensions, as Mr. Nixon ordered seven divisions of U.S. Marines ashore in the Dominican Republic in a wholly unexpected dawn invasion."

- General lede: "With only three weeks to go until Election Day, Richard Nixon seemed to be a President with all his options foreclosed. Saigon, Manila and Honolulu had fallen in successive weeks to 'Un-American elements,' the most recent Gallup poll had reflected a new if razor thin edge for George McGovern, and Pat Nixon had filed for a legal separation. In a bold (some say reckless) attempt to recoup his political fortunes, the President last week dispatched seven Marine divisions to seize control of the Dominican Republic."

Yes, it was definitely newsmagazine formula, but when done well it could be brilliant.

CHAPTER 9

"Joe—Surrender"

WHILE WE WERE GEARING UP for a second lawsuit, the women at the *Washington Post* were getting restless. Several years earlier they had complained about discrimination, including the lack of women in decision-making positions. That prompted Ben Bradlee, the paper's executive editor, to issue a directive in June 1970 underscoring the "equality and dignity of women." Promising to "use all our resources to combat discrimination against women," Bradlee decreed that words such as "divorcee, grandmother, blonde (or brunette) or housewife should be avoided in all stories where, if a man were involved, the words divorcee, grandfather, blonde or householder would be inapplicable. In other words, they should be avoided. Words like vivacious, pert, dimpled or cute have long since become clichés and are droppable on that account alone."

Two years later, on April 12, 1972, fifty-nine women at the *Post* sent a letter to Bradlee and Katharine Graham, among others, noting that women were losing ground at the paper. According to their statistics, women made up 15 percent of the *Post*'s staff in June 1970; in March 1972, they made up only 13 percent of the staff. There were no women assistant managing editors, news desk editors, or editors in the Financial, Sports, and Outlook sections, nor were there any female foreign correspondents or sports reporters. This time the *Post*'s management responded with specific goals and actions. Among other things, Bradlee promised "to increase substantially, and as fast as possible, the number of women on the newspaper, especially in top and middle management." He also insisted that "there is and shall be no discrimination in the assignment of women to breaking stories involving action and/or violence." The *Post* immediately established an internal equal employment opportunity committee and instituted a monthly status report on the employment of women and blacks. (The *Post* women ended up filing charges of discrimination two years later with the EEOC, which ruled in their favor.)

Also in April 1972, a group of black reporters at the *Post* called the Metro Seven filed a complaint with the EEOC charging the paper with racial discrimination in promotion and hiring, especially with regard to the lack of black editors. Bradlee and managing editor Howard Simons quickly negotiated a deal, hiring, among others, Dorothy Gilliam, a former *Post* writer whom they promoted to assistant editor. Gilliam was the first black editor of the reconfigured Style section. "It was shortly after [the Metro Seven settlement] that I was sought out," said Gilliam. "I can't help but think there was some connection."

Meanwhile, Kay Graham had undergone her own form of consciousness-raising. As one of only two women publishers of a major newspaper (the other was Dorothy Schiff of the *New York Post*), Kay was feeling isolated in the professional world, worried, as she wrote, that she would "appear stupid or ignorant when she was the only woman in a room full of men." Her close friend at the *Post* was Meg Greenfield, the deputy editor of the editorial page, who had achieved her success before the women's movement. (In her early days at the *Post*, Meg had a sign on her office door that read, IF LIBERATED, I WILL NOT SERVE.) But Meg, like Kay, was often the only woman in the room and together they decided to "think through" how they felt about women's lib. They started by reading books, among them *The Second Sex* by Simone de Beauvoir.

Then Kay met Gloria Steinem. Gloria had been writing a political column for Clay Felker at *New York* magazine when she began thinking about starting a feminist magazine (the first issue of *Ms.* magazine appeared as an insert in *New York* in December 1971). When Gloria was seeking an investor for her start-up, Felker introduced her to Kay. "She told me that if they put up money, they—the *Post*—would have to own it," Gloria told me later. But Kay gave her $20,000 in seed money and asked Gloria to talk to her about the new feminism. At the time, Kay wrote, "I couldn't understand militancy and disliked the kind of bra-burning symbolism that appeared to me like man-hating." But Gloria "more than any other individual, changed my mind-set and helped me grasp what the leaders of the movement—and even the extremists—were talking about." Around that time, Kay even asked her longtime executive assistant, Liz Hylton, who came from West Virginia, to please stop saying "yes, ma'am."

One day, Kay asked Gloria to come to lunch at the *Post*. "She wasn't being taken seriously by the men she employed," Gloria recalled. "She had invited Joe Alsop to lunch and asked me to explain this to him while she was sitting right there! I was trying to do Feminism 101 and be reasonable and persuasive about women's issues in general. It was as if she was calling me in to argue with someone she didn't want to argue with." Among the things they discussed was the fact that the *Post* wouldn't hire newsgirls to throw the paper on people's porches in Chevy Chase, Maryland. "After the lunch," said Gloria, "Kay told me that she had gotten so mad at some employee who told her they couldn't have newsgirls, she threw an ashtray at him. I was impressed because she was usually so reserved."

Kay also had Gloria talk to Oz Elliott about the *Newsweek* women. "I remember meeting Gloria in Kay's office and she was very helpful to me," he told me. "I was impressed with how constructive she was in suggesting how management should deal with the situation." When Kay discussed *Newsweek* with Gloria, however, "all I remember was trying to talk her out of being angry at Eleanor Holmes Norton," Gloria said. "Kay never really forgave Eleanor. She felt wrongly accused—her world had been wrongly accused—and Kay felt Eleanor crossed the line. She felt *Newsweek* was unfairly targeted, but separate from that was Eleanor and her style." Later on, when Gloria found herself on the opposite side of Eleanor on an issue, "I could see what Kay meant," she said. "Eleanor is scary, very scary. She's tough—and she should be."

I, too, felt Kay's disapproval—or perhaps it was disappointment. Because of my father, she probably felt that I was part of the *Post* family, which I felt as well. After all, she was responsible for my entrée to *Newsweek* and now I was the apostate suing her magazine. Many years later, when she was making a speech at *Newsweek* and recounting the history of the women's lawsuit, she stopped and said, "and some of the suers are in this room!"—and pointed to me. Whatever the reason, I thought she never forgave me for being disloyal and I felt a coolness in our interactions after the suit. It wasn't overt. She was always gracious to me, and from time to time she would ask me to come to her office to tell her how things were going with the women's movement at *Newsweek*. Over the years, I grew to admire Kay's courage, especially during Watergate, and as she became more confident, her sense of humor became more evident. At a *Newsweek* sales conference in Puerto Rico one year, Kay came out to walk with some of us on the beach. It had been a cloudy day, but when she appeared the sun suddenly came out. Kay looked up at the sky, opened her arms, and said mischievously, "Now you know why they call me the most powerful woman in Washington."

Primarily, however, I was concerned about my father's feelings since I now found myself in the unusual position of suing his boss. Dad loved and respected the Grahams and had a special fondness for Kay. When I called him after we filed the first complaint, he listened and never questioned or criticized my actions. At the same time, I knew he was worried about how Kay would feel. "He was nervous," recalled my brother Maury. "He didn't want anything that was untoward to happen to the *Post* and to Kay in particular." If he ever spoke to Kay—or she to him—about my role in the suit, he never told me. But I know he felt torn by his loyalty to her and his love for me. In 1974, Kay gave my father a gala dinner dance to celebrate his fifty years at the *Washington Post*. Before I flew down to Washington for the event, my father phoned me and gently asked whether I was planning to shake Kay's hand on the reception line, clearly wanting to avoid an embarrassing incident. "Of course," I said. "I'm not angry at her personally, just at the men who run her magazine." I think he was relieved, and it turned out to be a warm, wonderful evening.

Meanwhile, our negotiations with management were leading nowhere. After the March 1972 straw vote, the women met again and formally voted to once again take legal action, this time in two jurisdictions. On May 16, 1972, we announced that fifty women had filed a second complaint against *Newsweek* with the EEOC "because sex discrimination at the magazine remains essentially unchanged." Two weeks later, Margaret Montagno was the lead plaintiff on a complaint filed with the New York State Division of Human Rights "on her own behalf and behalf of the 50 or more female employees similarly situated." In a half-page, single-spaced paragraph, enumerating all the ways the magazine discriminated against women, Margaret charged *Newsweek* with unlawful discriminatory practice, ending the complaint saying, "Because I am a woman I believe I have no chance to become a senior editor or part of top management at *Newsweek*. Because I am a woman I believe I have very little chance to become a writer, bureau chief or reporter at *Newsweek*. I believe that to be a woman at *Newsweek* is to accept a permanent position in those lower paying and/or less prestigious jobs restricted to or predominantly held by women."

At the end of June 1972, Oz Elliott returned as editor-in-chief of *Newsweek* after serving on the business side. "I was astonished no progress had been made," he told me years later, "and I was surprised by the anger of the women. They were angrier than they had been two years before. One of the first things I did was to put the women's issues at the top of my list."

Oz immediately hired Shana Alexander as the first female columnist in the history of *Newsweek*. Shana had been the "first" in several publications: the first female staff writer and columnist for *Life* magazine and the first female editor of *McCall's*. But she quit *McCall's* in 1971, saying that it was a token job in a sexist environment. (Shana left *Newsweek* in 1974 and was replaced as a columnist by Meg Greenfield of the *Washington Post*.) As a concession to the women inside *Newsweek*, Oz also promoted Olga Barbi, the chief of research, to senior editor. The women were pleased for Olga but it didn't satisfy our demands to have a woman editing one of the major sections in the magazine. (On the business side, my friend Valerie Salembier was appointed *Newsweek*'s first female ad sales representative in May 1972.)

Then there was silence. Between May and September 1972, we had no meetings with *Newsweek*'s management. That summer, while the *Newsweek* women were being "trained" at the Famous Writers School, women from outside the magazine were being hired as writers without any trouble, and some without much experience. In July 1972, at the Democratic convention in Miami, Oz met Maureen Orth, a member of a guerrilla TV collective from San Francisco called TVTV. Maureen had graduated from Berkeley with a political science degree, had served in the Peace Corps in Colombia, and earned a master's degree in journalism at UCLA with an emphasis on documentary film. In 1971, she was pitching a story to *New York* magazine on the Cockettes, a group of celebrated hippie drag queens from San Francisco who came to New York where they were a big flop. "Clay Felker [the editor of *New York*] told me he'd pay me $500 and then have Rex Reed put his own lead on it and cut me out completely," she recalled. "I refused and gave it to the *Village Voice*." The story, one of a dozen she had written, ran on the front page.

Maureen came to New York in September and looked up her Berkeley schoolmate Trish Reilly at *Newsweek*. Trish asked whether she was interested in writing since the editors were desperately trying to hire women because of the lawsuit. Maureen had an interview with Rod Gander, and then spoke to Oz. "Oz said, 'Well, I think if we're going to hire women writers we're just going to have to make a decision to hire them,'" she recalled. She was sent to Jack Kroll, the Arts editor, "because I came from the West Coast and they thought he would 'get' me." Kroll said he would talk to Rod but added, "There's no way you can be hired as a writer because there are a lot of women waiting in the wings to be hired." Maureen told him about Oz's remark to just start hiring women.

A few weeks later, Kroll invited Maureen to lunch at the Gloucester House on East Fiftieth Street, the editors' favorite dining establishment for Saturday lunch. The expensive fish restaurant, staffed exclusively with black waiters, offered such *spécialités* as shrimp wrapped in bacon and French-fried zucchini strips stacked like Lincoln Logs. Over martinis, Kroll offered Maureen a job as a writer in the back of the book for $14,000 a year. She began in October 1972.

A month earlier, Linda Bird Francke, a contributing editor to *New York* magazine, was looking for a staff job when she got a call from Clay Felker, her boss. "He said, 'You've got a job at *Newsweek*,'" she recalled. "I was startled. I subscribed to *Time* and had never even read *Newsweek*, let alone considered it a job prospect. But Clay was insistent. 'Just call this number,' he said. 'They're waiting to hear from you.'" Linda went to 444 Madison Avenue, bought a copy of *Newsweek* in the lobby, quickly looked it over, and proceeded upstairs to meet with Russ Watson. "Without any preamble, he offered me any one of four sections: Life & Leisure, Nation, Foreign, and one other," she recalled. When she said that Life & Leisure sounded fun, he retorted, "No, no, that's considered a women's ghetto. You want to be on the front lines in Nation or Foreign, don't you?"

She reiterated that she preferred Life & Leisure, so he went on to discuss salary. "Well," he said, "I'm authorized to offer you anything up to $19,000, so let's make it simple and say $19,000. When can you start?" "And so," said Linda, "I commenced on my totally unexpected and unsought job without anyone looking at a single clip. Maureen Orth came in the same way. We were all hired in an instant to offset the women's suit."

Kay Graham, meanwhile, was feeling under pressure. With blacks suing the *Washington Post,* the *Post* women pushing for change, and now a second lawsuit by the *Newsweek* women, she called in Joseph A. Califano, Jr., the corporate attorney for the Washington Post Company. Califano was an old Washington hand, having served as special assistant to President Lyndon B. Johnson before joining the law firm of Edward Bennett Williams in 1971. "Kay said, 'I want you to straighten this out,'" Joe recalled. "She wanted it settled, no question about that, but we didn't want quotas. Nobody wanted quotas, certainly not Oz. I called Alan Finberg [*Newsweek's* general counsel] and said, 'Let me start by dealing directly with the women's lawyer.' That was Harriet Rabb."

Joe wrote to Harriet requesting a meeting with her and the women's committee on September 13, 1972. When we met, he had brought along a young associate, Rich Cooper, who seemed to object to every suggestion we had to move forward. In all our meetings that fall, Rich played bad cop and Joe, the avuncular good cop. Harriet was probably used to such legal maneuverings, and she had a few of her own. "I thought Harriet was a good lawyer," Joe said. "However, I have a recollection of her saying, 'I want you to listen to all these women to get you sensitized'—not something I appreciated her lecturing me about."

On October 6, Joe wrote Harriet a letter saying the September meeting "encouraged our hope that we are reasonably close on a number of the issues." But then he went on to shoot down almost every recommendation we made: a grievance procedure the women proposed was already provided in the Guild contract; he had investigated charges that back-of-the-book reporters were discriminated against as compared to bureau reporters, who did similar kinds of work, and concluded that "there is no substance to the suggestion"; and punitive enforcement provisions were not acceptable—instead management would provide detailed periodic reports for ensuring performance under the agreement. Joe ended the letter by stressing that it was in the interest of both *Newsweek* and the women to settle their differences amicably because "litigation is likely to be long, expensive and divisive."

By this time, "goals and timetables" had become common legal tools in job discrimination cases, and Harriet recommended them in her letter back to Joe that same day. She proposed that by December 1973, one-third of the writers and one-third of the foreign and domestic reporters should be women. She stated that priority should be given to in-house women for writing positions and that a woman writer should be placed in each of the seven editorial departments, including in the hard-news Nation, Foreign, and Business sections and not just in the feature-laden back of the book. The letter also stipulated that the percentage of male researchers should approximately equal the percentage of female writers on staff. There was a long section outlining procedures for recruiting and in-house tryouts. Finally, she insisted that one of the next three openings for senior editor should be filled by a woman.

That was the real sticking point. Mariana Gosnell, the Medicine reporter on our committee, pushed hard for a woman senior editor. "I remember saying that until they put a woman in the holy top bunch, they would have it in their heads that a woman couldn't be a Wallenda," she said. The editors refused, saying that the women couldn't dictate who would be in management. We said we wouldn't sign an agreement that didn't include a woman in the meetings where the decisions were being made.

"I went into the negotiations knowing we were going to end up with goals and timetables," Joe remembered. "In the beginning, Oz was not for that. He viewed goals and timetables as locking him into things he didn't want to do. But then we got into this argument about having one or two women senior editors. I'm not sure whether Katharine was or wasn't for them, but at some point I sat down with her and said, 'If you want to settle this you're going to have to do something like this. We're going to make sure that everybody knows they have a real opportunity and it's palpable, it's there. The only issue is who's going to get it and when.'" According to Joe, Kay's view was, "if we're going to do this, we want as much talent up in New York as possible so we can make the right pick."

Joe called *Newsweek's* Washington bureau chief, Mel Elfin, to find out whether any women on the magazine were qualified to be a senior editor. Mel recommended Liz Peer, who was working for him in the bureau. When she was in Paris in the mid-1960s, Liz had wanted to go to Vietnam, but *Newsweek* wouldn't send a woman to cover a war. Instead she returned to the Washington bureau in 1969, where she covered the State Department, the White House, and the CIA. "I think Katharine may have known Liz," Joe later said, "and I think she was more comfortable knowing that there was someone she knew who was capable of doing this, if she turned out to be the person. I was just surprised that Liz Peer was the only person outside New York that they thought worthy." (For her part, Liz confided to a friend that she felt Kay Graham didn't want her to be the first woman to succeed.)

Joe asked Oz to interview Liz Peer as a candidate for senior editor. "Mel had told Liz that it would cost, like, 25 percent more to live in New York than in Washington, and he told her, 'You gotta get more money and you gotta get this and you gotta get that,'" Joe recalled. "In the course of the meeting with Oz, Liz asked about salary and Oz, who was in the middle of a difficult divorce and sick and tired of talking to women about money, made some snide remark. When I asked Elfin about getting Liz to New York, he said it wasn't a good meeting. I think Oz was just very unhappy."

Once Joe was assigned the *Newsweek* case, I found myself in an awkward position as a member of the women's committee.

My older brother, David, was a law partner of Joe's at Williams, Connolly & Califano, so I didn't discuss our case with him. But at one point I was so annoyed with Rich Cooper's sarcastic remarks that I called David to ask about him. David said Rich really was a good guy, very smart, and then explained that he was just doing his job. Then David called me one day to tell me a story, laughing on the phone. Joe had come into his office complaining about the *Newsweek* negotiations. "These women are really tough," David recalled him saying. "They don't give an inch and your sister is one of the ringleaders. I don't know what to do." At this point David looked up from his desk and said simply, "Joe—surrender."

The negotiations carried on through the spring of 1973. On May 21, Mariana Gosnell noted in her diary that we "just spent the day negotiating with the lawyers about our women's agreement. It's still being haggled over and they keep backtracking and driving us mad. Men are REALLY pigs"—short for "male chauvinist pigs," the worst thing you could say about a man in those days. By June, Joe had finally convinced *Newsweek*'s management to accept goals and timetables for a female senior editor. "Katharine was fine so long as there was talent," Joe recalled. "I think Oz took it reluctantly, but he took it because Katharine was aboard. His divorce had an enormous impact on him. It was a bitter, bitter fight, and whatever was going on with his wife was consuming him."

On June 28, 1973, we announced that fifty *Newsweek* women had signed a second, twenty-two-page memorandum of understanding with management. We also withdrew our complaints with the EEOC and the New York State Division of Human Rights. The new memorandum stated that by December 31, 1974, approximately one-third of the magazine's writers and domestic reporters would be female and by the end of 1975, one of every three people hired or transferred to the staff of foreign correspondents would be a woman. We gave management more than two years—until December 31, 1975—to appoint a female senior editor in charge of one of the seven editorial sections of the magazine.

Newsweek also committed to providing writing and reporting training programs for women, an arbitration procedure, and reports three times a year on the magazine's affirmative actions. Editors now had to fill out forms on all the applicants for researcher, reporter, and writer vacancies, noting their age and gender, whether they had applied to or been approached by *Newsweek,* their experience and education, samples of their work, whether an interview was held and by whom, and the result: if rejected—why, if kept on file—why. The document, witnessed by Rich Cooper, was signed by Oz and Harriet and the six women on our committee: Connie Carroll, Merrill Sheils (McLoughlin), Margaret Montagno, Mariana Gosnell, Phyllis Malamud, and me. *Newsweek* paid Harriet $11,240 in costs and fees, payable to the Employment Rights Project at Columbia University.

According to Joe, Kay was pleased that it was settled. "She was sympathetic, but I had no sense of her being a feminist in any way at all during the *Newsweek* negotiations," he said. "She really was a business woman and a publisher, but she had a sense of fairness. I don't think she ever would have done anything she didn't think was right." We finally felt the system would change. One unnamed member of the women's committee was quoted in the press release saying, "All of the women at *Newsweek* worked very hard to bring this about, and we feel it's a great accomplishment, not only for us, but for other women in the media. The strength of this agreement—its specific goals, timetables and training programs—shows the strength of *Newsweek*'s commitment to equal employment for women. We think congratulations are due all around."

Again, we didn't ask for back pay. "It was a failure of will and imagination," said Harriet, looking back. "It was either your judgment or ours that if we asked for money, they wouldn't settle without litigation." At the time, recalled Harriet, the *Newsweek* case was fairly straightforward. "You all didn't have different job categories or salaries," she said. "You were a homogeneous class. Guys had better opportunities but they looked like you in background and qualifications."

Indeed, our case was relatively simple compared to Harriet's discrimination suits against the *Reader's Digest* in 1973 and the *New York Times* in 1974, both of which included women in different job categories and on the business side. The women at the *Reader's Digest* "were treated worse," said Harriet. "At the *Digest,* corporate was resistant because they felt they were good to women. There were women who worked in 'Fulfillment,' filling subscriptions—one of the least fulfilling jobs ever. In the morning, you could order dinner for two, three, or four people because Mother *Reader's Digest* wouldn't want you to go home without food, and women should feed their families well." But when it came to giving the women higher pay or promotions, the *Digest* was not so concerned. "There were end-of-the-year reviews with two lists of names—the editors and the ladies, who were also editors—and the factors for promotion. 'He's a family man, we need to help. She's a single woman, doesn't need more.'"

At one point, the *Digest* even went after Harriet. The plaintiffs had asked her to talk to an open meeting of other female employees who might want to learn about their case and either join or support them. Some *Digest* loyalists taped her remarks and turned the tape over to the company's lawyers. "The *Reader's Digest* filed a sanction against me saying I had breached legal ethics by encouraging people to litigate, that I was 'ambulance chasing' to get clients," Harriet explained. "It was scary because they were after my license. I wrapped myself in the flag and told the judge that management didn't want people to tell them their rights and that's what I did and I'm proud of it." The judge dismissed the *Digest's* motion from the bench. In the end, the *Digest* settled and 5,635 women plaintiffs got $1,375,000 in back pay—about $244 each.

In the case of the *New York Times,* said Harriet, "management really took off on the women and trashed them, unlike *Newsweek's* management, which didn't fight ugly. The *Times* women were angrier than the *Newsweek* women, in part because they were older and because many of them came out of the labor union movement. They also had seen their salaries because the union saw salaries, and there's nothing like money to make you angry."

The *Times* women began organizing in 1972, right after we filed our second suit in May. "Grace [Lichtenstein, a young *Times* reporter] kept saying, 'What are we doing sitting around like this when the *Newsweek* women are stirring things up?'" recalled Betsy Wade Boylan, the named plaintiff on *Elizabeth Boylan v. The New York Times Company*. In the spring of 1973, six *Times* women hired Harriet to represent them and in November 1974, filed a class action lawsuit. Management was furious. At one point, according to Harriet, Arthur Ochs "Punch" Sulzberger, Sr., publisher of the *New York Times* and a former trustee of Columbia University, called Michael Sovern, then dean of Columbia Law School, and asked whether he thought that what Harriet was doing with these cases in her law clinic was legitimate. "He led Michael to believe that he really wanted to stop the lawsuit, that he thought it was unfair," recalled Harriet. "Michael refused, and didn't tell me about it until the case was over."

Four years later, as the *Times* women were preparing for a September 1978 court date, a machinists union strike hit all three New York daily newspapers in August. The *Times* settled the suit in October, though the strike didn't end until November. The case had gotten so poisonous that going to court probably would have damaged not only the paper but also the women. Still, said Harriet, "I think they settled because if their defense was that the women weren't promoted because they weren't any good, then these were the same women—Nan Robertson, Marilyn Bender, Eileen Shanahan, Grace Glueck—whose bylines were in the paper." The *Times* ended up paying $350,000 to settle the suit, $233,500 of which went to back pay for the 550 women and $15,000 was divided among the plaintiffs and women who had testified in depositions. Employees with twenty or more years of service were given $1,000 with the others paid on a sliding scale down.

Afterward, several of the original editorial plaintiffs saw their careers stall—or worse. "We did a brave and a noisy thing and we knew it wasn't going to be for us," said Betsy Wade. Eileen Shanahan, a top financial reporter in the Washington bureau, left the *Times* in 1977, before the settlement. "I had repeatedly asked for editing jobs and couldn't get them," she later said. "That's one of the reasons I left. The other was knowing what retaliation was going to come from the suit." (Ironically, Shanahan went to work as the assistant secretary for public affairs officer for Joe Califano, who had become the secretary of Health, Education, and Welfare in the Carter administration). Grace Glueck, a gifted writer whose stories often ended up leading the culture page, was never made a top arts critic, while Joan Cook, a talented reporter, editor, and ideas person, was relegated to day rewrite, a backwater of the news department.

When she began organizing the women in 1972, Betsy Wade had been in a high-ranking position as head of the foreign copy desk. Getting nowhere, she took a position during the litigation as assistant travel editor so that she would be in a protected Guild job. She ended her career at the *Times* writing the "Practical Traveler" column, a secure but going-nowhere job. "I was sidelined because I was a woman," she recalled, "and I wasn't going to be promoted to the jobs that the people I trained were going to be promoted to."

"We were born ten years too early," said Grace Lichtenstein. "If I were born ten years later, I would have been a sportswriter. If Betsy were born twenty years later, she would have been managing editor or executive editor and certainly foreign editor." Although she felt disheartened by how little credit they got from young journalists "who don't understand all the opportunities that have opened up for them," said Grace, "we changed the way the *New York Times* looks at news." For Betsy Wade, the lawsuit "was the most important thing I did in my life." But she insisted it also had a broader impact. "It was important at the *Times* but it was even more important for the great newspapers out there," she said. "That's why the women at *Newsweek* were so important, because they were so early and people said, 'Holy Hosanna.' The *Newsweek* suit created a mold that showed that it could be done."

Anna Quindlen, who was hired at the *New York Times* at the age of twenty-four, considers herself one of the beneficiaries of the lawsuit. "I was convinced that I was hired because I was a whiz journalist," she said. "But I was hired there because of six courageous women who brought the women's suit. They weren't going to get a lot out of it, but I did. I call it the gift that keeps on giving. I was editor of the metropolitan section at twenty-nine and an op-ed columnist at thirty-three." Quindlen left the *Times* in 1995 to write novels, very successfully, and then went to *Newsweek* as a columnist in 1999, a position she held until 2009. "So you could say I was also the beneficiary of the *Newsweek* suit in taking over Meg Greenfield's spot on the back page."

At the *New York Times*, said Anna, "The women's suit changed the paper a lot! The content changed. Look at my 'Life in the 30s' column [which she wrote in the mid-eighties]. That was a direct result of the women's suit. One letter to my column said, 'I never thought the *New York Times* would write about what I was thinking about.' We understood the readers—a population that male editors had never known about." She also said the lawsuit changed who ran the paper. "Now we have women on the masthead," she added. "I never thought in my lifetime I'd see a woman on the *New York Times* masthead."

Gail Collins, the former editorial page editor of the *New York Times* and now an op-ed columnist and best-selling author, also credits the pioneering women. I first met Gail in 1973 when she invited me to speak to women journalists in Connecticut about our lawsuit. Gail was running the Connecticut News Service, which she had started in 1972 after covering the state legislature for the weekly *Fair Press*. "The idea of inviting you was not in the context of a suit," remembered Gail. "It was rather getting you to inspire everyone." But according to Trish Hall, the current op-ed editor at the *New York Times* who was then at the *New Haven Journal-Courier,* after my talk the women decided to sue. On October 4, 1974, fifteen women filed sex discrimination charges with the EEOC against the New Haven Register Publishing Company.

Gail was not part of that suit, but she extols all the women who put their jobs on the line. "I arrived in New York approximately one second after the women at places like the *New York Times* and *Newsweek* had filed lawsuits," she recalled. "The women who fought those fights were not the ones who got the rewards. People like me, who came right behind them, got the good jobs and promotions. I know many of the heroines of those battles and they aren't bitter. They're still very ticked off at their former employers, but they're very happy and proud of the women who came after and got the opportunities that rightfully should have been theirs. To me that's the definition of a great heart."

CHAPTER 10

The Barricades Fell

WOMEN'S PROGRESS TOOK a dramatic leap in the 1970s when Congress, the courts, and the media began responding to feminist demands. Between 1971 and 1974, Congress extended employment benefits to married women working in the federal government, prohibited sex discrimination in Social Security and other pension programs, and proscribed creditors from discriminating against women (until then, women couldn't get credit—or credit cards—in their own name). In 1972, Title IX of the Education Amendments Act banned sex discrimination in education programs and activities, giving women equal access to advanced math and science courses, medical and vocational schools, residential facilities, and in 1975, college sports. When twenty-nine-year-old Billie Jean King, who had been campaigning for equal prize money for women athletes, defeated fifty-nine-year-old tennis champion Bobby Riggs in three straight sets in the 1973 "Battle of the Sexes," she legitimized women's professional sports and inspired female athletes everywhere.

Politically, feminists were beginning to enter the national arena and their agenda was shaped around issues affecting women's lives. In 1964, Patsy Mink (D-HI) was the first Asian American elected to Congress, and in 1968 Shirley Chisholm (D-NY) became the first African American woman representative. They were followed by social activist Bella Abzug (D-NY) in 1970, civil rights leader Barbara Jordan (D-TX) in 1972, and a thirty-one-year-old lawyer named Pat Schroeder (D-CO) in 1973. Chisholm, Abzug, Betty Friedan, Gloria Steinem, and Eleanor Holmes Norton, among others, founded the National Women's Political Caucus in 1971 to increase the participation of women in political and public life. Two years later, the National Black Feminist Organization was formed. Its "statement of purpose" declared that

> the distorted male-dominated media image of the Women's Liberation Movement has clouded the vital and revolutionary importance of this movement to Third World women, especially black women. The Movement has been characterized as the exclusive property of so-called white middle-class women and any black women seen involved in this movement have been seen as selling out, dividing the race, and an assortment of nonsensical epithets. Black feminists resent these charges and have therefore established The National

Black Feminist Organization, in order to address ourselves to the particular and specific needs of the larger, but almost cast-aside half of the black race in Amerikkka, the black woman.

Meanwhile, sex discrimination suits were proliferating, including one against the giant telephone company AT&T. The largest employer of women, the Bell System (of which AT&T was a part) classified jobs by gender, prevented women from serving as line workers, and denied women the promotions it offered to men. The suit was settled out of court in 1972, when AT&T agreed to a multimillion-dollar payment to workers and promised to end the company's discriminatory practices.

In 1971, a young feminist attorney named Ruth Bader Ginsburg successfully argued before the US Supreme Court that an Idaho law giving preference to men as executors of estates was unconstitutional. That decision was the first time the court ruled that the Fourteenth Amendment's equal protection clause protected women's rights, which over the next thirty years was used to strike down many laws discriminating against women and men. In 1973, as a result of *Roe v. Wade,* the Supreme Court established that a woman's right to a safe and legal abortion, with certain qualifications, was a fundamental liberty under the US Constitution.

But there were several significant defeats. The Equal Rights Amendment, which passed Congress in 1972, failed to get ratification from enough states to become law. In 1971, Congress had approved the Comprehensive Child Development Act, which would have provided child care on a sliding fee scale to working parents as a matter of right. However, President Richard Nixon vetoed it, saying it would commit "the vast moral authority of the national government to the side of communal approaches to childrearing over against [*sic*] the family-centered approach."

At the same time, the mainstream media were spreading the feminist message in the public arena. By the end of 1971, stories on the new women's movement had appeared on the covers of *Time, Newsweek,* the *New York Times Magazine, Look, Life,* the *Atlantic,* and the *Saturday Review.* There was also a spate of "first" stories in the media—the "first woman" fire-fighter, police officer, stock broker, auto mechanic, telephone installer, you name it. The exploding coverage of the feminist movement not only was changing old institutions, it also was creating new ones. Feminist bookstores, magazines, coffee shops, and health care clinics were springing up, bringing women's previously private issues into the public domain.

Distrusting the coverage of the women's movement in the mass media, feminists focused their press on their own experiences and testimonies. Beginning in 1968, publications calling for social change—liberation or revolution rather than just equality—began to proliferate, including the *Voice of the Women's Liberation Movement* out of Chicago, *No More Fun and Games* in Cambridge, Massachusetts, *Lilith* in Seattle, and *Notes from the First Year* in New York (which published Anne Koedt's famous 1970 essay on "The Myth of the Vaginal Orgasm"). In all, more than five hundred feminist periodicals were published between 1968 and 1973.

Ms. magazine, which began publication in 1972, had a major impact on the media as the first mainstream publication written, edited, owned, and operated by women. It featured cover stories on domestic violence and sexual harassment, commissioned a national study on date rape, and publicized such issues as sex trafficking and the sexist portrayal of women in advertising. In 1973, a group of women in Boston who had been studying their own anatomy and sexuality published *Our Bodies, Ourselves,* which revolutionized how the world looked at women's health and popularized the radical notion that women's bodies were as worthy of research as men's.

Inside the traditional media, women at newspapers, television networks, and local TV stations were busy forming committees and filing lawsuits. In early 1972, the Federal Communications Commission granted a petition from the National Organization for Women requiring that women be included in affirmative action programs for radio and television stations as a condition for the renewal of their broadcast licenses. That same year, NOW filed a petition to deny the license renewal of WABC-TV in New York and of WRC-TV in Washington, D.C. In February 1973, fifty women at NBC filed a sex discrimination complaint with the EEOC, the US Department of Labor, and the New York City Commission on Human Rights, which "found cause to believe" the complaint had merit. NBC conceded that "the commission's report for the years 1967 to 1972 reflects the historical trends in American society—that women have been under-utilized in managerial positions and over-utilized in clerical positions." (The case would be settled in 1975 for $2 million, awarding $540,000 in back pay to 2,600 women—between $500 and $1,000 each, with more going to the original sixteen plaintiffs.)

Things were more complicated for the women at Time Inc., partly because they were older and better paid than we were and partly because the leaders of their movement didn't involve all the women employees from the very beginning as we had. (*Time* magazine, however, counted six women among its fifty-six writers.) In March 1970, a reporter for the British newsmagazine the *New Statesman* called a female *Fortune* employee and asked whether, after the *Newsweek* women sued, the women at Time Inc. were planning any action. That spurred a small group of women at several Time Inc. magazines to start meeting secretly. They decided to file sex discrimination charges with the New York State Division of Human Rights. When the complaint was ready to be signed, they called a meeting of the rest of the women to enlist their support. But, as one woman put it, it turned into "the Bay of Pigs," a similarly ill-fated mission. Some women who had made it out of the research ranks didn't feel discriminated against, others wanted to go to management first, and a number of women did not like having the decision imposed upon them.

A group of sixty Time Inc. women actually split off into a dissident group and drew up a petition simply to "bear witness" to the truth of the allegations of discrimination, which they presented to top management. Two months after our legal complaint, on May 1, 1970, ninety-six women at Time Inc. filed a sex discrimination complaint against *Time, Life, Fortune,* and *Sports Illustrated.* Seven months later, in February 1971, a conciliatory agreement was signed between 147 women and management stipulating, among other things, that the Human Rights Commission would monitor the company's progress in interviewing, hiring, and promoting women on a quarterly basis. We were envious of this legal accountability, but in the end, it fizzled out.

At *Newsweek,* we were moving ahead. After we signed the second memorandum of understanding with management in June 1973, more women were given tryouts as reporters and writers, and some were promoted. Lucy Howard, who had refused a bureau internship in 1972—"I was always the last person to try something," she explained—was sent to the Washington bureau in 1973 to fill in during Watergate. The following year, she returned to New York to work in the newly created Justice section. "Technically I was a researcher but I never checked a story—I was reporting," she recalled. "One of the women told me that according to Guild rules, if you don't check anything for six months they have to promote you." After six months, Lucy went to Ed Kosner, the managing editor, and showed him that she had not fact-checked a single story. She was promoted to reporter in 1974. "I was pushed into it," she said. "I was asked to do the reporting and I was a good girl, so I did it. I was competitive and I didn't want to get left behind, but I didn't think of this as a career until long after the suit."

Pat Lynden left the magazine in May 1971, when she got pregnant. Margaret Montagno ended up writing in Nation and

Religion before moving to *Newsweek*'s international edition, which, she said, "I preferred because it was much less pressure." Judy Gingold was given a writing tryout in "Where Are They Now?" but it didn't work out. As Judy's close friend, I was upset, knowing how smart and talented she was. I went to Ed Kosner and suggested that he give her a tryout editing the guest essays in the "My Turn" section. Until then, Ed had been selecting the pieces himself, but he was taking on more responsibility for editing the magazine, so he agreed. Not surprisingly, Judy was brilliant at it, especially handling famous contributors, such as Henry Kissinger and Lionel Tiger. She was promoted to "My Turn" editor in 1974.

When Mimi McLoughlin, the Religion researcher, had a writing tryout, she showed so much talent that Dwight Martin hired her. "If I have to have one of these women, I want to have a good one," he said. Mimi became the Education writer, where she proved to be a star. Mariana Gosnell, the Medicine and Science reporter, also tried out with Dwight, but after writing in Education and on *Newsweek International,* she languished and returned to her old position in the back-of-the-book. "I preferred reporting," she recalled. "I was always very verbose and didn't like to do the seventy-liners."

Even after she had turned down a promotion to be a reporter in the Los Angeles bureau, Trish Reilly found herself being groomed as a writer in the Arts sections. Her editor, Jack Kroll, kept giving her story assignments. "I don't know why I was targeted for success," Trish recalled. "I just assumed that Jack was under pressure to promote women." After a year or so, Jack told Trish he was going to promote her to writer and she panicked. "I felt so humiliated and ashamed that I was being given these opportunities and couldn't say, 'I don't want to be a writer,'" she explained. "I remember walking out of Jack's office saying, 'I've got to get out of here.'" In 1973, she bolted to CBS News.

I was doing better as a writer since my boss and nemesis, Joel Blocker, was fired in 1972. I felt vindicated. The senior editors who filled in liked my copy and in August that year, I was assigned my first cover story. It was on Halston, a young fashion designer who outfitted fashionable ladies, including Kay Graham, in chic Ultrasuede shirtdresses and sweater sets with wraparound skirts. I spent days hanging out with Halston, going to Studio 54, and interviewing his clients, including a heady lunch on his terrace with actress Liza Minnelli and photographer Berry Berenson, designer Elsa Schiaparelli's granddaughter. Given that we had sued *Newsweek* three months earlier—and kept asking to give the women a chance to succeed—I felt under enormous pressure. In a letter to my parents, my husband described my agony: "Lynn just wrote her first cover story. She had trouble sleeping at night and it was a sure sign of maturity. In the past, if she was nervous she would fall asleep in a second. Oz decided to cut short the chain of command and the article only went through one set of hands before he had a look at it. He was delighted with the story and gave it a very light edit." Afterward, Oz sent me a note that revealed questionable taste but unquestionable enthusiasm. It said, "Congratulations on losing your virginity in such style."

Over the next year, more women from outside were being hired as writers. Susan Fraker, who had graduated near the top of her class at Columbia Journalism School, got a job on *Newsweek's* international edition in August 1973, the only woman writer on that staff. "I learned about the women's suit months afterwards," she recalled, "but clearly that must have been why I was hired." That fall, Margo Jefferson became the first black woman writer at *Newsweek* and the first woman to write in the Arts department, an area populated in the general press by many female bylines. "I was a direct beneficiary of the women's suit," said Margo, who went on to become a Pulitzer Prize–winning critic for the *New York Times,* "and I was stunned by the systemic, genteel, upper-middle-class sexism of the place." When she was being interviewed by Jack Kroll, movie critic Paul Zimmerman wandered in to ask Kroll a question. Recognizing Margo from Columbia Journalism School, where he taught an arts writing course, he said, "You were one of Judy Crist's students. I wanted one of my best students to get an interview here but he didn't because he wasn't black or a woman." Margo was stunned. Kroll made a little joke that got Paul out of the office, "but that's how angry, how beleaguered and besieged and maltreated certain kinds of men were already feeling," she said.

By then, there were several black reporters at *Newsweek* and at least one bureau chief, but there was never any attempt to organize among them. "There wasn't a critical mass of blacks on the magazine," recalled Margo. "Although if there were more than two of us standing together talking, you could guarantee that someone would walk by and say jokingly, 'Planning an uprising?'"

When it came to finding a female senior editor, the editors first looked outside the magazine. I was told that they approached Gloria Steinem, who wasn't interested because she was editing her own magazine, *Ms.* Gloria later told me that she couldn't remember whether she was asked but, she added, "it would make perfect sense because at a certain point, I became like José Greco—I was the only Spanish dancer they knew." In the end, they decided to see whether a *Newsweek* woman could do the job. "I think after the Helen Dudar thing, they thought the women would be really mad if the first woman senior editor came from outside," recalled Ed Kosner. "And as for inside, there weren't too many candidates."

Oz offered Liz Peer a tryout as a senior editor in the summer of 1974. Liz had returned to New York in May 1973 as a swing writer in various back-of-the-book sections. In 1974, she won a Page One Award for her cover story on Barbara Walters (in her stylish prose, Liz described Barbara's probing interrogations as "some of the toughest questions in TV journalism— dumdum bullets swaddled in angora"). Liz was by far the most senior and most talented woman on the staff, and it was right that she would be the first to shatter *Newsweek*'s glass ceiling. But Liz was complicated. "Liz was very ambitious and not easy," said her close friend, sculptor Helaine Blumenfeld. "When the armor was on, she was clever, brilliant, and sassy. But nobody really knew her. She was so sweet, so vulnerable— just a gorgeous human being." With her spiked heels and conical bras, she always talked about her "beaux" and was famous for hanging a full-length ball gown—and feather boa—on her office door to show that she had better things to do after work. On seeing a dress hanging on her door one night, Dwight Martin popped into her office and said, "I know where you're going, Liz—to a women's lib meeting."

Oz had wanted Liz to be the first female senior editor. But although she was the consummate *Newsweek* writer and reporter, she wasn't cut out to be an editor. "She was very talented," recalled Ed Kosner, *Newsweek*'s managing editor at the time, "but she wasn't a good manager." She could be volatile. Her tryout ended when she threw an ashtray across the room because she was furious at someone or something. "They immediately said it was because she was a woman," recalled Nancy Stadtman, "but Russ Watson [another senior editor] used to throw things, too." (Betsy Carter said Russ once threw a typewriter at her.)

When Liz was trying out in the fall of 1974, I was on leave, trying to save my failing marriage. Unfortunately, the feature film that Jeff made had not done well and in 1973, he moved to Los Angeles to find work. For more than a year, we had been commuting back and forth every six weeks. Jeff desperately wanted me to move to LA, but I didn't want to give up my job until I was sure he could earn a steady living. In October 1974, I took a three-month leave of absence to see if we could make a go of it. Things were better there, and I felt that before any decision was made, we needed to live together again. In December, I came back to *Newsweek* and asked Ed Kosner for another, longer leave beginning February 1. I also offered to do some work out of *Newsweek's* LA bureau. Ed said fine.

As I was cleaning out my office in January, Ed called me down to his office. "I'm going to complicate your life," he said. "How?" I asked. "I want you to try out as a senior editor," he replied. I was surprised and, frankly, unnerved. How could I do this now? What would happen to my marriage? Would Jeff understand? Not to mention the job—was I up to it? Could I really do the work? Could I edit guys who had been my bosses and were far more experienced than I was? And, every editor's nightmare, would I be able to rewrite a cover story or a disastrous feature that needed to be turned around overnight? Not wanting to show my doubts or fears, I told Ed I was flattered and would talk it over with my husband.

I went home that night worried about telling Jeff the news. But as I mulled over Ed's offer, I found myself getting more and more excited just thinking about it. I had been working at *Newsweek* for ten years and writing for almost six. How could I turn down this opportunity to move up the ladder? To be the first woman senior editor? I knew Jeff would be disappointed, that he was counting on our being together in LA, as was I. But a tryout lasted only a few months and I wasn't sure I would get the job anyway—I just knew I wanted to try.

I called Jeff and told him about the offer. I said I had to stay in New York, that I felt I needed to prove to myself that I could—or couldn't—be an editor, and that if I never tried out, I would never know. There was silence and then Jeff said, "Either you come to Los Angeles or our marriage is over." I was shocked. I couldn't believe he really said that. He couldn't mean it. My stomach began to churn and it took me a minute to find my voice. Shaking, I told him that if he didn't understand how important this was to me after all these years at *Newsweek,* then he must not love me. He said that of course he loved me, which is why he wanted me in Los Angeles. We talked a few more minutes but there was nothing more to say.

The next day I had an appointment with my therapist at lunchtime. I remember walking into his office, sitting down, and saying, "Well, I guess my marriage is over." I was so confused between feeling elated by Ed's offer and feeling depressed that my husband couldn't understand the opportunity I was handed. It clarified some things in my mind that I had been talking about with my shrink: why our life always seemed to revolve around him and what I had to do for myself after spending so many years encouraging him. I walked out of the office still not believing that after seven years our marriage was actually ending. That night, Jeff called me from LA. He apologized and told me he loved me. He said he would come back to New York to be with me. The next month, he returned and found a job directing a soap opera.

My tryout lasted several months that spring of 1975. I was nervous and exhausted, staying late several nights a week to get the job done. But I quickly realized that I enjoyed editing more than writing. I felt more suited to it and it fit my nurturing personality. I had lots of ideas and a strong sense of structure, and I enjoyed working with talented writers, relishing the give-and-take in making their work better. What proved more daunting was being the only woman in the story meetings. Despite Ed's support, it was clear that most of the editors didn't take me seriously. In a room filled with testosterone and egotism, I had to learn to speak up and defend my stories and my writers. As I struggled to push myself forward, I was surprised by the passivity of some of the men. One of my former editors, who was always insisting that he had fought hard for our stories, just rolled over whenever he encountered an objection from the top guys. And he wasn't the only one.

My relationships with my writers were more rewarding. The most surprising was with Harry Waters, my old boss whom I now was editing. Mensch that he was, Harry couldn't have been more supportive or less threatened. We continued to work well together and I always valued his counsel. Ken Woodward was more skeptical of the decision to let me audition for the job. Ken was the longtime Religion writer at *Newsweek* and a man with old-fashioned values. But he was a good writer and an expert on religious topics. One day, Ken came into my office to tell me that initially he had been against my becoming a senior editor. He was against affirmative action and felt I was being considered only because I was a woman. But he had changed his mind after he realized I really was interested in the material and not just using the position as a stepping stone to get ahead, as had the men before me. He also told me that he had never asked to leave early to attend his son's baseball game because he was afraid to say that to a male boss; instead, he would say he had a doctor's appointment. But he felt that he could tell me the truth and I would understand. We had come to a truce.

That summer, Jeff and I went on vacation to Los Angeles to visit Mary Pleshette and Jack Willis, who had married and moved there. We decided to drive to the Grand Canyon and we were there when, on August 1, Oz announced that he would move up to become editor-in-chief and that Ed Kosner would be the next editor of *Newsweek*. When we got back to LA, Mary told me that Ed had phoned and to call him in New York. When I reached him, Ed told me his news. I was very happy for him and gave him my congratulations. Then he congratulated me. He told me that he had decided to promote me to senior editor and had already announced it effective September 1.

I'm sure I thanked him but I remember only that I was dumbfounded. I hadn't expected Oz to leave so soon, although it was clear that Ed was the next in line. Nor was I given any indication that I was even succeeding in my tryout. Although many of my ideas were picked up and my stories were getting through, I had no idea whether I was doing well. When I asked Ed years later, "Why me?" he said, "You had an editor's mind. You could see structure and you didn't have the kind of ego that had to be out there. The best editors were analytical and if our edited stories didn't sing, it was because we were on deadline and fixing a structural problem. And, no disrespect, but you had an iron ass. You would sit in the chair and work until it was done—late nights, late hours, and all."

I was pleased with Ed's confidence in me. He had been my mentor and was good to me, but it turned out that he wasn't exactly an equal-opportunity employer. When I returned to New York, Ed proudly told me that he was raising my salary from $27,000 to $32,000. Then I found out that Charlie Michener, another writer who had been promoted to senior editor in the Arts sections, would be making $40,000 a year. I couldn't believe it! Consciousness finally raised, I confronted Ed. He explained that my percentage raise was much higher than Charlie's, which meant only that I was making much less to begin with. Since Ed had already announced my promotion, I had him cornered. I told him that I wouldn't take the senior editor job unless I got the same amount as a man doing the same work. He reluctantly agreed and I felt great. When I called my parents to tell them the good news, my father was thrilled and cheered me on. My mother's response was true to form. "Now you'll never have children," she said.

Three weeks later, I encountered the editing nightmare I feared. On Monday, September 22, Jacqueline Kennedy Onassis announced she was taking a job as a consulting editor at Viking Press. *Newsweek* decided to crash a six-column story describing "Jackie on Her Own," to be reported and written by Liz Peer and edited by me. I was nervous about how Liz would respond to my editing her, but she was a pro. We discussed the story and she spent the week gathering information. On Friday evening, around six, I got the first half of her story. Unlike most of her pieces, this one just didn't work, and I was dismayed that Liz hadn't nailed it. I showed it to my top editor, Ed Klein, who agreed and told me the story had to be rewritten. Normally I would talk through the problems with the writer and let her fix it. But Liz was still writing the second half of the piece and I needed her to finish. So I shut my door and began to rewrite the copy. When Liz handed in the last part, she came into my office and I explained what I was doing and why. She took it well, but she was exhausted and said she didn't want to work on it anymore. I stayed until 4 A.M., returned early Saturday morning to finish the story, and handed it in by noon. It sailed through. I was relieved that I had passed the test, but I will always appreciate Liz's professional behavior. She never held it against me.

Becoming the first female senior editor in *Newsweek*'s forty-two-year history was a personal as well as a professional victory for me. I had never thought of myself as ambitious. I had been lucky in that most opportunities had come to me—I didn't have to ask for them. I pushed myself forward by looking around and saying, "Well, if that guy can do it, then I surely can." Now I had to recognize that I did have drive (my preferred word to "ambition") and some talent. I was anxious about succeeding in my new job, but for the first time I felt confident in my career, armed with the kind of outside affirmation that I—and many of the women I knew—needed. It was one thing for your parents or teachers to tell you how good you were; it was another for the world to chime in.

Professionally, my elevation broke the editorial barrier. Now women had a voice in the meetings, a representative in management, and an advocate for them and for their story ideas. There was still resistance. I was told that Bob Christopher, the executive editor, said that my becoming a senior editor was the worst mistake management ever made. But it didn't matter. This time, something truly had changed. We *Newsweek* women, who had never wavered in demanding our rights, had finally prevailed in our five-year fight for equality. I was amazed that as one of the women who had been a leader in the lawsuit, I was rewarded with being named the magazine's first female senior editor. That wasn't true for most women on the front lines in the media lawsuits. But the barricades were falling, and women were rushing in.

CHAPTER 11

Passing the Torch

B ETWEEN 1975 AND 1985, women pushed their way into
every position on the magazine except top management.
Liz Peer, who was promoted to Paris bureau chief at the end
of 1975, was sent to cover the war in Somalia in 1977 as
Newsweek's first female war correspondent. Elaine Sciolino,
hired as a researcher in the international edition in 1970, flew
to Iran in February 1979, on the same plane as the Ayatollah
Khomeini, where she covered the Iranian Revolution and
then the hostage crisis. (She later became Paris bureau chief for
the *New York Times*.) In December 1976, Eleanor Clift from the
Atlanta bureau rode into Washington with Jimmy Carter as
Newsweek's White House correspondent, the first female newsmagazine reporter to cover the president in the West Wing
(not the first lady in the East Wing).

Phyllis Malamud was promoted to Boston bureau chief in 1977 and Mimi McLoughlin became one of the magazine's star writers and editors. In the early 1980s, Mimi became the first female to edit the Business section and then National Affairs, the most important section on the magazine. Mimi had that natural newsmagazine talent: as a writer, she could synthesize pages of files on nuclear power and polish off a complicated and comprehensive cover story the next day; as an editor she had a nose for news and a keen ear for the language. She was also popular with her troops—tough when she needed to be but never leaving bruises—and we loved that she could drink any of the boys (including the "big boys") under the table.

During the years of our lawsuits, *Newsweek*'s coverage of women was beginning to change, although an August 1971 cover story on Gloria Steinem ("The New Woman"), reported by three women and written by Dick Boeth, "a writing minority of one," still carried the sexist subline, "A Liberated Woman Despite Beauty, Chic and Success." A content analysis of the magazine between 1969 and 1975 by a student at the University of Missouri showed that the number of lines devoted to women or women's issues nearly doubled in those six years, the greatest increases coming in the Sports and Business sections. Most sexist adjectives had been deleted, and when bylines were added in 1975, women writers and reporters were highly visible, especially in the Religion, Medicine, and Justice sections.

With more women reporting, writing, and editing, there were more diverse story ideas, more quotes from female experts, and fewer cheesecake photos in "Newsmakers." As fatigue from

Vietnam and Watergate took hold, the news focus began to shift inward and the back-of-the-book areas became more important. As we had predicted, women brought new ideas to the magazine. In my first few years as senior editor, I was averaging almost a cover a month in my five sections (News Media, Television, Life/Style, Religion, and Ideas), including "Who's Raising the Kids?" "Living with Dying," "How Men Are Changing," and "Saving the Family," the first newsmagazine special report on such family issues as stepfamilies, family therapy, and how the family is portrayed on TV.

Unfortunately, my family wasn't saved. In November 1976, after nearly nine years of marriage, Jeff and I separated. The confidence I had gained on the job allowed me finally to deal with the problems in my marriage. We had tried everything, including couples counseling, but nothing seemed to work. One day, when I was telling my therapist that Jeff wasn't giving me what I needed emotionally, my doctor simply asked, "Is he unwilling or unable?" That's when I realized I had to leave. I felt very sad but also relieved. I think Jeff knew it was over, too, and he moved back to California soon afterward.

I became consumed with work and as luck would have it, that paid off professionally and personally. Not only did I flourish as an editor, but I also found the right man. Steve Shepard was hired at *Newsweek* as a senior editor in the Business section in May 1976. Steve had been a top writer at *BusinessWeek* and was on leave at Columbia University's Graduate School of Journalism to direct the Walter Bagehot Fellowship, a mid-career business journalism program he had created with his friend Soma Golden from the *New York Times*. When he came to *Newsweek* in 1976, Steve was married, as was I, and we became friends, collaborating on several *Newsweek* covers and feature stories. Steve couldn't help but notice the close camaraderie on the magazine. "Gosh, there's so much sex at *Newsweek*," he said to me shortly after he arrived. Assuming this was standard practice at most weeklies, I asked whether this wasn't true at *Business Week*. "Not like this," he replied.

From the beginning, everyone respected Steve and he was regarded as a "comer" at the magazine. In story meetings, he was smart, sensitive, and supportive of his writers and reporters. I admired how he was able to cut through all the posturing and get to the essence of the idea. But I also thought Steve was cute. A great dresser, with a tall, slim body to show off his English double-breasted suits, Steve sported aviator glasses and longish hair that curled around his neck. Although he had grown up in the Bronx, he was nothing like those "pushy Jewish guys" from New York my Jewish mother had warned me about. He was soft-spoken and had an impish sense of humor. We got along well. He gave me wise advice about my writers and stories, and when he had his doubts, I supported his move to edit the National Affairs section in early 1977.

And that's where things stood when Steve's marriage ended in June 1977. I had been single for almost a year, going out with various guys but not really involved with anyone. (I did have a few dates with Warren Beatty, which set the office chattering for months.) In September, Steve asked me out. Although I was very tempted, I thought that dating a colleague, even one on an equal level, wasn't wise. We were in the same meetings every week and if things didn't work out, it would be awkward. So I refused several times. Finally he stopped asking. Annoyed, he told me that if I ever wanted to go out with him, I would have to do the asking.

The following month, in October 1977, Steve had proposed a cover story on "Is America Turning Right?," a prescient topic three years before Ronald Reagan was elected president. For the cover, he borrowed one of my writers, David Gelman, who could be eloquent on conceptual topics. The Friday night before the cover closed, I went down to the eleventh floor to see how David was doing. Unfortunately, the story wasn't in great shape, but Steve assured me that they would fix it and it would be fine.

At home on Saturday, I felt bad for Steve and David. But sitting alone in my bachelorette sublet on East Sixty-Ninth Street, I realized that what I really felt was stupid. Here was this great guy at *Newsweek* whom I really liked, and I was crazy not to go out with him. On the pretense of finding out how the story came out, I called Steve at the office on Saturday around 5 P.M. He assured me that David had turned the cover around and it was about to go to the printers. "Well, to thank you for all your hard work, I'd like to take you out to dinner," I said. There was a silence at the other end. Clearly he had other plans. Finally he said, "Okay, I can change some things and meet you for dinner."

We met at La Goulue, a little French bistro on East Seventieth Street, right around the corner from my apartment. Steve had the usual Saturday night dinner that editors often ordered to celebrate the magazine's closing: a martini, a big fat steak, french fries, and a glass of red wine. We chatted about the cover story and Reagan and all the *Newsweek* gossip. At dessert, I asked if he would like to share some profiteroles. Steve confessed that he had never had profiteroles, so we ordered some. I dug my spoon into the creamy pastry puff dripping with chocolate and offered him the first taste. Our eyes met and, as we say in Yiddish, it was *bashert*—destiny. We went back to my apartment after dinner, where I realized that not only did I like this man, I was falling in love with him. From then on we were a couple and to this day, we celebrate our first-date anniversary on the last Saturday night in October.

In the beginning, we kept our relationship secret. It helped that we worked on separate floors and reported to different Wallendas. Although as single senior editors there was no ethical issue, reporters are professional gossipmongers and we didn't want to deal with the rumors. In February, we decided to go on vacation to Virgin Gorda and the only people we told were our two bosses. At dinner the first Friday night at Little Dix Bay, we toasted each other, thrilled that we were looking at the moonlit Caribbean rather than working at *Newsweek* until two in the morning. Just then, a waiter brought over a bottle of wine. We looked around the restaurant and didn't recognize anyone. Bewildered, we finally saw the card. It read, "Enjoy! From all your friends at *Newsweek*." The surprise had been staged by my Sports pal Pete Bonventre, whose brother worked at Little Dix. Those *Newsweek* reporters were good! Steve and

I married in September 1979, and when I left on maternity leave in November 1980, I was given a big send-off at Top of the Week. It was another breakthrough—*Newsweek*'s first pregnant senior editor.

In the 1980s, *Newsweek* did better in hiring and promoting women than most media organizations, but progress was slow and painful. There were backtracks and broken promises, injustices and discrimination—and still no women were at the top. When I went on maternity leave, I told the editors to fill my senior editor slot, because I wanted to work part-time when I returned. But there were other candidates who could have risen up the masthead. Mimi McLoughlin, who had the talent and experience to become the first female assistant managing editor, left the magazine in 1986 when she and her husband, Mike Ruby, another *Newsweek* editor, departed for *US News & World Report*. In 1989, they became coeditors of *US News*, making Mimi the first woman to edit a national newsmagazine. Annalyn Swann, a music critic at *Time*, was hired at *Newsweek* as a writer in the Arts sections and took over as senior editor in 1983. At one point Kay Graham, a friend of Annalyn's family, had encouraged her to think about becoming a Wallenda. But, Annalyn later recalled, in talking to Rick Smith, then the editor of *Newsweek*, "He told me that any Wallenda should be seasoned by front-of-the-book experience as well as back-of-the-book."

In 1986, Rick changed his mind. He hired Dominique Browning from *Texas Monthly* as the senior editor for my old sections. Two years later—and eighteen years after our first lawsuit—Rick promoted Dominique to assistant managing editor (AME), the magazine's first female Wallenda.

After Dominique left in 1992, several women became AMEs, but none of them made it to the very top. Alexis Gelber, a former National Affairs editor and AME, was a strong contender, but she was married to Mark Whitaker, who became the editor of *Newsweek* in 1998, the first African American to lead a national news magazine. That put Alexis out of the running. Ann McDaniel, who ran *Newsweek's* award-winning Monica Lewinsky coverage as Washington bureau chief—and held the title of managing editor—was a favored candidate, but she didn't want to leave D.C. In 2001, Don Graham hired her as vice president of the Washington Post Company. Dorothy Kalins was hired in 2001 as *Newsweek's* executive editor, the number-three position, but as an accomplished lifestyle editor and founder of *Metropolitan Home, Saveur,* and *Garden Design* magazines, she clearly would never become the top editor of a newsmagazine.

Every masthead is a snapshot of a moment in time: women do better at some times than at others. That's natural, as long as progress flows as well as ebbs—and that usually depends on the person at the top. Some editors, such as Rick Smith and Maynard Parker, worked well with women and hired or promoted many of them. Others seemed to feel more comfortable with a circle of men. In 2008, Don Graham appointed Ann McDaniel to the newly created position of managing director of Newsweek Inc., overseeing both the business and editorial sides of the magazine. It was the second time, since Kay Graham, that *Newsweek*'s editor reported to a woman.

*****

AND THAT'S WHERE things stood in October 2009, when Jessica Bennett, Jesse Ellison, and Sarah Ball persuaded their editor to let them write a story about young women in the workplace today. Since the piece was bound to be controversial, the editor, Marc Peyser, kept it under wraps until it was ready. "The three of us had so much fun working on the story," said Jesse. "We felt like there were echoes of what you all had done forty years earlier—the secrecy of it and the sisterhoodness of it!" They decided not to put their names on an early version that went to the top editors. Instead, they bylined the story "the Dollies," the patronizing name given the Nation researchers of old. "Marc was worried about repercussions and he thought it would be safer if we didn't sign it, just for the first draft," explained Jessica. "He thought it would make the editors think more about who—and how many people—were saying this. But his biggest concern was that they could hold it against us and if it never ran, it would hurt us."

The women submitted the story to the editors right after Thanksgiving. Then they heard nothing. In January 2010, various editors responded with particular points and fixes they wanted made. The story went from 2,500 words to 6,000 words, then to 3,000 words and finally back to 2,000 words. When Peyser felt it was ready, he resubmitted it. That's when

Newsweek's editor, Jon Meacham, decided to recuse himself from overseeing the story. "That was a perfect, silent way of killing it," explained Jessica, "because nobody would make any decisions without Meacham's approval."

For two months there was no word from the top, and the fortieth anniversary of our lawsuit was approaching in March. "At that point, I was physically ill, going from lethargic to depressed to angry," said Jessica. "Jesse lost her voice, Sarah was crying, and we were a mess. We felt if this didn't run we would have no faith in humanity." As a reminder of the history of discrimination at *Newsweek* and the fortieth anniversary news peg, the three women pinned up copies of the 1970 "Women in Revolt" cover over their desks.

At one point, *Newsweek*'s general manager, Ann McDaniel, asked to see them. "She was coming from a management perspective," recalled Jesse. "She wanted to see if we had legitimate complaints about the way we were treated, but we didn't say anything. She talked about convening monthly lunches where we would talk about the women, but none of that happened. It was good to talk to her but it was unclear what her motives were."

Then they met with Mark Miller, *Newsweek*'s editorial director, and begged him to run the cover. Miller asked whether the women had been personally discriminated against. "Our strategy was to be positive," said Jesse. "We felt that the more we said we were discriminated against, the less [likely it was] they would run the piece. So we talked about how it's not really about *Newsweek*, it's bigger than *Newsweek*, it's a cultural thing."

Marc Peyser was upset that the women hadn't relayed their personal grievances. He called Miller and told him about the women's experiences—and the piece got going.

The four-page story, "Are We There Yet?," finally ran in the March 22, 2010 issue, almost forty years to the day that we had charged *Newsweek* with sex discrimination. Leading with our landmark suit, the women questioned how much had actually changed for women since 1970, not only at the magazine but in the workplace in general. They cited statistics showing that full-time working women who *haven't* had children still make seventy-seven cents on the male dollar and that in their first job out of business school, female MBAs make $4,600 less per year than male MBAs. In the media, they wrote, "female bylines at major magazines are still outnumbered by seven to one; women are just 3 percent of Fortune 500 CEOs and less than a quarter of law partners and politicians."

They also wrote about *Newsweek*. In 1970, women made up 25 percent of the editorial masthead; forty years later that number was 39 percent. (Overall, they pointed out, 49 percent of the entire company was female.) But perhaps the most damning statistic they cited was that "men wrote all but six of *Newsweek*'s 49 cover stories last year—and two of those used the headline 'The Thinking Man'" ("The Thinking Man's Guide to Populist Rage," for example). Then, to cover their tracks, they wrote,: "We should add that we are proud to work at *Newsweek*. (Really, boss, we are!) We write about our magazine not because we feel it's worse here, but because *Newsweek* was once ground zero for a movement that was supposed to break at least one glass ceiling." The women explained how "somewhere along the road to equality, young women like us lost their voices. So when we marched into the workforce and the fog of subtle gender discrimination, it was baffling and alien. Without a movement behind us, we had neither the language to describe it nor the confidence to call it what it was." Recognizing that sexism still exists, they said, "is one of the challenges of the new generation."

The response inside *Newsweek* was overwhelmingly positive from the young female and male staffers. "One woman said, 'I can't believe you guys did this—I truly thought there was no chance in hell it would see the light of day,'" recalled Jessica. "The only negative response we got was hearing that the middle-aged editors thought we were very entitled, that we were just complaining and didn't appreciate what we had. But it sparked a lot of conversation among the young women in the building." After the story came out, several women got promotions and there were more covers about women, written by women. Jon Meacham never spoke to the women about the story.

Five months later, in August 2010, the Washington Post Company sold *Newsweek* for $1 plus its liabilities to ninety-two-year-old audio pioneer Sidney Harman. The magazine had been hemorrhaging revenue and readership for years, but Harman thought it had value and he had the money to invest in it. After a very public search for a new editor, Harman made news again. In November 2010, he announced that Tina Brown, the first female editor of *Vanity Fair* and the *New Yorker*, would become editor-in-chief of *Newsweek* in a joint venture with her website, the *Daily Beast*. It happened almost by accident, but forty years after forty-six terrified young women sued *Newsweek* for sex discrimination, there was finally a female name at the very top of the magazine's masthead. Tina tipped her hat to us in her press interviews. "A merger has created what the lawsuit couldn't," she told National Public Radio. In her first editor's letter, she said she was "honored to be the first female editor of *Newsweek*," but unaware of the behind-the-scenes details of our lawsuit, she also wrote, "I'm both humbled and grateful to know that the trail was blazed long ago, and that Kay Graham blazed it. This issue is dedicated to her memory and inspired by her example."

But Tina couldn't make a go of it. *Newsweek* folded its print edition on December 31, 2012, and went digital. Five months later, owner Barry Diller said he was exploring a sale of what was left of *Newsweek*. It was an inglorious end to a once great magazine.

Today many women hold senior positions at other news organizations, but few have made it to the top. The *New York Times* has the best record. Janet Robinson was president and CEO of the New York Times Company from 2004 until 2012 and in June 2011, Jill Abramson was appointed to the paper's highest editorial position. The *Washington Post* has a female publisher, Katharine Weymouth, Kay Graham's granddaughter; Gracia Martore is president and CEO of Gannett; Mary Junck is chairman, president, and CEO of Lee Enterprises; Kathleen Carroll is the top editor of the Associated Press; and Debra Adams Simmons, an African-American, is editor of the

Cleveland Plain Dealer. At one time, the *Chicago Tribune*, the *Oregonian*, the *Philadelphia Inquirer*, the *Des Moines Register*, and the *St. Paul Pioneer Press* all had women editors, but none do today. *Time* magazine has never had a female managing editor nor has a woman run the news operations of ABC, CBS, CNN, MSNBC, or Fox News. In July 2012, Patricia Fili-Krushel became chair of NBCUniversal News Group, and in May 2013, she appointed British ITV editor Deborah Turness as president of NBC News—the first woman to head a network news division.

It's hard to believe that two generations later there are still so few females in the executive suite. Who would have thought it would take so long? We believed the lack of advancement was merely a pipeline problem: once there were enough women in the workforce, they would naturally advance—all the way to the top. We didn't realize how hard it would be to change attitudes and stereotypes. There still are not enough stories on women's issues, not enough women quoted as sources, and not enough women editorial writers and commentators. Perhaps most important for women's advancement, there still is no private or public support for working families, who rely primarily on mothers to care for the children. According to the 2011 Global Report on the Status of Women in the News Media, conducted by the International Women's Media Foundation, the regions with the most women at the top of their news organizations are those with the best support system for parents: the Scandinavian countries, Europe, and Eastern Europe.

Oz Elliott once said that the two most important things that happened in the twentieth century were civil rights and women's rights. As in the civil rights movement, the women's movement didn't solve all the problems, but our actions at *Newsweek* continue to have an impact. "Finding out about the lawsuit and writing the story was a real turning point for me," said Jesse Ellison, who took the *Newsweek* buyout in December 2012 and is now a freelance writer. "It was hugely empowering and put a finger on what we were feeling—tremendous self-doubt. Once I understood that things aren't just my problem, they're *a* problem, it made me bolder, more willing to push for my stories and realize that I am as smart as the dude sitting next to me." Jesse found that in working on the *Newsweek* story, "there was an element of personal growth in our own journey and how that compared to—and was reflected in—learning about your journey. As we kept rewriting the *Newsweek* piece, it made the story more effective and strengthened my voice."

For Jessica Bennett, now a freelance journalist and editor-at-large for Sheryl Sandberg's Lean In Foundation, "It was our modern 'click!' moment," she explained. "Now I see almost everything through a gender lens. I'm writing a lot about women's issues. Part of me doesn't want to be pigeonholed as the women's writer, but I am naturally drawn to these stories in ways I never was before." Learning the history of our lawsuit, she said, was a "sub-education—it's become so useful to me, thinking about stories, knowing the background and how things evolved. It's enabled me to understand what's changed and what hasn't."

Sarah Ball didn't consider herself a feminist before she started working on the *Newsweek* story. "I'm just young enough not to have ever been in a situation before *Newsweek* where there were more men than women," she said. "I only knew 'feminism' as a denigrating term. Doing the story, it was fascinating to dive back to its beginnings and understand how feminism was—and is—such a necessary term to use and to espouse. I'm now aware that we didn't just get this one day. There were a lot of women who got this for us and I'm glad I will never be ignorant of what came before."

Sarah was particularly moved by a fortieth reunion of the original *Newsweek* plaintiffs at my home in June 2010. "I'm so grateful that I can put a face to the people I owe this incredible debt," she told me. "I had so many meaningful conversations that night with very smart, educated women who have a lot of history and a lot of experience. There was something about the way that experience resonated with you all—it was so important a cause, so much bigger than yourselves, and so selfless risking the job you already had rather than just protesting from outside. I don't know if anything would make women coalesce like that today. It made me feel very jealous, as if our generation missed out on something."

Jesse and Jessica acknowledge they also feel a bond with us, although we are old enough to be their mothers. "There was a sense of a *Newsweek* culture that hadn't really changed—even to calling the editors the Wallendas—so we could share these stories from forty years apart," said Jessica. "We have a great feeling for the women who came before us, who were proud of what we were doing and were supporting us in our fight. I used to keep the 'Women in Revolt' cover over my desk and it still gives me chills when I see it. It was an honor to be associated with it."

The women's movement is an incomplete revolution. Many issues remain unsolved for this generation, including the continuing stereotyping of women, the increasing sexualization of society, and the infighting that still exists in the women's movement. After the *Newsweek* piece was published in March 2010, the feminist blog *Jezebel* attacked the young women for a narcissistic "focus on your magazine and its past covers, and your childhood, and your issues with the F-word." It also excoriated them for not including women of color in their story. "If the actual staff of *Newsweek* doesn't include much in the way of diversity," *Jezebel* opined, "isn't it time to utilize those reporting skills of which the traditional media is supposed to be the last guardians?"

Stunned by the criticism from their fellow feminists, Jessica and Jesse answered *Jezebel* in a blog they had started called *The Myth of Equality*. They pointed out that the women they interviewed for the piece were either directly involved in the suit, wrote about it, or had recent books, articles, or studies related to women in the media and in the workplace. "We should also note—and this was one of many things that didn't make it into the final piece—that the women of color at *Newsweek* didn't sign onto the suit in 1970, for various reasons," they wrote. The *Jezebel* experience cut deep. "You can argue about sexism," said Jesse, "but in the feminist blogosphere, there's a strange infighting that happens that's destructive. When *Jezebel* attacked us,

I felt like I lost a best friend. Nobody can be feminist enough. I see so much of that on these sites. Feminism takes on an exclusionary sensibility and competitiveness."

This year, the political attacks on reproductive rights have begun to galvanize this generation. "Just as we grew up being told we could 'do anything we put our mind to,' we took having freedom over our bodies for granted," said Jessica. "Plan B [the morning-after pill] has been around since I was a teenager, available over the counter. I'm sure the Right would like to argue this made me a bigger slut—it didn't—but it did make me assume that these kinds of rights would always be available to me. So here we are, suddenly having to fight for something we never had to think much about."

As they see their friends having babies, these young women also worry about how to balance work and family. "The idea of being able to 'have it all' is still prevalent," said Sarah Ball, who left *Newsweek* in 2010 and is deputy editor of Vanityfair.com. "It's become easier because you can work remotely, but it still eats at your core. It's what a lot of my friends talk about." Free and accessible child care has always been a fundamental demand of the women's movement, but the legislative efforts to pass such measures have failed. "Everything that our generation asked for as feminists was getting the identical things of what boys had—access to the Ivy League or professional schools or corporate America," said psychiatrist Anna Fels. "Women now are up against a much deeper structural problem. The workplace is designed around the male life cycle and there is no allowance for children and family. There's a fragile new cultural ideal—that both the husband and wife work. But when these families are under the real pressure of having a baby or two, there's a collapse back to old cultural norms and these young parents go back to the default tradition."

While women are increasingly taking on leadership positions in what are considered "caretaking" professions—medicine, social work, teaching, and even politics—in other professions, such as business and law, said Fels, "there's still a huge backlash against women who are openly ambitious and there are fewer women at the top. The data show that once you're a mother you're written off in terms of a career. Some of it is prejudice and some of it is reality. If husbands don't change their roles, if family structure doesn't change, and if corporate attitude toward families doesn't change, then women are in a lose-lose situation."

Facebook's Sheryl Sandberg agreed. "We reward men every step of the way—for being leaders, for being assertive, for taking risks, for being competitive," she said in 2012 at the World Economic Forum in Davos, Switzerland. "And we teach women as young as four—lay back, be communal. Until we change that at a personal level, we need to say there's an ambition gap. We need our boys to be as ambitious to contribute in the home and we need our girls to be as ambitious to achieve in the workforce."

Jessica, Jesse, Sarah, and many of their friends are already working on these problems. "Five years ago we didn't really talk about women's issues," said Jessica. "Only when we got to the workforce did we start to care about gender issues. Now a lot of young women are realizing sexism still exists. They're writing about it and starting blogs about it. I think something's happening."

This recognition of sexism in the workplace perhaps explains why this young generation loves *Mad Men*. My generation identifies with the sexualized office culture, the subjugation of women, the 1960s clothes, and the scotch-soaked parties. That was our life. I always thought that younger women viewed the TV series simply as a historic costume drama. But they understand that the most compelling part of the show takes place in the office and they relate to that. They see how Peggy, the talented, ambitious secretary who becomes the first female copywriter, and Joan, the smart, voluptuous office manager, battle sexism at work. "Peggy's having this feminist awakening," said Jessica, "and many of the things she talks about are things women still debate."

In 1970, we challenged the system and changed the conversation in the news media. For the women who participated in the lawsuits, the struggle rerouted our lives, emboldened us, and gave many of us opportunities we never would have had. It made *Newsweek* a better place to work and a better magazine. Like us, today's young women are challenging assumptions and fighting their own, more complicated battles in the workplace. They, too, are having a feminist awakening. We are standing in their corner and rooting for their success. For we now see that as with *Mad Men*, our history isn't just history. It has become a legacy for the young women who followed us.

EPILOGUE:

WHERE THEY ARE NOW

IT HAS BEEN FORTY-THREE YEARS since we became the first women in the media to sue for sex discrimination. All of us are proud of the historic role we played but the effect of the lawsuit on our lives has been mixed. For some women, it opened doors and offered career choices they never would have imagined. For others, it remains the high point of their professional lives. For a few, it's a bitter reminder of regrets and never-realized ambitions. But for all of us, now in our sixties and seventies, it was an experience that changed our perspectives about ourselves, about men and women—and womanhood—and about justice and ambition.

Judy Gingold. As with many of the women on the front lines of a legal complaint, the mainspring of our movement never fully benefited from her courageous act or her enormous talent.

Judy's last job at *Newsweek* was editor of the "My Turn" section, which she enjoyed, shepherding essays from prominent experts and everyday readers. In 1982, she left the magazine and went to Los Angeles with her husband, David Freeman, a screenwriter. In LA, Judy did some book reviews for the *Los Angeles Times* and freelance pieces for the *Wall Street Journal*. She continued her interest in feminism as a fellow at the Institute for the Study of Women and Men in Society at the University of Southern California, where Betty Friedan led a feminist think tank, and at the Center for the Study of Women at the University of California at Los Angeles.

In 1996, Judy wrote a groundbreaking piece on liposuction, which was published in the *Atlantic*. Recently, she has worked on several health topics and written some lighter, more humorous pieces. "The *Newsweek* suit was the most worthwhile thing I've ever done," she told me. "I can't think of anything I've done subsequently that comes close." Looking back at her role in starting it all, she said, "I am very proud of my part in the suit. Pride is what enables people to make that psychic switch, whether it's black pride, gay pride, or women." Though Judy feels that the suit didn't help her professionally, she believes it helped her grow personally. "I was a good girl," she said. "I learned something about the world and found the courage not to be a good girl."

Lucy Howard. Lucy spent her entire career at *Newsweek*. After reporting for the Justice section in New York, she returned to the Washington bureau in 1976 and worked as a correspondent there for ten years. When Lucy came back to New York, she wrote for the Periscope section and eventually was promoted to senior writer. Lucy took a buyout in 2002, leaving *Newsweek* after thirty-nine years. "I should have pushed myself more," she said, "but I'm not going to look back and say, 'Boohoo.' I have no regrets about staying, but the most enduring pleasure is the amazing range of people I worked with, and the lasting friendships I made." Lucy went back to her roots: she bought several small shares in racehorses and became active in environmental issues in Maryland. She never married.

Margaret Montagno Clay. Although Margaret enjoyed her stint writing on *Newsweek*'s international edition, "I never really thought of myself as a journalist nor thought I had a future as a journalist," she said. In the summer of 1978, she married Pete Clay, a scientist and inventor, and left *Newsweek* later that year. Since 1981, Margaret has lived in Los Alamos, New Mexico, where she has raised two children and done volunteer work.

"To me the situation at *Newsweek* was glaringly unfair and totally at odds with the editors' liberal views," she said. "When Oz said this wasn't discrimination but a long-held tradition, it was staggering." At the time of the lawsuit, Margaret recalled, "I knew this was not a just way to run the world but I didn't have a vehicle for it. I went to some early consciousness-raising groups where everyone sat around until they arrived at some consensus. The lawsuit seemed like a better route to change. You could actually do something about it with people whose abilities were known to you. It was the most concrete thing I've ever done."

Pat Lynden. Pat was going to be a journalist no matter what, just not at *Newsweek*. She was still a reporter in the New York bureau when she married Allen Gore, a police detective, in August 1970, the month we signed our first memorandum of understanding. She left *Newsweek* in May 1971, when she was pregnant with her son, Richie. Pat has worked as an editor on several magazines, including *Viva, Connoisseur,* and *Longevity,* and freelanced for others, including *New York Woman,* founded and edited by Betsy Carter, a former *Newsweek* researcher. Now divorced and a grandmother, she is a freelance writer and editor and is currently writing a novel.

Pat looks back on *Newsweek* with mostly positive feelings. "I loved the smart, interesting people, the lifelong friends I made," she said. "But I don't feel good about the fact that journalistic advancement for us didn't come from hard work and talent, as it did for the men. I adored reporting and would have given anything for a foreign bureau assignment, but that was out of the question. To this day I'm sad that I never got a crack at that professional experience."

For Pat, the lawsuit was a vindication of our belief in ourselves. "During those many nervous-making months when we were planning our action—right up to the day of the press conference—we proved to ourselves, and finally to the guys, just how smart and capable we were," she said. "It was amazing how clueless and dumbstruck they were by what we pulled off!

Of course, our action took place in the cauldron of the women's movement that was roiling every household in America. But we contributed a nice piece to that history and I'm glad I was part of it."

Fay Willey. Fay was an example of why the women's movement at *Newsweek* didn't necessarily work for everyone. Fay never wanted to be a writer, but feeling pressured by several women to move up the ladder—and seeing others try out who knew far less than she did—she relented, tried out, and was promoted to a writer in the Foreign section in May 1973. Her pieces were smart, especially on Communism, but rarely led the section. When *Newsweek* started a Japanese-language edition in 1984, the editors asked Fay to teach the Japanese how to make a newsmagazine. Two years later, she returned to the Foreign section as a writer. Although Fay was always proud of her part in the lawsuit, she has said that she regretted being talked into becoming a writer. She felt she didn't have the overall influence at the magazine that she once had as chief researcher. In 1988, Fay took a buyout with sixty-four other staffers. After a brief marriage in college, she never remarried and continues to be actively involved in the world of foreign affairs and the arts in New York and in London, where she lives for several months a year.

Merrill (Mimi) McLoughlin. Mimi is an example of what women can accomplish if given the chance. From Religion researcher to writer to the senior editor for National Affairs,

Mimi had a meteoric rise at *Newsweek*—and then rose higher. In 1986, she left to go to *US News & World Report* with her husband, Mike Ruby, also a *Newsweek* editor, where they became coeditors in 1989. Mimi was the first woman to edit a national newsweekly. In 1999, they left *US News* and are now living in the Southwest, writing and coauthoring books.

"The women's movement at *Newsweek* was definitely a turning point for me,'" said Mimi. "Had it not opened the doors, I probably wouldn't have hung on—I would have looked for another thing to do with my life. I wanted to be a doctor or I might have become a full-time mother. I didn't want to be an editor, ever—even at *US News*—but I liked writing." For Mimi, the lawsuit was a great confidence builder. "Coming together in a group was a very liberating experience," she said. "I can't imagine doing it on my own, but we had that sense that we were acting together and that it was a just cause." "When you look back," she added, "*Newsweek* ended up in a very good place."

Trish Reilly. Trish was so smart and talented, yet she was unable to benefit from the women's movement. In 1973, she left *Newsweek* in a panic but found herself just as anxious at CBS News. "I wound up doing very well there," she recalled, "but it still didn't change who I was. With every success, I became more depressive." After her three-year contract ended, Trish married and moved to Los Angeles. Six years later, she got divorced and moved back to Northern California, where she got a license doing real estate appraisals for probate court until she retired in 2000. "I never pursued anything that would make me a star or put me out there like that," she said. "Working for probate court didn't threaten my image of myself as a 'good girl' who didn't seek attention, who didn't seek higher achievement. I had that fire of youth that propelled me out of Alameda, but I never could overcome that other part of myself that said, 'Who do you think you are?' I understand the other part of this—the women who didn't push themselves."

Looking back at her *Newsweek* experience, Trish said, "Ultimately the women's movement helped me relate to men like an equal, but I was so entrenched in traditional values that it wasn't until my forties that I finally realized it. On the one hand I'm very sad about what could have been for me, but I don't feel regret. There are women who never tried. I can take pride in what I did do."

Liz Peer. Liz was at the top of her game in the 1970s. She had been a star reporter and writer at *Newsweek* and was promoted to Paris bureau chief, covering Western Europe and North Africa. In 1977, she finally got her wish to be a war correspondent—in Somalia. Liz won an award for her reporting there but riding in a Land Rover with no springs, she suffered a broken coccyx, causing a cycle of chronic pain. That same year, her father committed suicide—seventeen years after her older brother was found dead in a New York City rooming house, also an apparent suicide.

In 1978, Liz married at the age of thirty-nine. She continued to write in the back of the book, but her pain began to affect her personality and slow her journalistic skills. She became more erratic, more difficult, and more depressed, and by 1982 her marriage had disintegrated. In April 1983, according to a *Manhattan Inc.* article by Gwenda Blair, Bill Broyles, the new editor of *Newsweek,* terminated Liz but offered her a deal: *Newsweek* would help her find a new job and if she couldn't find one, she could freelance and do consulting work for the magazine. Liz was distraught. "What always concerned me about Liz was that her identity was completely with *Newsweek,*" recalled her friend Linda Bird Francke, a former *Newsweek* writer. "She would start every sentence with 'We feel, we know, we think'— meaning her and the magazine. You can't lose yourself so much. When she got fired, I knew terrible things would happen. That completely destroyed her."

Liz was negotiating with the magazine for health insurance and was even considering suing *Newsweek* when the editors, seeing her deterioration, offered to hire her back. According to Gwenda Blair, when they didn't promise her a level of work comparable to what she had done in the past, she turned them down. She was to go on permanent medical disability in July 1984, but on the evening of May 26, Liz put on a pale blue negligee, laid out her favorite ball gowns, and propped her feather boa around a mirror. Listening to French songs on the stereo, she wrote letters to her mother and her estranged husband. "I don't like the person I've become," she wrote to her husband. "I'm dog-tired living with an ice pack belted to my rear and I can't bear the sense of failure that stretches from my first waking moment until I fall asleep. . . . When friends ask why, tell them it's simply seven years of pain."

She drank some wine and swallowed pills. She was forty-eight years old.

"They could have kept Liz," said Linda Francke, still bitter today about what happened to Peer, as many *Newsweek*ers are. "She could have written something. She would have taken less pay. She would have done anything. They didn't need to fire her but they did. After speaking at her funeral, I walked out of the church and burst into tears. Several editors were there, looking stricken, and they came up to me and said. 'We didn't know, we didn't know.' And I said, 'You're assholes for not knowing.'"

Mary Pleshette Willis. During Mary's writing tryout for Jack Kroll, which was going nowhere, her fiancé, Jack Willis, was hit by a wave while body surfing off Long Island and broke his neck. It was July 1970, two months before they were to marry. Mary immediately took a leave from the magazine until November and, she recalled bitterly, "Kroll never called once to find out how Jack was."

Luckily, Jack Willis recovered, and he and Mary married the following year. In 1972, the couple wrote a book about their experience, *But There Are Always Miracles*. "When the advance was more than I was making at *Newsweek*, I quit," said Mary. In 1975, Mary and Jack moved to Los Angeles when their book was optioned for a television movie, which they cowrote as well as several other made-for-TV films. They moved back to New York in 1978 with their two daughters, and Mary freelanced and wrote afternoon TV specials. She published her first novel, *Papa's Cord*, in 1999, still freelances, and is writing another novel.

"I felt I was one of the early guinea pigs," said Mary, looking back on her *Newsweek* experience. "Had I stayed, I might have gotten some of the benefits of the suit, but I left before there was really any change. The highlight of my time at *Newsweek* was filing the lawsuit."

Diane Camper. Diane was one of the black researchers who decided not to join the lawsuit. In 1971, she was sent on a summer training program to the San Francisco bureau and the following year was promoted to a reporter in *Newsweek's* Washington bureau, covering the Watergate break-in and trials. Diane took a leave in 1976 to go to Yale, where she earned a master's degree in law. She returned to the Washington bureau the following year to cover the Supreme Court. In 1983, the *New York Times* editorial board hired Diane to write on education, welfare, and other social issues. She left journalism briefly to go to the Annie E. Casey Foundation as public affairs manager in 1997. In 2004, Diane went to the *Baltimore Sun* as assistant editorial page editor until June 2008. She is currently communications officer at the Public Welfare Foundation in Washington, D.C. She never married.

Thinking about the situation of women then and now, Diane said, "Whatever oppression I felt then, I identified [it] more as a racial thing. But I do know that women, particularly black women, have suffered. To that extent, I think we could have identified on both a racial and gender basis without compromising the racial piece of it. I have probably benefited by being both black and female, so I identify now in a more positive way with both race and gender."

Elisabeth (Lala) Coleman. Lala had been a reporter in *Newsweek*'s San Francisco bureau for three years when she was hired away by KQED-TV in 1973. The following year she went to work for ABC News before becoming press secretary to California Governor Jerry Brown in 1976. She resigned in 1978, when she married Rock Brynner, Yul Brynner's son. Lala came back to New York, got divorced, and started working for a media communications firm. She joined American Express in 1990, rising to vice president of international public affairs and communications before retiring in 2004. She is currently writing a memoir.

"The *Newsweek* lawsuit played a huge role in my life," said Lala. "I was immediately dispatched to a bureau and then given the first bureau reporter opening. If we had not filed, others probably would have, but I suspect they would not have been as successful as we were."

Phyllis Malamud, Jeanie Seligmann, and **Mariana Gosnell** were *Newsweek* lifers. Phyllis was promoted from New York reporter to Boston bureau chief in 1977 and returned to New York in 1983, where she became editor of the "My Turn" section. In 1986, at the age of forty-eight, Phyllis married *Newsweek*'s longtime Medicine editor, Matt Clark. She and

Matt took a buyout in 1988 and have since retired. "The suit was helpful in getting me the Boston bureau chief position," said Phyllis, "and that was helpful in terms of establishing myself as a manager."

Jeanie Seligmann worked at *Newsweek* for twenty-eight years. After being promoted to writer in 1971, she became editor of the Letters section in 1999 and took a buyout in 2002, retiring at fifty-seven. She never married. "Without the women's suit, I don't think I would have had the gumption to push for a tryout," said Jeanie. "I was much more of a follower than a leader. I guess my consciousness got raised."

Mariana Gosnell left *Newsweek* in 1988, after twenty-six years. "I often thought about leaving but I couldn't figure out a better job," she said. On her off-hours, Mariana got a pilot's license and in 1961, she bought a single-engine airplane. At one point, she took a three-month leave of absence and flew solo across the country. In 1994, when she was sixty-two, Mariana published a book about her bird's-eye journey in her plane, *Zero Three Bravo*. In 2007, she wrote another called *Ice: The Nature, the History, and the Uses of This Astonishing Substance*, which the *New York Times* reviewed and pronounced "remarkable." "I wasted too many years at *Newsweek*," said Mariana, who had a long-term relationship but never married. "It was a lack of knowing one's possibilities and a lack of belief in your capabilities. Doing the flying book gave me more of a sense of accomplishment, but the reporting at *Newsweek* determined a lot about how I write." Sadly, Mariana died unexpectedly in March 2012.

Eleanor Clift. One of Washington's most respected reporters and commentators, Eleanor credits the *Newsweek* women's suit with giving her the first boost. "It was this great unseen hand in New York that gave me the entrée to ask for a reporting internship," she recalled. In 1970, Eleanor was the Girl Friday in the Atlanta bureau. After her reporting internship in the summer of 1971, she was promoted to correspondent in Atlanta and started covering Georgia Governor Jimmy Carter. Her big scoop was getting Hamilton Jordan's game plan for how Carter could win the presidency. In 1976, Eleanor followed Carter to Washington as *Newsweek's* White House correspondent. She left *Newsweek* briefly in 1985 to go to the *Los Angeles Times* but returned to the Washington bureau thirteen months later. She covered Capitol Hill and then the White House again from 1992 to 1994. Eleanor is currently a contributing editor at *Newsweek* and a regular on the syndicated TV show *The McLaughlin Group.*

Married to Brooks Clift (Montgomery Clift's brother) from 1964 until their divorce in 1981, Eleanor has three sons. In 1989, she married fellow journalist Tom Brazaitis, who died of kidney cancer in 2005 at the age of sixty-four. Three years later, she wrote *Two Weeks of Life: A Memoir of Love, Death, and Politics,* which weaves the experience of Tom's death with the events surrounding the Terri Schiavo case during a two-week period in March 2005.

When she first heard about the women's suit, Eleanor recalled, "I thought there was a lot of anger at *Newsweek* on the part of the men and the women. But in the end, I think it changed the chemistry of the magazine and how we looked at gender. It wasn't about ego—this was before bylines. It was about women wanting to be in the game and it was a group effort."

Jane Bryant Quinn. Jane was the only woman to hold positions at opposite ends of the *Newsweek* masthead. After leaving the *Newsweek* clip desk "with great pleasure" in 1962, she went to *Look* magazine and then was hired by McGraw-Hill to cofound a personal finance newsletter for *BusinessWeek* magazine. She was listed on the masthead as J. B. Quinn, "because women weren't thought to know anything about personal finance." A young mother in need of a job, she reluctantly agreed to the byline, but "I compensated by listing my entire staff—male and female—by their initials, too." Six years later, when she became the newsletter's publisher, she switched the masthead to full names.

In 1974, Jane started writing a personal-finance column for the *Washington Post* syndicate and in 1979, she was hired back at *Newsweek* as the magazine's first female business columnist, alongside economists Paul Samuelson and Milton Friedman. "To come back to *Newsweek* as a respected columnist was a wonderful feeling," said Jane. "I always loved *Newsweek*, but I was angry and sorry there had not been a place for me there."

In addition to *Newsweek*, Jane wrote for many publications and authored several books. She married again, had another child, and after her husband died, remarried in 2008. In 2009, Jane and her husband, Carll Tucker, started what is now The

Daily Voice, an online community news company. "Although I wasn't active in the women's movement," she said, "I was—and am—proud to declare myself a feminist. I love and respect all those rude and noisy women whose protests—even the silly protests—achieved so much for women's freedom and choice. It wouldn't have happened if the movement had been left to polite girls like me, who said 'please' and 'thank you' and imagined we could advance, in a man's world, on merit alone. We and our daughters and our granddaughters are all standing on the shoulders of those tough and insistent personalities who wouldn't be appeased. Equality is never given, it is taken—and they took it for all of us."

Eleanor Holmes Norton. Still a firebrand, Eleanor Holmes Norton continues to fight for civil rights, women's rights, and the rights of the residents of Washington, D.C. After representing the *Newsweek* women in their first lawsuit, Eleanor became head of the New York City Human Rights Commission in 1970, where she held the first hearings in the country on discrimination against women. In 1977, President Jimmy Carter appointed her to chair the Equal Employment Opportunity Commission, the first woman to hold that position. Eleanor returned to her hometown and in 1990 was elected a delegate to Congress for the District of Columbia. In her position she serves and votes on committees but is not permitted to vote on the final passage of legislation. In 1993, Eleanor divorced her husband after an income-tax scandal. She continues to serve in Congress and as a tenured professor of law at Georgetown University.

Looking back on her first meeting with the *Newsweek* editors, Eleanor said, "they were so awkward and didn't know how to deal with you, the women, or with me. Oz became a good friend and so did Katharine Graham, but here they were, the pillars of progressive America being confronted with a discrimination suit—how embarrassing." One thing Eleanor regrets is not speaking to the black researchers about joining our suit. "I would have convinced them, I know I would have," she said. "At that time, it was very hard to go behind you all, but I'm sure they would have all been with you today."

Eleanor still regards our lawsuit as a seminal case for women. "This was a case that some would say that you could not win because there was no precedent," she explained. "But discrimination is discrimination and your case paralleled any case in which there were qualified blacks at the bottom and whites at top. I didn't understand why this should be any different."

Harriet Rabb. After the *Newsweek* case, Harriet became the go-to lawyer for sex discrimination lawsuits. She represented the women at the *Reader's Digest* in 1973 and those at the *New York Times* in 1974. Harriet continued as director of the Employment Rights Project at Columbia Law School until 1978, where she also served as a professor, director of clinical education, assistant dean for urban affairs—the first woman dean—and vice dean. In 1977, when Joe Califano was appointed secretary of Health, Education, and Welfare in the Carter administration, he called up his old *Newsweek* adversary and asked whether Harriet would be interested in working for him. She declined, but the offer came around again. In 1993, Donna Shalala, the new secretary of Health and Human Services in the Clinton administration, hired Harriet as her general counsel. Harriet returned to New York in 2000 and is the vice president and general counsel of Rockefeller University.

"Look at what we took on," said Harriet. "The *Washington Post* and the *New York Times*—it doesn't get any tougher than that. What you all did gave other people the courage to do it as well. The *Newsweek* women were not waiting for God to descend and fix it for all of us. A pool of New York journalists rising up made a picture for every woman in other papers around the country."

Harriet believes not only that our case was important, but that it continues to be relevant. "It's not over," she said, "and it's never going to be over—the realization that people always have to have somebody who's the other, that justice is so hard to come by, that fairness is so hard to come by. You hope that it will get better, and it does get better. But backsliding is so much easier than forward progress and there always has to be somebody who's willing to step forward. You provided the role models. You all had options. You could have personally had an easy row to hoe. But it just wasn't who you all were. For you, it was the integrity of the case, to do the right thing. It's not that there wasn't courage involved. It took courage, but it was just some well of integrity and decency that says this isn't right. And that's at least as great a virtue as courage."

Oz Elliott. Although his first impulse was to justify the discrimination of women at *Newsweek* as "a newsmagazine tradition going back almost fifty years," Oz turned out to be a quick and lasting convert to our cause. After we had negotiated our first memorandum of understanding in August 1970, Oz thought the mechanisms were in place for progress. When he returned to the editorial side in June 1972, just after we had sued the second time, he made women's advancement a priority. At that point, Oz was going through his own transition. He was getting divorced and had just started seeing Inger McCabe, who had been married to a *Newsweek* correspondent in the Far East. Inger was an independent woman—a talented photographer and entrepreneur who started a successful design business called China Seas. "Oz loved women," said Inger, who married Oz in 1974. "He adored women and yet he didn't pay enough attention to them. He wasn't thinking!"

When Oz left the magazine in 1976 to become New York City's first deputy mayor in charge of economic development, there was a big party at Top of the Week. As he recalled in his memoir, "The women of *Newsweek* who had fought so strenuously for their rights gave me a suitably sexist scrapbook chronicling their victory." In 1977, Oz became dean of the Columbia University Graduate School of Journalism, stepping down in 1986. He also chaired the Citizens Committee of New York, an organization he helped found in 1975 that encourages local volunteerism. He died of cancer in 2008.

To his credit, Oz was always honest about his role in *Newsweek*'s discrimination against women. When he became friendly with Ellen Goodman in later years, she recalled, "He was the first to say, 'God, weren't we awful? Can you believe that it was like that then? All those [talented women] who left, as well they should have—why did they ever stay?' Oz would preempt the discussion but in my mind, there would still be this connection to the women whose careers were basically ended by that [discrimination]. People did something and it had terrible effects on other people. Then they changed and the world changed and Oz certainly changed. I was very fond of him."

We all were. Just before he died, I asked him if there was anything he regretted. "Looking back," he said, "I would have been more sensitive about what it was all about before the storm broke. And in retrospect, I'm sure I would have said something different than that it was a newsmagazine tradition!"

As for me, I always say I am an affirmative-action baby and proud of it. After being promoted to *Newsweek's* first female senior editor in September 1975, I worked in that job until I left on maternity leave in November 1980, when our daughter, Sarah, was born. When I returned six months later, I negotiated a three-day week to work on special projects. During that time, I packaged seven *Newsweek* cover stories into books, helped turn one of them into a CBS Reports television documentary, and launched *Newsweek on Campus* and *Newsweek on Health,* specialty magazines that were distributed on college campuses and in doctors' offices. In 1982, Steve and I had our son, Ned, and two years later I returned full-time as a senior editor, often filling in as a Wallenda.

In 1991, after twenty-five years at *Newsweek,* I left to become editor-in-chief of *Working Woman,* a monthly magazine started in the mid-1970s when women were flooding into the workforce. I loved having my own magazine, especially one geared to professional and business women, but it was severely underfinanced (it closed in 2001). In 1996, I took a job as East Coast managing editor/senior executive producer of MSNBC.com, a new Internet–cable TV news venture created by Microsoft and NBC. Working in New York, my team was responsible for creating the Internet content for NBC News and MSNBC cable programs and personalities. It was exciting to be in this new world of digital journalism and I learned a lot. But since broadband—so critical for NBC's video—wouldn't happen as quickly as we had hoped, I started to get restless. After a brush with breast cancer (I'm fine), I decided to leave MSNBC.com in March 2001. Since then I have freelanced, tutored in a public school, and been active on the boards of the Women's Rights Division of Human Rights Watch and the International Women's Media Foundation, which supports women journalists around the world.

My husband, Steve Shepard, left *Newsweek* in 1981 to become editor of *Saturday Review,* a weekly literary magazine with a distinguished history. But it was on its last legs and folded a year later. Steve was wooed back to *BusinessWeek* as executive editor and became editor-in-chief in 1984, a position he held for twenty years. In 2004 Matthew Goldstein, chancellor of the City University of New York, asked him to create a new Graduate School of Journalism at CUNY. As a product of public schools in New York and a graduate of City College, Steve was thrilled to design the only publicly funded graduate school of journalism in the entire Northeast and he has been the founding dean ever since. We have been blissfully—and blessedly—married for more than thirty-three years.

My father, who died in 1998, continues to have an enormous influence in my life. He suffered from a damaged heart valve but was writing up to the very end, at nearly ninety-three. The day before he died, on June 4, 1998, he wrote his last column, which was published alongside his obituary. His seventy-five-year writing career provided a front-row seat to the most awe-inspiring sports moments of the twentieth century, yet his columns had never been collected. In early 2003, my brothers and I decided to edit a collection of his sports columns, along with George Solomon, former sports editor of the *Washington Post* who had worked with Dad for twenty-five years. *All Those Mornings . . . At the Post* was published by PublicAffairs in 2005, on what would have been my father's hundredth birthday.

I was fortunate to be working and without children when the women's movement came along. If it hadn't been for the lawsuit, I never would have become a senior editor at *Newsweek*, a thrilling job that taught me so much about the world, about managing people, and about myself. I am forever grateful to the women who pushed us, the lawyers who represented us and the men who supported us. The lawsuit not only changed my life, it changed my thinking about women: about how we are raised, how we realize our ambitions, how we balance the demands of a career while raising a family. It also set a path for me for the rest of my life: to help other women. In telling our history, I hope our daughters come to understand that sisterhood is powerful, that good girls can revolt, and that change can—and must—happen.

THE GOOD GIRLS
WHO SIGNED ON FOR THE GOOD FIGHT

THE FORTY-SIX WOMEN WHO FILED THE FIRST EEOC COMPLAINT (IN THE ORDER IN WHICH THEY SIGNED), MARCH 16, 1970:

Virginia Adams
Susan Agrest
Holly Camp
Elisabeth Coleman
Barbara Davidson
Nancy Dooley
Valerie Gerry
Marianna Gosnell
Judy Gingold
Lucy Howard
Janet Huck
Patricia Lynden
Phyllis Malamud
Margaret Montagno
Mary Pleshette
Noel Ragsdale
Trish Reilly
Sylvia Robinson
Susan Sands
Merrill (McLoughlin) Sheils
Joan Spack
Nancy Stadtman
Lynn (Povich) Young
Sheila Younge
Jeanne Voltz
Jean Seligmann
Abigail Kuflik
Harriet Huber
Lynn Allegaert
Eileen Pond
Judy Harvey
Madeleine Edmonson
Joanna Cole
Ellen Jurow
Karla Spurlock
Marjorie Lester
Helen Willingham
Fay Willey
Ann Ray Martin
Diane Zimmerman
Jean MacGregor
Alden Cohen
Marie Whiteside
Constance Bessie
Constance Carroll
Sunde Smith

**THESE FOURTEEN WOMEN
ADDED THEIR NAMES ON
MARCH 24, 1970:**

Priscilla Baker
Deborah Beers
Pat Conway
Dale Denmark
Joyce Fenmore
Susan Fleming
Constance Guthrie
Alison Kilgour
Janet MacDonell
Madlyn Millimet
Ann Schumacher
Ruth Werthman
Lisa Whitman
Gwendolyn Wright

**THE WOMEN WHO SIGNED
THE SECOND EEOC COM-
PLAINT, MAY 16, 1972:**

Katrine W. Ames
Linda B. Backstein
Bonnie K. Bell
Andrea Besch
Connie Bessie
Susan Braudy
Barbara Bright
Barbara Burke
Holly Camp
Constance W. Carroll
Babette W. Carter
Alden D. Cohen
Barbara L. Davidson

Allison W. Dimond
Madeleine Edmonson
Susan (Moran) Fleming
Jane M. Friedman
Sandra Gary
Judith Gingold
Marianna Gosnell
Constance Guthrie
Hilary Horton
Clare Howard
Lucy Howard
Janet Huck
Sally Hunter
Alison Kilgour
Lorraine Kisly
Abigail Kuflik Kimball
Laurie Lisle
Jean L. MacGregor
Anne N. McGinn
Phyllis Malamud
Ann Ray Martin
Werner Michel
Margaret Montagno
Patricia C. Reilly
Sandra Salmans
Ann M. Schumacher
Jean A. Seligmann
Merrill (McLoughlin) Sheils
Nancy Stadtman
Elizabeth Wasik
Marie Whiteside
Lisa Whitman
Fay Willey
Lynn (Povich) Young

ACKNOWLEDGMENTS

W HEN I LEFT *NEWSWEEK* in 1991 after twenty-five years, I took
home the documents surrounding our 1970 lawsuit. By then, no
one seemed interested. I was going to send them to the women's archives
at Radcliffe's Schlesinger Library, which had requested the material, but
I got sidetracked. In 2006, when I finally had time, I realized that to make
sense of the papers I had to write a narrative. I started contacting the
women involved. When the history grew to 30,000 words, I knew this
was a story that should be told.

Interviewing people about what happened forty years ago, however,
was a challenge. My own memory proved inaccurate in several instances
and other people's recollections contradicted one another. I have tried my
best to reconstruct what happened using documents, interviews, and research. However people remember it, I am hoping that, as T.S. Eliot said,
"the end of all of our exploring will be to arrive where we started and know
the place for the first time."

I interviewed over forty people who were at *Newsweek* at the time, including, just before he died, Oz Elliott. All of them contributed facets of
the story and I deeply appreciate their help. But this tale could not have
been told without the testimony and insight of Judy Gingold, Lucy
Howard, Peter Goldman, Pat Lynden, Margaret Montagno, Trish Reilly,
Mary Pleshette Willis, Harry Waters, Mariana Gosnell, Franny Heller
Zorn, Betsy Carter, Phyllis Malamud, and Elisabeth Coleman. I am indebted to them for their time and their support. I also want to thank our
two inspiring lawyers, Eleanor Holmes Norton in the first lawsuit, and
Harriet Rabb, whose files on the second lawsuit were invaluable.

In capturing what *Newsweek* was like in the early sixties, I relied on
the vivid memories of Jane Bryant Quinn, Ellen Goodman, and Nora

Ephron. Gloria Steinem, Betsy Wade, Anna Quindlen, and Gail Collins provided essential information on the tenor of the times.

When I started reporting, I didn't know Jessica Bennett, Jesse Ellison, and Sarah Ball, three young women working at *Newsweek*. I am so grateful to them for keeping our story alive. I am also proud that they now call themselves feminists and are passionately carrying on the fight for women's rights. At *Newsweek/Daily Beast*, Sam Register, director of the library, and photo editor Beth Johnson were especially helpful.

I want to thank my friend Peter Osnos, founder of PublicAffairs, who was an early supporter of the project, and PublicAffairs' publisher, Susan Weinberg, and senior editor and marketing director, Lisa Kaufman, who were enthusiastic about the book from the very beginning. I am particularly indebted to Lisa, my editor, for her sage advice and suggestions in helping me shape the story. Managing editor Melissa Raymond kept me on track, and assistant director of publicity Tessa Shanks provided creative and expert guidance. My lawyer, Jan Constantine, general counsel at the Authors Guild, shepherded me through the contract and made smart recommendations.

Throughout this project, I was encouraged by many close friends. I am especially grateful to Jack Willis, Sarah Duffy Edwards, Rosemary Ellis, Polly McCall, and Letty Cottin Pogrebin who urged me to keep going whenever I got stuck.

I could not have written this book without the loving support of my husband, Steve Shepard, a brilliant editor who makes everything in my life better. As I was laboring with my book, Steve began to write a memoir of his life in journalism, from *Newsweek* and *BusinessWeek* to the CUNY Graduate School of Journalism. It's called *Deadlines and Disruption: My Turbulent Path from Print to Digital*. As luck would have it, our books were being published in the same week.

Our children, Sarah and Ned, bring joy and meaning to my life every day. May this story inspire them to speak up and make a difference.

NOTE ON SOURCES

M OST OF THE INFORMATION in this book comes from my interviews, original documents or copies of documents, and books, which are listed in the bibliography. All other sources are cited by chapter.

All quotations from Susan Brownmiller are from her book *In Our Time: Memoir of a Revolution* (New York: Dial Press, 1999).

Here, in alphabetical order, are the people I interviewed:

Leandra Hennemann Abbott, Katrine Ames, Sarah Ball, Jessica Bennett, Helaine Blumenfeld, Susan Braudy, Kevin Buckley, Joe Califano, Diane Camper, Betsy Carter, Susan Cheever, Phyllis Malamud Clark, Margaret Montagno Clay, Eleanor Clift, Elisabeth Coleman, Kate Coleman, Gail Collins, George Cooper, Madlyn Millimet Deming, Dorinda Elliott, Inger Elliott, Osborn Elliott, Jesse Ellison, Nora Ephron, Karla Spurlock Evans, Anna Fels, Joe Ferrer, Penny Ferrer, Susan Fraker, Linda Bird Francke, Rod Gander, Judy Gingold, Peter Goldman, Ellen Goodman, Mariana Gosnell, Trish Hall, Lucy Howard, Liz Hylton, Margo Jefferson, Vajra (Alison) Kilgour, Ed Kosner, Lynn Langway, Grace Lichtenstein, Diana Elliott Lidovsky, Pat Lynden, Ann Ray Martin, Merrill McLoughlin, Joe Morgenstern, Eleanor Holmes Norton, Barbara Bright Novovitch, Maureen Orth, Anna Quindlen, Jane Bryant Quinn, Harriet Rabb, Noel Ragsdale, Trish Reilly, Elaine Sciolino, Jeanie Seligmann, Steve Shepard, Sunde Smith, Ray Sokolov, Nancy Stadtman, Gloria Steinem, Annalyn Swan, Rich Thomas, Jeanne Voltz, Betsy Wade, Harry Waters, Fay Willey, Mary Pleshette Willis, Diane Zimmerman, Franny Heller Zorn.

PROLOGUE: WHAT WAS THE PROBLEM?

Page xiii   **Hadn't Maria Shriver's report:** Maria Shriver and the Center for American Progress, *The SHRIVER Report: A Woman's Nation Changes Everything,* ed. Heather Boushey and Ann O'Leary, October 16, 2009; www.american progress.org/issues/2009/10/womans_nation.html.

Page xiv   **A crumpled Post-it note marked the chapter:** Brownmiller, *In Our Time,* 140.

Page xv   **Joe Halderman, a CBS News producer:** Richard Huff, George Rush, and Samuel Goldsmith, "David Letterman Reveals $2M Sex Affair Extortion Plot; CBS News Producer Robert [Joe] Halderman Busted," *New York Daily News,* October 2, 2009; www.nydailynews.com/entertainment /television/david-letterman-reveals-2m-sex-affair-extortion -plot-cbs-news-producer-robert-halderman-busted-article -1.379822#ixzz1oYaHuIBT.

Page xv   **That same month, ESPN analyst Steve Phillips:** Jeane MacIntosh and Dan Mangan, "ESPN's Steve Phillips in Foul Affair with Production Assistant," *New York Post,* October 21, 2009; www.nypost.com/p/news/national/item _bLw9UoSAQJwJLU4ZDXvvDO#ixzz1oYWPQC9L.

Page xv   **In November, editor Sandra Guzman:** Sam Stein, "*New York Post* Lawsuit: Shocking Allegations Made by Fired Employee Sandra Guzman," *Huffington Post,* November 10, 2009; www.huffingtonpost.com/2009/11/10/shocking -allegations-levi_n_352314.html.

Page xv   **"At this moment, there are more females":** Nell Scovell, "Letterman and Me," Vanityfair.com, October 27, 2009; www.vanityfair.com/hollywood/features/2009/10/david -letterman-200910.

Page xvii   **"the problem that had no name":** Betty Friedan, *The Feminine Mystique* (New York: W.W. Norton and Co., 1963), p. 57 in later editions.

Page xviii   **In the 1950s, full-time working women:** Borgna Brunner, "Help Wanted—Separate and Unequal," *The Wage Gap: A History of Pay Inequity and the Equal Pay Act,* Infoplease

.com; www.infoplease.com/spot/equalpayact1.html#ixzz1o
YPDhqqg.

Page xviii   **Until 1970, women comprised fewer than 10 percent:**
Claudia Goldin and Lawrence F. Katz, "On the Pill:
Changing the Course of Women's Education," *Milken Institute Review* 3 (2nd quarter 2001): 14; www.economics
.harvard.edu/faculty/goldin/Papers.

CHAPTER 1 "EDITORS FILE STORY: GIRLS FILE COMPLAINT"

The description and quotes about the *Ladies' Home Journal* sit-in are from
Brownmiller, *In Our Time*, 83–92.

Page 9   **In the next few years, women sued:** Kathleen L. Endres
and Therese L. Lueck "Media Report to Women," in
*Women's Periodicals in the United States: Social and Political
Issues* (Westport, CT: Greenwood Press, 1996), 202.

Page 9   **In 1974, six women at the *New York Times*:** Nan Robertson, *The Girls in the Balcony: Women, Men, and the New
York Times* (New York: Random House, 1992), 168.

Page 9   **in 1975, sixteen women at NBC:** Arnold H. Lubash, "$2
Million NBC Pact Is Set as a Settlement with Women of
Staff," *New York Times,* February 17, 1977.

Page 10   **When Oz Elliott and *Newsweek* chairman Frederick
"Fritz" Beebe telephoned her:** Katharine Graham, *Personal History* (New York: Alfred A. Knopf, 1997), 425.

Page 11   **In her insightful book:** Anna Fels, *Necessary Dreams: Ambition in Women's Changing Lives* (New York: Pantheon
Books, 2004).

Page 12   **Sheryl Sandberg, chief operating officer of Facebook:**
"Sheryl Sandberg Sees Global 'Ambition Gap'" Bloomberg
News, January 30, 2012; www.bloomberg.com/video/85189
956-sandberg-sees-global-ambition-gap-for-women.html.

Page 13   **"It was, all in all, a benevolent version":** Gail Collins,
*When Everything Changed: The Amazing Journey of American
Women from 1960 to the Present* (New York: Little, Brown
and Company, 2009), 105.

CHAPTER 2 "A NEWSMAGAZINE TRADITION"

Page 15   **Classified ads were still segregated by gender:** "*Pittsburgh Press v. Pittsburgh Commission on Human Relations,*" http://aclu.procon.org/view.resource.php?resourceID=3124.

Page 16   **That infamous "tradition" began in 1923:** Robert T. Elson, *Time Inc.: The Intimate History of a Publishing Enterprise, 1923–1941* (New York: Atheneum, 1968), 72.

Page 24   **Liz later told him:** Osborn Elliott, *The World of Oz: An Inside Report on Big-Time Journalism by the Former Editor of Newsweek* (New York: Viking Press, 1980), 143.

Page 24   **Returning to the office at night:** Gwenda Blair, "The Heart of the Matter," *Manhattan Inc.,* October 1984, 73.

Page 31   **In 1965, Karen was sent out:** "Divorced. Alan Jay Lerner," *Time,* December 23, 1974.

CHAPTER 3 THE "HOT BOOK"

Unless otherwise noted, information about Osborn Elliott comes from his memoir, *The World of Oz: An Inside Report on Big-Time Journalism by the Former Editor of Newsweek* (New York: Viking Press, 1980).

Page 34   **"Ozzy baby, I know where the smart money is":** Elliott, *The World of Oz,* 3.

Page 35   **To get Phil Graham interested:** Ben Bradlee, *A Good Life: Newspapering and Other Adventures* (New York: Simon & Schuster, 1995), 224.

Page 36   **"Visually they are a nightmare":** *Newsweek,* February 24, 1964; Charles Kaiser, "A Magazine That Mattered," *Radar* online, May 6, 2010; www.hillmanfoundation.org/blog/newsweek-sale.

Page 36   **"With Kermit, we had a Jewish intellectual":** Alex Kuczynski, "Kermit Lansner, 78, Former *Newsweek* Editor," *New York Times,* May 22, 2000.

Page 39   **"No doubt the war":** Elliott, *The World of Oz,* 101.

Page 42   **Describing the weekly routine:** Carole Wicker, "Limousine to Nowhere . . . If You're a Girl at a News Magazine," *Cosmopolitan.*

Page 43   **"The dialogue was eighth grade":** Robin Reisig, "Is Journalism an Air-Brushed Profession?" *Village Voice,* May 16, 1974, 24.

Page 46   **Nation researcher Kate Coleman:** Kate Coleman, "Turning on Newsweek," *Scanlan's Monthly,* June 1970, 44.

CHAPTER 4 RING LEADERS

Page 52   **The famous "click!":** Jane O'Reilly, "The Housewife's Moment of Truth," *Ms.,* December 1971.

Page 54   **At that time, the Marshall:** "History 1960–1991," Marshall Scholarships; www.marshallscholarship.org/about /history/1960–1991.

Page 54   **the Rhodes wasn't extended to women:** "Second Class Citizens? How Women Became Rhodes Scholars," Rhodes Project; http://therhodesproject.wordpress.com.

Page 60   **In the fall of 1969, Judy Gingold:** Daisy Hernandez, "A Genteel Nostalgia, Going Out of Business," *New York Times,* February 23, 2003.

Page 62   **She was a "red-diaper baby":** Patricia Lynden, "Red Diaper Baby," *New York Woman,* August 1988.

CHAPTER 5 "YOU GOTTA TAKE OFF YOUR WHITE GLOVES, LADIES"

Page 77   **In October 1964 Otto Friedrich:** Otto Friedrich, "There Are 00 Trees in Russia: The Function of Facts in Newsmagazines," *Harper's,* October 1964, 59–65.

Page 79   **Fay wrote a scathing letter:** Fay Willey, "Letter to the Editor," *Harper's,* December 1964, 4.

Page 81   **The great-granddaughter of a slave:** Joan Steinau Lester in Conversation with Eleanor Holmes Norton, *Fire in My Soul: The Life of Eleanor Holmes Norton* (New York: Atria, 2003). Unless noted, biographical information about Eleanor Holmes Norton is based on *Fire in My Soul.*

Page 85   **The provision protecting women:** Gail Collins, *When Everything Changed: The Amazing Journey of American Women from 1960 to the Present* (New York: Little, Brown, and Company, 2009), 76. Feminist Jo Freeman argues that "sex" was not added to scuttle the bill. "How 'Sex' Got into Title VII," www.jofreeman.com/lawandpolicy/titlevii .htm.

Page 86   **"Congressman Smith would joyfully disembowel":** Don Oberdorfer, "'Judge' Smith Moves with Deliberate Drag," *New York Times Magazine,* November 12, 1964.

CHAPTER 6   ROUND ONE

Page 94   **At one point Vice President Spiro Agnew:** Spiro Agnew, "Speech to Alabama Chamber of Commerce," *American History Online,* Facts on File Inc., November 20, 1969.

Page 95   **"I idolized her":** Helen Dudar, *The Attentive Eye: Selected Journalism,* ed. Peter Goldman (Bloomington, IN: Xlibris Corporation, 2002).

Page 98   **Lucy was insulted:** Susan Donaldson James, "Newsweek Still Wages Gender War, 40 Years Later," *ABCNews.com,* March 23, 2010.

Page 101   **"My idea of a cold-sweat nightmare":** Brownmiller, *In Our Time,* 145.

Page 103   **As she wrote in her remarkably candid, Pulitzer Prize –winning autobiography:** Graham, *Personal History,* 340, 418.

Page 104   **Kay replied that she encouraged her employees:** "Kay in Miami," *Women's Wear Daily,* March 24, 1970.

Page 107   **Carrying hand-lettered signs:** "'Liberation' Talk of the Town," *New Yorker,* September 5, 1970, 28.

Page 108   **Describing the event on the ABC evening news:** Susan Jeanne Douglas, *Where the Girls Are: Growing Up Female with the Mass Media* (New York: Three Rivers Press, 1994) 163.

Page 109   **In a *New York Times* story about the agreement:** "Newsweek Agrees to Speed Promotion of Women," *New York Times,* August 27, 1970.

CHAPTER 7   MAD MEN: THE BOYS FIGHT BACK

Page 116   **When Katharine Graham suggested:** Graham, *Personal History,* 424.

Page 117   **Hef's memo as to why he didn't like:** Carrie Pitzulo, *Bachelors and Bunnies: The Sexual Politics of Playboy* (Chicago: University of Chicago Press, 2011), 142.

CHAPTER 9 "JOE—SURRENDER"

Page 140   **The *Post* women ended up filing:** Chalmers M. Roberts, *The Washington Post: The First 100 Years* (New York: Houghton Mifflin, 1977), 429.

Page 141   **"It was shortly after [the Metro Seven settlement]":** Dorothy Gilliam oral history, *Washington Press Club Foundation,* 1992–1993; http://beta.wpcf.org/oralhistory/gill4 .html.

Page 141   **Her close friend at the *Post*:** Graham, *Personal History,* 421.

Page 156   **The case had gotten so poisonous:** Robertson, *Girls in the Balcony,* 203, 205.

Page 159   **On October 4, 1974, fifteen women filed:** *Media Report to Women,* ed. Dr. Donna Allen, December 1, 1974.

CHAPTER 10 THE BARRICADES FELL

Page 162   **Its "statement of purpose" declared:** "The National Black Feminist Organization's Statement of Purpose, 1973," University of Michigan–Dearborn; www-personal.umd .umich.edu/~ppennock/doc-BlackFeminist.htm.

Page 163   **The largest employer of women, the Bell System:** Crista DeLuzio, ed., *Women's Rights: People and Perspectives* (Westport, CT: Greenwood Publishing Group, 2009), 197.

Page 163   **In 1971, a feminist attorney named Ruth Bader Ginsburg:** Ruth Bader Ginsburg, "Breaking New Ground— *Reed v. Reed,* 404 US 71 (1971)," Supreme Court Historical Society; www.supremecourthistory.org/learning-center /womens-rights/breaking-new-ground.

Page 164   **However, President Richard Nixon vetoed it:** Abby J. Cohen, "A Brief History of Federal Financing for Child Care in the United States," *Future of Children Journal* 6, no. 2 (Summer/Fall 1996): 32; http://futureofchildren.org /futureofchildren/publications/docs/06_02_01.pdf.

Page 164 **By the end of 1971, stories on the new women's movement:** Ruth Rosen, *The World Split Open: How the Modern Women's Movement Changed America* (New York: Penguin Books, 2006), 302.

Page 164 **Distrusting the coverage of the women's movement:** Patricia Bradley, *Mass Media and the Shaping of American Feminism, 1963–1975* (Jackson: University Press of Mississippi, 2003), 49.

Page 164 **Beginning in 1968, publications calling for social change:** Martha Allen, "Multi-Issue Women's Periodicals: The Pioneers," Women's Institute for Freedom of the Press; www.wifp.org/womensmediach3.html.

Page 164 **In all, more than five hundred feminist periodicals:** Kathryn T. Flannery, *Feminist Literacies, 1968–75* (Champaign: University of Illinois Press, 2005), 23.

Page 165 **That same year, NOW filed a petition:** "Broadcasting Cases," National Women and Media Collection, Donna Allen (1920–1999) Papers, 1920–1992 (C3795), State Historical Society of Missouri, University of Missouri, Columbia; http://shs.umsystem.edu/manuscripts/invent/3795.html #broa

Page 165 **In February 1973, fifty women at NBC:** "City Rights Unit Finds NBC Sexism," *New York Times,* January 24, 1975.

Page 165 **The case would be settled in 1975 for $2 million:** Arnold H. Lubash, "$2 Million NBC Pact Is Set as a Settlement with Women of Staff," *New York Times,* February 17, 1977.

Page 166 **In March 1970, a reporter for the British newsmagazine:** Lilla Lyon, "The March of *Time*'s Women," *New York Magazine,* February 22, 1971.

CHAPTER 11 PASSING THE TORCH

Page 193 **"A merger has created":** "Daily Beast, *Newsweek* to Merge," *Morning Edition,* National Public Radio, November 12, 2010.

EPILOGUE: WHERE THEY ARE NOW

Much of the information on Liz Peer came from Gwenda Blair, "The Heart of the Matter," *Manhattan Inc.*, October 1984, 73.

BIBLIOGRAPHY

Bradlee, Ben. *A Good Life: Newspapering and Other Adventures*. New York: Simon & Schuster, 1995.

Bradley, Patricia. *Mass Media and the Shaping of American Feminism, 1963–1975*. Jackson: University Press of Mississippi, 2003.

Brownmiller, Susan. *In Our Time: Memoir of a Revolution*. New York: Dial Press, 1999.

Carter, Betsy. *Nothing to Fall Back On: The Life and Times of a Perpetual Optimist*. New York: Hyperion, 2002.

Chamberlain, Mariam K. *Women in Academe: Progress and Prospects*. New York: Russell Sage Foundation, 1988.

Chambers, Deborah, Linda Steiner, and Carole Fleming. *Women and Journalism*. London and New York: Routledge, 2004.

Collins, Gail. *When Everything Changed: The Amazing Journey of American Women from 1960 to the Present*. New York: Little, Brown and Company, 2009.

DeLuzio, Crista, ed. *Women's Rights: People and Perspectives*. Westport, CT: Greenwood Publishing Group, 2009.

Douglas, Susan Jeanne. *Where the Girls Are: Growing up Female with the Mass Media*. New York: Three Rivers Press, 1995.

Dudar, Helen. *The Attentive Eye: Selected Journalism*. Edited by Peter Goldman. Bloomington, IN: Xlibris Corporation, 2002.

Echols, Alice. *Daring to Be Bad: Radical Feminism in America, 1967–1975*. Minneapolis: University of Minnesota Press, 1989.

Elliott, Osborn. *The World of Oz: An Inside Report on Big-Time Journalism by the Former Editor of Newsweek*. New York: Viking Press, 1980.

Elson, Robert T. *Time Inc.: The Intimate History of a Publishing Enterprise, 1923–1941*. New York: Atheneum, 1968.

Ephron, Nora. *I Remember Nothing and Other Reflections*. New York: Alfred A. Knopf, 2010.

Flannery, Kathryn T. *Feminist Literacies, 1968–75*. Champaign: University of Illinois Press, 2005.

Friedan, Betty. *The Feminine Mystique*. New York: W.W. Norton and Co., 1963.

Fels, Anna. *Necessary Dreams: Ambition in Women's Changing Lives*. New York: Pantheon Books, 2004.

Graham, Katharine. *Personal History*. New York: Alfred A. Knopf, 1997.

Kosner, Edward. *It's News to Me: The Making and Unmaking of an Editor*. New York: Thunder's Mouth Press, 2006.

Lester, Joan Steinau, in conversation with Eleanor Holmes Norton. *Fire in My Soul: The Life of Eleanor Holmes Norton*. New York: Atria, 2003.

Pitzulo, Carrie. *Bachelors and Bunnies: The Sexual Politics of Playboy*. Chicago: University of Chicago Press, 2011.

Redstockings of the Women's Liberation Movement. *Feminist Revolution, an Abridged Edition with Additional Writings*. Edited by Kathie Sarachild. New York: Random House, 1975, 1978.

Roberts, Chalmers M. *The Washington Post: The First 100 Years*. Boston: Houghton Mifflin Company, 1977.

Robertson, Nan. *The Girls in the Balcony: Women, Men, and the* New York Times. New York: Random House, 1992.

Rosen, Ruth. *The World Split Open: How the Modern Women's Movement Changed America*, rev. ed. New York: Penguin Books, 2006.

Trillin, Calvin. *Floater*. New Haven, CT, and New York: Ticknor & Fields. 1980.

A READER'S GUIDE TO
THE GOOD GIRLS REVOLT

We are providing the following supplementary materials—the 2010 *Newsweek* article discussed in the prologue, a Q & A with author Lynn Povich, and questions for discussion—to enhance your reading of *The Good Girls Revolt* and provide a jumping-off point for reading group discussions. For more information about PublicAffairs books, visit us at publicaffairsbooks.com, at facebook.com/PublicAffairs, or follow @public_affairs on twitter.

***

In the prologue to The Good Girls Revolt, *Lynn Povich introduces Jessica Bennett, Jesse Ellison, and Sarah Ball, three young women working at* Newsweek *in 2009, who unexpectedly found themselves struggling against gender discrimination. After Jessica, Jesse, and Sarah learn about the landmark gender discrimination lawsuit that Lynn and her colleagues filed against the magazine in 1970, they become "determined to write a piece for* Newsweek *questioning how much had actually changed for women at the magazine, in the media, and in the workplace in general" (p. xvii). Here is the piece they wrote, which* Newsweek *published in March of 2010.*

ARE WE THERE YET?

In 1970, 46 women filed a landmark gender-discrimination case.
Their employer was Newsweek. Forty years later, their contemporary
counterparts question how much has actually changed.

By Jessica Bennett, Jesse Ellison, and Sarah Ball

They were an archetype: independent, determined young graduates of Seven Sisters colleges, fresh-faced, new to the big city, full of aspiration. Privately, they burned with the kind of ambition that New York encourages so well. Yet they were told in job interviews that women could never get to the top, or even the middle. They accepted positions anyway—sorting mail, collecting newspaper clippings, delivering coffee. Clad in short skirts and dark-rimmed glasses, they'd click around in heels, currying favor with the all-male management, smiling softly when the bosses called them "dollies." That's just the way the world worked then. Though each quietly believed she'd be the one to break through, ambition, in any real sense, wasn't something a woman could talk about out loud. But by 1969, as the women's movement gathered force around them, the dollies got restless. They began meeting in secret, whispering in the ladies' room or huddling around a colleague's desk. To talk freely they'd head to the Women's Exchange, a 19th-century relic where they could chat discreetly on their lunch break. At first there were just three, then nine, then ultimately 46—women who would become the first group of media professionals to sue for employment discrimination based on gender under Title VII of the Civil Rights Act. Their employer was *Newsweek* magazine.

Until six months ago, when sex-and gender-discrimination scandals hit ESPN, David Letterman's *Late Show*, and the *New York Post*, the three of us—all young *Newsweek* writers—knew virtually nothing of these women's struggle. Over time, it seemed, their story had faded from the collective conversation. Eventually we got our hands on a worn copy of *In Our Time*, a memoir written by a former *Newsweek* researcher, Susan Brownmiller, which had a chapter on the uprising. With a crumpled Post-it marking the page, we passed it around, mesmerized by descriptions that showed just how much has changed, and how much hasn't.

Forty years after *Newsweek*'s women rose up, there's no denying our cohort of young women is unlike even the half-generation before us. We are post–Title IX women, taught that the fight for equality was history; that we could do, or be, anything. The three of us were valedictorians and state-champion athletes; we got scholarships and were the first to raise our hands in class. As young professionals, we cheered the third female Supreme Court justice and, nearly, the first female president. We've watched as women became the majority of American workers, prompting a Maria Shriver–backed survey on gender, released late last year, to proclaim that "the battle of the sexes is over."

The problem is, for women like us, the victory dance feels premature. Youthful impatience? Maybe. But consider this: U.S. Department of Education data show that a year out of school, despite having earned higher college GPAs in every subject, young women will take home, on average across all professions, just 80 percent of what their male colleagues do. Even at the top end, female M.B.A.s make $4,600 less per year in their first job out of business school, according to a new Catalyst study. Motherhood has long been the explanation for the persistent pay gap, yet a decade out of college, full-time working women who *haven't* had children still make 77 cents on the male dollar. As women increasingly become the breadwinners in this recession, bringing home 23 percent less bacon hurts families more deeply than ever before. "The last decade was supposed to be the 'promised one,' and it turns out it wasn't," says James Turley, the CEO of Ernst & Young, a funder of the recent M.B.A. study. "This is a wake-up call."

In countless small ways, each of us has felt frustrated over the years, as if something was amiss. But as products of a system in which we learned that the fight for equality had been won, we didn't identify those feelings as gender-related. It seemed like a cop-out, a weakness, to suggest that the problem was anybody's fault but our own. It sounds naive—we know—especially since our own boss Ann McDaniel climbed the ranks to become *Newsweek*'s managing director, overseeing all aspects of the company. Compared with the *Newsweek* dollies, what did we have to complain about? "If we judge by what we see in the media, it looks like women have it made," says author Susan Douglas. "And if women have it made, why would you be so ungrateful to point to something and call it sexism?"

Yet the more we talked to our friends and colleagues, the more we heard the same stories of disillusionment, regardless of profession. No one would dare say today that "women don't write here," as the *Newsweek* women were told 40 years ago. But men wrote all but six of *Newsweek*'s 49 cover stories last year—and two of those used the headline "The Thinking Man." In 1970, 25 percent of *Newsweek*'s editorial masthead was female; today that number is 39 percent. Better? Yes. But it's hardly equality. (Overall, 49 percent of the entire company, the business and editorial sides, is female.) "Contemporary young women enter the workplace full of enthusiasm, only to see their hopes dashed," says historian Barbara J. Berg. "Because for the first time they're slammed up against gender bias."

We should add that we are proud to work at *Newsweek*. (Really, boss, we are!) We write about our magazine not because we feel it's worse here, but because *Newsweek* was once ground zero for a movement that was supposed to break at least one glass ceiling. Just as our predecessors' 1970 case didn't happen in a vacuum, *Newsweek* today is neither unique nor unusual. Female bylines at major magazines are still outnumbered by seven to one; women are just 3 percent of Fortune 500 CEOs and less than a quarter of law partners and politicians. That imbalance even applies to the Web, where the founder of a popular copywriting Web site, Men With Pens, revealed late last year that "he" was actually a she. "I assumed if I chose a male name [I'd] be viewed as somebody who runs a company, not a mom sitting at home with a child hanging off her leg," the woman says. It worked: her business doubled once she joined the boys' club.

We know what you're thinking: we're young and entitled, whiny and humorless—to use a single, dirty word, feminists! But just as the first black president hasn't wiped out racism, a female at the top of a company doesn't eradicate sexism. In fact, those contradictory signs of progress—high-profile successes that mask persistent inequality—are precisely the problem. Douglas describes those mixed messages as "enlightened sexism": the idea that because of all the gains women have made, biases that once would have been deemed sexist now get brushed off. Young women, consequently, are left in a bind: they worry they'll never be taken as seriously as the guys, yet when they're given the opportunity to run the show, they balk. A recent Girl Scouts study revealed that young women avoid leadership roles for fear they'll be labeled "bossy"; another survey found they are four times less likely than men to negotiate a first salary. As it turns out, that's for good reason: a Harvard study found that women who demand higher starting salaries are perceived as "less nice," and thus less likely to be hired. "This generation has had it ingrained in them that they must thrive within a 'yes, but' framework: Yes, be a go-getter, but don't come on too strong. Yes, accomplish, but don't brag about it," says Rachel Simmons, author of *The Curse of the Good Girl.* "The result is that young women hold themselves back, saying, 'I shouldn't say this, ask for this, do this—it will make me unlikable, a bitch, or an outcast.'"

Somewhere along the road to equality, young women like us lost their voices. So when we marched into the workforce and the fog of subtle gender discrimination, it was baffling and alien. Without a movement behind us, we had neither the language to describe it nor the confidence to call it what it was. "It's so much easier when you're the generation that gets to fight against [specific] laws than it is to deal with these more complicated issues," says Gail Collins, the *New York Times* columnist. In a highly sexualized, post-PC world, navigating gender roles at work is more confusing than ever. The sad truth is that when we do see women rise to the top, we wonder: was it purely their abilities, or did it have something to do with their looks? If a man takes an interest in our work, we can't help but think about the male superior who advised "using our sexuality" to get ahead, or the manager who winkingly asked one of us, apropos of nothing, to "bake me cookies." One young colleague recalls being teased about the older male boss who lingered near her desk. "What am I supposed to do with that? Assume that's the explanation for any accomplishments? Assume my work isn't valuable?" she asks. "It gets in your head, which is the most insidious part."

Recognizing that sexism still exists despite its subtlety is one of the challenges of the new generation—though it doesn't hold a candle to what the dollies of 1970 pulled off. When they filed their legal complaint, the bottom tiers of the *Newsweek* masthead were filled almost exclusively by women. "It was a nice place—especially if you were a man," says Nora Ephron, a *Newsweek* "mail girl" in 1962. The women reported on the murder of a colleague, the State Department, and the 1968 campaign. But when it came to writing, they were forced to hand over their reporting to their male colleagues. "It was a very hopeless time," remembers Brownmiller. "After a while you really did start to lose your confidence. You started to think, 'Writing is what the men do.'"

Over dinner one night, a young researcher poured out her frustration to a lawyer friend, who ordered her to call the Equal Employment Opportunity Commission. She did, and slowly her colleagues signed on to a class-action suit. They found a fiery young lawyer—now D.C. Congresswoman Eleanor Holmes Norton—and they waited, nervously, until the time was right. "We were very staid, ladylike, not guerrilla-theater types," says Pat Lynden, one of the group's early organizers, who wrote cover stories for *The Atlantic Monthly* and *The New York Times Magazine* even while she wasn't allowed to write for *Newsweek*. "But eventually we just couldn't take it anymore."

A year later, as the national women's movement gathered steam, *Newsweek*'s all-male management decided to put feminism on their cover. Oblivious to the rebellion brewing at home, they looked past the legions of *Newsweek* women and went outside the building for a writer—to the wife of one of their top brass, whom they would ultimately describe, in an editor's note, as "a top-flight journalist who is also a woman." It was the final straw. The night before the issue hit newsstands, the *Newsweek* women sent a memo announcing a press conference. They pooled their money to fly a colleague to Washington to present a copy to Katharine Graham, the magazine's owner, who later asked, "Which side am I supposed to be on?" Then on Monday, March 16, 1970, the *Newsweek* women did what journalists do best: they took their story public. Crowded into a makeshift conference room at the ACLU, *Newsweek*'s "news hens" (as a local tabloid called them) held up a copy of their magazine, whose bright yellow cover told their own story: "Women in Revolt." Two days later the women of *The Ladies' Home Journal* would stage their own sit-in; others were soon to follow.

It was a moment of hope, one that set the stage for a wave of progress that continued rapidly through the 1990s. Twenty years after the *Newsweek* dollies rose up, mothers were entering the workforce in unprecedented numbers, women's organizations such as NOW saw surges in membership, and expanded affirmative-action programs ensured that girls had equal access to education. "Girl power" became the new female mantra, and young women's empowerment groups sprang up at YWCAs. By 2000, when the female employment rate peaked, many women thought the job was done.

In the years since, there has been what Douglas describes as "a subtle, insidious backlash." In the face of 9/11, two wars, and now the Great Recession, gender equality—and stereotyping—became a secondary concern. Feminism was no longer a label to be worn with pride; Britney Spears and Paris Hilton now dominated airwaves. But the changes were more than cultural. The Global Gender Gap

Index—a ranking of women's educational, health, political, and financial standing by the World Economic Forum—found that from 2006 to 2009 the United States had fallen from 23rd to 31st, behind Cuba and just above Namibia. Companies may have incorporated policies aimed at helping women, but they haven't helped as much as you'd think. "The U.S. always scores abysmally in terms of work-life balance," says the WEF's Kevin Steinberg. "But even here, [women] still rank 'masculine or patriarchal corporate culture' as the highest impediment to success." Exhibit A: the four most common female professions today are secretary, registered nurse, teacher, and cashier—low-paying, "pink collar" jobs that employ 43 percent of all women. Swap "domestic help" for nurse and you'd be looking at the top female jobs from 1960, back when want ads were segregated by gender.

The women of *Newsweek* thought, or hoped, they'd begun to solve these problems four decades ago. Yet here we are. "It's sad," says Lynden, now 72. "Because we fought for all that." There's no denying that we're enjoying many of the spoils of those women's victories. We are no longer huddled in secret; we're reporting for a national magazine, and we're the ones doing the writing. We have a president whose first act in office was to sign a law that promises equal pay for equal work. Yet the fact that such a law is necessary makes the point: equality is still a myth. "We've got the entire weight of human history behind us, making us feel like we're kind of lucky to have jobs," says writer Ariel Levy. "And I think it takes a lot of fearlessness to think, 'F—k it, go ahead and yell at me, I'm going to fight for what I deserve.'" We've come a long way, baby. But there's still a long way to go.

With Sam Register and Tony Skaggs

Reprinted courtesy of *Newsweek*

© 2010 The Newsweek/Daily Beast Company LLC

A CONVERSATION WITH LYNN POVICH

What inspired you to write The Good Girls Revolt—*and what worried you about writing it?*

I'm at the age when one looks back more than one looks forward. I realized that the *Newsweek* lawsuit had been one of the most influential events in my life—and no one knew about it. The history of our lawsuit had been lost and our legacy as the first women in the media to sue for gender discrimination had been forgotten. I wanted to tell the story of these brave women who opened the doors for so many female journalists—and many other women—so that at least my children, if not the next generation, would know.

However, I worried that no one would be interested in a lawsuit that happened forty years ago—important as it was. There has been great progress for women and people don't think about filing lawsuits as we did in the "protest decades" of the Sixties and Seventies. That was then—this is now. So I was blessed when I got a call in 2010 from three young women working at *Newsweek* who were experiencing similar obstacles in the workplace as we had forty years earlier. They had just found out about our lawsuit and were eager to hear about it. I realized our story still resonated and had relevance to young women in the workplace today.

How hard was it to interview people forty years after the event and did anyone object?

I wouldn't advise doing it! Some people have excellent memories but most of us are very selective in what we remember. Although I had the legal papers from the lawsuit, there wasn't any other original material so I had to report most of the book and reconstruct the story from interviews. The problems arose when someone's "clear" memory conflicted with another's "clear" memory. At those times I tried to triangulate and call others to see what they thought. And when I couldn't figure out which story was truly accurate, I resorted to saying, "As so-and-so remembered it."

Almost all of the women I interviewed were happy to talk because, like me, they wanted the story to get out. Only one woman, who gave me a long and very helpful interview, asked me not to quote her, so I didn't. But I knew a lot of her story from my own experience and others did too, so she is well represented in the book and is an important character.

What did you learn in writing the book?

There were stories women told me that truly shocked and dismayed me. The researcher who was not only stalked by her senior editor, which I did know, but who was told that if she didn't marry him she would have to leave, which I didn't know. Trish Reilly's story of turning down two promotions, panicking, and leaving *Newsweek*. And the story of Oz Elliott calling Fay Willey—twice—the night before we were going to sign our lawsuit to ask her to stop it and suggest that if we filed it, it would contribute to the Nixon administration's war on the "Eastern establishment elitist press."

I also learned a lot from the young women in the book who were working at *Newsweek* in 2010. It was interesting to me that when they came upon obstacles at work they didn't identify it as a gender issue. Like us forty years earlier, they thought it was them—they just weren't good enough. That surprised me because this generation was raised in the era of Girl Power. They were also told that you can be anything, you can do anything, the sex wars are over and there's a level playing field, which may be true for girls in school—but not so much in the work world. So learning about our story and meeting us changed their lives, too, and brought me in touch with this next generation of working women.

What surprised you about the responses to the book—positive and negative?

I figured that women who lived through the sixties and seventies would respond positively to the book because we all have these stories—and they have. Many are reading *The Good Girls Revolt* in their book clubs and giving it to their daughters so that they will know what the times were like for women and what their mothers went through.

What surprised me was how positively young women have responded to the book. I've been asked to speak to many colleges and universities, to people who have no idea of what women were up against back then. And they are fascinated. One reason is they can't believe how bad it was! It's like reading about the middle ages—people actually said that? But they are also interested in the personal struggles we went through because they are going through them, too—struggles about ambition, career, family issues, and managing it all—and, of course, sexism, which still exists even on campus.

I haven't heard too many negative responses. When I have it's from people who think women have succeeded and there isn't much gender discrimination anymore. If anything, they say we have to worry about the men.

What do you think about the current public discussion on women in the workplace today, the issues raised by Yahoo CEO Marissa Mayer and Facebook COO Sheryl Sandberg?

I give Sheryl Sandberg a lot of credit. When I was editor-in-chief of *Working Woman* magazine, I interviewed a lot of female CEOs and almost none of them wanted to be called a female CEO nor did they want to talk about women's issues. So I applaud her putting herself on the line for feminism and raising these issues. She restarted an important conversation and look, we're still talking about it.

Sheryl Sandberg's book, *Lean In*, has a lot of research and advice about gender bias in the workplace. Her book is about getting women into leadership positions so she focused a lot of the book on how women hold themselves back as well as the institutional barriers. And she raises very interesting points about women—especially younger women—not pushing themselves forward, not taking on riskier assignments, holding themselves back because they're considering having a family. And many younger women are grateful for her advice. One more thing: Sheryl Sandberg talks about an "ambition gap"—that women have to be more ambitious at work and men more ambitious at home. I think what she really means is that women have a "confidence gap"—still—and that's what I find fascinating.

As for Marissa Mayer, like all women at the top, everyone is looking at her and she's got big problems at Yahoo. So I understand that her priority is to make Yahoo successful. She felt she had to have everyone in the office to do that so she cancelled Yahoo's flexible hours policy. I think there are more reasonable ways to get people into the office without penalizing everyone and I don't think that is the way the workplace is evolving. All the research says that flexible hours increase productivity, health, and morale.

What happened to the three young women who were working at Newsweek *in 2010, Jessica Bennett, Sarah Ball, and Jesse Ellison?*

They all are doing very well in journalism but not at *Newsweek*. Sarah Ball is the deputy editor of Vanityfair.com. Jessica Bennett is a freelance journalist and editor-at-large for Sheryl Sandberg's "Lean In" foundation, which aims to increase the number of women in leadership positions. Jesse Ellison is now doing freelance journalism. Sadly, in December 2012, *Newsweek* printed its last magazine edition and is now available only in digital form.

QUESTIONS FOR THOUGHT AND DISCUSSION

1. What motivated the *Newsweek* women to sue their bosses? Do you think they should have aired their complaints to management first? Would you have joined the group? Do you think your mother would have joined? Your daughter?

2. What did you think about the choice *Newsweek*'s black researchers made not to participate in the suit?

3. What was the impact of the women's movement on the *Newsweek* women? How was feminism portrayed through the leading characters in *Good Girls Revolt*: the researchers, Liz Peer, Fay Willey, Eleanor Holmes Norton, Katharine Graham, and Lynn Povich herself?

4. How did the legal styles of Eleanor Holmes Norton and Harriet Rabb differ and why?

5. Why was the lawsuit ultimately so effective? What were the factors that contributed to the *Newsweek* women's success? And why do you think their case was largely forgotten over the years?

6. How do the *Newsweek* women change over the course of the narrative? What did you think about the women who couldn't make the transition to being "liberated" professional working women?

7. In the interview with Lynn Povich included in this reading guide, she makes a distinction between an "ambition gap" and a "confidence gap" inhibiting women in the work world. Do you agree? What, if anything, do you think inhibits you?

8. Have you had an insight or experience that ended up changing you, the way Lynn's and her colleagues' recognition that the "rules of work" were unjust changed them?

9. What do you think about the attitudes of the young women working at *Newsweek* in 2010? What do you think has changed and hasn't changed for women in the workplace today compared to forty years ago?

10.   In telling the story of the first and the second rounds of the lawsuit, Povich draws a distinction between legal change and cultural change; between "official policy" and how things actually happen on the ground. What stories in the book illuminate that distinction? Have you recognized or experienced similar "disconnects" and discrepancies in your own life, or see them in the world around you?

11.   If you saw something illegal or immoral happening in your workplace today, what would you do about it?

INDEX

Lynn Povich is an award-winning journalist who has spent more than forty years in the news business. She began her career at *Newsweek* as a secretary. In 1970, she was one of forty-six women who sued *Newsweek* for sex discrimination. Five years later, Povich was appointed the first woman senior editor in the magazine's history. Povich left *Newsweek* in 1991 to become editor-in-chief of *Working Woman* magazine, the only national business magazine for women. She joined MSNBC.com in 1996 to help launch the twenty-four-hour news and information cable/Internet venture, overseeing the web content of NBC News as well as MSNBC cable.

Povich has received numerous honors, including a 1976 Matrix Award from Women in Communications for Exceptional Achievement in Magazines. In 2005, she edited a book on her father, famed *Washington Post* sports columnist Shirley Povich, called *All Those Mornings . . . At the Post.* A native of Washington, D.C., Povich graduated from Vassar College, where she was executive-in-residence in 1996. She serves on the advisory boards of the International Women's Media Foundation and the Women's Rights Division of Human Rights Watch. She is married to Stephen B. Shepard, former editor-in-chief of *Business Week* and founding dean of the Graduate School of Journalism of the City University of New York. They have two children.

PublicAffairs is a publishing house founded in 1997. It is a tribute to the standards, values, and flair of three persons who have served as mentors to countless reporters, writers, editors, and book people of all kinds, including me.

I. F. STONE, proprietor of *I. F. Stone's Weekly*, combined a commitment to the First Amendment with entrepreneurial zeal and reporting skill and became one of the great independent journalists in American history. At the age of eighty, Izzy published *The Trial of Socrates*, which was a national bestseller. He wrote the book after he taught himself ancient Greek.

BENJAMIN C. BRADLEE was for nearly thirty years the charismatic editorial leader of *The Washington Post*. It was Ben who gave the *Post* the range and courage to pursue such historic issues as Watergate. He supported his reporters with a tenacity that made them fearless and it is no accident that so many became authors of influential, best-selling books.

ROBERT L. BERNSTEIN, the chief executive of Random House for more than a quarter century, guided one of the nation's premier publishing houses. Bob was personally responsible for many books of political dissent and argument that challenged tyranny around the globe. He is also the founder and longtime chair of Human Rights Watch, one of the most respected human rights organizations in the world.

•   •   •

For fifty years, the banner of Public Affairs Press was carried by its owner Morris B. Schnapper, who published Gandhi, Nasser, Toynbee, Truman, and about 1,500 other authors. In 1983, Schnapper was described by *The Washington Post* as "a redoubtable gadfly." His legacy will endure in the books to come.

Peter Osnos, *Founder and Editor-at-Large*

MARJORIE GRENE

SARTRE

NEW VIEWPOINTS
A Division of Franklin Watts, Inc.
New York, 1973

Library of Congress Cataloging in Publication Data

Grene, Marjorie (Glicksman) 1910–
    Sartre.

    Bibliography: p.
    1. Sartre, Jean Paul, 1905–
B2430.S34G724   194   73-1311
ISBN 0-531-06358-5
ISBN 0-531-06487-5 (pbk.)

Cover design by Nicholas Krenitsky
Book design and original art by Rafael Hernandez

To my students
and especially to Kit,
who helped a lot

ACKNOWLEDGMENTS

It is a pleasure to acknowledge the assistance of two UCD graduate students, Mrs. Kathleen McLaughlin and Mrs. Susan Denning, in the preparation of this essay. Mrs. McLaughlin helped me immeasurably in our discussions of philosophical problems in *Being and Nothingness* and the *Critique,* by reading and criticizing the drafts of each chapter in turn, and with bibliographical work. Mrs. Denning read the manuscript with great care and accuracy and caught many of my errors. Professor Philip Thody read the whole book and made a number of interesting comments and criticisms; unfortunately, the manuscript was already in the hands of the publishers when I received his comments, so that I have not been able to incorporate all of them. The series' former editor, Professor James Edie, made some excellent suggestions, and Professor David Olmsted, who also read the complete manuscript, gave me invaluable assistance in carrying them out. I am deeply indebted to them all.

I also wish to put on record my gratitude to the Philosophy Department's able administrative assistant, Mrs. Charlotte Honeywell, and her staff, who typed the manuscript in several drafts, and to the University of California, Davis, for research grants in the years 1970–1971 and 1971–1972 which enabled me to secure the assistance of Mrs. McLaughlin and Mrs. Denning.

I am grateful to the American Philosophical Association for permission to reprint my Presidential Address to the Pacific Division (1972), which was based on part of Chapter Five. Braziller and Company have kindly given me permission to quote from the Frechtman translation of *Les Mots,* and Literary Masterpieces, Inc., to quote from Hazel Barnes's translation of *L'Etre et le Néant.*

Cambridge, England
August 1971

My final chapter is concerned with the first two volumes of Sartre's work on Flaubert. Since I completed the manuscript, in August 1971, the third volume has appeared (Gallimard, 1972). A cursory reading suggests that it is pretty straight Sartrean "Marxism"; it therefore neither confirms nor (wholly) falsifies my final prognosis.

Boston
January 1973

CONTENTS

SARTRE

chapter one: the man of words

No philosopher, one suspects,
has ever produced so elegant, eloquent, and effective an introduction
to his own works as has Jean-Paul Sartre in
the autobiography of his childhood appropriately
named *Words* (*Les Mots*). Mercilessly and brilliantly,
he has pinned on his own collecting board the child that

was himself. It would ill befit an ordinary teacher and writer of philosophy to try to better his performance. Yet if Sartre were right about the relations of man to man, it would be only the outsider, the third man, who generates these relations: who generates, in this case, the relation of Sartre, famous writer of fifty-five, to Jean-Paul, small boy of five. Or, to reduce the terms to two, it is, according to Sartre's theory of literature, the reader who enters into a compact of freedom with the writer and so completes the work.

I want, then, in the spirit of either of these enterprises—as third man to the Sartre–Jean-Paul relation, or simply as reader—to take *Les Mots* as *entrée* to the examination of Sartre's vocation as a writer. But why examine this again, you may ask, when Sartre himself has given us so lucid and precise an account of the nature and origin of his calling? Because I want to show, if I can, that, in the light of that very account, Sartre is fundamentally a philosophical writer, who has sometimes embodied his arguments in literature, rather than a literary man who happens to philosophize. There are two reasons to argue at some length this rather obvious thesis. For one thing, *Les Mots* is not only a superb work of literature, which repays study in itself; it is, as I have already indicated, the best possible introduction to Sartre's philosophy, both its style and its doctrine. And for another, it is worth arguing that Sartre is first and professionally a philosopher, because as philosopher he is a self-acknowledged "existentalist," and existentialism has often been tagged (on occasion by myself among others) as more "literary" than "philosophical." Sartre himself, ten years ago in the *Critique,* publicly branded existentialism an "ideology," Marxism being, he swore, the only philosophy of our time, with existentialism its faithful ideological servant. More commonly, especially among its English-speaking expositors, existentialism has been labeled as a style of literature rather than a form of philosophy, not because it serves some higher school of thought, but because it is, allegedly, scarcely thought at all. It exclaims instead of arguing, so it is said; it rants instead of analyzing. Its themes, therefore, such critics aver, are best expressed in novel and drama, not in the sober guise of philosophical reflection. Thus if you want to know what Heidegger as existentialist has to say (even though he has never been one), read Tolstoy's *Ivan Ilyich.* If you want to know what Sartre as existential philosopher has to say, read his literary corpus, not his long-winded theoretical writings. If you want to know what the lot of them have to say, read Dostoyevsky, or Beckett, or heaven knows whom; but don't trouble with their supposed "philosophy." It is neither logic nor science, neither ordinary-language analysis nor pure, exact and exacting, phenomenology. So forget it!

Now, apart from the question of existentialism in general, whatever that may be, this is, for philosophically interested readers of the works of Jean-Paul Sartre, very bad advice. For the philosophical work of Sartre—*Being and Nothingness* in particular, but even, in part at least, that much reviled and admittedly prolix tome, *The Critique of Dialectical Reason*—repays close and repeated attention. One may disagree with it totally, but if one likes philosophy and is patient, one will find in it a surprising wealth of subtle and ingenious argument. What more can a philosophical reader ask? Truth, perhaps. But for us smaller fry, and indeed, even for the rare original thinker in philosophy, one way to truth is through the errors of one's great predecessors and contemporaries. Such is the case with Sartre. His work embodies, I believe, more incisively and more ingeniously than any other, the intellectual crisis of our time. It is worth wrestling with, both because we meet in it a philosophical intellect steeped, by training and by temperament, in the great European tradition, and because we can learn through it to grapple better with our own philosophical problems, which we have inherited from the same tradition.

But back to my thesis, which is to show, on the ground of Sartre's own "confession," that he is, and in what sense he is, a philosophical writer.

The epithet "man of words" that gives this chapter its title is adapted from the remark of Maurice Merleau-Ponty, Sartre's one-time friend, critic, and passionate admirer, that he was "too much of a writer." That remark has been amply substantiated by Sartre's own account of his vocation, its discovery and development. Picture the curly-haired three-year-old Jean-Paul in a sixth-floor Paris apartment, the adored child of his young widowed mother, the object of approval and admiration by the grandparents with whom they live:

> . . . there is no lack of applause. Whether the adults listen to my babbling or to *The Art of the Fugue,* they have the same arch smile of enjoyment and complicity. That shows what I am essentially: a cultural asset. Culture permeates me, and I give it off to the family by radiation, just as ponds, in the evening, give off the heat of the day.[1]

Sartre's grandfather, Charles Schweitzer, purveys French culture to the Germans, German culture to the French. Every year he re-edits his German reader. The whole family shares in the suspense of waiting for the proofs, and murmurs soothingly when, inevitably, he reviles his publisher. His study, filled with the French and

German classics, is a cultural shrine. There are grand-mother's lending library books, too, and Jean-Paul's own books that his mother reads to him ("I began my life," he says, "as I shall probably end it, amidst books"), but it is grandfather's study that sets the proper tone:

> In my grandfather's study there were books every-where. It was forbidden to dust them, except once a year, before the beginning of the October term. Though I did not yet know how to read, I already revered those stand-ing stones: upright or leaning over, close together like bricks on the bookshelves or spaced out nobly in lines of menhirs. I felt that our family's prosperity depended on them. They all looked alike. I disported myself in a tiny sanctuary, surrounded by ancient, heavy-set monuments which had seen me into the world, which would see me out of it, and whose permanence guaranteed me a future as calm as the past.[2]

Jean-Paul had to break into that closed, magic world. At three he learned to read:

> I would climb up into my crib with Hector Malot's *No Family*, which I knew by heart, and, half reciting, half deciphering, I went through every page of it, one after the other. When the last page was turned, I knew how to read . . . I was wild with joy. They were mine, those dried voices in their little herbals, those voices which my grandfather brought back to life with his gaze . . . I was going to listen to them, to fill myself with ceremonious discourse, I would know everything![3]

It was, then, words that made him, and it was through words that he, creator and magician, could in turn make things: ". . . the Universe would rise in tiers at my feet and all things would humbly beg for a name; to name the thing was both to create and take it. Without this fundamental illusion I would never have written." [4] However he has changed, that "illusion" has stayed with him. Nor iş it wholly an illusion, for it is his truth. It was through words that, for him, things acquired their reality, not, as for "practical" people, the other way around. Although, like most Parisian middle-class children, he spent summer vacations in the country, his reality was on the sixth floor, 1 rue de Goff, among the books:

> In vain would I seek within me the prickly memories and sweet unreason of a country childhood. I never worked the soil or hunted for nests. I did not gather herbs or throw stones at birds. But books were my birds and my nests, my household pets, my barn and my countryside.[5]

Even as ordinary an object as a table, he insisted later, got its reality from the name that evoked it.

And if words as read had "the thickness of things," so much the more power had they when, at six, he began to write. By the age of nine he had firmly established his calling as a writer. If, as he had thought, "to exist was to have an official title somewhere on the infinite Tables of the Word," then "to write was to engrave new beings upon them or—and this was my most persistent illusion—to catch living things in the trap of phrases: if I combined words ingeniously, the object would get tangled up in the signs, I would have a hold on it." [6]

He began, he says, in the Luxembourg, by charming himself with a bright simulacrum of a plane tree. "I did not observe it. Quite the contrary: I trusted to the void, I waited. A moment later, its true foliage would suddenly appear in the form of a simple adjective or, at times, of a whole proposition: I had enriched the universe with quivering greenery." [7]

Not that these words were written down, or even, as the child supposed they would be, remembered, but they gave him, he says "an inkling of my future role: I would impose names." [8] If words made him, he, by naming, made things. Not that he really made them, of course: that is the illusory part of it; but what he really made was—himself. If he has lost the illusion that there is real efficacy in words, if they have lost their "thickness," if he is convinced to the core of his being of his own view of the negativity of imagination, of the emptiness of his self-made world of words, he still writes, and will until he dies. Why? Well, why not? And besides, *that,* he confesses, is his character. Some time between 1911 and 1914, the die was cast. The child of words made himself their maker, made himself a writer.

What sort of writer? In terms of his own relation to words as he describes it, and in terms of his own contrast between poetry and prose, one would at first suppose: a poet. "The poetic attitude," he wrote in *What is Literature?,* "considers words as things and not as signs." [9] The ordinary speaker is "beyond words and near the object, whereas the poet is on this side of them." [10] For us ordinary speakers, meanings take us straight back toward the reality from which we had started, and which we are seeking to maneuver and control. Meanings for the poet, on the other hand, lack this practical vector; they cling to the words themselves. Meaning "is no longer the goal which is always out of reach and which human transcendence is always aiming at, but a property of each term, analogous to the expression of a face, to the little sad or gay meaning of sounds and colours. Having flowed into the word, having been absorbed by its sonority or visual aspect, having been thickened and defaced, it too is a thing, uncreated and eternal." [11]

Thus for the poet "language is a structure of the external world." [12] He considers words, not as signs to guide him to others and their activities, but "as a trap to catch a fleeting reality. . . ." [13] "In short," Sartre says, "language is for him the mirror of the world." [14] But so, for Jean-Paul, was his grandfather's library: "The library was the world caught in a mirror. It had the world's infinite thickness, its variety." [15] And when he came to write, it was the beings of his imagination that peopled his world. He lived outside ordinary things, through language, as poets do. For the poet, he was to write, "sees words inside out, as if he did not share the human condition, and as if he were first meeting the word as a barrier as he comes towards men." [16] That seems, to judge from his own account, the attitude through which he himself came to language and to literature.

Yet Sartre has never been a poet; he has never, since he began at six to compose romances, aspired to be one. Master of his native tongue as he can be when he likes, it is French prose of which he is master. True, there is poetry as economical in its style as *Les Mots,* the book now before us and as good an instance as any of Sartre's writing at its best. True, the poet can turn ordinary words, even ordinary sentences, into poetry. But in *Les Mots,* working the other way around, Sartre assimilates images which in another's hands might serve poetic ends, to the incisive economy of great prose. "Griselda's not dead," he writes at the conclusion, "Pardaillan still inhabits me. So does Strogoff. I'm answerable only to them, who are answerable only to God, and I don't believe in God. So try to figure it out." [17] The whole story in a nutshell, complete with worm inside. Or take as an example of the terseness and pregnancy with which he can write (not that he always or even often does so) the phrases in which he embodies the atmosphere of the smug middle-class environment of pre-World War I, reflected in the self-satisfaction of an idolized child: "My grandfather believes in Progress, so do I: Progress, that long, steep path which leads to me." [18] But alas, as a mere philosopher I feel myself helpless before a style, whether of poetry or prose. Read *Les Mots* and you will see: you will find set out before your eyes a rigid analytical frame in which a child and his environment are held fast to view—the man of words making out of his own words the picture of the incipient word-magician that was to be, and still is, himself.

Sartre, then, is a man of words, but of prose, not poetry. What sort of prose? we have next to ask. The passages I have quoted about poetry come from his essay *What is Literature?,* originally published as a series of articles in *Les Temps Modernes* after the war, when the journal was new and Sartre, as its founder and editor, was passionately engaged in formulating its mission and presenting it to the world. In the pages of *Les Temps Modernes* he contrasted the detachment of the poet, insulated from action by words and images, with the commitment—primarily the social commitment—of the prose writer. The poet, like the painter, Sartre believed, may dwell in his creation; so may his reader or viewer. Prose writing, he insisted, lacks that moment of passivity. It is first and last a compact between two freedoms, the writer's and the reader's. The prose writer wants by his writing to act on others, and to enjoin upon them action in their turn. Admittedly, the exact role of the writer varies from society to society. He may have—and had in the Middle Ages or in the French seventeenth century—the task of upholding the established order; he may have, and more appropriately has, the role of proto-revolutionary. It is he who holds up to critical light the inequities of his own society, even of his own class, and so, indirectly, calls for change.

Is Sartre, then, a prose writer in this sense? In his own account of the vocation which, from childhood, shaped his character we have seen how his relation to language, his life of imagination, cut off as it was from everyday reality, resemble the state, in his literary theory, of the poet. Yet, on the other hand, his picture of the young Jean-Paul romancing in the shadow of Charles Schweitzer's library is also the picture of the writer who seeks and needs a public. For one thing, the vocation imposed on him by his elders ("He will be a writer") was a social role. A conservative role, to be sure, as they saw it: he would be a teacher, like his grandfather, and supplement his salary by his pen, all safely inside and on behalf of the cultural establishment. More important: the child himself, if we believe Sartre's reconstruction, always thought of his productions as performances for an audience. He wanted, he says, to give men the reading matter they desired. In his mind's eye he saw his own great-nephew, round about 1980, poring over and admiring the message of his works. It was, it seems, one freedom calling to another yet unborn, a variant at least of the prose writer as conceived in *What is Literature?*

And of course, much of Sartre's production does fit this formula, appealing, not indeed to posterity, but to his contemporaries, as, according to his own theory, the writer is supposed to do. His best short stories embody social themes: the civil war theme of loyalty and betrayal in "The Wall," the bad faith of the bourgeoisie and contrasting apparent good faith of madness in "The Room," anti-Semitism in "L'Enfance d'un Chef." In each case the writer puts before us a social commitment and a critique of society to which, in reading him, we in turn are to commit ourselves. His plays, too, clearly exemplify the character of the new theater as set forth in *What is Literature?* Not individual characters, but ideas themselves, he tells us there, now walk upon the stage. It is the ideological, political arena that we enter when we watch a play. It is political and social issues that the dramatist has personified and that the audience relives in watching. True, the issues change as Sartrean theater and thought develop. In *The Flies,* Orestes seeks *his* act; the characters of *Huis-Clos* embody hell-as-the-others. These plays represent through action the Sartre of *Being and Nothingness,* the doubter of humanity, as he puts it in *Les Mots,* who proved man impossible but as doubter presumed to claim exemption from his own proof. Later, when he turned more explicitly to the external, material and social conditions, even (almost) determinants, of individual action, he put upon the stage more explicitly political conceptions. This is clear in *Les Mains Sales,* where party loyalty is at issue, in *La Putain Respecteuse,* where American racism is the theme, and so on. But the archetype of appeal from freedom to freedom is still exemplified.

Yet there is something—indeed, there are several things—wrong with this picture. For one, there is something too contrived about the theory of *What is Literature?* itself. As with much of Sartre's theoretical writing, the *aperçus* are many, yet the theme is too self-conscious, too abstract. Merleau-Ponty remarked that while of course the writer can write about writing, the painter cannot (at least not quite so directly) paint about painting. But do writers who are primarily imaginative writers, makers of literature, not of argument, write so reflectively about their works? Poets don't. When Emily Dickinson writes poetry about writing poetry, it is the poem that speaks to us, and the poet speaks from within it; it is not the reflection of the poet that speaks to us over and above the poem. Sartre might agree; but the prose writer, he insisted in the 1940's, is someone quite different—and so, in his recent essays on Flaubert he still seems to insist.

Is that correct? Is the novelist really so very different from the poet in his relation to his language on the one hand and to experience on the other? Granted, the lyric poet evokes, ideally, a *moment* of experience in which language and feeling resonate almost statically with one another, while the novelist ideally evokes a whole world into which one enters with him and in which one lives, sharing not only the here and now, but also the formerly and the not-yet of his characters and their concerns. Yet although the temporality is different, the aspect of indwelling within the work belongs to the reader, or hearer, in both cases. As we may feel with Yeats, for example, the poignancy of aging, so we live with Tolstoy in the Rostovs' ballroom, with Alexey in battle, with Natasha now nearly eloping, at last happily examining the newest baby's diapers. Tolstoy, no more than the lyric poet, urges us to action. We do contract with him; there is a compact of freedoms, but a compact to surrender, to see and to live, neither to accept a society nor to change it, but freely and in imagination *to be there.*

In short, the literary artist, whether poet or prose writer, does not come from outside his own vocation with a theme, exemplify it through his invention, and then ask us to wrestle with it. From within himself he is driven to reconstitute his experience imaginatively in language, and he asks us to do so with him. There can be a theater of ideas, indeed, as Sartre argues and has demonstrated by his own practice, but the novel of ideas, it seems to me, hardly ever succeeds as novel. Both Sartre and Beauvoir have suffered as novelists from having too clear and self-conscious themes which they proceed to impose upon their works and too clear and self-conscious ends for writing. It was not (to use the same example) the author of *What is Art?* who wrote *War and Peace* and *Anna,* but his younger predecessor. Sartre, on the contrary, comes to his literary task, as expounded in *What is Literature?,* from the outside, reflecting in terms of abstract principles on what literature ought to be and deciding to do it that way. Visually (except perhaps for *Nausea*), he is a philosopher who has determined on principle that plays or novels are the proper thing to write.

Besides, even it we take his own statement of the aim of literature at its face value, we find the vocation of the prose writer as he sets it out there in important ways unlike the calling that the young Sartre recalled in *Les Mots* had envisioned for himself. As I have already indicated, the one appeals to his contemporaries, the other to posterity. Further, while the one speaks from within a situation, the other is essentially apart from it.

As to the first point: the child romancer, imagining the destiny of his works, envisaged himself sometimes as discovered old and poor and belatedly acknowledged, but usually as dying in obscurity, leaving behind him a long row of volumes for the admiration of his "great-nephews." (Never grandsons; make what you like of that!) As Sartre rationalizes that singularly unchildlike childhood vision, he thought of himself as dead because he had no wish to live. To write, yes; to be admired, yes; but admired once the living writer, the maker of those immortal objects, was safely buried. That is far from the committed writer of *What is Literature?*. Not, of course, that the account of *Words* must be literally true; it is too contrived a piece of Sartrean existential analysis for the story to have been quite like that. Yet as an account of Sartre's vocation as a writer it has much more plausibility than does his theory of committed literature, of the writer as "permanent revolutionary." True, the author of *Being and Nothingness,* turning to political thought, must and can only become a revolutionary theorist: against the alleged values of his, or any so far extant, society, seeing human relations as he does in terms of alienation, oppression, conflict. But the kind of revolutionary he is and has become is not the natural outgrowth of a deep historical commitment; it is rather the necessary logical consequence of the way in which, in *Being and Nothingness,* and even in his early literary work (notably *Nausea*) he sees human freedom as the for-itself over against an alien-in-itself, radically in opposition to it, complete, yet completely other. This Sartrean freedom, total, yet so totally denial of what it is not and of what is not it, this freedom is the freedom of a Cartesian intellect. Beauvoir says of herself and Sartre when they were students: "We were encouraged by Cartesian rationalism, . . . we believed ourselves to consist of nothing but pure reason and pure will." [19] Descartes opened his *Meditations* (published when he was forty-five) "happily free of all cares and disturbed by no passions." His aim, it will be recalled, was to put aside all his former opinions, all his youthful prejudices, and to make a wholly new beginning in the cold clear light of an emancipated reason. This is the freedom of an adult intellectual, of an adult, indeed, who seems never to have been a child. And, *Les Mots* tells us, that is just what Sartre never was. True, he had eventually some ordinary years as a day boy at school. But that was not what counted most in making him the writer he is. What counted was the leap to the imagined *œuvre* as the objectification of the finished life. If the man has changed, as he insists he has, if he found, in the war and the resistance, in the injustices of postwar years, in Algeria and Vietnam, in Stalinism and Hungary, a social and political situation which he had to face; if he became, as he hoped, a writer for his day, nevertheless, his character—and his mind—are still that of the word-spinner cut off in time from the world around him, in a future which he can "totalize" precisely because it is separate in time from the day-to-day occupations that he has yet to live.

If, further, Sartre was cut off in time from his own "childhood" years, he was separated in space as well from his contemporaries. There he is, sitting with his mother on a bench in the Luxembourg, a puny wall-eyed child, detesting his own ugliness. (Why, he used to ask himself, must I always see that same face in the mirror every day?) Round about the affectionate pair other boys are playing together. Don't you want to play with them? asks Anne-Marie. No, says Jean-Paul. Shall I ask their mothers if you could play with them? Doubly no! The vision is devastating. But then there is his own world, 1 rue de Goff, up on the sixth floor, where he is himself, ruler and creator, where he reads his books and writes his romances:

> When my mother took me to the Luxembourg Gardens—that is, every day—I would lend my rags to the lowlands, but my glorious body did not leave its perch; I think it's still there. Every man has his natural place; its altitude is determined by neither pride nor value; childhood decides. Mine is a sixth floor in Paris with a view overlooking the roofs. For a long time I suffocated in the valleys; the plains overwhelmed me: I crawled along the planet Mars, the heaviness crushed me. I had only to climb a molehill for joy to come rushing back; I returned to my symbolic sixth floor; there I would once again breathe the rarefied air of belles-lettres.[20]

Of course, this description is not to be taken too literally. Sartre has his place also in Paris, not only on the sixth floor rue de Goff. The locales of *Being and Nothingness,* that café from which Pierre is absent, that apartment where Pierre hopes to dominate Thérèse or Thérèse Pierre, the Luxembourg itself: they are also Sartre. So is Rousseau, the Bastille, the Terror, so is the Fall of France, the Resistance, French Colonialism, the French Communist Party which he never joined: he is part and parcel of all these and they of him. But also Parisian is the very quality of his detachment: these roofs have an otherness, a belonging in otherness, that no other roofs could have. Compare, for instance, Sartre's relation to Paris with that of Joyce to Dublin. (Admittedly, Joyce belongs to the category, despised by Sartre, of "poet-novelist" or "novelist-poet," but the comparison is perhaps for that very reason so much the more apt.) Joyce, who was of course more literally an exile, never returned to his city after 1909. When asked why he never went back to the place that so haunted him, he answered: "Have I ever left it?" Sartre has lived all his life in Paris and one cannot imagine him elsewhere, yet his being *of* it is a looking down up*on* it, a detachment such as only a Weltstadt, perhaps only Paris, would permit. That is partly the difference between Dublin and Paris. Yet it is also the difference, I think, between an artist (poetic prose writer, or prose-writing poet, as you like), and a philosopher. The one, though in self-imposed exile, has never left his city; the other, at home, is always on the sixth floor, not quite down there at all.

That Sartre's relation to writing is reflective and philosophical is confirmed by an interview on "The Artist and his Language," in which he describes to his interlocutor his own attitude to words.[21] He does not live *in* language, he says. Nor has he interiorized it, so as to gesture with it, to use it simply; he *possesses* words. Egged on by his questioner, he explains this out of the peculiarity of his bourgeois childhood. "Property" is of course a bourgeois category. Words were his peculiar property because, he says, they were all the child Jean-Paul possessed. Living with his grandparents, without his own home, he became the proprietor of—the French language. The explanation is too pat; but the fact it seems to explain is important. For Sartre neither sets words between himself and things, to dwell in them poetically, as it were, nor does he simply use them as transparent signs, as his committed writer ought to do. They are his portable property; he manipulates them, he controls them. They serve neither to evoke images nor to point out paths of action. They are the wise man's counters; they convey concepts. Their primary use, in other words, is philosophical.

Not, of course, that Sartre is only a philosophical writer. Far from it. He himself remarks in the same interview: "I write so many languages," [22] the languages of literature, of the theater, of philosophy. But his own description here of philosophical style is precisely the description of the proprietor of words, who uses them as his own instruments in order from them to come to things. He distinguishes philosophical from scientific language by suggesting (not quite correctly, but that's beside the point) that scientific concepts have been stripped wholly of the ambiguity of natural language. Philosophical language, on the contrary, has a residue of ambiguity. The philosopher does not relish this unclarity of sense, however, as does the poet —who, indeed, lives by it. The philosopher tries to clarify and purify his concepts so that through them he can come to the reflective understanding of experience itself. That is the sixth-floor attitude, to the life. Armed with one's verbal tools, one comes down occasionally to look and measure, and even to share up to a point, then one goes back to one's perch aloft, sharpens and refines the tools themselves, the better to cope with one's little excursion below, and looks out over the roofs with a serene and distant understanding of the scurryings they conceal.

That is a caricature of philosophy if you like, though no more so than Lucretius' "well-fortified sanctuaries, built up by the teachings of the wise, whence you may look down from the height upon others and behold them all astray. . . ." But my point is twofold. First, whatever his undeniable powers as dramatist or prose stylist, Sartre's attitude to language is primarily reflective and philosophical rather than literary. And secondly, his attitude to language reveals him, not only as *a* philosopher, but as *this* philosopher. Both the manner and the matter of his philosophy are just what one would expect of the author, and subject, of *Les Mots,* and his story of the birth of his vocation sheds on his philosophy a most gratifying light. Much that was obscure becomes clear once one reads *Les Mots;* much that was clear but infuriating appears inevitable and coherent, even if not therefore true.

Philosophy, being sustained reflection on experience or some sector of experience, must be detached and must be abstract. But the detachment and the abstraction of Sartre's philosophical method are extreme. That seems a strange remark to make about an "existentialist." For "existentialism" is supposed somehow to deal with "concrete situations," to avoid the speculative system-building or the detached analytical ingenuities of other philosophical styles. Besides, apart from slogans like "man is a useless passion," which, Sartre himself admits, are literary intrusions into what should be a purely conceptual structure, what is most striking at first sight about his philosophical *magnum opus* is precisely his concrete descriptions: one misses Pierre at the café, one is discovered listening at the keyhole, one throws down one's rücksack too tired to hike further, and so on. Yet if we look more carefully we find that these phenomenological jewels are carefully placed in the setting of a highly abstract and ingenious argument. The major premise is: there is no human nature. The tools with which Sartre elicits the consequences of this starting point are the two concepts of his title: being and nothingness. I am, I make myself, as nihilation, as the denial of being; being is what I am not, by its very being it threatens me with non-being, yet not-being-it is precisely what I am. Even within consciousness the very "nature" of my being (which of course is precisely not a "nature") is to *want:* to be what I am not and to not be what I am. Out of the most abstract of dialectical contraries, being and nothing, positive and negative, inner and outer, self and other, Sartre has built his own philosophical edifice. It is as if one tried to construct the whole of Hegel's dialectic out of its first two steps, being and non-being. Anything else would compromise the self-contained isolation of the sixth-floor world.

Indeed, Sartre's early philosophical development seems to consist of a series of negative insights, or insights into negativity. Or if that is too sweeping a statement, there are at any rate two steps in his development which are clearly negational in character, and a third that is easily assimilated into the peculiar brand of "negative dialectic" that was to come.

Sartre spent a year in the French House in Berlin in 1934–1935. There he studied Husserl, and the lesson he derived from phenomenology was: that the ego is an illusion. This at least is the thesis that he developed in *The*

Transcendence of the Ego, published in 1936.[23] Like all good Frenchmen, he had set out from the Cartesian *cogito,* the "I think" which was for Descartes the starting point of all knowledge. This was meant to be a self-contained moment of consciousness. I am thinking about my thinking; subject and object are, in this indubitable moment, directly and indubitably at one. Husserl had shown, however, that all consciousness is *intentional;* it is *of*—an object (not a real object, that's beside the point—but of a target of my consciousness which alone makes it the consciousness it is). In itself, consciousness is an empty locus. Consciousness, for Sartre, however (being still Cartesian, even if drained of its content), is also momentary. I am no Cartesian substance; I have to make myself; but I make myself *ex nihilo* at every moment. Thus there is no stable ego, no self with a history. The real I is empty, the full I a mistake. For Sartre, then, the lesson of Husserl's intentionality is: that *nothing* has been inserted into the *cogito,* and dwells at the very heart of its being. Nothing is the engine that makes it run.

During these same years Sartre had been commissioned to write a survey of theories of imagination (also published in 1936), a survey which led him to develop his own conception of the imaginary. (The original part of the work, rejected by the first publisher, was published separately in 1939). [24] Here again, indeed, even more emphatically than in *The Transcendence of the Ego,* negativity is the operative concept. What is imagined is *not.* The life of imagination is the life of denial, of *de*-tachment par excellence. The work of consciousness, creation at every moment out of nothing, is also, in the thing created by the imagination of the artist, creation *of* nothing. Sartre has held faithfully to this view. Thus two of his most admired artists are, in the verbal arts, Genet and, in the visual, Giacometti. In Genet the "absence of connection with external reality," he writes

> is transfigured and becomes the sign of the demiurge's independence of his creation. . . . In the realm of the imaginary, absolute impotence changes sign and becomes omnipotence. Genet plays at inventing the world in order to stand before it in a state of supreme indifference.[25]

And Giacometti, he remarks, "became a sculptor because he was obsessed by vacuum." "Ironic, defiant, ceremonious and tender," Sartre writes,

> Giacometti sees empty space everywhere. Surely not everywhere, you will say, for some objects touch others. But this is exactly the point. Giacometti is certain of nothing, not even that. For weeks on end, he has been fascinated by the legs of a chair that did not touch the floor. Between things as between men, the bridges are broken, and emptiness seeps in everywhere, every creature concealing his own.[26]

In any medium, to imagine is to deny the real world, to make one's own non-space.

Yet all action is *in* the world; if the ego is empty, it is because my consciousness is out there, in things. To imagine is to make un-things which are nevertheless posited as negations *of*—the real. My being in itself is empty; it is wholly out there in the world, but as action: as wanting to make the world other than it is, in order, by that making, to make myself other. Thus my action, which is all I really am, is also negational: it is basically a posture of othering, of making what is —and thereby myself, who am nothing but my relation to that being out-there that I am not—of making what is into what it is not, or conversely of making what is not into what is. This conception of the finality of human being, which is fundamental to Sartrean philosophy, already lies at the basis of the third essay I want to refer to here: his *Sketch of a Theory of the Emotions,* published in 1939.

Emotion, Sartre argues there, is magical behavior, or more exactly, it is "an abrupt drop of consciousness into the magical." [27] I am always in the world, always acting to make myself over against the demands of the world. But the world has traps in it. It's like a pinball machine; you put in a coin, the balls start running here and there, but sometimes they run into blind alleys, fall into holes—anything but hit the jackpot. Ordinarily, of course, the metaphor of a game of chance is not *quite* accurate, for we treat the things in our world as manageable on the whole, we set ends and work toward them. Sometimes, however, the difficulties are too great; there is no rational action we can take. Sartre gives an example, or better a relatively trivial analogue:

> I extend my hand to take a bunch of grapes. I can't get it; it's beyond my reach. I shrug my shoulders. I let my hand drop, I mumble, "They're too green," and I move on. All these gestures, these words, this behavior are not seized upon for their own sake. We are dealing with a little comedy which I am playing *under* the bunch of grapes, through which I confer upon the grapes the characteristic of being "too green" which can serve as a substitute for the behavior which I am unable to keep up. At first, they presented themselves as "having to be picked." But this urgent quality very soon becomes unbearable because the potentiality cannot be realized. This unbearable tension becomes, in turn, a motive for foisting upon the grapes the new quality "too green," which will resolve the conflict and eliminate the tension. Only I cannot confer this quality on the grapes chemically. I cannot act

> upon the bunch in the ordinary ways. So I seize upon this
> sourness of the too green grapes by acting disgusted. I
> magically confer upon the grapes the quality I desire.[28]

Here, he says, "the comedy is only half sincere." But if the
situation is more serious, and the incantation seriously
meant (though not, be it noted, grasped reflectively, with
full consciousness), then emotion results. Take the example of fear:

> I see a wild animal coming toward me. My legs give way,
> my heart beats more feebly, I turn pale, I fall and faint.
> Nothing seems less adapted than this behavior which
> hands me over defenseless to the danger. And yet it is a
> behavior of *escape*. . . . Here the fainting is a refuge.
> . . . Lacking power to avoid the danger by the normal
> methods and the deterministic links, I denied it. I wanted
> to annihilate it. The urgency of the danger served as mo-
> tive for an annihilating intention which demanded magical
> behavior. And, by virtue of this fact, I did annihilate it as
> far as was in my power. These are the limits of my magi-
> cal action upon the world; I can eliminate it as an object
> of consciousness, but I can do so only by eliminating
> consciousness itself.[29]

Of course not every emotion is quite like this: there is active as well as passive fear—I may run away. I can grieve,
too, either actively or passively. Basically, however, the
structure is always the same. Either "consciousness is
degraded and abruptly transforms the determined world
in which we live into a magical world" or—as in horror—
"the world itself sometimes reveals itself to consciousness as magical instead of determined, as was expected
of it." [30]

Thus emotion appears as an escape-mechanism, a
sharp alternative to the rational control of my environ-

ment. Its paradigm case is hysteria, or a child's tantrum: if you can't have the candy, scream! I *have* to act in the world, and if I can't act in a straightforward instrumental fashion, then I re-act: I cast a spell, I become a magician and the world becomes the kind of world that a magician needs. I make myself afraid and the world fearful; I make myself angry and the world infuriating.

This seems, at first sight, an all-or-none alternative of the same kind that we have found, in different contexts, in *The Transcendence of the Ego* and *The Imaginary.* Although the essay on the *Emotions* is intended to be phenomenology, or phenomenological psychology, its spirit is dialectical. Emotion is action as the refusal of action, the active anti-action of the sorcerer. But surely, one may object, the alternative of rationality *vs.* magic is not one recognized by the person who feels the emotion at the time he feels it, so how can this be correct phenomenology? Sartre in fact sees this very clearly. Emotion is a structure of consciousness, he argues, but not of self-consciousness. It is a structure of non-reflective, non-thetic consciousness which accompanies and underlies the central thrust of awareness. This is a theme elaborated in *Being and Nothingness,* perhaps the principal conceptual link that ties Sartre's abstract dialectic to the real flow of real experience, as, he says in *Les Mots,* the elevator at 1 rue de Goff tied his imaginative eyrie to the street below.

I shall return to the problem of non-thetic consciousness and its role in Sartre's philosophy of man when we come to *Being and Nothingness.* Both there and here, in these preliminary writings, however, it is the all-or-none spirit of Sartrean dialectic that prevails. I make myself each moment *ex nihilo;* in imagination what I make is also —nothing. Emotion is action as the denial of action. All my ways of being, as he was to put it in *Being and Noth-*

ingness, manifest freedom. Why? Because they are all ways of being my own nothingness. Action itself is always negating: making what-is-not be and making what-is-not-be. And emotion, the exorcising of the world, the negation of action, is still the action of negating. And so on.

Man of words, indeed! A juggler of words, perhaps, who means next to nothing by them? Faced with this sort of conceptual ping-pong, as it looks to be, one can sympathize with the student who described the subject-matter of contemporary continental philosophy as "perfectly perverse." But in philosophy even perversity, when perfected, can be, not only entertaining, but illuminating. It is astonishing what a complex and intricate structure Sartre has built out of his over-detached, almost nihilistic starting point. Assimilating for his own uses, yet with rare understanding, the philosophies of the past, he has produced in *Being and Nothingness* one of the treasure-houses of Western philosophy: a text one returns to again and again, not only for its catch phrases or for its strange truncated dialectic or for its occasional pieces of brilliant phenomenological description, but for the subtlety of its detailed arguments. It is surprising how complex and delicate this web of abstract words can be, and, indeed, how many real problems, out of its very detachment, it catches in its net. It is not only himself that the man of words, in *Words,* has caught (to change metaphors) in his pitiless mirror. In the conceptual mirror of man that he has set before us in his philosophical writing, although there is a basic distortion, an obsession with nothingness that strangely transforms the realities, there is also, even in the very set of the disproportions, much that is revealed.

Let *Words* have the last word. The man of the sixth

floor describes his career, both its constancy and its change:

> Today, April 22, 1963, I am correcting this manuscript on the tenth floor of a new building: through the open window I see a cemetery, Paris, the blue hills of Saint Cloud. That shows my obstinacy. Yet everything has changed. Had I wished as a child to deserve this lofty position, my fondness for pigeon-houses would have to be regarded as a result of ambition, of vanity, as a compensation for my shortness. But it's not that; it wasn't a matter of climbing up my sacred tree: I *was* there, I refused to come down from it. It was not a matter of setting myself above human beings: I wanted to live in the ether among the aerial simulacra of Things. Later, far from clinging to balloons, I made every effort to sink: I had to wear leaden soles. With luck, I occasionally happened, on naked sands, to brush against submarine species whose names I had to invent. At other times, nothing doing: an irresistible lightness kept me on the surface. In the end, my altimeter went out of order. I am at times a bottle imp, at others a deep-sea diver, often both together, which is as it should be in our trade. I live in the air out of habit, and I poke about down below without much hope.[31]

For those of us who live down below, the results are worth studying, on both levels.

chapter two: sartre and his predecessors

I. descartes and the phenomenologists

introduction

Sartre, we have argued,
is in the first instance a philosophical, rather than imaginative, writer. He
works with concepts first and moves from
and through them to experience. The philosopher, however, does not snatch his concepts out of
thin air. In large part, he inherits them. He takes what men

have thought or are thinking and molds it into a new shape. Even his innovations—concepts christened with new names—usually have some affinity with the problems of his predecessors, and, as he sees it, their erroneous solutions. Ever since Plato, or even Parmenides, Western philosophy has been firmly rooted in its own history. Sartre is no exception. The derivations of his thought are clear, and clearly acknowledged.

At the same time, one must admit that, from Plato onward, original philosophers, though philosophizing in one way or another out of the history of philosophy, have often been bad historians. What they want, after all, is not so much to understand their predecessors as to use them. They have their own problems, which, though generated by the tradition, have been transformed by their own time and character. Using the concepts and arguments of the past for their own purposes, they fail to see and understand them as such, as the historian must try to do. In this respect, Sartre *is* an exception. He does indeed use the thinkers of the past (and present) for his own ends, but at the same time he sees them with extraordinary clarity. In his references, say, to Kant or Spinoza, he not only uses their thought as a springboard for his own, but also exhibits a solid and scholarly penetration into their principles and views. His relation to Marx is less straightforward, as we shall see, but in general one finds in his philosophical works an interweaving of themes in which the original strands stand out for themselves with unusual distinctness, while at the same time they are being worked into a characteristically Sartrean pattern.

Compare Sartre in this respect with Heidegger. Much more than Sartre, Heidegger considers himself a philosopher in and of the history of Western thought. Sartre does, indeed, take Descartes's *cogito* as a necessary starting place; but to the tradition before that dramatic turning point he seems to be indifferent. Besides, he takes even the *cogito* as an eternal, not a historical, absolute. Heidegger's thought, on the contrary, is rooted in the first historical soil of Western thought—in the meanings of "truth" and "being" at the very beginning of our intellectual history. If he seeks "the destruction of metaphysics," he does so, not for any crass positivistic purpose, but out of reverence for history as such. For what he wants is to renew the beginning of Western thought itself. He wants to get back into the tradition so deeply that he can teach us how to live again its profound and fateful source. Yet from the point of view of historical scholarship, Heidegger is, in the main, a scandalous historian. His *Kant and the Problem of Metaphysics,* for example, illuminating though it can be, if used judiciously, for the study of the first *Critique,* is nine-tenths Heidegger. Much of his treatment of Greek philosophy, in the *Introduction to Metaphysics,* for example, is based on far-fetched etymologies embedded in the pompous profundities of the German Herr Professor at his worst. Though historically oriented, Heidegger is no "historian."

Admittedly, Heidegger himself would dismiss any demand for "scholarly accuracy" as superficial and irrelevant. It is a much deeper historicity, the very destiny of Being, that he is after. And woe betide us, not him, if we fail to follow him. So be it. My point is simply that Heidegger's "history," though at the heart of his method, is scarcely recognizable as history to the ordinary student of Western thought. Sartre, on the other hand, although he does not see his philosophical task as explicitly historical, appears to the philosophically schooled reader as, not only an original thinker, but, in a more humdrum way, a thoroughly competent professional philosopher with a sound historical schooling. For this reason, the relation of his own thought to the philosophers he most relies on comes through to the reader with unusual distinctness, and his own method appears, not indeed simply as eclectic, but as an idiosyncratic interweaving and re-making of familiar concepts and themes. It should help us, therefore, in approaching his philosophical work to look first at the use he makes of other thinkers both past and present.

Sartre's major predecessors—that is, the philosophers he most relies on in his own reflections—may be divided into two groups: Descartes and the phenomenologists on the one hand, and the dialecticians on the other. I am taking "phenomenology" here as the name of the school derived from Husserl and "dialectic" as designating the method of Hegel and his successors. True, one of Hegel's major works is also entitled "Phenomenology" (i.e., *The Phenomenology of Mind*), but it is from the modern "phenomenological method" that Sartre's practice derives, while it is the dialectical aspect of Hegel's philosophy that he adopts. Granted, the contrast I am making may, historically, be unfair to Hegel as phenomenologist; but in terms of influences on Sartre it is certainly plausible, and in terms of the major emphasis of Hegel's developed system it seems to me also not only permissible, but on the whole correct.

Descartes holds a peculiar position in this contrast. It is a residuum of Cartesian metaphysics which both limits the scope of Sartre's phenomenology and, in large measure, dictates the subject-matter as well as the style of his dialectic. Descartes is therefore Sartre's first, and, so to speak, constitutive forerunner. Yet the Cartesian *cogito* is also, as Husserl himself insisted, the necessary starting point of phenomenology; so in a way Descartes belongs with and among the phenomenological influences. But it is the *cogito,* with the idealism inherent in it (much as Sartre would deny such an allegation) that fatefully controls Sartre's dialectical reasoning as well as his phenomenology. The shadow of Descartes, therefore, presides over both sides of Sartrean method. More than the *cogito* alone, moreover, it is his Cartesian starting point in a number of its aspects—Cartesian freedom, Cartesian dualism, Cartesian temporality—that forms the framework of his thinking. In other words, the influence of Descartes is broader and deeper than simply the influence of the *cogito* as first principle and therefore of Descartes as phenomenologist or forerunner of phenomenology.

With this partial asymmetry in mind, however, I shall take Descartes along with Husserl and Heidegger as constituting one set of influences and the three great nineteenth-century dialectical philosophers, Hegel, Marx, and Kierkegaard, as forming another. Indeed, it can be seen in Sartre's early book *A Sketch for a Theory of the Emotions,* that the first three had already formed his thinking while the dialectical strand had just begun its work. The *Emotions* is a text in Cartesian phenomenology. Sartre there ranks himself quite by the way and automatically among those for whom the Cartesian *cogito* is an absolute, the necessary starting point of any sound philosophy. And in the introduction he sketches the contributions of Husserl and Heidegger, whose method he claims to be carrying forward in this essay.

Descartes

Sartre complains frequently about the bourgeoisie. He is, but hates being, a French petit bourgeois intellectual, and yet the class he despises has, he avows, nevertheless made him what he is. But much deeper and much harder to shake off in every French philosopher than the class he was born into is the influence of Descartes, the first and greatest French philosopher. Merleau-Ponty spent a lifetime fighting Descartes. Until very recently at least, Sartre never even wanted to fight him. Of course Sartre has long ago given up the Cartesian God. The old man receded into a Parisian sky one day when Jean-Paul was twelve or so, and he has never come back—except insofar as, for a committed atheist like Sartre, God has to be there to be denied. As a matter of fact in *Being and Nothingness* it is the traditional *definition* of God, *causa sui,* that man seeks to realize and cannot. But this is a Spinozistic rather than Cartesian formula, and it is probably Spinozistic being rather than Descartes's non-deceiving manipulator of all things that Sartre has in mind. In fact, it seems to me, the God of the *Meditations,* even for Descartes, was more a device to keep the divided world together than a genuine object of belief and worship, let alone a pervasive ontological foundation like the God of Spinoza. He is not hard to get rid of and Sartre has done the job thoroughly.

Cartesian substance, too, Sartre has eliminated, and by the same move to atheism. It is the *cogito,* this moment of my awareness which, though I doubt, even as doubter I must *be,* that is for him firm, unique, and the fulcrum of all philosophy. But that I as thinker am a substance, an independently existing thing worthy of immortality: that thesis can be supported only by my confidence that God created me at conception and will conserve me to sing psalms to Him in the hereafter. Departing, He has taken the substantial immaterial self away as well. But doesn't that leave the material world? Not as substantial. As every reader of the *Meditations* knows, the sixth meditation forms the weakest step in the series. That there are real external things I have succeeded in doubting at the very start so thoroughly that only God can reinstate them at the end—and even He can vouchsafe them only "practical," not perfect certainty. Usually, when my mind tells me "my leg hurts," it is in fact (if God's general rules are valid, and they must be if He is no deceiver), that piece of stuff out there whose aging veins are misbehaving. But there are, Descartes noted, amputees whose "leg" hurts. One can't be sure, as one is sure of mathematical truths, that the leg is *there*. So the whole of Cartesian cosmology, God and with Him the two finite substances, are easily dispensed with. Born into a late and secular century, conventionally Catholic in a Protestant household, Sartre can stop with the *Second Meditation* and let the rest go.

It is the first two *Meditations,* on the contrary, that establish the Cartesian method, that lay down as philosophical axiom the priority of pure consciousness and with this axiom a small but fateful cluster of metaphysical concepts which accompany it. All these Sartre has assimilated to his very bones.

First, the *cogito* itself : the pure consciousness of being conscious as the necessary beginning of philosophy. My senses sometimes deceive me; even about the most certain mathematical truths, given a deceiving demon to play tricks on me, I *could* be wrong. But my consciousness that I am now conscious of that consciousness—even if I were dreaming—could not be wrong. This self-contained now of self-consciousness is absolutely indubitable. It is the first and stable something, as Descartes put it, of which even the doubter of all traditional opinions and attitudes could have no doubt.

What is implied for philosophical method in this starting point? First, the primary tool of philosophy is intuition, not argument. The *cogito* is not an argument: in the

Meditations, there is no "therefore" between "I think" and "I am." I am, I think, Descartes declares, this is true every time I say it. What philosophy is after is the *aperçus* of consciousness into itself. True, as we shall see shortly, Husserl, claiming to follow Descartes's method, will transform the *cogito* into *cogitationes,* the thinking into thoughts, and Sartre will try (with important differences) to follow him in this. But what is common to all three, Descartes, Husserl, and Sartre, is the insistence that philosophical knowledge begins from a pure, evident, self-guaranteeing intuition and remains on (or recurrently returns to) the intuitive level so long as it is correctly executed. Indeed, for Sartre, not only philosophical knowledge (though that *par excellence*) but all knowledge is intuitive, as it was for Descartes. Argument is subordinate to insight and must be brought back to it.

Such insight, it should be remarked by the way, must be distinguished from the "understanding" (*Verstehen*) of the modern social scientist, sometimes associated with phenomenological method. We shall find in Sartre's *Critique* that "comprehension" (*Verstehen*) is a second-order instrument, secondary to the reflective awareness of the individual's nature and destiny. Only after a series of complex dialectical maneuvres can we achieve the "comprehension" of social functions and structures and of men as agents in society. The primary intuitions, the insights we have to cultivate first, are not sociological comprehension, but the self-awareness of a pure reflective consciousness.

For the ideal of philosophical knowledge, with Sartre, as with Descartes and Husserl, is absolute certainty: "apodeicticity," that is, *necessary* truth. This is not of course physical necessity, which is always hypothetical, contingent upon postulates and upon given circumstances. Physical laws always say, if such and such were given, then so and so would happen. Nor is it logical necessity, which says, if A, then not non-A, and so says nothing real. The necessary truth of the phenomenologist from Descartes through Husserl to Sartre must be luminousness itself: the self-evident. That was the basic methodological insight of the *cogito* which all pure phenomenologists have still to follow: they seek the self-guaranteeing, the pure light of reason illuminating itself by its own rays and leaving out of account all the universe outside that beam. The metaphor betrays itself: for light always falls on *something,* not itself—we will return to that point with Husserl—yet the ideal remains—only the self-evident is worthy of acceptance as philosophical truth.

Empirically, however, we can easily see that the insights we have into social action, into the ordinary situations of others' lives and of our own—for as living embodied beings we have always been, since our prenatal existence, dependent on others, influencing them and being influenced by them—we can see that these everyday insights fall short in their ordinary operation of such apodeicticity. Day by day, in our bodily situations, we are fallible. Even logicians and mathematicians, let alone ordinary mortals, make mistakes. Three centuries after Descartes's *Fourth Meditation* we still fail to confine our wills within the bounds of our understandings. We still judge probabilistically, we gamble and go wrong. How can I escape, as philosopher, this seemingly universal fallibility and achieve self-evident truth? Only—again Sartre agrees with Descartes in the seventeenth century and Husserl in the twentieth—by a disciplined reflection which detaches the reflecting consciousness from its factual enmeshment in the contingent givens of the factual world. That world, Sartre believes, is indeed all I have, and I am always out there in it. But I philosophize by detaching myself from it, setting myself, as consciousness conscious of itself, over against it. Only in this way can the necessary purity of philosophical thought be initiated or maintained.

It may be objected that I am unfair to Sartre in putting him so unequivocally inside the tradition that seeks for philosophy unadulterated apodeictic truth. He himself has called Husserl's search for necessary truth, his attempt to construct a range of apodeictic philosophical sciences, madness—though the madness of genius. Yet in the *Critique* Sartre himself is still seeking "apodeicticity," and even if he never finds it (though in the *Critique* he thought he had), it remains his ideal. If it is an empty ideal, so much the more strenuous is his search for it, so much the more emphatic his insistence on the intellectual development that could alone implement its fulfillment.

The peculiar detachment of the Cartesian philosopher is evident in Sartre's case if we compare, briefly, his style of philosophical reflection with that of two other twentieth-century writers. Take, for example, C. I. Lewis, a philosopher very far from Sartre in method and interests. Lewis, too, recognized explicitly that the method of philosophy is "reflection." But the reflective method for him is that of a practical man in a world of practical concerns, both ethical and intellectual—for the intellectual interests even of the pure scientist are for Lewis ultimately linked to practice. Here we are, in this humdrum, murky world, trying to find out, from within, what it is all about. The achievements of science, the moral dilemmas of our fellow men, are all grist to our philosophic mill; but we never lose the awareness of being one of our fellows ourselves. From within society and its demands, we withdraw a little, to look around us and ask on what principles our actions, both more and less immediately practical, might be based. But we have never radically doubted—could never doubt—the evidence of our bodily senses, from which, after all, all our "external" information flows. The empirical and the conceptual, though on reflection we find them to be logically independent, are not sharply separated in fact and we attempt no method to achieve their radical separation. It is in empirical situations, both developments in physics and the givens of ethical life, that we try to separate abstractly these conceptual strands. Embodiment, fallibility, contingency, and immersion *in* the real world are all essential to this kind of pragmatic reflection from the start. Pure consciousness, the tool and the medium of phenomenology, is here neither the starting point of philosophical reflection nor its desideratum.

Much closer to Sartrean philosophizing, and indeed deeply motivated by the need to come to grips with it, is the thought of Merleau-Ponty. But the same contrast obtains. For Merleau-Ponty, perception, which expresses my embodied being with and in the world, is what comes first. Perception, as he constantly argues, is primary, in its epistemological status and its ontological import. Reference to the *cogito,* the moment of pure reflection in which I as pure consciousness am purely aware of being conscious, comes late in the text of his *Phenomenology,* and remains, in its purity, an object of thought, not an achievement, let alone a starting point. Here I am, he says, thinking about Descartes's *cogito.* But when I think about myself thinking about the *cogito*— or about anything else—what I find is no pure consciousness at all but a situated, historical, embodied stretch of thinking, feeling, listening, seeing in all the ambiguity of my being-in-the-world. And Descartes's own *cogito* must in fact have been like that: Descartes, after all, was a mathematician with certain interests and aspirations—in particular, the aspiration of finding a secure and permanent foundation on which to build, first, mathematical physics and then, flowing from it, a universal science. His dream of finding a new and infallible method of reflection was guided by his own mathematical genius and by the confidence of the new scientists of his day that a revolutionary method of knowledge could and must be found to keep the new discoveries on a secure and systematic path. Only in that historical situation was there a Cartesian *cogito*. But in that situation it was not in fact the *cogito* it seemed to be. It was the claim of a historical, thinking-and-feeling human being—a claim which, in its full implications, has proved, as so many of our claims prove, to be illusory.

Now Sartre, of course, if he has abandoned the metaphysical superstructure of the *Meditations,* God and finite substance, is also far from the intellectual interests of the historical Descartes. His conception of the method of physics (which is not Descartes's conception of it) does, as we shall see in connection with the *Critique,* have a certain influence on his own method. But it is far from central, and at the stage of his development when he wrote *Being and Nothingness* it is hardly operative at all. What interests him is not what in fact interested Descartes, the discovery of a new method on which to found the sciences, or what was to interest Husserl, the discovery of a new method on which to found the philosophical sciences and, through this foundation, to justify the positive sciences also. What interests Sartre is the *cogito* itself as the moment of pure determined self-awareness. It is this, in and of itself, this moment which for a more pragmatic or more empirically oriented thinker does not exist, even as an ideal—it is precisely this moment which for him is the unique and necessary starting point of philosophical thought.

But, it will be objected, the starting point of *Being and Nothingness* is not really the Cartesian *cogito,* totally aware of its own self-awareness, not the reflective *cogito* which is the first sure step to a unified science, but the pre-reflective *cogito,* a consciousness (of) self which is in fact self-forgetting. The example Sartre gives in *Being and Nothingness* is, counting my cigarettes: there are twelve. Thetically, that is, in terms of the center of my attention, it's the cigarettes I'm thinking of, not myself as counting them. But if you ask me what I'm doing, I say automatically, "Counting my cigarettes." So I *was* aware, though "non-thetically," of my own consciousness as well as, "thetically," or explicitly, of its object. This move to the non-thetic, non-focal consciousness (of) self had been made, in fact, already in the *Transcendence of the Ego* and *The Emotions.* Is not this a fundamental, non-Cartesian, even anti-Cartesian move? I shall of course return to the pre-reflective *cogito* and its place in Sartre's philosophy when I come to analyze the argument of *Being and Nothingness.* But against this objection one can say here: first, Sartre does expressly take the *cogito* itself (even though he is going to transform it) as an absolute beginning. And secondly, the Sartrean *cogito,* even though it will have lost the explicitly reflective character of the original, still carries with it many of the implications of the Cartesian first principle. Sartre not only retains, as I have been arguing, the ideal of intuitive, detached, pure self-evident knowledge (to be attained, presumably, in *Being and Nothingness,* when he turns in Chapter III of Book Two, from the pre-reflective to the reflective level). He retains also, as I have suggested, the corollaries of the *cogito:* Cartesian freedom, Cartesian dualism, and the Cartesian concept of time. In this, indeed, he goes much further than does Husserl in his loyalty to the essential Cartesian strategy of the *Meditations.* Before I go on to consider Sartre's relation to Husserl, therefore, let me look briefly at these three, Cartesian co-ordinates, so to speak, of his thought.

First, freedom. God, Descartes had said, gives laws in the universe as a king gives laws in his kingdom. For Sartre, there is no God, every man is king, and king just as Descartes's God was king. Man is wholly free. In his introduction to a collection of Cartesian texts, Sartre expressly celebrates this Cartesian concept,[1] and *Being and Nothingness* may itself be considered a long paean to Cartesian freedom. We are indeed *condemned* to be free: our destiny of freedom is a burden, for the comforting substantiality of the Cartesian self is no longer ours to attain. When we try to fill our freedom in, so to speak, to give ourselves stability and content, we betray ourselves: we borrow from elsewhere, from the past, from social convention and myth, we fall into bad faith. And yet we remain free: consciousness surging up over against the world, bringing negation into the world, making ourselves at every moment. No look of the Other, no torture, no past commitment can negate that fundamental fact: at every instant *I* and only I decide. Sartre says that he has changed. His Orestes now shocks him. He knows how determined by his society, his class man is. Yet even in the *Critique* he insists that every man is sovereign. There is, he claims, no *foundation* of sovereignty, as political theorists have tried to argue. Why not? Because, though through very devious dialectical channels, the derivation of the sovereignty of "the Sovereign" is from the sovereignty of man as such, which is total and, though always alienated, still inalienable. If you genuinely start with the *cogito,* that is how it has to be. This pure moment of consciousness, self-dependent and self-sustaining, is the first foundation of thought and of being, of knowledge and of reality.

But is it? If you really start with the *cogito,* you start by *cutting out all else.* The *cogito,* the moment of freedom, of self-choice, of the project through which I surge up as my self, has to be over against all that is not this moment, all that is not my self. To accept the *cogito* is to accept dualism, not, indeed, a dualism of substances, but a dualism of consciousness against what is rejected: the out-there, the extended and external, the other-than-myself-here-now-aware-or-myself-here-now. Within this basic, radical dichotomy of self and other, of act and object, as we have already seen and will see yet again, all Sartre's thinking—however socio-political, however dialectical it may become—is sternly and uncompromisingly confined. Both the to-and-fro dialectic of *Being and Nothingness* and the more tortuous but still largely negational dialectic of the *Critique* take their direction and their character from this Cartesian starting point: the opposition of consciousness as "for-itself" and the "in-itself," the "mere" being, to which it is opposed. The man of the *cogito,* of detached self-consciousness, over against his objects, the man of the sixth floor, remains. He is still Orestes, making himself by his own act, for, but also against, his city. He is still Roquentin—however thick the forest of chestnut roots (even, as he calls it in the *Critique,* the human forest), they are still nauseating. They threaten him, because as himself he has to be their Other, their denial, and they are his denial because he has to be, if he is to be at all, pure consciousness, self-making and self-maintaining over against all else.

Can he so make and so maintain himself? Of course

not. Hence, as we shall see, the dialectical in-and-out that is to follow. But he can seem to—for a moment. The *cogito,* of course, is momentary. I am, I think, *whenever* I am aware of thinking. Beyond thought, I need God to recreate me. Time itself is a string of beads, of which I have one only at any time. As we shall see in *Being and Nothingness,* the Cartesian instant haunts Sartre's argument. Though he denies it, he wants it. Good faith could exist, Orestes could really make himself, only if he could find that instant. Like the apodeicticity of Cartesian knowledge, the instant remains as the ideal. And so it must for any pure phenomenological method whatever, even, I would venture to suggest, with Husserl, despite the subtleties of his description of temporal consciousness. For what is intuited as evident must be presented—and what is presented must be present *in* the present. The past is no more, the future is not yet, it is the unique moment of present truth at which phenomenological description aims.

Again, on these three concepts—freedom, mind-body dualism, and the atomic concept of time—it is instructive to contrast Sartre and Merleau-Ponty. Merleau-Ponty rejects all three of these Cartesian notions. In the first instance, he abandons dualism, seeking to found our being-in-the-world squarely in the thoroughgoing ambiguity of a psychophysical existence. But the ambivalence of our existence as embodied beings lends indirection and qualification also to our freedom. "We never see our freedom face to face." The fact that I live in and out of this body and this bodily situation means that my choices rise up *within* a given set of contingent circumstances, *within* what Sartre would call "facticity," not over against it. Similarly, time for Merleau-Ponty is not a string of moments, but truly historical from the start. He attempts, with some modification, to follow the lead of

Husserl's *Inner Time Consciousness;* he is certainly not in pursuit of a Cartesian present moment.

Husserl

So far I have been speaking of Sartre's Cartesianism, which is the starting point of his phenomenological method; it also provides the boundaries as well as the first principle for his philosophical reflections and achievements from his first to his most recent publication: from the *Transcendence of the Ego* through the *Critique* to his work on Flaubert. In *Emotions,* however, and in *Being and Nothingness* as well, he makes it plain that he has derived a great deal also from the twentieth-century phenomenologists Husserl and Heidegger. Having already touched on Sartre's debt to Husserl in connection with *Transcendence of the Ego* and *The Imaginary,* let us now look a little more systematically at the connection between Sartre and Husserl, mediating the connections by comparing Descartes and Husserl.

Descartes's first *Meditation* puts into operation what has come to be known as the principle of methodological doubt. To approach a new and certain beginning of knowledge, he prepares the way by taking as false, for the time being, all opinions which he had previously accepted on dubitable grounds. Husserl, without denying, even *pro tem,* the beliefs of ordinary life, follows an analogous method insofar as he holds such beliefs in abeyance. He "brackets" the whole of "reality" as accepted by the natural standpoint. He performs an *epoché*—that is, a holding in suspense of everyday beliefs. He thus puts to one side, also, the philosophical problem of the reality of the external world, eliminating the transcendent, in the sense of what lies beyond consciousness, altogether from his inquiry. In this, indeed, he is more radical than Des-

cartes, who will try to reinstate this other-than-conscious-
ness, both God and matter, in the third and sixth *Meditations* respectively.

Secondly, beyond and before and immune to doubt,
we find the *cogito.* This move, at least in the *Cartesian
Meditations,* Husserl accepts, like Descartes, as the only
proper beginning for a sound, necessary, and "scientific," philosophy. Yet Husserl accepts Descartes's principle in a spirit that is not Cartesian. His starting point is
different from Descartes's in two significant aspects.
First, the *cogito* for Descartes is uniquely self-guaranteeing because it is self-reflective. I am thinking now about
my thinking now. The idea and its object collapse into one
another in perfect unity. What Husserl constantly speaks
of in his *Meditations,* however, is not the *cogito,* but *cogitationes,* not the "I think," but thoughts. What characterizes consciousness for him is *intentionality,* the fact that
thought is always directed toward a target. It is never
purely and simply self-identical as the Cartesian *cogito* is.
Descartes had found as his firm and secure starting point
a unique moment of thinking cut off from anything beyond its own identity with itself. Although Husserl, too,
wants to bracket, to hold off from consciousness all that is
not purely conscious, it is not just this unique self-identical
moment he wants to examine. It is *any* phenomenon of
consciousness in its unique intuited structure that interests him. Looking at consciousness in this way, he finds,
not a pure and collapsed self-reference in which thinking
and thought are one, but a vastly complex structure of
thinking and its target—a structure which can be opened
out, he hopes, into a wide range of phenomenological sciences. This move promises not only much knowledge, but
secondly, the avoidance of much error. Descartes
thought to move from the *cogito* to transcendent objects

and thus he re-embarked, despite his inspired beginning, on the speculative metaphysic that has led so many philosophers astray. But the new phenomenological method, Husserl believes, with its self-conscious reduction, is not accessible to the mistaken path that Descartes takes as he proceeds from the *cogito, via* God, to reconstruct the world. All the discoveries of phenomenology, Husserl insists, are to remain definitively within the sphere of consciousness. There is to be no advance to dogmatic metaphysics, to the assertion of trans-conscious realties as such. There is plenty of work for philosophy to do within the sphere of immanence, in examining the *cogitationes* both in their active and their passive aspects, seeing them in their essential structures, and inquiring into their constitution by consciousness itself.

How does Sartre stand in relation to all this? Although he does not start from an explicit position on either methodological doubt or its cousin the *epoché,* he seems to accept something like it, at least insofar as he begins in *Being and Nothingness* within consciousness, with the "pure phenomenon," which could only have been reached by some such method. Yet he has not seriously executed the Husserlian reduction. He has not put himself faithfully on the level of consciousness so as to remain there. I shall return to this point shortly.

But the chief peculiarity of Sartre's phenomenology, and of his dialectic too, stems from the way in which he takes the *cogito.* For he both accepts Husserl's revision of the *cogito* to *cogitatio* and refuses to accept it. Thought *is* of an object, he has argued in the *Transcendence of the Ego,* so the thinking as such is empty. Yet he cannot resign the *cogito* itself. If it is always *of* something other than my thinking that, in the first instance, I am thinking; nevertheless, non-thetically, in a peripheral or submerged fashion, so to speak, I am also, conscious (of) myself as doing so. (Remember the cigarettes already referred to!) Now I could of course think thetically about my thinking and even about my thinking about my thinking by turning to a higher, reflective level. In this case the object of my thinking would be a previous thought or previous thinking. The same move could be made by Husserl, or Descartes if he thought about it, but such reflective regression does not alter the fundamental structure of thought as intentional—or, for Sartre, of the *cogito* as pre-reflective. In fact, for him the regressive reflection would be viciously infinite, could one not cut it short with his *cogito* as a non-reflective absolute. And it is on this structure, the pre-reflective *cogito,* that the argument of *Being and Nothingness* rests.

Moreover, Sartre not only retains the *cogito,* if in altered form; he takes the object of the *cogitatio,* not as the immanent target of thinking, but as outside it. He reintroduces—has never really abandoned—the Cartesian extended thing. He has, indeed, as we have seen, abandoned its substantiality, but its sheer exteriority, its otherness-than-consciousness remains. In fact, consciousness, emptied by the insight into intentionality, turns out to be nothing but the *other of that otherness:* the in-here as a negation of the out-there. The move to intentionality in Sartre, therefore, is not a move within consciousness to open up its immanent complexities; it is a leap which both empties consciousness and places its object transcendently out in the world. Thus Sartre seems to have taken from Husserl just one insight: thought is always of an object. At the start he has retained a pre-reflective *cogito* as surrogate for the Cartesian and has taken the intentional object as transcendent rather than reduced, thus generating out of a phenomenological base the dialectic of Nothingness and Being from which no God, whether benevolent or deceiving, will rescue him.

Yet Sartre is a phenomenologist. If he accepts a minimum of Husserlian doctrine, he is—or at least has been on occasion—a superb practitioner of the descriptive method in philosophy. Without anticipating in detail the argument of *Being and Nothingness,* let me try to illustrate if I can what this method, stripped of Husserl's technicalities, amounts to, and how Sartre uses it.

The slogan of phenomenology is "back to the things themselves." But "things," of course, after the *epoché,* are not transcendent things: phenomenologists are not asking whether what there is is "really" mind or body or something different from either. They are trying to look without philosophical or scientific prejudice at the content of experience as experience, both on the side of the experiencing, in memory as against perception or imagination, for example, and of what is experienced, as physical object, person, animal, art work, space, time, and so on. The principal function of "bracketing" from this point of view is to turn the philosopher's attention from distracting—often even insoluble—speculative problems to the domain of consciousness, where he can seek to inspect impartially and accurately what he does unquestionably have: the whole field of his own consciousness as he is conscious of it. He can seek to describe fully and soberly the content of his experience and the manner of experiencing it. It is out of this medium of consciousness, after all, that all the pronouncements of the so-called positive sciences have to be elicited. Without the consciousness of mathematicians, in its peculiar style and with its appropriate conceptual objects, there would be no mathematics; without the consciousness of physicists, no physics; without the consciousness of social scientists, no social science. It is a given style of experience, with its peculiar targets and its peculiar ways of taking them, that constitutes a given kind of positive science. The same goes for segments of the field of consciousness before and beyond science: aesthetic experience, religious experience, the experience of everyday life in all its manifold aspects. Phenomenology as pure description is the *sine qua non* of all philosophical criticism or justification.

"Pure description," however, has been cultivated in the main by literature and psychology. If we are to take phenomenological description as it is intended—as philosophy, not literature or empirical science—we must consider briefly how it is distinguished from both of these —admitting that it is also, of course, connected with both.

Phenomenologists may use examples from literature, and the literature of consciousness lends itself peculiarly to this use. Phenomenologists like, for example, to quote Valéry's *M. Teste.* Sartre in particular borrows numerous descriptions from Proust. And of course, being an imaginative as well as a philosophical writer, he can either produce a story with a philosophical lesson or place a phenomenological description within a literary text. In *Nausea,* for example, he is doing both: writing a philosophical argument in fictional form, and using descriptions that might well find their place in a more conventional philosophical text—for instance, the description of listening to a hit tune on the gramophone—in the context of the novel. Similarly, in *L'Enfance d'un Chef,* the description of the child's consciousness in relation to his mother could easily be transposed into a phenomenological account of intersubjective experience as such. Yet there is a difference, even though it may be difficult to specify it exactly.

For one thing, it is a question of the proportion between imagination and intellect. The phenomenologist uses his imagination systematically, and abstractly, in "eidetic variation." That is, he *imagines* the present experience, both its content as experienced and the manner of experiencing it, shifted slightly one way and another. And he does this in order to cultivate a vision that is primarily *intellectual,* the vision of essences as such. True, the novelist, too, however precisely he may describe the feel of a given conscious moment, produces a work that is also in some sense "eidetic." If "Marcel's" (or "I's"?) consciousness or Bloom's consciousness were *only* "Marcel's" or Bloom's, no one could read *Remembrance of Things Past* or *Ulysses.* There must be enough generality to permit imaginative participation by the reader. But in literature, however "universal," it is the *imaginative* participation that is primary.

Further, it is *participation* that the novelist has to seek, whereas with the phenomenologist what is sought is *re-enactment.* It is not Husserl's "primordial world" that I enter into in reading his *Cartesian Meditations;* if I read Husserl seriously, it is my own consciousness that, in following him, inspects itself. I am with Bloom on the way to Glasnevin or with the great-aunts acknowledging the gift of wine. In inspecting, with Husserl, the nature of the *cogitatio,* I am with—myself. To put it philosophically, the tool of the literary reader is Humean sympathy, while the tool of the philosophical reader is Cartesian self-awareness. Even when Husserl comes to the problem of intersubjectivity—or when other phenomenologists like Scheler or Stein describe the phenomenon of "empathy"—it is *my* awareness of others as mine that is being investigated. Thus, for literature and phenomenology, both aim and process differ.

Is phenomenology, then, the same as introspective

psychology? Husserl is emphatic in rejecting such an identification. And in the *Emotions* Sartre, too, though he is by no means obsessed with method as was Husserl, emphasizes the distinction between phenomenology and phenomenological psychology. It is the latter, he says, that he is partly practising there, but with the aim of a phenomenology, not a psychology, of the emotions in mind. Psychology, even when introspective, is an empirical science. It asks the subject to report exactly his conscious state under certain contingent experimental conditions. Admittedly, the phenomenologist may sometimes seem to be doing the same thing. In his lectures on "First Philosophy," for example, Husserl keeps referring to the fact that if I eat santonin everything appears yellow. A simple empirical generalization, it seems, or, in a given instance, abstracting from the empirical conditions, a simple introspection: everything looks yellow. And the phenomenologist may indeed simply bracket the question of existence and describe in detail his consciousness at this very moment. But that would be in itself of little interest to any philosopher. What really interests him is the essential structure of, say, visual perception on the one hand (as distinguished from memory or imagination), and the color yellow on the other, as distinct from red or from a "bright" sound. Such insights he seeks, not by a simple description of this very experience here-now, as experienced here-now, but rather by the method already mentioned, that of "eidetic variation." In other words, he systematically imagines alterations in his present experience. If he does this carefully and well—and of course always within the "reduced" field of consciousness, with all extraneous "factual" questions held in abeyance—he will come to exercise the chief occupation of phenomenological research: the inspection of essences. It is in this method of eidetic variation that his skill chiefly resides, and it is a vast and systematically related range of essences, all within the field of consciousness itself, that he claims to grasp.

Note: these phenomenological essences are not Platonic forms, subsisting in some remote transcendent place; they are necessarily as they in fact appear *within experience itself.* The phenomenologist does not seek to explain the existence of material objects, for example, as Plato did by calling them "participants in some higher reality." Indeed, he refrains from asking *whether* they exist at all. He takes the experience of a material object, which he, like every one, has, and asks what kind of experience this is. Now, short of the sophistications of the physicist, material objects are of course experienced chiefly through perception; so he is asking on the one hand what perception is and on the other what perceptible objects are. Varying his actual (but reduced) experiences slightly and systematically in his imagination, he finds, for example, that perceiving essentially contains anticipations of gradual and coherently interrelated variations in the aspect of the perceived object from "different points of view." He also finds that for perceiving, unlike memory or imagination, these variations are never finished: there is always an aspect *to be perceived,* there is an open horizon of perceptibility inherent in the very nature of perception itself. Abstaining from speculation even in the rudimentary sense in which he accepts "on faith" that there is a world and he is in it—though of course noting the inherence of that primordial faith in his ordinary consciousness—he simply but precisely and exhaustively describes the essential structures of the experience itself as such.

To banish metaphysics, to stick to experience itself, was of course the aim of empiricism. But phenomenology is neither empirical in its method nor empiricist in its intent. Husserl himself, however, acknowledges the kinship: the great empiricists, he believes, were trying to describe the givens of consciousness, but they were too deeply committed to the speculations of the "new corpuscular philosophy" and too naïve about the relation of philosophical to experimental method to succeed in carrying out their program. Only in the twentieth century has philosophy acquired the necessary methodological self-consciousness to carry through what Locke or Hume had attempted—that is, the systematic investigation of the pure field of consciousness by consciousness itself with the aim of discovering the full range of its essential structures. It is description in this systematic and philosophical spirit that the phenomenologist undertakes.

It should be remarked parenthetically that eidetic description is, for Husserl, still only a way-station, though a vast and fruitful one, in the development of phenomenology as a whole. Ultimately, for him phenomenology seeks not only to describe the structures of consciousness, but to *found* them. Phenomenology, ultimately, is *transcendental* phenomenology, in which I see not only the manifold "objects" of experience and the manifold ways of experiencing them, but my own *constitution* of both these out of myself as "transcendental ego." Thus it seems that the "I" *almost* makes the world. This apparently idealist issue of phenomenology Sartre never accepted, and it need not concern us, at least not directly, in dealing with the influence of phenomenology on his philosophy. Insofar as Sartre pursues phenomenological method, it is the descriptive techniques of this tradition, not its transcendentalism, that he is following.

Let me illustrate this here by taking just one example, not the famous "look" in which I am caught at the keyhole, but a description which precedes it in Sartre's development of the experience of the Other. There is, he says, clearly a direct and immediate relation to the Other which occurs in my ordinary life. I can point to it, but to understand it I must examine more carefully its ordinary appearance. Very well. "I am in a public park," says Sartre:

> . . . Not far away there is a lawn and along the edge of that lawn there are benches. A man passes by those benches. I see this man; I apprehend him as an object and at the same time as a man.[2]

What does this mean? Sartre asks. What do I mean, when I affirm that this object is a man? This is plainly a philosophical question. What concerns Sartre, however, or any phenomenologist, is not the use of the word "man" or the sentence "There is a man," but the structure of the experience itself as such. Try eidetic variation: think of him as inanimate, as a puppet. In that case:

> . . . I should apply to him the categories which I ordinarily use to group temporal-spatial "things." That is, I should apprehend him as being "beside" the benches, two yards and twenty inches from the lawn, as exercising a certain pressure on the ground, etc. His relation with other objects would be of the purely additive type; this means that I could have him disappear without the relations of the other objects around him being perceptibly changed. In short, no new relation would appear through him between those things in my universe: grouped and synthesized from my point of view into instrumental complexes, they would from his disintegrate into multiplicities of indifferent relations.[3]

By contrast with this imagined variant—that is, seeing him as an object—to perceive him as a man is to grasp

"things" and the world in a different organization: ". . .
Perceiving him as a *man* . . . is not to apprehend an additive relation between the chair and him; it is to register an
organization *without distance* of the things in my universe
around that privileged object." [4] The original external relation of things to things remains, indeed, "the lawn remains two yards and twenty inches from him," but it is now
coupled with another, a distanceless relation: the lawn is
"also as a *lawn* bound to him in a relation which at once
both transcends distance and contains it." Thus:

> Instead of the two terms of the distance being indifferent,
> interchangeable, and in a reciprocal relation, the distance
> *is unfolded starting from* the man whom I see and *extend-
> ing up to* the lawn as the synthetic upsurge of a univocal
> relation. We are dealing with a relation which is without
> parts, given at one stroke, inside of which there unfolds a
> spatiality which is not my spatiality; for instead of a
> grouping *toward me* of the objects, there is now an orien-
> tation *which flees from me*.[5]

This is only the beginning of Sartre's analysis. He will assimilate this description and others to the ontological
thrust of his basic categories. But at crucial points in its
development, it is often on these descriptions of experienced structures that his argument rests. Even the ten-
dentious epithet "hemorrhage" applied to the Other's appearance in my world has its foundation in that
description in which suddenly my centeredness in my
own thoughts and perceptions runs off, loses its centrality,
as I am taken into his perspective and so lose hold of my
own. My own everyday life world, which lets the whole of
my surrounding field revolve around me as center, suddenly loses its ordinary structure. It flows away, immediately and unpleasantly, like uncontrollable bleeding. Or-

dinarily I control my world, just as ordinarily my body contains and bounds my blood. I don't usually notice this; indeed, I live in and by not noticing. But suddenly the center shifts: I run off into a mere peripheral item organized around another center, and by that very running off I see myself as usually the center of my own world of action— as in a hemorrhage, I feel by shocking contrast the "normal" containment of my circulating blood which has suddenly gone out of bounds. It is flowing off and I am flowing with it.

Admittedly, as my speculation on "the Other as hemorrhage" indicates, such phenomenological foundations are in Sartre's case quickly elaborated in a style controlled by his overriding dialectical interests. And, indeed, many of the sections of *Being and Nothingness* entitled "Phenomenology of—" are more dialectical than descriptive. Take one further instance. In the section on the past in the "Phenomenology of the Temporal Dimension" Sartre chooses as an example the statement: "Paul in 1920 was a student at the Polytechnic." [6] What is it, in terms of the structure of consciousness, to experience what is intended by such a statement, to be aware that something *was?* There is a phenomenological core to the inquiry, but the answer is given—and argued for—in a style as speculative as St. Augustine's. For Sartre does not just describe, he argues in terms of concepts like being and non-being, facticity, contingency, and of course the for-itself and in-itself dichotomy. He comes to grips with others' theories (in fact he starts from a reference to "theories of memory"), with James and Claparède, with Descartes, Bergson, and Heraclitus. Thus even what Sartre calls phenomenology, in his own philosophising, has been taken up into a highly speculative enterprise. The strictness of Husserl's descriptive method is not his style. Yet the phenomenological foundation is there. Sartre has adopted from phenomenology, not only the methodological thesis that philosophy must begin from and remain within the field of pure consciousness, not only the thesis of the intentionality of consciousness —the principle that every consciousness is *of* an object —but also the use of accurate description of moments or aspects of consciousness, combined with eidetic variation, as a philosophical tool.

Heidegger

So far, so good. But Sartre acknowledges indebtedness to two contemporary phenomenologists: Husserl and Heidegger. The two influences are hard to combine, and the way in which Sartre in fact combines them shows this to be the case. Heidegger was also Husserl's student, and *Being and Time* is still recognizably a phenomenological work, but with the very great difference that it has wholly renounced any Cartesian starting point. Methodological doubt, the *cogito,* consciousness as the medium of philosophy—all this Heidegger has systematically bypassed. Consciousness is not a category he needs or uses; the starting point is being-there—Dasein, the individual human being—in and with the world. Husserl found, in a philosophy of immanence, a clever way to evade the question of "the reality of the external world." Heidegger, starting with my being *in* the world, among things ready-to hand for my use, was shocked that the question was ever asked. I am *there* from the start.

Rejecting the Cartesian starting point of phenomenology, moreover, he has cast aside all the more emphatically the metaphysical remnants of the Cartesian universe that we have found Sartre retaining. Both on Cartesian dualism and Cartesian temporality, and even freedom (though more obscurely), his position is plainly and radically different from Sartre's.

Since he is working with *Dasein,* or human being, not with consciousness, Heidegger has in fact gone beyond—or behind—the kind of philosophising for which the mind-body problem arises. He does not, like Merleau-Ponty, try to wrestle with the problem of embodiment from a post-Cartesian point of view; he has simply made a detour around it. Now as far as body goes, this may be a serious omission. The relation of man to his body would seem to many philosophers as well as psychologists an essential problem for any account of human existence as such. It would seem to demand a place among what Heidegger calls the "Existentialen," the fundamental categories of my being as such. Be that as it may. The point here is simply that Heidegger is working within a single basic category, being-in-the-world; he is concerned neither with body as body nor with mind as mind. Sartre, on the contrary, while remaining a Cartesian, cannot start from being-in-the-world as a neutral third. He is a *cogito* man; he must start from consciousness. Yet he does make heavy use of the basic Heideggerian concept. How can he do so? He does it, I think, by combining being-in-the-world with Husserl's intentionality, and identifying consciousness of—an object, with my being in—a world. But to do that, to read being-in-the-world in the spirit of the *Meditations,* Descartes's and Husserl's, rather than of *Being and Time,* is precisely to break the world apart. Instead of a unified world-in-which-I-am, we have the for-itself (*pour-soi*) against the in-itself (*en-soi*). The "inness" of the "in," though captured sometimes along the way in some of Sartre's best descriptions, is always pushed aside again by the "over-against" of the detached consciousness confronting its Other.

Heideggerian *Dasein,* secondly, is essentially historical and belongs in its lived world precisely because it is historical. Heidegger's concept of temporality is, again, radically anti-Cartesian. Time for Heidegger, that is, "lived" or "existential" time, is the stretch of a personal history which thrusts itself into the future as what it is resolved to be, doing so out of its past—the past, at the same time, of the world into which it has been thrown—yet always drawn aside from this primary aim by its attraction to the present. *Dasein,* even inauthentic, everyday *Dasein, is* because it "temporalizes," living its past toward its future, despite its present, or, if it attains authentic existence, resolved to make its past truly inwardly historical in its assimilation of the authentic present to its destiny. Sartre, on the other hand, is in search of a Cartesian instant which, could he find it, would be, if temporal at all, withdrawn from the stretch of time.

And yet, as we shall see in more detail later, there is much that Sartre has taken over from Heidegger's account. Man has to make himself: he is his future as his possibility. Sartre's "project" is a translation of Heidegger's "resolve," which is directed to what is yet to come. But though making himself he is not his own foundation: he has to make himself out of his past, out of what contingency provides him with—these bodily endowments, this family, these neighbors, this society. All this is past, a translation, again: Sartre's concept of "facticity," of radical contingency, is, at first sight at least, but a Gallic rendering of Heidegger's "throwness," or *Geworfenheit,* which expresses the sedimentation of the past.

Yet even where Sartre speaks in temporal terms, the relation between the three temporal modalities is fundamentally different in the two philosophers. For Heidegger, the primary tense is future: it is his self-transcendence, his being-ahead of himself that primarily defines man. The synonym of transcendence is existentiality: for self-transcendence is fundamentally what existence *is*. So for Sartre, one may say, is the project: if there is for him any one most basic philosophical axiom, it is that man must make himself; he has to be in aspiration what he is not in fact, and that means, to *not* be what he is in his own projection of himself. But even for the project, the ideal is instantaneous self-creation, choice NOW. And in the light of this ideal, temporalization is the *loss* of the instant. It is flight. So he describes it, again and again. The moment of the pre-reflective *cogito,* the moment of pure reflection, difficult, if not impossible, of attainment: these moments of conscious being are what I forever flee. I escape from self-making into a past to which I gave a false substantiality: it is my history, my ego, as a thing. I escape into the future, into an imagined—and therefore nihilating—vision of what I am not. Sartre does indeed borrow much from Heidegger on temporality. But from all his excursions into Daseins-analysis he is pulled back, every time, by the lure of the instant. Except for dread, which is momentary— which is perhaps the only true instant I might, with luck, achieve—he sees the span of time, in Heidegger's terms the original structure of time, in the last analysis as a falling off, an escape from what ideally ought to be into what (alas) is. From the thought of the Cartesian pure self-conscious moment he darts out as far as it will let him in the direction of Heideggerian being-in-the-world, only to be pulled back, time and again, to the center that holds him fast. He is, to use a favorite word of his own, haunted by the instant. The primacy of time as stretching and stretched eludes him.

In the case of freedom the situation is more difficult to disentangle. For one thing, Sartre's concept of freedom is Cartesian through and through. Cartesian freedom is not just there as ideal, hovering over his thought, so to speak; freedom for him is Cartesian freedom, substantively, to its very core. And for another thing, freedom explicitly appears, in *Being and Time,* only in the description of authentic existence, as "Freedom to Death." But this concept of Being to Death is one that Sartre emphatically rejects. (My death *is* something to others rather than to me.) It is the description of being-in-the-world at the everyday level that Sartre seems chiefly to follow, and this is not, explicitly at least, an analysis in terms of freedom as such. Nor does Sartre's use of "freedom" resemble its development in Heidegger's "On *the Essence of Ground"* where it is a central concept. On the contrary, Heidegger has there begun to make more explicit the rooting of human being in Being, in this case through an identification of freedom and "ground," a relation which, though already present in *Sein und Zeit,* has come more and more to dominate much of his later work. Such a conception of being Sartre would certainly reject.

Nevertheless, the portrait of the for-itself, free yet caught by facticity, making itself yet always out there in the world, plainly derives much from Heidegger's analysis of human being. If the bone structure of Sartrean freedom is Cartesian, much of the physiognomy bears a Heideggerian stamp. First, as I have already pointed out, Sartre's concept of man's self-making is conceived in terms that run closely parallel to Heidegger's. Not that the "project" *really* is Heidegger's "resolve." The being-in-the-world of *Being and Nothingness* is a very different condition from that of *Being and Time.* As we have already seen, even the "in" is different. So is the world: primarily, it is the inertial, the pure exteriority of classical physics. The "things ready to hand" which are the "nearest things to me" in Heidegger's version have, in Sartre's case, to be derived by a complicated argument revealing first my body, then the Other, and finally the human world as a set of techniques which I can use. Again, Descartes's *thinking mind* and *extended matter,* if de-substantialized, remain to haunt, and dichotomize, the world. But many of the single concepts, though woven into a characteristically Sartrean pattern, are, as we have seen, certainly derivative from *Being and Time.*

Sartre follows Heidegger, moreover, in distinguishing an inauthentic from an authentic style of existence—in distinguishing, in other words, our fundamental freedom from the enslavement to which we (freely) bind ourselves in our ordinary lives. The insistence that at one and the same time we have as free beings to make ourselves, and invariably fail to do so, is one of the principal themes of what is usually called existentialism, and its outstanding recent expositors have been precisely Heidegger and Sartre. Of course here, too, there are differences. For example, in Heidegger's account, "forfeiture," my loss in the "they," is inescapable. Even the rare authentic individual cannot escape it. Sartre's bad faith, on the other hand, would, one gathers, be left behind by the true self-creator, could such a one arise. And authenticity itself has a different goal: it is being to death in the one case, and in the other the pure choice of myself. Dread, the dizzying sense of nothingness, has the same function for both philosophers: it is the unique experience which may raise to true freedom him who faces it. But, again, its object is different: for Heidegger, my own finitude, my annihilation in death; for Sartre, the non-being, the emptiness of the "self" I have to make.

How then can we sum up the relation of Sartre to Heidegger? Best, perhaps, in terms of Sartre's relation to

Descartes and Husserl as well. Fundamentally Cartesian in sympathy and starting-point, Sartre has taken the turn to intentionality, from *cogito* to *cogitiatio,* and within the medium of consciousness, wholly alien to Heidegger's own thought, has interjected a number of central Heideggerian themes. They are still recognizable, yet, transposed into consciousness, also altered, if not in their appearance, then in their ontological import.

Such an interweaving of disparate themes could be achieved, however, only with philosophical tools alien to phenomenology itself. They have to be treated dialectically. And indeed it is the dialectical strand in Sartre's thinking, derived from a different tradition, that carries his argument even in *Being and Nothingness* and has since come more and more to dominate his thought. It is to that other line of influence that we must turn before we can see how the two principal inheritances are worked together in *Being and Nothingness* itself and later (though with a very different balance of ingredients) in the *Critique.*

chapter three: sartre and his predecessors

II. the dialecticians

dialectic

Being and Nothingness
bears the subtitle *An Essay on
Phenomenological Ontology*. Phenomenology as such, however, at least in Husserl's sense, stringently abstains from ontological
inquiry. The "things themselves" it seeks to describe
are "things" as consciously experienced; their "being" be-

yond or before the *epoché* is not in question. To become ontology—an inquiry into being—philosophical reflection must move beyond description; the philosopher must question what he sees about its being. To put such a question would be inappropriate to a method of pure description. Admittedly, Heidegger began as a phenomenologist, yet his philosophizing is directed, first and last, to "the question of being"; indeed, he asks about human being only because this is the only being for whom its being is in question. But what Heidegger starts from, as we have seen, is not the "data" of pure consciousness; it is being-in-the-world that is the medium of his inquiry. And being-in-the-world already entails an "understanding of being" which gives the ontologist matter to look at in what might still appear a quasi-phenomenological fashion. If one starts, like Sartre, with the *cogito,* however, no such recourse is available. To move from the *cogito* to the question of being, one must move from description to some other style of philosophical inquiry.

The means Sartre has chosen for this movement is dialectical. Indeed, in the *Critique,* as its title implies, the dialectical method has come to dominate his thought. The whole argument of that book is in fact a defense of "dialectical reason" and an attack on its contrary, "analytical reason," as the possible tool of social and political understanding. But even in *Being and Nothingness* it is the admixture of dialectic with description—or, better, the weaving of description into a dialectical argument—that characterizes the peculiar mode of Sartrian phenomenology. I have already given an example of this process in the case of Sartre's "phenomenological" study of the past. Now let us see if we can establish at least approximately what "dialectic" consists in, first in general—at least in post-Kantian philosophy—and then in the particular case of Sartre in so far as his method is related to that of his predecessors, especially to Hegel, the founder and greatest practitioner of this method of modern philosophy, and through him to his two great critics (and followers), Kierkegaard and Marx.

Hegelian dialectic, like phenomenology, though it came a century earlier, was meant to liberate philosophy. Phenomenology was intended to take us back to the things themselves, to a broader vision of the content and activities of conscious life than conventional methods or the prejudices of traditional metaphysics and epistemology had permitted. Nineteenth-century dialectic had also undertaken a liberating return—not in the first instance to things, but to thought. Where phenomenology was to seek intellectual vision, dialectic had attempted to enter into the life of thought itself in its inmost and living development. Kierkegaard complained of Hegelian dialectic that the System was never finished. At its best, it was not meant to be. It was Thought itself as alive, as moving, not as completed, even in the profoundest insight. Dialectic is a process, not a state; it is a movement of concepts. Yet it is not the movement of proof. Dialectic is not, in the logician's sense, logic. A logical argument is always equivalent to the statements "A is A" or "Not both A and non-A." If it contains more than this tautology, it is invalid. For in strict logic one can elicit from the premises of an argument only what is already contained in them. But dialectic is the *development* of concepts: they grow under the philosopher's touch; at the end of his reflection they are not what they seemed to be at first—and yet they are also more than they seemed to be.

That may sound like nonsense. Surely, it may be objected, a concept must be precisely defined. What follows from it, follows, and what doesn't, doesn't. If one fails to admit such rules of logic, not only does one talk nonsense, one cannot talk at all. Of course, in fact "one's mind wanders"; one starts out thinking about one thing and is "reminded" of another. I look at the pampas grass in my garden and am reminded of the pampas grass staff carried by the leader of the "vizards" at an Irish Halloween. But this is a purely contingent and external conjunction. Experience, atomic in its elements, produces by the "gentle force of association" (or, in modern terms, "conditioning") the conjunction of disparate contents. One can hardly call this a "concept" "developing". Pampas grass is pampas grass, wherever I happen to have seen it or to whatever use it happens to be put. Now it must indeed be admitted that ordinary logic is uniquely binding; to abandon it altogether would mean to abandon discourse of any reasonable kind. And it must also be admitted that experience often ranges externally and associatively over logically stable and disparate units. But are the units we conjoin in thinking really atomistic in their nature, and is the movement of joining them exclusively associative in its procedure? It seems that to get somewhere, at least somewhere new and interesting, thought must move in a fashion somehow different from this.

Here I am, for example, thinking about dialectic. I have to write a chapter about its influence on Sartre. Every time I start a chapter, there is blank paper and myself, and I can't imagine what led me to think I could fill it in with anything that makes sense. I had an outline in mind for the whole book, but each time I begin on a part of it there seems to be next to nothing there. When I think of Hegelian dialectic, in particular, I think first (by association if you like) of formulae like "substance must become subject," which, I must confess, means to me nothing or worse than nothing: it means a lot of word-juggling and pretended system-building. But then I think of the concept of a growth of thought, and I wonder if this process of writing isn't, on a small scale, an instance of dialectic in that sense. When I tried, for example, in the preceding chapter, to explain the difference between a phenomenological and a literary description of consciousness, I found, in talking about the relative weight of the imaginative and intellectual components, that there was also a difference between participation in the one case and re-enactment in the other. I hadn't known that before; my concept of phenomenological description had developed. And here I am, it seems, hoping to go through the same process with "dialectic." So my thinking seems to instantiate the Hegelian conception: the concept I am thinking about develops as I think about it in ways I hadn't dreamed of. Before this the Hegelian method had always seemed to me almost a pure fraud; now I find that there is something it's about—namely, the very process I am going through in trying to understand it. Perhaps, then, the best model for Hegelian dialectic is heuristic: thought in search of what it does not yet know. Formal, logical proof is a device to encase thought *found:* when we know what we have and want to find it an elegant dress. Even in mathematics there is that duality. The great German mathematician Gauss is said to have remarked that he first discovered a theorem and then tried to prove it. And the most famous account of discovery, of the search for the unknown, is by the mathematician Henri Poincaré. But if there is a growth of thought even in the most formal science, how much more must this be so for philosophical reflection. One lets a concept germinate; it flowers, not as some seed catalogue had promised, but surprisingly. It is this notion of a self-unfolding, a self-development of thought that forms the core—at least to non-Hegelians, the intelligible core—of the dialectical method. Instead of starting at the outset with precisely defined concepts, one starts with a concept and watches it develop, engages oneself in its development, so that the concept itself is richer at the close of one's inquiry than it appeared at the beginning. Dialectical argument in philosophy, then, is (minimally) argument in which the concepts themselves are transformed as the argument proceeds.

Let me give an example of this from the history of philosophy. Immanuel Kant was a philosopher who certainly did not consider himself a dialectical thinker. For Kant, "dialectic" means fallacious argument; the Dialectic of Pure Reason for him is a set of invalid speculative arguments which Reason inevitably but unsuccessfully develops. Yet as the British Hegelian Edward Caird demonstrated, Kant's *Critique of Pure Reason* is itself a dialectical work in the sense I have just suggested. This is clearly so, for example, in Kant's treatment of "space" and "time." These two concepts first occur, in the Aesthetic, as the twin forms of all appearance: all outer sense is spatial, while all sense, outer and inner, is temporal. In the Analytic, however, this symmetry is broken. In his analysis of the activity of mind in organizing (or having organized) experience, Kant gives time first place as that from which the argument proceeds. Taking subjective temporal experience as the minimal starting point, he shows that it is the categorial rule-giving of the mind, ultimately held together by the fact that I *could* unite all my experience by an "I think," which has always already transformed such a pure subjective flow of "experience" into the experience of objects: of an organized nature in objective space and time. Thus time as subjective is the minimal starting point, and the objective space-time of nature the issue of the argument. Temporality and spatiality themselves have developed from the parallelism of the Aesthetic to their roles as principium and issue respectively of the Analytic. And of course time itself develops in the Analytic also: from the purely inner-sense time of the Subjective Deduction through the homogeneous temporal patterns of the Schematism to the objective time that is produced as correlate of space in the Objective Deduction and the Principles. Any argument whose concepts thus develop as it proceeds is dialectical in the sense we have been considering here.

Nevertheless, this is a minimal concept of dialectic as Hegelians intend it. For if Kant's method is one of "isolation," this means that the whole panorama was there from the beginning. Experience is structured as the whole *Critique* finds it to be. If our understanding develops as we follow its argument, the structure of experience was always already there, eternally, as it is and as we are coming to see it. Hegelian dialectic is much more radical than this. For Hegel insists that, if thought develops, its object too develops, and by the very same process. Or if it doesn't, it's an inferior object, fit only for the maneuvers of ordinary logic, not for philosophy. In real conceptual thought, Hegel insists, the "firm ground" that ordinary (logical) reasoning possesses in the ordinary logical subject at rest "begins to sway," and this swaying movement itself "becomes the object of thought." [1] Thus the very development of thought, Hegel alleges, is at the same time the development of its object—or better, perhaps, the development of thought is thought's own object.

But is this so? Can one identify thinking and what it is the thinking of, and say that the development of thought is also the development of what the thought is thought of? The concept of the atom, for example, has developed almost out of recognition since its inception in Ancient

Greece with Leucippus and Democritus. But whatever the foundation in nature, which, through atomism, man has been seeking to understand, *that* surely is still the same. Even if nature itself is basically process, its development is not to be identified with the development of our own conception of it. However theory-laden scientific concepts, laws, and principles may be, and however deeply theories are influenced by the *Zeitgeist* of a given discipline in a given period, what such concepts, laws, and principles aim at is an understanding of something that transcends the act of understanding, of something that lies beyond the theory's understanding of it. Scientific knowledge has often been equated with prediction and truth with verifiability. That would perhaps be a truncated Hegelian concept, for if the truth of a matter is what we will be able to verify about it, then the object (what is known) does develop with the subject—in this case, the experimental scientist. But that is precisely what science does not do. It seeks to find out how things work, not how scientists work. Even a pragmatic concept of truth, when carefully formulated, like C. S. Peirce's, makes it plain that what knowledge (at least natural knowledge) is after is not prediction for prediction's sake, but the indefinite range of unforeseeable future consequences which are the mark of the real. Our thoughts *about* a natural phenomenon may develop indefinitely, but the phenomenon itself always outruns our thinking about it; the two are never identical, the development of the thinking is never identical with the development, in nature, of what it is the thinking about.

Now up to a point—or beyond a certain point, perhaps—I think Hegel would have had to admit this. Whatever his merits in other fields, that is why he is such a superficial philosopher of nature. But what if we are thinking about experience itself rather than about its external objects? Then, surely, our very experience is transformed by our thinking about it. Experience reflected on can never again be naïve; it has been transformed by my thought about it. It is the experience it was—it is presented in memory, or at least leaves its "traces" in my life history, even if not remembered. But it has also irrevocably vanished; I can never, having reflected, have that non-reflective immediate experience again. Yet at the same time, since it has acquired a new dimension through my reflection, my experience has also been enriched. That is in fact the chief movement of Hegelian dialectic, embodied in the ambiguity of the German *"aufheben":* a given reality is cancelled, yet preserved and elevated to a higher level of reflection. And for the individual's experience there seems, at least with respect to the relation of naïve to reflective experience, to be something in it.

The range of Hegelian dialectic, however, far outruns individual consciousness. It is humanity, not the schoolmaster of Jena or even the Berlin professor, whose "development" Hegel claims to be re-creating. In his *Logic,* the systematic crown of the Dialectic, he even claims to be re-creating "the thoughts of God before creation." Is this an empty boast, or is there really a content in Hegel's work to match this claim? It is sometimes said that the merit of Hegel is in fact the rich empirical content of his writing. Because of the very generality of his fundamental concepts he can fill them in with a mosaic of what would now count as sociology or psychology much more illuminating than the narrow philosophy of the Enlightenment could provide. And the movement of the dialectic, exhibiting the manifold phases of a given kind of experience, may prove applicable when one turns from it to the real world to find instances of the structures one has been expounding. Sometimes, on the other hand, it is history that Hegel is said to illuminate most profoundly: the development of "the Western mind" from Greece through Rome and Christianity, to the French Revolution. Now admittedly all this may indeed be mined out of Hegel's work. Yet his own claim, and that of his chief philosophical followers, has nevertheless been more dogmatic. It is not only the empirical or historical, but the eternal unfolding of Being itself as absolute mind, that he constantly insists on as the ontological foundation of his method. One ought not to save him for common sense by ignoring entirely his own claim.

In any case, it is Sartre's debt to the dialecticians, not "dialectic" as such, that interests us here. And what Sartre takes over from Hegel is not the empirical content of his work, though he sometimes treats of some of it, nor his insight into history; what Sartre adopts from Hegel goes much deeper than any particular bits of information or ways of classifying them. Admittedly, the Hegelian influence comes relatively late in Sartre's career, but it goes deep. Sartre is Hegelian, and has become increasingly so, first in his style of philosophizing, in the way he uses concepts. Further, the central concepts he uses both in *Being and Nothingness* and in the *Critique,* also belong, if not to Hegel, then certainly to the German idealist tradition. And finally, however emphatically he may claim to reject systematizing speculation in general and idealist systems in particular, there is also something in Hegel's ontology itself that Sartre retains. Let us see if we can sort out these three aspects of his debt, focusing chiefly on *Being and Nothingness,* but with an occasional glance at the *Critique* for confirmation or contrast.

Sartre and Hegel

First, his method. The structure of Sartre's argument, in both his major philosophical works, *Being and Nothingness* and the *Critique,* is dialectical in the minimal sense described above. He opens up avenues along which he can let his basic concepts move—in a movement which is also to alter them, so that they become, at the end of the argument, different and richer than they were at the beginning. He does not (at least in *Being and Nothingness*) set up premises from which to draw correct logical conclusions; instead he sets up starting points from which to move to surprising, even contradictory, positions, which nevertheless combine with what precedes to take him along to still further surprising combinations. Granted, again, even the most inspired dialectician cannot abandon ordinary logic; if he did, he could not argue anything in any style. But "ordinary logic," for the dialectician, is an uninteresting, dead skeleton of thought. It is thought's growth that interests him.

Compare, for example, Sartre's ontological argument, proving the existence of Being in itself, with the traditional one, proving the existence of God. The most perfect being, St. Anselm said, must exist. For suppose you think of a most perfect being which does not exist. Non-existence is an imperfection, a lack; so this is not the most perfect being: you can think of a more perfect being —the one who does exist. The argument is, on the face of it, a *reductio ad absurdum.* A non-existent most perfect being is a non-perfect most perfect being; therefore the very concept "most perfect being" already entails the existence of the entity of which it is the concept. Now of course it has often been argued—either against Anselm or even for him (in the first instance by Anselm himself in his reply to Gaunilon)—that this is no "argument," but the elucidation by one of the faithful of his faith. If I did not believe in God as the real, existent, most perfect being, I could not work the argument. But that (*contra* Kant) is just what makes it a *good* argument, not a bad one. I, the believer, am eliciting, in logical style, the implications of the proposition: there is God. The non-believer cannot follow my argument, not because it does not follow from my assertion, but because he has not made the assertion. Indeed, he asserts its contradictory; so how could he possibly draw the same conclusion? The argument may be a *petitio principii,* but it is so only in the sense in which all sound arguments contain in their premises what will follow in the conclusion.

Now look at Sartre's ontological argument (or a very free paraphrase of it). His starting point is consciousness, here-now, as the consciousness it is. But consciousness *is* not simply; it is *"for-itself,"* that is, aware of itself. There is a doubleness, a reflexivity, about consciousness. The lawn in the park is just there, the man passing by it is there too, but by knowing he is there he has both doubled its being there and separated himself from it: he *could* be elsewhere. And yet it is not really himself the man passing by is (thetically) aware of. What he is aware of is that, strolling through the park, he is on his way home. Consciousness, Sartre has learned from Husserl, is never simply of itself, but of something which it is not. Thus the very reality of the man passing by, as the reality of a consciousness, is for-itself *as* directed toward what is not for-itself—toward the simple reality, the "being in-itself," of the lawn, the park, the apartment over beyond the park that he is walking *toward*. The for-itself in its very nature as for-itself points to the in-itself. Thus if we understand the for-itself, if we really think about *its* nature, we are directed from it to the in-itself, to its essential target. But the for-itself does not *contain* the in-itself, as a premise contains its conclusion, as God (who, if He is, is in—and for—Himself) contains His own existence. No: we move, we are moved, from the for-itself *to* the in-itself, whose otherness, whose negation, the for-itself is. The man is not the lawn; as a conscious being he is the being who makes the lawn, who makes the park, the-stretch-to-be-traveled between himself and home. It may *be* as the pleasant green sward that he can stroll across before he has to trudge the less pleasantly resilient pavement; it may *be* as the short-cut he can take to hurry belatedly to an important rendez-vous. In either case, indeed in any case, it is what he takes it for; and yet however he takes it, however he possesses it, he takes it as what is not himself—at leisure or in haste, contentedly or nervously—but the space he has to cross to get where he is going, and he is the consciousness he is as its other, as the need to transcend it, to get to the other side. Thus the for-itself refers us away from itself to the in-itself as its necessary other, the not-for-itself to which, in its being as for-itself, it is necessarily directed.

Now, admittedly, in this to-and-fro movement from consciousness to its contrary, from for-itself to in-itself, as Sartre calls it, we already have, in little, the whole argument of *Being and Nothingness.* In this sense one could say that Sartre, like any philosopher, is only going to elicit from his premises what is already contained in them. And even in the *Critique,* as we shall see, though he has dropped the concepts "for-itself" and "in-itself" as basic categories, he is laboring deviously and painfully to elicit a social theory from the same premises from which he had been arguing in the earlier work. But the premises themselves, I think it is fair to say, are clearly dialectical. For it is the contradiction between consciousness and nature, between for-itself and in-itself, that makes the whole thing work. The logical use of contradiction, as in Anselm's argument, is to eliminate an impossible—because a self-contradictory—position, and so, indirectly, to support the position one wishes to defend. But in dialectical argument it is "contradiction"—or at least contrariety—that makes a new position possible: thought takes a position, finds it "contradicting" itself, takes a new position modifying, and thus in a sense "denying," the first, a position which, opening onto a new "denial," leads to a new position, and so on. Only by seeing the second position as "contradicting" the first and by assimilating it as a new position are we enabled to move at all. In this sense, illogical though it may sound, dialectical argument uses contradiction, not indirectly, through the *reductio,* but directly, as the very engine of its movement. It is not just any statement of what there is, any set of primitive propositions, from which Sartre is seeking to deduce first his theory of the individual and later of society. It is the living relation of intentionality to its object, the relation of consciousness to what it is consciousness of, which is not what it is and is what it is not: it is this relation, vexing and in appearance contradictory, yet capable of application to every field of conscious life, that Sartre is exploring and developing— if in different modes, as well as with different content—in both his major works.

In *Being and Nothingness,* as we have seen, phenomenological descriptions—Pierre not in the café, the girl "innocently" letting a would-be lover hold her hand, the exhausted hiker throwing down his rücksack—are the perches, so to speak, from which the flight of the argument takes wing. The description is opened out so that a movement of concepts develops from it. Pierre's absence haunts the café: it is not just this collection of faces and table and waiters and chit-chat, it *is*—where Pierre is not. In the scene itself the looseness from what is, the otherness than being, that marks the human condition becomes apparent to us. One may wonder, perhaps, what would have happened if Pierre had been there. Would we have had a plenum of being and so have missed the move to otherness which makes the argument go? No, of course not. Pierre would have failed me somehow. He would have denied the favor I had come to beg of him; or he would have aged since our last meeting twenty years ago. Somehow Pierre-not-being-my-idea-of-Pierre would have haunted our meeting, even had we met. But the descriptions Sartre uses are nevertheless characteristically those that will most effectively make the ferment of contradiction work. And similarly, his arguments work by finding contradiction as their outcome. Thus out of the move to being as what consciousness is directed to, he raises the question of the question—and the question, it appears, is that to which one may obtain a negative reply. I seek, and may not find. Surely sometimes I seek and find. But such a quietus of consciousness is not what would help dialectic, and especially Sartrean dialectic, on its course. The to-and-fro of position and negation is what makes the argument move, from start to finish.

So far I have been trying to characterize Sartre's method as dialectical; but inevitably the concepts he is working with have also already been exhibiting their characteristically Hegelian stamp. The overall movement of Hegelian dialectic is from mere being, in-itself, through consciousness, for-itself, to what Hegel considers the ultimate ground of all reality—the Concept as Being-in-and-for-itself. Sartre, good Cartesian as he is, begins with consciousness, the for-itself, but is directed by Husserl to its target, which, in Hegelian fashion, he describes as sheer being, as the in-itself. The for-itself-in-itself is then what his for-itself is in search of. Being in the mode of what is other than being, it longs to be simply, or rather to be what it is—that is, to be for-itself and so not to be simply, and yet to be for-itself as being is, as being pure and simple. The major Hegelian concepts, therefore, take on a new movement and lead us to a different, and much less self-satisfied, finale. But they are the very same Hegelian counters, though used in a different context and with a different intent.

Indeed, the very concepts "Being" and "Nothingness," as Sartre uses them, are Hegelian. Compare, for example, in its very broadest outlines, the ontology of Sartre's *Being and Nothingness* with that of Heidegger in *Being and Time*. Both works are concerned with Being; both works make a great deal of Nothing or of a sense of Nothingness—of what Sartre calls nihilation—as somehow essential to human life. And both works are phenomenological: they seek to describe the essential structures of human existence as being-in-the-world. For Heidegger, however, Being is the framework of the investigation from the very start, temporality is discovered as its essence, nothing as the end—in death—to which its temporality must ultimately relate. In one phase of the work after another, he is recurrently boring into some part of a total structure which is always already there from the start. Sartre, on the other hand, uses Nothingness to open up Being: it is Nihilation that makes the for-itself the being it is—namely, the being that has to be what it is not and not be what it is. Instead of digging down into *Dasein,* as Heidegger does to uncover the temporality on which it has always already rested, a temporality which had been half seen in the inadequate understanding of Being characteristic of the human manner of being in the world,

Sartre takes a pair of contraries, Being and Nothingness or Being and non-Being, and lets them work on one another to show us the kind of being we have to be. Being and time are not dialectical opposites; far from it. Time, for Heidegger, is the inmost sense of being; "nothing" serves, through dread, as agency to reveal that truth. "Being" and "Nothingness," on the other hand, are the dialectical contraries par excellence: the first pair of the whole Hegelian system, out of which all else is made to grow. It is temporality, indeed, that comes between, in this case, as my consciousness flees its own nothingness, trying vainly to find a solider being in the pseudo-substantiality of my past or the deceptive promise of my future. Thus though Sartre calls his work "phenomenological ontology," that description applies more clearly to Heidegger's magnum opus, while in Sartre's case even the phenomenological aspect is in large part a means of access to an argument that is Hegelian, not only in method, but also in the conceptual apparatus with which it works.

In the *Critique,* moreover, Hegelian concepts as well as Hegelian method have become even more strikingly dominant. The phenomenological and even the long historical descriptions are ruthlessly assimilated into a series of moves with concepts like necessity, intelligibility, alienation: concepts that have characterized modern dialectical philosophy from Hegel to the present. We shall see more of these concepts when we examine the arguments of both books. But the point here is simply this: even the "Being" of Heidegger's and Sartre's titles differs profoundly, precisely through the Hegelian character of the latter. Heidegger's "Being" is typically his own— though allegedly Parmenidean, Nietzschean, or what you will, it is decidedly not Hegelian. It is not the opening counter in the series of dialectical moves, but the all-en-closing medium, the Being through which all beings are. Sartre's "Being" *is* Hegelian: the other-than Non-Being in relation to which the Being of human being in its very non-being, in its alienation from being, is to be exposed.

If Sartre's chief concepts are Hegelian, moreover, so, in a sense, is the ontology that he builds with them. Of course he is not, like Hegel, an "absolute idealist," or so he vigorously insists. Yet there are remnants in his thought even of this: both of the "absoluteness" of Hegelian thought and of its idealism, the former in both *Being and Nothingness* and the *Critique,* the latter chiefly in the argument of the later work.

First, as to Hegelian "absolutism," or the hope of an all-inclusive issue of philosophy in identity with an all-inclusive reality: this issue Sartre admittedly despairs of, yet, as a desideratum, it dominates his thought. In *Being and Nothingness* man wants to become God, and fails. In the *Critique* Sartre tries to lay the groundwork for understanding history, and that would mean, he makes plain, to understand it as a *whole:* as totalization. By why, if I seek anything—and of course, as human, I do—must I seek *absolute* Being? Why, to understand history, must I understand it *all?* Only the spirit of Hegel—and the Spirit of Hegel, the Absolute Mind which all reality imperfectly reveals—could give the answer. That spirit—of needing totality, even while admitting our inability to achieve it—plainly broods over Sartre's work.

But what about Hegel's idealism? This, surely, Sartre has relentlessly abandoned. In terms of *Being and Nothingness,* the for-itself is always out there—in the world, with the in-itself, as its negation to be sure, but with no content other than that negation. In that sense—as what is there to not be—it is the in-itself that makes the for-itself be what it is not. Even if, as we shall see, my body is known as all consciousness, it works the other way too; my consciousness, as to its content, is all body. And in terms of the *Critique:* well, Sartre is allegedly a Marxist. The dialectic is material; there is no reality except the existent, practical, biological organism, and the non-living inert matter in which it finds, and through which it tries to fulfill, its material needs.

Yet there is an idealistic aspect to both arguments, more emphatically (if paradoxically) in the explicitly "Marxist" one. Body comes in late in *Being and Nothingness,* not as lived, but as known, as the explicit object of knowledge. It is consciousness that is both starting place and framework of the whole; consciousness in its quintessential being as choice, as agency, is firmly opposed to its other: passivity, exteriority, or body. Even the emotions, as we have noted in Sartre's early treatise on that subject, and as is still the case in the account of *Being and Nothingness,* are not "bodily passions" invading consciousness, but modes of choice, magical devices of consciousness for acting on the world. Consciousness is no longer substance, as for Descartes, acting, and sometimes being acted on by, that other substance, body, to which it is so strangely and closely allied. Consciousness is pure act, always act, it never stops acting: we are "condemned to be free." And so Hegel is vindicated. Substance has become subject with a vengeance.

In the *Critique,* moreover, the whole point of the argument is to prove that there *is* a dialectic which can be understood in history: and that means not just a movement of class-antagonisms over and above the people who suffer from this movement. It means a movement in which the "practical organisms" engaged in action and in suffering understand, out of and in their own actions, the movements of which they form part. What Sartre claims to object to in Marxism is that it leaves out of its dialectic the individual existent, the freely self-chosen project of the for-itself. But what he really seems to be objecting to as the argument proceeds is the alleged failure of Marxism to make dialectical necessity "intelligible"—and that seems to mean, for him, a failure to identify dialectical processes with the self-understanding of the agents who shape them and are shaped by them. A process that is truly dialectical must be intelligible. But what does it mean to be intelligible? To be intelligible must mean to be of the nature of reason; it must be the understanding of itself by itself. Substance, again, becomes subject: only the reflective coalescence of the material happening with its conscious, its ideal meaning, makes it what it really is. However grounded in matter, in need, in scarcity, in the facts of economic and political life, this is still idealism. In its ontological import, as well as in important aspects of its method and in the provenance and meaning of its central concepts, Sartre's philosophy owes to the Hegelian at least as much as it does to the phenomenological tradition.

Sartre and Kierkegaard

With this very sketchy account of his relation to Hegel, however, we have not finished with Sartre's debt to the Hegelians. We must take account of his debt to Kierkegaard and Marx, Hegel's two greatest nineteenth-century critics. For Sartre's dialectic uniquely combines themes from all three.

The kinship of Sartre's philosophy with Kierkegaard's is obvious, and has been much discussed. Kierkegaard was the first "existentialist"; Sartre is the greatest latter-day "existentialist." True, the label was thrust on Sartre, but he has accepted and even adopted it. Kierkegaard, finding in Hegel's dialectic an empty play with ideas, had insisted that what matters is the dialectic, not of essence, but of existence—and by this he meant human, indeed, subjective, existence. Taking dialectic not only in its methodological, but also in its ontological aspect, he urged his reader to plunge into the real development, not of some "Absolute," but of his living, suffering self. And a century later Sartre remarks: ". . . we ought to oppose to Hegel Kierkegaard, who represents the claims of the individual as such." [2] The emphasis on dread (*angoisse*), moreover, as liberating mood, stems, historically, through Heidegger from Kierkegaard. True, in each of the three cases the situation that arouses dread is different. For Kierkegaard, dread is of my nothingness before my infinite Maker; for Heidegger, dread is of my coming nothingness in death; for Sartre, it is of my total responsibility for my own choice of myself, which, as nihilism, rests on—nothing. Yet dread in each case is somehow dread of nothing and it is dread in each case that can uniquely awaken the individual to his own true resolve.

All that is by now commonplace. Yet to speak of a major "influence" here seems questionable. That the first dialectic of the individual is Kierkegaard's is not to be denied, and Sartre acknowledges this priority. But all the influences that have been dealt with so far—Descartes's, Husserl's, Heidegger's, and Hegel's—form essential and inextricable strands of Sartre's thought. He has assimilated their thinking, or aspects of it, as deeply as he had assimilated in imagination the daring of his childhood heroes. His kinship with Kierkegaard, however, seems to me in the last analysis rather a parallelism than an influence. The individual in search of himself, finding himself, in that search, before an abyss of nothingness: that is, after all, the characteristic of our time. Its source could be said to be Nietzsche as much as Kierkegaard, or Dostoyevsky as well as a host of lesser literary figures. Or, as Raymond Aron does, one could refer it to Pascal, substituting the absence of God for God. Admittedly, Sartre not only refers to Kierkegaard in this connection, but also acknowledges the influence, if not of Kierkegaard directly, at least of Jean Wahl's existentialism. And at the beginning of his *Questions de Méthode* he treats briefly of Kierkegaard's existentialism in contrast to that of others, such as Jaspers. Yet one cannot imagine Sartre really steeped in the reading of Kierkegaard as one is sure that he has steeped himself in the writings of his other sources. The two thinkers differ too extremely both in interest and in philosophical style.

Kierkegaard considered himself primarily—as Louis Mackay has ably argued—"a kind of poet," one who uses philosophy for poetic ends.[3] Sartre, we have seen, is certainly not a poet, and, at least as we are considering him here, he is not even primarily an imaginative prose writer. He is a philosopher who has sometimes cast his arguments in fictional or dramatic form. True, both men have produced a corpus of literary-philosophical works which form in each case a coherent whole. But to understand what Sartre has to say as philosopher we can use the tools of philosophy: the conventional knowledge of the history of thought, imaginative re-enactment of philosophical description, conceptual participation in the course of dialectical argument. To understand what Kierkegaard has to say, except in a few sections of his most "philosophical" writings, in particular the *Philosophical Bits* and *Unscientific Postscript,* we have to read him as we would a poet: lingering in his moods, revelling in his language, his wit and humor, his irony.

Moreover, Kierkegaard is a religious poet, while

Sartre's philosophy is programmatically atheistic. Kierkegaardian dread stems from the individual's dizzying awareness of his distance from the Maker to whom he owes his very Being. The Sartrean individual is utterly alone, wholly responsible, making himself as the negation of a barren field of being, in itself wholly devoid of meaning, or even, in its inertia, of power. When the Sartrean for-itself is threatened, moreover, it is primarily by the Other, who rises up as an alternative center of existence. Kierkegaard, it seems, never really noticed the human Other, even as Hell. It is Abraham confronting God that moves us in *Fear and Trembling;* Isaac is a stick. It is the seducer who matters in the aesthetic stage of *Either-Or;* Cordelia is a null. It is Judge William, the ideal married man, who is supposed to matter in the ethical life, though he is stuffy and unreal enough; his wife can scarcely be said to exist at all. My inner consciousness, miserable sinner that I am—and God; these are the entities celebrated in Kierkegaard's poetry. It is the poetry of worship and of prayer, of an ingrown, breast-beating worship and prayer, alien or exaggerated even to many Christians, let alone to a thinker so far removed from religiosity as Sartre. Even as a negative limit of the for-itself's development, as suggested earlier, God, for Sartre, is the cause of itself, the for-itself-in-itself, Spinoza's one infinite, wholly complete, and wholly actual substance. For Kierkegaard, He is Father, Maker, and Master, stern Judge, and Merciful Pardoner of Sins. It is not His self-sufficiency which matters, but His overwhelming power and overflowing goodness. *"Causa sui"* would be from a Kierkegaardian point of view an empty phrase. So it is for Sartre, too, in the sense that it refers to no real entity; I cannot point to any Being that is or could be its denotatum. But as the ideal of what I seek and can *not* find it is significant, and crucially so, whereas God the Father for Sartre is simply an old gentleman whose acquaintance he made, briefly and superficially, in childhood, and with whom, he confesses, he might, given other circumstances, have got on well enough, but who in fact bowed out of his social circle long ago. Indeed, he not only doesn't know him any more; he has demonstrated that He can not exist—or rather that *causa sui,* his philosophical alias, is non-existent. The living God of Kierkegaard or Pascal is, for him, not even a worthy target for disproof.

Even as dialecticians the two writers differ, at least in the overall direction of their respective dialectics. Granted, they are both Hegelian, and as such their philosophical interests and arguments are similar, often strikingly so. Thus Sartre's use of modal concepts in *Being and Nothingness,* for example, is reminiscent of Kierkegaard on possibility and necessity in the *Bits.* In general, indeed, modal concepts seem to be dear to the hearts of dialectical philosophers. Sartre's account of the immediate structures of the for-itself, again, strikingly resembles Kierkegaard's account of the self in *The Sickness to Death.* Thus Kierkegaard, in a passage which is both a parody of Hegelian method and its apotheosis: "The self is a relation which relates itself to its own self, or it is that in the relation . . . that the relation relates itself to its own self; the self is not the relation but . . . [the fact] that the relation relates to its own self." [4] Sartre similarly detaches the self from substantial status, and makes it, though more negatively, relational: "The for-itself is the being which determines itself to exist in as much as it can not coincide with itself." [5] For both philosophers, moreover, this self-related being, the being which *is* the stretch of its own relation to itself, is grounded in a being other than itself. Kierkegaard writes: "Such a relation which relates itself to its own self (that is to say, a self) must either have constituted itself or have been constituted by another. . . . Such a derived, constituted relation is the human self, a relation which relates itself to its own self, and in relating itself to its own self relates itself to another." [6] And Sartre: "The for-itself in its being is failure because it is the foundation only of itself as nothingness. In truth this failure is its very being, but it has meaning only if the for-itself apprehends itself as failure in the presence of the being which it has failed to be; that is, of the being which would be the foundation of its being and no longer merely the foundation of its nothingness—or, to put it another way, which would be its foundation as coincidence with itself. . . . Human reality is its own surpassing toward what it lacks; it surpasses itself towards the particular being which it would be if it were what it is. Human reality is not something which exists first in order afterwards to lack this or that; it exists first as lack and in immediate synthetic connection with what it lacks." [7] In the one case, to be sure, the transcendent Being to which we are referred is the Hebraeo-Christian God, and in the other, inert exterior Being-in-itself; yet both the movement of their thought and the insight it carries are closely parallel.

In short, the concepts both philosophers are working with have the kind of generality which characterizes Hegelian philosophizing, and their use is the kind of quick to-and-fro that, again, marks dialectical argument. One wants to say: word-juggling. How else can one characterize Kierkegaard's, "The disrelationship of despair is not a simple disrelationship but a disrelationship in a relation which relates itself to its own self"; [8] or Sartre's, "In order for being to be lacking or lacked, it is necessary that a being make itself its own lack; only a being which lacks can surpass being toward the lacked." [9] Yet there is not only brilliance in the juggling, in its speed and skill; through it one sometimes gains insight that the more moderate methods of analysis fail to achieve. It is irritating that this is so; there is surely something about the method too facile to be true, the concepts it uses are surely too entirely general to convey anything about concrete reality. Yet they do sometimes convey something: in this case, of the self-and-other relatedness of human being, a thesis fundamental to any adequate philosophy of man. In Kierkegaard's case, moreover, there is immense variety of psychological insight in his typology of despair; and there are similar observations of special cases here and there in *Being and Nothingness.* To make such comparisons here, however, would be tedious and irrelevant. I want simply to emphasize that both these philosophers are in fact practitioners of Hegelian dialectic at its best.

Yet they are dialecticians with a difference, both in their interests and in the devices they use to implement them. Kierkegaard, once more, is a religious poet: his aim is to bring himself—or his reader, could he find him—to tremble before God, to live *in* that terrible yet glorious confrontation. Sartre is an ontologist: however much he claims to stress the individual, it is the *Being* of the individual, his having to be what he is not and not be what he is, that he wants to exhibit and make intelligible. Kierkegaard seeks *indirect* communication: hence his host of pseudonyms. What he has to say is really the unsayable, one either lives it after him or fails to hear it. For Sartre, on the contrary, "all is significance." In its very nihilation, in its contradictions, human reality brings meaning to the world, makes even the in-itself intelligible. Reason must triumph. Even passion, we have seen, must be interpreted as action, because it must be rational: it must be some way, even if an absurd one, of making sense. If man "tries to become God and fails," at least he tries, and he must be able to give reasons for his efforts. Given these different aims, finally, their means of attaining them differ accordingly. However abstract Kierkegaard's manipulation of concepts in passages like those quoted, his aim is always existential: it is self-inspection and self-transformation that he is after. True, Sartre, in *Being and Nothingness* at least, taking off from phenomenology, often uses examples more concretely within his arguments, yet he seeks a much more general and conceptual issue. Kierkegaard engages his fictitious characters, scenes or stories, as well as his dialectical arguments, in the one aim of self-development of the religious life. Sartre devotes both description and dialectic to the cause of ontology: of seeking to understand the being of myself and the being other than myself that is the in-itself. "What we desire to appropriate in an object," he writes, "is being and is the world." [10] This is a Hegelian aim, as it has been the aim of all systematizing thinkers; it is the aim against which Kierkegaard rebels. Sartre, whatever concepts he has borrowed from Kierkegaard, and whatever methods he shares with him, far from abandoning the goal of the System, has made it his very own.

Sartre and Marxism

There remains the question of Sartre's relation to Marxism. This is a question I shall deal with more thoroughly when we come to the *Critique,* but let me put it briefly here in order to complete my account of Sartre's dialectical predecessors.

If Kierkegaard turned the dialectic to the individual's inner existence, Marx turned it, not only "right side up," but outward: to the material conditions of life, to labor and its exploitation by capital. How can one thinker coherently make both these moves at once—both inward to my consciousness and outward to the class struggle? Yet that is just what Sartre claims to have done. Indeed, he seems to have come to Hegel through Marx; it was dialectical materialism that led him to dialectic—but to existential dialectic, of all things. The three dialectics assumed their roles in his thought contemporaneously; if the Marxist one—in its peculiar Sartrean form—takes the stage more conspicuously in the *Critique,* it had been patiently waiting in the wings for its cue.

Sartre himself has told the story in the opening pages of the *Critique,* or rather of *Questions de Méthode,* the treatise on method written in the 1950's for a Polish journal, which forms its introduction. His formal education, he says there, though officially "idealist," had included no initiation into dialectical thought. The famous lectures of Kojève on reading Hegel took place between 1933 and 1939, when Sartre was already teaching philosophy in a *lycée.* In 1925, on the contrary, he writes, "the horror of dialectic was such that even Hegel was unknown to us." [11] Marx and Marxism, he says, were only referred to from the outside: Marx must be read "to be refuted." Even the communist students dared not refer to such topics in their official lives; they would have failed their examinations. Sartre did read *Capital* and *The German Ideology* in this period, but though he "understood it luminously," he confesses, he nevertheless understood it not at all. "To understand is to change, to advance on one's own; that reading did not change me." [12] Marxism came to him, not as political or social theory, but as a "reality": "the heavy presence, on my horizon, of the working masses, an enormous and sombre body that *lived* Marxism, that *practiced* it and that exercised from a distance an irresistible attraction on the petit bourgeois intellectuals.'' [13] This has been its primary role for Sartre all along: it is a reality that lures him, that moves him—he longs to serve it, to *be* it; but it is not *his* reality. At the time, he says, its philosophy did not seem to him and his contemporaries to have any privileged position. ''We said to ourselves; 'Here are the conceptions of a German intellectual who lived in London in the middle of the last century.' '' [14] And despite his later insistence that Marxism, or rather the position of Marx himself (as he interprets it) is the *only* philosophy of the twentieth century, this external relation to Marx has never been overcome. His very adulation of Marxism in the *Critique* and other postwar writings rings not quite true. ''Marxism'' as he conceives it seems still to be his Other, the Other to which he must surrender, yet on his own terms.

And these terms are still, as they were at the outset, existential. The reaction of his contemporaries to their idealist training, Sartre recalls, was to embrace against the smooth system of their teachers a darker and theoretically (though only theoretically) more violent mood. They revelled in Unamuno's ''tragic sense of life.'' They celebrated Wahl's *Toward the Concrete,* seeking, however, to take ''concreteness''—life in its full richness, in its individuality—as starting point, not conclusion. This was the turn to existence—to the sense of individual crisis, even of individual despair—which Sartre, like so many contemporary writers, did indeed ''advance to on his own,'' and from which, Marxism or no Marxism, he has never retreated. This position, with its stress on the inner quality of experience, its sense of human isolation, of the ''darkly felt split between things as they are and things as they ought to be,'' all this he could indeed assimilate, whether as Cartesian individualist, as phenomenologist concerned to describe the data of consciousness in all their purity, or as the man who had been that lonely child recalled in *Les Mots.* (No, maman, don't ask the other boys to play with me; but perhaps I can imagine how miserable, deep down inside, each of them too must be!)

Philosophically and politically, Sartre recalls, the position he and his friends took at this period was a kind of pluralism: a position essentially of the right, which refused to "totalize," refused to subsume the crisis of the present under its proper dialectical, and Marxist, rubric. It was the war and the occupation, he says, which taught them better. Or, if one follows Simone de Beauvoir's account, it was first the Spanish Civil War (where after all the officially Marxist state was on the side of justice) that brought political events emphatically to the attention of these young academicians. Between Franco and Hitler they came to see (so they allege) that pluralism is fascist. They were rescued by the tragic events of the 1930's and 1940's. They fled from the bourgeois right to the banner of revolutionary socialism, which, though without ever embracing any party of the left, they still proudly fly.

Is this a true story? Yes and no. First, parenthetically, let us put to one side the equation of pluralism with fascism. If fascism has a theory at all, it is a "totalizing," not a "pluralistic" one. Liberal democracy, the official theory of the bourgeoisie, is a far cry either from the clericalism of the Falangists or the blood-and-soil mysticism of the Nazis. By the weakness and folly of its adherents it did indeed permit their rise; but that does not make it philosophically their equivalent. To insist as uncompromisingly as Sartre does on the dichotomy of fascism = pluralism versus Marxism = "totalization" is to indulge once more in the same kind of dualistic either-or that makes him so fundamentally unpolitical, indeed, so unhistorical a thinker. Nor am I contradicting myself here. Sartre is an excellent historian—of philosophy. But it is precisely the imprecisions, the half-lights, the muddles of *real* history that he fails to see.

Yet his account is convincing in so far as it concerns, not the history of our time, but his own development. It illuminates the intimate relation of the existential to the "Marxist" aspect of his thought, and enables us to understand how both the general intent of his philosophy and some of his central concepts could take on a quasi-Marxist slant. First, the existentialist's "tragic sense of life" became for him the conceptual instrument through which he sought to recognize, alongside the politicians of the left and the masses they claimed to represent, the real oppression and injustice of the real world. He sees the step to existentialism now as the revolt of a petty bourgeois intellectual against the dominant class to which, nevertheless, he still belonged. He and his friends expressed their rebellion, at the time, in what he later found to be inadequately practical terms: they talked of "essences" and "ideas"; even the violence of their revolt was purely conceptual. However, in Sartre's case at least, it seems to me, the reason for the intellectual cast of his rebellion was not, in the last analysis, the fact that he was still a bourgeois, expressing his dissatisfaction with the establishment of the day by denying its monistic (idealist) solution in favor of a looser, pluralistic position. His rebellion was intellectual because it was an intellectual's, indeed, a philosopher's, rebellion, not that of a practical man. Though he still seeks to found the whole panorama of history on *praxis* or the action of the individual, his own *praxis,* as *Les Mots* makes very clear, is verbal and conceptual. It has none of the spirit of calculation that all politics, even revolutionary politics, demands. He insists on "man in situation," but theoretically; the messiness of the practical situation eludes him. He has indeed been a committed writer, not admittedly in the sense of commitment to a party, but in the sense that he has publicly and emphatically espoused, over and over, the cause of the exploited or the oppressed, and the cause of revolutionaries who seek to overthrow exploitation or oppression. He does indeed support those who man the barricades. But it is not his métier to tear up the paving stones himself. This is the posture of the *theoretical* revolutionary, the man who simply and loudly says "no" to what there is, but it can also be the posture of the existentialist, certainly in the Sartrean form of existentialism: an existentialism, without transcendent values, without God, in which the lonely individual sees over against his own project, his own aspirations, the nauseating insufficiency of what in fact *is* to his own ideals.

There is, it seems to me, something in common with Marxism in this existentialist attitude, both in its general intellectual strategy and in some particular concepts that Sartrean existentialism and at least some forms of Marxism share.

In general, the in-itself/for-itself dichotomy lends itself, in a very abstract fashion, to a "Marxist" position in social and political philosophy. If one seeks to go beyond the purely subjective dialectic of the inner man, the alternative is—totalization. Over against myself as agent is the in-itself as meaningless, indefinitely extending exteriority, as threat to myself as for-itself, and this "in-itself" includes the dehumanized "humanity" of social institutions. True, I can take the world as a complex of techniques for my action; but I can also take it, alternatively, as a vast snare to objectify me, to deny my humanity. Indeed, society as institutionalized *is* the inhuman. It is expropriation, act become inertial. I swing back and forth, therefore, between my aspiration to an impossible good faith, to pure act, in here, and the threat, the wickedness of all that is out there. I am by no means asserting that this is Marxism; but it does share with Marxism its utopian component. Either all is well or nothing. And since it is never the case that all is well, one must take up a position of revolutionary nihilism: don't fool yourself, all there is is rotten. If Sartre is to take a political stand, that is the only one his existentialism, his search for the purely active act, could possibly allow him.

Certain concepts, moreover, which play a crucial role in the argument of *Being and Nothingness,* are already, if not Marxist, at least surrogates for their Marxist analogues. An obvious candidate is "alienation." If Marxist alienation was a function of capitalism, of the laborer's possession by the machine, for Sartre alienation, in the sense of the flight from the instant of pure activity, is the human condition as such. The two conceptions have in common, if nothing else, the Rousseauist thesis that man, born free, is everywhere in chains, and chains of his own making. Freedom is the true humanity, but men are fated to lose it through their own agency. Dialectical materialism sees this loss in economic history and the exploitation of the working class by capital. In *Being and Nothingness* Sartre sees it in the individual's own self-deception. But the formal alternative is the same: free action is humanity, and it is lost by human agency.

A second parallel, finally, is the concept of class struggle. Though he approaches it in *Being and Nothingness* by a course very different from any Marxist argument, and though he has to prove with immense circuitousness in the *Critique* that there can be "struggle," Sartre sees the togetherness of human beings as arising primarily from conflict. In *Being and Nothingness,* there is no "we-subject" except indirectly. A and B and C all hate the D's, for example, who want to objectify and thus exterminate them. They are united as a we-subject by common hatred of the us-object whose *raison d'être* is to make such an object of them. Thus the understanding of social history becomes essentially the understanding of the class struggle. And out of such hatred, the envisagement of political action is the envisagement of revolution, of overthrowing the exploitation that is the Other's use of me, or, indirectly at least, of us. Again, if Sartre's individualism lends itself to any political philosophy, it will be some sort of theory in which exploitation and the revolt against exploitation are at the heart of the interpretation of social structures.

In these limited senses then, Sartre's "Marxism" and his existentialism, however far apart these two traditions may appear, form equally integral aspects of his philosophy even before the expansion of the "Marxist" theme. Yet if we look back at the influence of the three dialecticians, it is Hegel who wins hands down. Both the dialectic of the for-itself and the dialectic of social *praxis* Sartre develops, ultimately, with a virtuosity, an ontological persistence, that seem to be inspired, through contact with existentialism and Marxist literature, in the last analysis by Hegel himself. If his dialectic is narrower than Hegel's in empirical content or poorer in concrete historical insight, what limits it is not so much Kierkegaardian introspection, let alone Marxian concern with the realities of economic life; what limits the scope of his dialectic, as it limits his phenomenology, is the presiding genius (perhaps the evil genius) of French philosophy: the spirit of Descartes. In both his major works of philosophy of date, Sartre is, or has become, a Hegelian dialectician whose speculation is nevertheless confined within the bounds of Cartesian dualism and of a truncated Cartesian rationality. That this is so—and in what respect—will become apparent as we follow the argument of *Being and Nothingness* in its main movement, and look more carefully at some of the problems that loom up before us in its course.

chapter four: being and nothingness

the argument

from the phenomenon to being

It is fashionable nowadays
to identify philosophy with something called "conceptual analysis."
Conceptual analysis is certainly a tool of philosophy; but what is it used *for?* The answer to
that question seems to divide philosophers into two di-
vergent camps. First, there are those who reflect upon, and

within, experience in order to seek a clearer understanding of experience itself, of the ordinary world, whether of everyday life or of some specialized discipline. But then there are also, recurrently, those who philosophize in order to seek, beyond and behind everyday experience, some special insight into the really real. As things appear to us, they are forever changing. Is there not some permanent reality behind them which they somehow express and which, if we follow the right method, we can come to understand? Philosophers, it seems, habitually return to this question, yet never come to a final answer—an answer that once and for all will put the search to rest. Kant found an ingenious solution, which, as it turned out, merely exacerbated the problem. There are really real entities, "noumena," he claimed, behind the phenomena, but, though we keep trying to grasp their nature, it is *our* nature never to succeed, and, as far as claims to knowledge go, we should stop trying. We can know things only as they appear, not as they are "in themselves." Kant's was a most unstable "solution." There, over the fence, are the things in themselves, but we must be content to nibble away at our phenomenal meadow, with the greener grass of reality exasperatingly out of bounds. The two greatest movements of European philosophy since Kant, Hegelian dialectic and Husserlian phenomenology, were both concerned to eliminate the Kantian dichotomy. The question of how Hegel in fact meant to do this—by bringing everything (in the *Phenomenology of Mind*) within the scope of experience, or by swelling out the human, experiencing person (in the *Logic* and elsewhere) into a kind of suprahistorical super-superego— that difficult question, fortunately, need not concern us here. It is in the phenomenology of the twentieth century that Sartre had found the cure for the ailment Kant had bequeathed to us. Husserl has abolished the noumenon. If thought is always of—an object, that object is not the hither side of some hidden "X"; it is simply, as object of thought, what it appears as, and no more. But that is plenty. For the phenomenologist's "phenomena" are not the mythical "impressions" of Hume or the sense data of the positivist's dream. They have the full richness of experience itself; stripped of speculation, without conventional superstructures, they can be studied accurately and systematically, so that a structured range of objects and modes of experiencing them are displayed, all luminously appearing as they are—since it is appearances that they are. It was with confidence in this enterprise that Sartre had written his sketch on the emotions and had discovered how affective consciousness, normally nonthetic, can serve on occasion as magical surrogate for the rational control of objects. The position he reached there remained as starting point of *Being and Nothingness*. Not only is non-thetic or "pre-reflective" consciousness the first principle of that work and the subject matter of its first major theme; the theory of the emotions is also retained, recurring, as we shall see, in the last, most frankly "ontological" phase of the argument. Or, to make a more general point, Sartre firmly maintains his affirmation of Husserl's success in doing away once and for all with the shadow of Kant's thing-in-itself. It is from that achievement and its implications that his argument begins. Sartre draws a clear distinction between the Kantian phenomenon, which relates to the noumenon as appearance to being, and Husserl's theory of the phenomenon, which holds that there is nothing behind the appearance: the phenomenon, supported by nothing other than itself, refers only to itself and to the total series of appearances. If we start honestly within consciousness, within experience as experienced and experiencing, there is no question of any hidden reality. "Consciousness has nothing substantial; it is pure appearance in the sense that it exists only to the degree to which it appears." [1] And even when we move, *via* the ontological proof, from consciousness to being, it is not noumenal being that is in question, but the transphenomenal being of phenomena—the being of this table, of this package of tobacco, of this lamp, the being of the world implied by consciousness. Thus, the phenomenon, freed of its inacessible noumenal alternate, is before us in its complete being as the pure appearance that it is.

Yet the resolution of the Kantian dichotomy turns out to be itself unstable, or so Sartre argues in the Introduction to *Being and Nothingness.* Concurring in modern philosophy's rejection of the noumenon, his Introduction nevertheless proceeds to demonstrate the instability of phenomenology and to transcend it in the direction of an ontological inquiry. The argument is condensed and obscure, but worth disentangling, since it lays the foundation for the structure of the work itself. I shall therefore examine it in some detail before going on to trace in much more general outline the course of the argument that follows.

In Section One, Sartre begins, as we have seen, by accepting modern thought's banishment of the Kantian noumenon. Much of what he says in this section applies, incidentally, as much to "phenomenal*ism*" as to phenomenology. It is the rejection of speculative metaphysic, even in its most vestigial form, that he is referring to, a rejection common to many schools of thought. Thus he speaks here of Poincaré and Duhem as well as of Husserl. But since he describes his own enterprise as "phenomenological ontology," it seems reasonable to read this opening argument also as that of a philosopher starting from what he believes to be Husserl's method and modifying it in his own way. In any case, what matters here, first, is simply the rejection of the noumenon, a step on which phenomenalism, with its modest empiricism, and phenomenology, with its more ambitious aims, agree.

Beginning, then, with this fundamental thesis of modern philosophy, Sartre proceeds to make a number of opening moves which set the stage for what follows. First, he examines, and apparently validates, the claim that modern thought by "reducing the existent to the series of appearances" has overcome a number of "dualisms." First, it has transformed the contrast of internal and external: there is no inaccessible "inside" to objects "behind" their apparent surfaces. Instead there is simply the appearance contrasted with a series of appearances equally apparent. It has also abolished the contrast between appearance and reality: the phenomenon is the existent, there is no lurking "really real" of which it is the appearance. For if the phenomenon is relative to some one, yet it is nevertheless absolutely itself; it is at least relative-absolute. Nor, thirdly, does the duality of potency and act survive; behind the act there is no power or disposition "in view of which" the act is possible. What about essence and existence? Here, too, there has been a change. We have the appearance of the existent, or the existent as it appears, still contrasted with its essence, but the latter, being simply "the manifest law of the series of appearances," is equally apparent. It is not an essence off in some other world, as "essence" once was thought to be.

Through all these alterations, Sartre proceeds to argue, we have not so much abolished all dualities as we have converted them into a single new contrast, that of finite and infinite. The existent, we have already seen, manifests itself in a series of appearances. Each such appearance is finite, but the series must be infinite. Why? The series must be infinite, first, Sartre insists, simply because each appearance appears to a subject. For even if an object should manifest itself through only one aspect or "profile" (*Abschattung*), even if I always perceived only that one aspect, only this side of G. E. Moore's inkwell, for instance, I always have the possibility of perceiving it from other points of view. That is what "perceiving" means. From the side of the appearance itself, secondly, we can also draw the inference that the series of appearances cannot be finite, for this would mean, Sartre argues, "that the first appearances do not have the possibility of *reappearing,* which is absurd, or that they can all be given at once, which is still more absurd." [2] What, then, has the theory of the phenomenon accomplished? What it has done in fact is to replace *reality* (belonging to things) with *objectivity* (belonging to phenomena), and, Sartre points out, it has justified this change by an appeal to infinity. Again, this statement would be equally characteristic of Husserl's account of perception as the series of profiles of an object systematically interrelated by receding into an infinitely expanded horizon, and of a phenomenalist formula like John Stuart Mill's "permanent possibility of sensation," since a finite series could not be "permanently" possible. Sartre proceeds to gloss this thesis in characteristically Cartesian fashion.

What is "reality"? "The reality of that cup is that it *is* there and that it is *not me*." [3] Now in modern terms we interpret this to mean "that the series of its appearances is bound by a principle which does not depend on my whim." [4] This statement in turn is interpreted both from the *subject* and the *object* side. First, the appearance in itself would be simply a "subjective phenomenon," this appearance to me here now. To achieve a principle of organizing appearances, therefore, the subject must transcend this appearance in the direction of the series: "he must *seize Red* through his impression of red," [5] where by "Red" is meant precisely the principle of the series. Or, similarly, he must seize the electric current through the electrolysis—that is, through its manifestations. But all this, though achieved through the subject's transcendence of the appearance, in fact establishes the objectivity of the object. So we can equally well argue, from the object side, that "on principle an object posits the series of its appearances as infinite." [6] So the appearance, too, not only the subject to which it appears, itself demands that it be "surpassed to infinity." Without that surpassing it could not be apprehended as "an appearance of what appears," as appearance of an object, albeit a phenomenal object.

The new opposition, therefore, replaces all the traditional dualities. So Sartre declares. But he now proceeds to reinstate them all within this single principle—to reinstate them, indeed, as more radically opposite than they had been before. First, external/internal: the object, of which each appearance is one aspect, is totally *in* this aspect (since there is no "real" thing behind it), yet at the same time totally *outside* it (since the series itself, which is infinite, and the principle of which makes the object objective, never as such appears in any one aspect). Similarly for potency and act: if the appearance is what it is, and potency is banished, a new "potency" returns—the potency "to be developed in a series of real or possible appearances." [7] Finally, essence and existence are again, and more radically, divorced. For Plato, for example, who represents for most of us the most extreme "two-world" philosophy, forms do indeed exist apart from the phenomena, yet the phenomena share in that higher being. Indeed, they have such existence as they have in view of that very sharing. Now, however, we have abolished participation, since the essence is that which is manifested by an infinite series of manifestations. But then it is never manifested, even imperfectly, in any one. Thus we have, within the theory of the phenomenon, not only a single dualism, but an aggravation of all the old ones. In every case, in fact, an original polarity has been transcended or replaced, only to give way to a sharper opposition, if not an outright contradiction. This conclusion, concealed within the compression of the initial argument, Sartre will draw out to its full paradoxical consequences in the seven hundred pages to come.

The process is prefigured in the remaining sections of the Introduction. Section Two cuts apart "the phenomenon of being" and "the being of the phenomenon," and presents in little the theme to be elicited from the next section. We find that even the pure appearance can be questioned about its being, and, indeed, must be so: the two are not identical, nor does the phenomenon as such, even the phenomenal object as such, of itself reveal its being. True, there is no "being" *behind* the phenomenon. As phenomenon, as existence, and even, in the principle of its appearances, as essence, it is coextensive with its being. Yet it is also different from its being, since, transphenomenally, we can ask—indeed, cannot avoid asking—what its being is. The phenomenon reveals itself; that it is, is the condition of its revelation. Yet if, in turn, we take *that* phenomenon: that it is, *the phenomenon of being,* as a revelation, we want in turn to ask about the being *on the basis of which* it is revealed. Thus, the phenomenon, even the purest phenomenon, transcends itself in the direction of ontology.

Two points should be noted about this brief section, one parenthetically, the other as a fundamental premise of the whole argument. First, when Sartre considers the possibility of a direct revelation of being as phenomenon, he finds being disclosed to us by an immediate access which is affective rather than intellectual (typically, Sartre cites "boredom" and "nausea"), and ontology becomes the description of being as it presents itself directly to us. We may put aside here the question why Sartre prefers "boredom" or "nausea" rather than, say "wonder" or "ecstasy." But essential to the very structure of the argument is a remark tucked into the final paragraph of the section, which both anticipates the thesis that "all knowledge is intuitive" and indicates the way in which Sartre's ontology is to transcend knowledge. This move, beyond or behind knowledge to some other relation to being on which it rests, is fundamental to the structure of the argument to come. Yet Sartre seems to introduce it almost unawares. We have to establish first of all, he writes, "the exact relation which unites the phenomenon of being to the being of the phenomenon." [8] To do this, he continues, we should "consider that the whole of the preceding remarks has been directly inspired by the revealing intuition of the phenomenon of being." [9] In other words, we have tried to take being not as the mere *condition* of appearance, but as itself "an appearance which can be determined in concepts"—as other appearances can be determined if we either list their properties or move toward their "meaning," that is, their essence as the principle of the series of appearances ("Red" through red . . . etc.). But this attempt has shown us that in the case of being we cannot make such a reduction: the phenomenon of being exceeds our grasp either through properties or meaning; it still points to being as *trans-*

phenomenal. So, Sartre says—and this is the fateful step—"we have understood . . . *that knowledge cannot by itself give an account of being.*" [10] In other words, knowledge is the direct presentation of phenomena; it is intuition, "the act of a clear and attentive mind," in its si-mon-pure self-contained direction toward what it sees. The reach beyond appearances to being, therefore, is a reach beyond knowledge. The phenomenon of being not only leads beyond the phenomenon to its being, "requir-ing a foundation which is transphenomenal": [11] in leading us that way, it also leads us beyond knowledge itself to some fundamentally non-cognitive attitude. Sartre con-cludes:

> What is implied by the preceding considerations is that the being of the phenomenon, although coextensive with the phenomenon, can not be subject to the phenomenal condition—which is to exist only in so far as it reveals itself—and that consequently it surpasses the knowledge which we have of it and provides the basis for such knowledge.[12]

It is in the next section, on "The Pre-Reflective Co-gito and the Being of the Percipere," that we decisively make this move from the secure inspection of the phe-nomenon *as known* to a precognitive foundation for knowledge. At the same time it should be noted that the two theses established in the previous section, the trans-phenomenality of being and its precognitive import, will be confirmed in radically divided areas. It is conscious-ness that will reveal to us a precognitive dimension, and it is being as such, being-in-itself as radically other than consciousness, that will take us beyond the phenomenon to ontology. The phenomenon has twin transphenomenal roots, but they are far from identical twins. The phenomenon appears to—consciousness, and that consciousness, as knowing consciousness, is founded in the pre-cognitive moment of the not-yet-reflective *cogito:* I am counting my cigarettes, non-thetically aware of myself as counting. The phenomenon which appears, on the other hand, *is,* and as being *it* demands the transphenomenal, demands a being other than consciousness as the condition of its appearance. Thus consciousness is tied to itself behind and before knowledge in the pre-reflective *cogito,* and at the same time catapulted into the obscurity of sheer being, being which is coextensive with appearance, yet at the same time its ontological obverse.

Sartre opens this next stage of his preliminary argument by proposing to consider once more the possibility of resting in the phenomenon, of accepting the Berkeleyan identity *"esse est percipi,"* "To be is to be perceived." It will not work, he holds, for two reasons, one in the nature of the *percipere,* of perceiving, one in the nature of the *percipi,* the perceived.

The examination of the former makes more explicit the view of knowledge hinted at in the previous section and establishes its first and primary consequence. Knowing, Sartre holds, is the explicit, intentional confrontation of the act of knowing with what it knows. But is knowing itself known? If it were, we would be started on an infinite regress, from the idea to the idea of the idea and so on indefinitely—a regress which, once started, would never stop. I would know my knowing and in turn my knowing of my knowing and my knowing of my knowing of my knowing and . . . Only an initial resting place, a rooting of knowledge in something other than knowledge, could cut off this intolerable regression before it starts. I have already mentioned, in discussing Sartre's Cartesianism, the transformation of the *cogito* from reflective to pre-reflective, which he effects in order to cut short this regressive process; but I must recapitulate briefly here in order to put the Sartrean "absolute" where it belongs, at the head of his argument.

We start from the phenomenon as apprehended, that is, as known. What knows, however, is consciousness: "The law of being in the knowing subject is *to-be-conscious.*" [13] *This* being—"to-be-conscious"—will turn out on the one hand to be entirely phenomenal: consciousness *is,* utterly lucid, it is pure appearance, its existence is its appearance. But on the other hand, it is also transphenomenal, for it is the being *of* the knowing subject. Yet it is not being *simpliciter,* for it is the being of consciousness. And consciousness, of course, is inescapably intentional. It is always consciousness *of*—. Not that all intentionality is cognitive; there are also, for instance, Sartre admits, "affective states of consciousness"; they, too, are *of*—, but in some other way. But here it is the pure phenomenon—that is, the object of knowledge—from which we have started; so it is knowing consciousness, which is always consciousness of—its object, that we are interrogating, and it is the precognitive foundation of knowing consciousness that we are about to discover.

Sartre's argument here is brief, definitive, and, I believe, invalid, slipping in an unwarranted minor premise which, though unstated, suffices to impose on all that is to follow, both in this work and later, the bias, sometimes slight, sometimes extreme, but always distorting, that characterizes his philosophy.

"The necessary and sufficient condition for a knowing consciousness to be knowledge *of* its object," he asserts," is that it be *consciousness of itself* as being that knowledge." [14] That it is a sufficient condition is clear enough, for "my being conscious of being conscious of that table" does indeed suffice for my being conscious of it—not for its existence in itself, but for its existence for me, insofar as I *am* conscious of it. But why is this "self-consciousness" a necessary condition? This is where Sartre's argument is obscure and, indeed, as I see it, fatally misleading. This is where he ought to have renounced his Cartesian heritage, but failed to do so.

Being conscious of itself as being the knowledge of its object is a necessary condition of a knowing consciousness's being consciousness of its object, Sartre argues, because "if my consciousness were not consciousness of being consciousness of the table, it would then be consciousness of that table without consciousness of being so. In other words, it would be a consciousness ignorant of itself, an unconscious—which is absurd." [15] Granted, the concept of an unconscious consciousness is indeed a contradictory and thus an absurd one. But why must a consciousness conscious of something other than itself, as, following Husserl, Sartre agrees all consciousness is, be, because ignorant of itself, not conscious at all? Consciousness is defined as other-directed; that doesn't make it unconscious. On the contrary, it is just its vectorial character, its consciousness of what is not itself, and therefore, one might suppose, its lack of consciousness of itself, its "ignorance" of itself if you will, that *makes* it conscious. Husserl may be mistaken—or, better, Husserl as interpreted by Sartre may be mistaken—in holding all cognitive consciousness to be thetic, positing its object explicitly and centrally. It may be—and I believe it is—the case that there is always a non-thetic foundation, a foundation of what Michael Polanyi calls subsidiary awareness, at the root of even the most plainly intuitive, positional (or, in Polanyi's language, focal) awareness of an object. But why must that non-thetic residue be introduced, as Sartre introduces it, as consciousness (of) *self?* On the contrary, the non-thetic ground of consciousness is, in most of our dealing with the world, a set of clues on which we rely, from which we move, in order to make out, through them, the outlines, the meaning, of our focal object in the world, not of ourselves. The subsidiary is indeed interiorized, it is *mine,* but it is not *me,* or no more so than is the focal object I comprehend through it and with its aid. It is the crutch I lean on to advance out there into and with the world. To attend *from* it, and by means of it, *to* the world is indeed the necessary condition of knowledge—but that is by no means the same thing as to turn from the world to awareness, even subsidiary awareness, of myself. Nor is forgetting myself in my concentration on what, *via* the non-thetic, I seek to posit, to be identified with unconsciousness. Quite the contrary: the outward thrust of subsidiary awareness is the very transcendence of self that makes intentionality possible.

Why does Sartre fail to see this? Why does he argue that a non-self-conscious consciousness would be unconscious? Clearly because for him, in *Being and Nothingness* as already in the *Emotions,* the *cogito* has been taken as the unique and indispensable starting point of all philosophy. And the *cogito,* unlike Husserl's *cogitationes,* is self-referential. In moving the content of consciousness out into the world, Sartre has nevertheless retained the Cartesian thesis that the first unique moment of thought must be thinking about thinking: consciousness, to be consciousness, must be self-directed and self-contained. This moment has indeed lost the lucidity of the Cartesian original, for the light of consciousness now looks outward. It is, in itself, contentless, merely, as Sartre puts it, "an operative intention"; but it must operate *on itself,* it must reverberate somehow within itself, else, he believes, despite the thesis of intentionality, it would not be consciousness at all. True, in Sartre's view, this merely operative intention cannot be cognitive, since knowledge is always directed to an object, not to itself. So it is prior to knowledge; indeed, Sartre concludes, it is the precognitive absolute, the transphenomenal being on which, as its being, consciousness as phenomenon rests. The consciousness of consciousness, not as thetic but as nonthetic, is "the immediate non-cognitive relation of the self to itself" on which the very possibility of consciousness depends. This pre-reflective *cogito,* then, is the condition of the Cartesian *cogito,* as of every *cogitatio.* It is the absolute beginning of philosophy.

But, again, it is precisely here, in founding philosophy on this immediate, non-cogitating *cogito,* that Sartre has foundered. He has cut off once more the bridge from thinker to thought that Husserl's method had established and has insulated the empty self against any impact, except through negativity, from or on the world. Yet the very example he uses to illustrate his pre-reflective *cogito* could have led him beyond this initial, and, for him, ultimate impasse. In counting my cigarettes, he tells us, I do not know myself as counting, witness the fact that "children who are capable of doing a sum spontaneously can not *explain* subsequently how they set about it." These tests of Piaget's, Sartre continues, "constitute an excellent refutation of the formula of Alain—To know is to know that one knows." [16] Indeed they do; but what they indicate is simply the tacit ground of all knowledge, not a tacit knowledge of one's *self.* They suggest that at the basis of knowing-that, there is a tacit knowing-how (an "operative intention"!) which cannot be made wholly explicit. They suggest a revision of the conception of knowledge to include that other-directed tacit base. But to follow this suggestion would mean denying both the self-referential being of immediate consciousness and the wholly positional character of cognitive consciousness. It would mean, moreover, denying not only these Cartesian principles, but their corollaries also: the concept of consciousness as wholly active and as instantaneous. But to all these theses, as we saw earlier, Sartre is committed from the start, too deeply committed to question them even at the hand of an example which so plainly illustrates their contrary. The child's "knowing how to add"—which he cannot specify—is nevertheless knowledge; it is directed to the numbers he is adding, not to himself; it is both something he does, as agent, and a giving of himself to a task, as patient. Finally, as the action-x-passion of an embodied being, it takes time; it is not, it does not even aim at being, instantaneous, as the *cogito* is alleged to be. On all these counts, then, the Piaget experiment should lead us to substitute a non-thetic vector toward and within the world for any *cogito,* even a "pre-reflective" one. That move, however, Sartre is unable to make; and so we will find his assimilation of themes from Hegel, from Heidegger, and from Husserl, as well as his own phenomenological descriptions, confined and cramped, over and over, by the barrier of this first Cartesian step.

To return to Sartre's argument: his search for the being of the percipient has led him, he believes, to a non-reflective awareness (of) self as a non-substantial absolute. This is, primally and originally, how consciousness is: it simply surges up as non-thetic consciousness (of) itself. It is its own beginning. That is why one can, and must, say of it that its existence implies, and precedes, its essence—not, indeed, as the particular realization of some abstract possibility, but in its very rising into being, consciousness creates its essence, that is, the "synthetic order of its possibilities." [17] Without the existence of consciousness, there cannot even be nothingness. Consciousness is limited only by itself. Yet its existence, of course, is far from substantial; it simply is as it appears: "it is precisely because consciousness is pure appearance, because it is total emptiness (since the entire world is outside it), it is because of this identity of appearance and existence within it that it can be considered as the absolute." [18]

So much for the *percipere*. We have found its transphenomenality in the concrete subjectivity of consciousness itself. Have we then founded, in consciousness, the being of the *percipi* as well? Far from it. As the lines just quoted indicate, consciousness has "the whole world" —that is, its object—"outside it." Granted, what is perceived is relative to the perceiver; it is passive, there to be acted on. But though passively awaiting the activity of consciousness, and though existing, as perceived, in relation to consciousness, it does not *derive* from consciousness, for it is, as perceived, *before* consciousness. Intentionality reasserts itself. The very being of consciousness, as non-thetic (self) awareness, points to its other as what, thetically, it is consciousness *of.* For consciousness, existence is primary; its essence follows from its existence. For being-over-against-consciousness, however, its very essence—to be over-against-consciousness—leads us to infer its necessary existence. Consciousness leads us to its object, the being of the phenomenon which confronts it, and the ontological proof leads us, dialectically, as noted earlier, from the essence of such a being to its existence.

This is the argument of sections IV and V (on the

being of the *percipi* and on the ontological proof), which is expanded, finally, in the tentative description of being-in-itself. Consciousness, we will find, exists as for-itself, in immediate, pre-reflective yet nevertheless doubling reflection *of* (not *on*) its being. But thetically it is of, and necessarily leads us to, its very opposite: being which simply is, is in-itself, is what it is. We have distinguished, therefore, two absolutely separated regions of being: on the one hand, the being of the pre-reflective *cogito,* and on the other, the being of the phenomenon, of which we had earlier been in search. Overcoming the dualisms of ontological tradition, we have reached the acme of all dualisms: the sheer, active upsurge of consciousness, against the meaningless plenum of sheer being-as-such. Nor can either idealism or realism help us overcome this gap. Idealism would derive being from consciousness; but being does not flow from consciousness, it confronts it. Realism would derive consciousness from being; but consciousness has no derivation. It simply springs up. "Nothing" is its cause. Its way of being (though not its being) is self-contained. It is in the way that consciousness has to be—and that, as we shall see to the point of satiety, is precisely *not* the way that being is. Sartre concludes:

> A multitude of questions remain unanswered: What is the ultimate meaning of these two types of being? For what reasons do they both belong to *being* in general? What is the meaning of that being which includes within itself these two radically separated regions of being? If idealism and realism both fail to explain *the relations which in fact unite these regions which in theory are without communication,* what other solution can we find for this problem? *And how can the being of the phenomenon be transphenomenal?* It is to attempt to reply to these questions that I have written the present work.[19]

Yet philosophical questions seldom hide surprising answers. The answers to Sartre's questions are already packed away in the questions themselves. The dialectic that elicits them takes, from the start, an inexorable course.

The Major Movement of the Argument

Part I, "The Problem of Nothingness," forges the tool by which Sartre will connect—always in *dis*connection—his two disparate spheres of being. The problem is no abstract one. What the Introduction has led us to, out of the restriction of philosophy to the pure phenomenon, is the concrete reality of *this* man as being-in-the-world. For it is part and parcel of the very structure of being-human that it is, on the one hand, its own immediate, pre-reflective "self"-awareness and (but not merely additively "and") its relation to the other realm of being, the being-in-itself that it is not.

Paradigmatic for this relation—the relation of consciousness to being, or of man to world—is the attitude of the *question*. First, if I knew the answer I could not ask; therefore in questioning I assert the non-being of my knowing. Second, if the world had already given me the answer, I could not ask; therefore the question also entails the possibility of non-being in being itself. And third, the question implies the existence of a truth sought as answer. But this, too, Sartre insists, entails negation; for the true reply will be "thus *and not* otherwise." The positive delimitation of truth from falsity will therefore constitute, as much as a negative answer would do, an introduction of non-being into the undifferentiated plenum of being-in-itself. The very nature of inquiry, therefore, including *par excellence* the present ontological inquiry, leads us to negation as the theme we need to pursue in order to find the two great realms of being emerging in the concrete bond between them that constitutes man. Waiting for Pierre in the café, we find how "nothingness haunts being." Studying the conceptions of nothingness in Hegel and Heidegger, we move toward an insight into the origin of such negation. It is through man that nothingness comes into the world; and, indeed, that *is* the reality of man: that through him nothingness comes into the world. But the reality of man is freedom; and freedom is in fact, Sartre tells us, the human being putting his past out of play by secreting his own nothingness.

Nihilation as a *cleavage* between my immediate psychic past and my present is the act by which I make myself as free. The consciousness of that cleavage is *dread:* the dizzying mood in which I recognize myself, not only as not being what I was, but also as being, in the mode of *not* being it, the future that I will, or ought to, be. This is the mood from which, in my everyday, "serious" existence, I am everywhere in flight. Evading the nihilating revelation of dread, which exhibits me as an emergent freedom, responsible in this very instant for my own being, for the values which "start up like partridges before my acts," [20] I hesitate in the false instantaneity of bad faith. Thus Sartre asks at the close of his first chapter, "what consciousness must be in the instantaneity of the pre-reflective *cogito,* if the human being is capable of *bad faith?*" [21] The inquiry which follows in Chapter Two, however (the chapter entitled "Bad Faith"), already makes it plain that it is in fact bad faith which is the predominant alternative. Social role-playing, for example (the way the waiter *is* a waiter, yet without *being* so in the straightforward way in which the inkwell is an inkwell), invariably exemplifies the "inner disintegration" of my being, not the transcendence of that disintegration toward the in-itself which, were it possible, would be its correct alternative. Thus we are already moving toward the final question of the book, not whether bad faith is possible, but whether some attitude different from it can in fact be realized. Man is freedom as nihilation, but is that freedom ever achieved? Can being as for-itself and being-in-itself ever be reconciled in the free act of a being which achieves its being for-itself as truly being? The thrust of the ontological inquiry initiated in the Introduction and the pathos of the self-destroying vision of man that this inquiry generates will emerge inseparably through the intervening variations on the central theme.

In Part One, then, the study of the "question" has opened up the perspective of nihilation, found dread as the instrument of self-recognition, and bad faith as its apparently inevitable alternative. Out of the initial positional consciousness of an object, supported by a non-positional consciousness (of) myself, the contrast of the in-itself as plenum and the for-itself as opposing that plenum—as a "hole in being"—has opened up. Part Two proceeds to examine the structures of the (in the first instance non-thetic but non-reflective) for-itself.

First, let us deal with its immediate structures. We discover the "presence to itself" which "supposes that an impalpable fissure has slipped into being. If being is present to itself, it is because it is not wholly itself. Presence is an immediate *deterioration* of coincidence, for it supposes separation [my italics]." [22] What brings about this separation, however, is precisely nothing: this *is* the "fissure," the "hole in being," the "fall of the in-itself to the self," "by which the for-itself is constituted."

How can such nothingness come to be? Only by what Sartre calls an *ontological act,* the "perpetual act by

which the in-itself degenerates into presence to itself."
Sartre describes this act as an absolute event in which
nothingness—that is, consciousness—comes to being
and is sustained by being; it is the very putting into question of being by being. As being is complete in itself, isolated in its plenitude, it cannot, for Sartre, be caused by
any other being, nor can anything affect it. Its unique possibility is nothingness, which, as nothingness of being, is
sustained by being. This being we see in human reality,
which, since it is defined by the "original project of its own
nothingness," is a being whose being is founded on nothingness.

Out of this original foundation of nothingness, then,
Sartre elicits the further structures of the for-itself. First,
its facticity, its character as *an unjustifiable act.* Secondly, its character as *lack:* human reality is the being
which has to not-be what it is and to be what it is not. It is
the over-against-being through which negation, through
which lack appears in the world. To assert this lack, it
must itself *be* a lack. But a lack of what? Of "the impossible synthesis of the for-itself and the in-itself." [23] Making
itself as a *lack* of being, human reality is *on principle* both
the aspiration to *be* (what it is not) and incapacity of such
being, since it is precisely as *not* being that it *is.* To anticipate a later formulation, "we are condemned to be
free." [24] We choose ourselves, we make ourselves be, as
the unrealized and, by the very logic of our being, unreal-
izable completion of ourselves.

In this nihilating act, thirdly, consciousness not only
posits value, it is *as* value. Value is the lacked which the
for-itself lacks. It is the empty "for" of the for-itself: "The
being of value qua value is the being of what does not
have being. . . . Value is beyond being. . . . Value taken

in its origin, or the supreme value, is the beyond and the *for* of transcendence . . . the meaning and the beyond of all surpassing.'' [25]

Notice, we are still with the pre-reflective *cogito.* Value at this stage is not *known;* it is not an object posited before consciousness, but rather is itself this non-thetic transparency, this consciousness of being which exists everywhere and nowhere. Value is lived concretely as my lack, which constitutes the meaning of my being, continually present, always out of reach. Thetically, as the object of consciousness, value must be grasped reflexively, and along with it the for-itself it accompanies. In this reflective consciousness, Sartre distinguishes two elements: first, the *Erlebnis* upon which we are reflecting is posited as a lack; and second, value is thus seen to be the unattainable meaning of what is lacked. It is in this way that Sartre can term reflective consciousness, moral consciousness; for whenever I reflect, I am concerned with the meaning of what I lack as for-itself. Here again, Sartre ensures human freedom, for as reflective consciousness I am free to consider certain values and to ignore others, to occupy myself with this or that object, yet my more or less studious attention to these values does not in any way affect the fact of their existence. Note also that by implication the all-or-none of honest and unhappy dread or of the relaxation into bad faith is already given as our only pair of alternatives. Either on the level of reflection I shall rise to face myself as pure lack—in freedom, anguish, total responsibility— or sink into a complacent taking of my values (which are *really* lacks) as substantive realities.

Short of the ultimate statement of this duality, Sartre adds here to facticity and value the concept of *possibility* as *''the something* which the For-itself lacks *in order* to be itself," [26] a something already shown to be unattainable in terms of its starting point. Finally, the dialectic of the for-itself and the possible (*its* possible) is shown to produce the "circuit of selfness" in which the self seeks itself by its own surpassing, and in which the *world* appears as the fugitive structure, "haunted by possibles," which I *live.*

The argument has been confined, so far, to the limits of the pre-reflective *cogito;* yet it has transcended these limits in that direction towards its possibles, which constitutes the for-itself's nihilating upsurge. It becomes necessary, therefore (in Part II, Chapter II), to elicit the temporal structure of the for-itself. Given the instantaneity of the *cogito* from which it started, however, Sartre can find in temporality only *flight,* "the refusal of the instant." [27] Consciousness temporalizes itself as what it *was,* in sheer contingency, and *is not,* and as the future which is its lack, and which again it is not. Yet even so, as the very being which has to not-be what it is (was) and to be what it is not (yet), the for-itself, even as denial, is nevertheless primarily present. In this Sartre differs from Heidegger, for whom the Future is the dominant dimension or *ekstasis.* Thus Sartre argues that the Present, although it is conditioned by the Past and the Future just as much as it conditions them, forms the nothingness essential for the negation of the Past (when the for-itself discovers it is its Past as that which it has to surpass) and the Future (when the for-itself discovers itself as lack, as what it is not and has to realize). The present is "the mould of indispensable non-being for the total synthetic form of Temporality." [28]

All this, in the life of consciousness, is still primarily non-thetic. I may try, in pure reflection (this is presumably what Sartre is attempting here), to seize on the character of original temporality itself: on the nihilating, empty eruption of the for-itself as *historicity.* More frequently, however, consciousness falls prey to *impure* reflection, where, with their shadowy being, the structures of duration, of psychic life, of the "person" are spun out.

In Chapter III of Part II, "Transcendence," Sartre returns, in the light of the exposition of the for-itself, to the question he had posed in the Introduction of the phenomenon and its knowledge. ("Transcendence" here, it should be noted, is not the transcendence to the future, Heidegger's "existentiality," referred to in the "Temporality" chapter, but the transcendent relation between the for-itself and the in-itself.) We are now moving from the for-itself as the non-thetic *conscience* (*de*) *soi* to the thetic consciousness of—an object. What does the being of the for-itself have to be in order to be knowledge of the in-itself?

There is, Sartre announces (and as I have already mentioned) only intuitive knowledge, and intuition is the presence of consciousness to the thing. But presence-to —is, we have found, essentially negation. The for-itself puts itself in question as *not* being the being of the object. Knowing, though opposed to being, is also a form of being; it is the for-itself as realizing its own being, and its otherness than being, in its internal negation of itself. We meet, in other words, in the clear light of positional consciousness, the exacerbation of the for-itself/in-itself, *pour-soi*/*en-soi,* conflict. The world as known refers us either to absolute being, when we consider knowledge to be subjective, or to ourselves, when we want to grasp this absolute. Consciousness is everywhere surrounded by being: being which is itself and nothing else. When the for-itself attempts to grasp being, it is thrown back on itself. Knowledge, rising between the for-itself and the in-itself, between non-being and being, is itself defined in terms of what it is not; to know being as it is would mean to be the thing itself. Yet, if I were to be the thing, then the whole question of knowledge would vanish, for the "such as it is" would have no meaning and according to Sartre could not even be thought. He denies that this is either skepticism (for this would place the "such as it is" on the side of being) or relativism (for there is truth in knowledge). But, although in knowledge we find ourselves in the presence of the absolute, the truth of knowledge is a human truth. "The world is human." [29]

Within this to-and-fro, all-or-none context, Sartre has handled, in this chapter, a surprising number of traditional (and some untraditional) epistemological categories and problems: quality, quantity, abstraction ("the revelation in profile of my future"), space, time, and perception ("a conductor in the circuit of selfness"). He has elaborated, with a slight twist, Heidegger's theory of the instrumentality of things. And he has returned to value, the in-itself-for-itself, which, as the "perpetually indicated but impossible fusion of essence and existence," [30] is apprehended as beauty. The beautiful is, for Sartre, the ideal, the completion and perfection of the world which would correspond to the totalization of the for-itself, the identity of consciousness and being. It is because we apprehend our own being as a lack, and thus long for plenitude, that we are able to apprehend the world itself as incomplete, as lacking beauty, and can transcend the actual state, positing its ideal realization in the realm of the imaginary. Ordinarily, Sartre argues, we do not thetically posit beauty, but rather, as he has already said of value in general, we grasp it intuitively, discovering it through its absence, as something lacking, as the imperfection of the world. This is a *Symposium* emptied of content. It is true for Sartre, as for Plato, that only he who has seen beauty itself will breed true virtue, because he alone is in contact not with illusion but with truth; and, indeed, that all others are imitators of imitations. But the Sartrean ideal is vacuous, even self-contradictory. The for-itself is in its very being the nihilation of being, and its ideal reunion with being—the for-itself-in-itself—is thus by its very nature the self-canceling denial of itself. Could it come to an issue—which it cannot—it would be the pinpoint-being, the *un*being of A·~A which it had achieved. Wittgenstein at the close of the *Tractatus* threw away his ladder: exact speech issues in total silence. Sartrean existence *is* the ladder, forever aimed at its own extinction, or, in the downward direction, forever fleeing it. Indeed, on the ground of the *cogito,* of the claim to wholly self-contained and wholly explicit knowledge, that is the only existence we can have, or can be. Human reality, temporalization, is, and can only be, flight, deterioration, from the eternal perfection of an unattainable ideal. This is historicity confined within the iron grip of the *cogito;* but the *cogito,* deprived of supernatural or rational support, has itself collapsed into nothingness.

From this ground, further, in Part III, the compulsive dialectic of the Other and of the body necessarily follows. True, Sartre sometimes mentions a non-thetic awareness of body, which would, if he had started with it, have led him, as it did Merleau-Ponty and Marcel, to a different and more hopeful issue. But he begins, fatally, as we shall see in more detail presently, with the body as the known; and on his premises—and on the premises equally of traditional rationalism or empiricism, on the premises also of phenomenology—that is where he must begin. The pre-reflective *cogito,* being purely self-directed, is impotent to reach the body; it is only through thetic consciousness, through "knowledge," that the body comes into view. It appears as the alienated aspect of myself, the congelation into a thing of my facticity. But as object, secondly, it comes into view essentially as what the Other knows. Indeed, even taking my body as myself, my brain as my mind, as a materialist like J. J. C. Smart would do, I therewith take myself in effect as known by another. And as the Other's object, finally, my body becomes the opener for me of the dizzying spectacle of another's subjectivity: of another for-itself which degrades me to mere being, unless in my turn I succeed in so degrading it. (I shall deal with these matters in more detail in the next chapter. I want here only to indicate how this problematic develops within the overall structure of the work.)

Finally, Part IV is a deepening and elaboration of the ontological foundations laid down in the argument so far. The for-itself, totally free, responsible even for its own being, and indeed for the meaning of being itself, in the teeth of its ineluctable contingency, of the fact that it is not its own foundation, is essentially agent, actor, and maker. Yet for Sartre action in the last analysis is possession. Being sheer activity, as sheer nihilation of the alien object and the alien Other, it seeks to absorb the in-itself into itself, and so to escape its own non-entity. Even knowing, the act by which the for-itself posits its negation in the object, becomes a kind of having, a digestive process by which I seek to devour the alien world. Yet the for-itself, being in its nature nihilation, cannot possess its object; whether in practice or theory, the in-itself forever escapes it. So I either strive vainly and absurdly for an empty authenticity or relapse into bad faith and "the spirit of seriousness." Either way my action is suffering, my aspiration failure: man is a useless passion.

The upshot, in summary, is this: we are a negation, a hole in being; our manner of existing is a disintegration of a unity, a flight from ourselves, and, inexorably, a failure.

And in this condition the only honest attitude is dread: a mood which swings, it seems, between blind arrogance —*I* am responsible, *I* give meaning, *I* make the world— and blind despair—I am nothing, an unjustifiable fact, a contradiction, prey to the Other's look, a mere means to the Other's end. Wherever we turn, we find an impasse.

Yet, as we noticed in discussing the pre-reflective *cogito,* there might have been a simple way out of that impasse. Non-thetic consciousness is essential, not only to the being of the for-itself, but to knowledge—that is, to the relation of the for-itself and the in-itself. It is not pre-reflectively reflexive, but outward directed; it directs the for-itself toward the in-itself. To see this, however, would have meant for Sartre a radical denial of his Cartesian starting point. And then he would not be Sartre. That is not to deny the power, or even the greatness, of his argument, both in *Being and Nothingness* and elsewhere, nor, for that matter, its direct and dramatic bearing on our own philosophical problems. For if the tragic outcome of Sartre's philosophy stems from its Cartesian beginning, we have after all, since 1641, all begun there. And if we can succeed in evading once and for all the consequences of Cartesianism, we owe a debt to Sartre for the appalling honesty with which he most of all twentieth-century philosophers has faced the consequences of our common crisis.

chapter five: the problem of the other

the other, the body, the emotions

In the preceding chapter
I presented in profile, so to speak,
the argument of *Being and Nothingness,*
analyzing the Introduction in some detail
and sketching very briefly the main movement of
its dialectic. Now I want to look more closely at some
of its special themes, in particular the problem of the
Other and in relation to it the problem of the Body.

Fundamental to both these expositions, however, is the theory of the emotions which Sartre has carried over from his early work—and to which he returns explicitly in Part IV of *Being and Nothingness.* Indeed, as F. Jeanson emphasizes in his book on Sartre, the themes of both *The Imaginary* and *The Sketch on the Emotions* are still operative in *Being and Nothingness*—and Sartre himself suggests as much in the opening sentence of Part III. We have been working so far, he says, with the *cogito* by means of a study of negating action and have thus come to understand consciousness as for-itself.[1] But "negating" is the move undertaken in the study of imagination—the image is what is not—and as we have seen, it is, in *Being and Nothingness,* the force of negativity that makes the dialectic move. Moreover, the pre-reflective *cogito,* Sartre's variant of the Cartesian original, *is,* I think it is not too much to say, the magic consciousness identified with emotion in the earlier essay. This identity should become clear as we proceed—and I shall return to it finally in connection with Sartre's exposition of action in Part IV.

The Second Cogito

In the chapter on "Transcendence," Sartre has completed his study of the structures of the for-itself, grounded in the discovery of the pre-reflective *cogito.* Then in the same chapter he goes on to consider some structures characteristic of reflection as well. The whole movement, however, has been confined to *one* consciousness, whether thetic or non-thetic. We have not yet evaded—or even discovered in our path—what Sartre calls "the reef of solipsism." Nor, as I noted above, have we discovered the body: since the body, Sartre insists, is in the first instance "that which is known by the Other." We must first learn (1) how there can be the Other; and (2) how my being is related to the being of the Other.[2] These questions, in Sartre's view far more difficult than any he has asked so far, must be answered before we can understand the body, whether "for-itself" or "for-others." Thus Part III is entitled "Being-for-Others," and "The Body" is sandwiched between the "Existence of Others"—since it appears first as known by others—and the "Concrete Relations with Others," of which the body serves as vehicle (and victim). Meantime, at the beginning of Part III, we are still in the realm of the *cogito,* interpreted (with the help of the study of negation) as for-itself.

Having set the problem, Sartre proceeds (in Section 2) to consider the reef of solipsism, noting the inability of both realism and idealism to steer their way past it. "Realism" in the Cartesian tradition is a philosophy based on intuition; but it provides (as Gilbert Ryle, too, has argued) no intuition of the soul of the Other. Thus, as far as knowing a real Other is concerned, it gives way to idealism. But idealism, at least in its Kantian form, also fails to deal with persons; it gives us no critique of social experience. Nor can the Other be explained as a Kantian "regulative idea," a mere guiding maxim: the Other has to come precisely from *outside* my experience, as no item in Kant's cognitive landscape is allowed to do. The Kantian "solution," therefore, ultimately gives way, in its turn, to an ungrounded realism. So both these positions fail: both (Cartesian) realism and (Kantian) idealism have had to leap to the Other by an unintelligible and purely external negation. Or if philosophers have tried to substitute an *internal* relation, they have moved, like Leibniz or Spinoza, to God as foundation of the I-Other relation. What we must do, however, Sartre argues, is to find some positive solution which neither falls back on God as all-absorbing reality nor surrenders to solipsism.

Sartre now looks (in Section 3) to his predecessors for guidance. He finds in Husserl a purely cognitive approach which still leaves open the road to solipsism. Hegel has recognized rightly that the problem is one of *being,* not of *knowing,* and these two categories will stand in sharp contrast throughout Sartre's own argument. But despite this seminal insight, Hegel too fails, Sartre insists, since he neglects the place of the individual in the inquiry, and therefore the place of the *cogito.* Heidegger too neglects the *cogito;* yet even his existent, for all the emphasis he places on *Mitsein,* remains isolated. From these historical reflections Sartre draws four conclusions. We must start from the *cogito,* though of course from his *prereflective cogito,* which is prior to knowledge. If I am seeking the Other in a sphere anterior to the worked-up thesis of a knowing attitude, moreover, I am seeking him somehow *not* as object. Yet at the same time I am seeking him, further, insofar as he reveals himself as not being me, even though this "not-being-me" is not the familiar in-itself of the knowable material world. On the contrary, this is a new kind of not-being-me: not that of the cup-which-is-not-myself but that of the One Who, though neither myself nor my object, yet looms up, before and behind knowledge, as uncannily Someone Else.

The most important lesson Sartre gleans from his investigation, however—most important, at least, for our understanding of the argument to come—is the one he lists first, before the three just mentioned. The Other must be approached, he tells us, not by any abstract argument (all these have failed), but *by a second cogito.* And this move, from the original *cogito* to the *cogito* by which I apprehend the Other, he likens to Descartes's move in the Third Meditation from himself to God.

The parallel is worth thinking about. *Via* the methodological doubt of the First *Meditation,* Descartes moved in the Second *Meditation* to his indubitable starting-point, the self-guaranteeing awareness of his own existence in any moment of awareness. Whenever I pronounce it, the sentence "I think, I am," cannot fail to be true. And this pellucid moment of self-contained self-awareness is the unique beginning of philosophy. But what comes next? As he explains in the *Regulae,* Descartes's method consists in establishing a first and simplest intuition, "an act of a plain and attentive mind, so clear that no doubt remains concerning that which is apprehended," then in moving step by step from this first intuition to the next simplest and so on, until he has covered, surely and carefully, the whole range of human knowledge. At the outset—until a goodly portion at least of the whole system is established —he must proceed, he insists, in this heuristic manner, not, as ancient mathematicians pretended to do, by the method of axiomatization and proof. And he has himself confirmed in the *Replies to Objections,* that it is this method of discovery—the synthetic method, as it was traditionally called—that he is using in the *Meditations.* As the title of the work declares, he is going through a series of *meditations,* schooling himself to move, and moving, from one perfectly established, self-contained intuition to another. At the start of Meditation III he has reached the first of the series, and now needs to find a path to a second, which must be equally indubitable, equally susceptible to direct apprehension by the mind. If he is to achieve knowledge of an external world, moreover, this second idea must be something outside himself. And in particular, if he is to trust his clear and distinct ideas beyond the self-evident, momentary presentation of any one of them, it must be the idea of an all-good, all-powerful God. Now on the view of Husserl or any pure phenomenologist, the first of these two demands misleads him, since it takes him beyond pure consciousness to metaphysics. But the second demand, ever since the publication of the *Meditations,* has raised the question of the "Cartesian circle." Descartes needs God to guarantee his clear and distinct ideas, yet he has to use clear and distinct ideas to prove the existence of God. How, if at all, can this peculiar move be justified? For our purposes we may safely set aside the scholarly debate on this subject, and concentrate on one very simple point. All we need for our present purpose is to recognize that, logically speaking, this *is* a very peculiar argument, precisely because it is not so much an argument, in the logician's sense, as it is the *strategy* of a discoverer. The philosopher in his meditation must direct his attention from his first, self-contained, self-conscious intuition to another equally self-sustaining intuition. For all the complications of the Third Meditation, with its "formal" and "objective" realities, its modified causal principles, and so on, what the whole thing amounts to is *one* straightforward step from intuition I (the *cogito*) to intuition II (God). Once the thinker has that, once he has looked with total attention at the idea of God that his own mind innately contains, he will have what he needs to go on again: the guarantor of his clear and distinct ideas, the shield against error, the patron of a unified knowledge of nature and of man. All this will follow. But in itself the step from the *cogito* to God is simply the turning of attention from one direct presentation to another equally direct.

What of Sartre? The external world is already with him in the in-itself whose negation the for-itself is. And he is certainly not moving from his (pre-reflective) *cogito* to God; for him God is not only non-existent but impossible. That solution to solipsism, which he has rightly recognized as typical of the tradition, he certainly cannot adopt.

Moreover, his original *cogito,* being non-thetic, was not *known,* as the Cartesian *cogito* is; it was only *lived.* Nor is the move to the second *cogito,* the *cogito* of the Other, a cognitive move. As I have already said, Sartre contrasts throughout *being* and *knowing,* and the move here is from *being* to *being,* not, as for Descartes, from one moment of knowing to another. In all these respects the situation here is very different.

Yet the parallel Sartre draws between his argument and Descartes's is exact. He has been working so far, if with far-ranging dialectical instruments, on the ground of *one* self-contained, unique beginning, the pre-reflective *cogito,* the consciousness (of) self which is, for him, the fulcrum of all intentionality, of all outward-directed, and indeed all reflective, thought. It is this first and unique *cogito* which supports all the structures of the for-itself. But the for-itself, like Descartes's moment of self-aware-ness, is, and must be, *alone.* Another for-itself would be for-*itself.* How then can the for-itself discover such a con-tradictory double of itself? Only by a new, separate, equally absolute "intuition," or quasi-intuition, which looms up in experience as direct and overwhelming, but not for-me. Descartes has first discovered an idea of him-self; he has secondly—has always had—an idea of an all-good, all-powerful Deity. With reverence he looks at this idea, and behold, God *is.* He has but to inspect this idea and all that he needs will follow. Sartre has first dis-covered a different and non-thetic *cogito;* and he has no idea of God to which he may next proceed: he cannot re-cover the old gentleman who receded from the Parisian rooftops so long ago. But he does have, as Descartes does in Meditation III, an experience which reveals to him directly a second directly apprehended presence. That presence is the presence of the Other, and the experience through which he apprehends it is the experience of *shame.* Although he acknowledges three Other-revealing emotions—shame, fear, and pride—in the course of this chapter, it is shame he starts from, not only in the description of the Look—in the scene at the keyhole—but in the very beginning of the argument. I make an awkward gesture (say, picking my nose), and suddenly I find myself observed. The Other is there. In the *Meditations,* the believer looks with reverence to his God and acknowledges His being as the source of all being. The for-itself is ashamed, and the being before whom he is ashamed is discovered to him as the Other, the monstrous for-itself that is not *my* for-itself, which by its very being threatens me with degradation to objectivity. Just as the intricacies of the Meditation III reduce to one move from the *cogito* to the apprehension of the idea of God, so the complexities of Sartre's argument on the Other reduce to one move from the first, pre-reflective *cogito,* the *cogito* of the for-itself, to the "second *cogito,*" the *cogito* that reveals the Other.

Shame, Fear, Pride

We have already looked at the main steps of Sections II and III, on solipsism and on Husserl-Hegel-Heidegger. In Section IV, The Look, Sartre returns to shame as his starting-point, and asks in detail his two original questions: on the Existence of the Other, and on my relation to it—both, remember, as questions of *being,* not of knowing. In other words, the problem is not, as philosophers often put it, how I *know* other minds. On the level of probability I could manage that as I can the inferential knowledge of any other object. But the scandal is this: the world is organized around me, while the Other as Other claims to organize the world around him. Yet if, as it is, the world is my world, made the world it is by my self-projection, how can such an Other *be?* And how, in my being, do I relate to him? These are the questions Sartre has to ask.

There are three main divisions of his exposition. First is the phenomenology of the Look, which reveals the Other and my relation to him. Second comes the ontology of the Other: who is the Other, what is his being and the being of my relation to him? Finally, there is the metaphysical question, why is there an Other, a question which leads us back to the temporal dimensions of past, future, and present, and introduces briefly the problem of "mind" as an (im)possible totality of consciousnesses. I shall not try to trace in detail this complex and often obscure argument, but shall only stress some of its chief, and debatable, themes.

The description itself is among the best known sections of *Being and Nothingness:* the jealous watcher at the keyhole (let's call him Pierre), wholly engaged in spying out those within. This is the paradigm of the "situation" as Sartre here defines it. Pierre's jealousy *is* his absorption in the conjecture that Thérèse may be in there in bed with Paul. That is Pierre's world; the fact that he is the lover of Thérèse, who is having an affair with Paul is what *makes* him jealous, and thus makes his jealousy, makes *him* as a jealous man. But these "facts" are facts of a human situation only through his jealousy. Were he wholly indifferent to Thérèse and indeed away making love to Annette, they would not be the facts they are. Situation always has this dual character. I live the world in and through my (non-thetic) consciousness (of) self—in this case, for Pierre, through *being* jealous. But, on the other hand, my consciousness (of) self, in this case Pierre's jealousy, *is* projected, through the keyhole, into the room where Thérèse and Paul may be in bed together.

This duality of non-thetic consciousness, reflecting

the way I am in the world through my emotion, so that my emotion is just my way of being-in-the-world and yet at the same time makes the world what it is, makes the grapes sour or my mistress unfaithful—this duality of situation is universal, as we shall see later when we return to Sartre's treatment of the emotions in Part IV. But there are certain emotions which uniquely reveal the Other, reveal him not as a probable object in my world, but as lived by me in his very being. These emotions, once more, are shame, fear, and pride: in the keyhole case, of course, shame. Pierre has been looking through the keyhole; suddenly he feels himself looked at; someone is coming; he freezes; instead of the impassioned mediator of an all-absorbing situation, he becomes—a spy. Suddenly he is degraded to an object, a puppet with a role, the nasty role of sneak. He acquires a "character": a man who doesn't trust his mistress. And that degradation happens, not just through a change of mood, from jealousy to shame, but through the upsurge of the Other whom his shame reveals. Shame is shame of myself before the Other; through it the Other is there as He Who Makes Me Ashamed. Of course jealousy, too, it may be objected, is jealousy of Another. But, Sartre would insist, it is not other-related in the same way as shame. In jealousy I am conjuring away through my emotion the escape of one of my possessions—wife or mistress. A loved object is, in Sartre's terms, just that: an object, and no more. Jealousy, therefore, is my magical way of keeping what is mine. But shame takes me from myself —and my possessions—and drops me, dizzyingly, into a place in the Other's world: he sees before him—a jealous lover. Thus I become a character in his drama, an object in his world.

Fear, too, reveals the Other directly and immediately as there. It transforms the world I was engaged in into the Other's world, in which I may be a victim. A soldier reconnoitering in a valley feels himself looked at from a farmhouse on the hill, and is afraid. He is afraid because somebody may be looking; and somebody's being there —eyes looking—is what is revealed through his fear. Before that, he was curious, on the lookout. Suddenly he is instead a possible target for a sniper's bullet. That is what it *is* to be afraid. In other words, the Other, seeing me, also sights me; I am no longer myself, but the target in his sight. As the Other looms up as He Who May Shoot Me, so I become, in fear, He Who May Get Shot. And with this revelation I lose my freedom. For it is the predator who freely stalks his prey; the prey, on the contrary, however fast he runs, is prey, not out of his own free choice, but because the Other makes him so. Thus the Other reveals himself by robbing me of my freedom: it is, suddenly, his freedom I have to live, not mine. That is why, Sartre follows Gide in saying, the Other plays the Devil's part. That is why, to quote Sartre's own familiar maxim, "Hell is Other people." The revelation of the Other is the loss of freedom, the fall of the self into the Other's world. This is the second *cogito* Sartre was seeking:

> Just as my consciousness apprehended by the cogito bears indubitable witness of itself and of its own existence, so certain particular consciousnesses—for example, "shame-consciousness" bear indubitable witness to the *cogito* both of themselves and of the existence of the Other.[3]

And this second *cogito,* it must be emphasized once more, is still—or again—on the level of being, not knowing. Although, admittedly, the character the Other gives me, that is, the object I become in his world, is an object of knowledge, it is primarily something *he* knows. I may indeed know it, too, and even accept it as "my" character. Yet it *is* not I. It is separated from me by an infinite gap: the gap between my projection of my possibilities and the Other's projection of his possibilities, including this strange double that is "me." Thus as being-for-Others I am radically, inalienably alienated from myself. Over against the Other, in the light of the second *cogito,* that is how I am. Moreover, the whole of Sartrean sociality consists in attempts to evade this fate: in ruses to make the Other keep his objectivity in the world of my freedom, and so to prevent my relapse into objectivity in the world that *he* freely constitutes. From instant to instant of the for-itself's existence, one or other of two I-Other relations is bound to prevail: either the sadism that objectifies the Other or the masochism that perversely accepts my own reduction to an object through the Other's Being. A third possibility—namely, that *we* are together—is, on Sartrean premises, wholly impossible. We shall have to examine later the question whether Sartre has really changed his position in the *Critique,* but in *Being and Nothingness* there is no question: the Other is the Devil, he is out to destroy me, either he wins or I do.

All this is crystal clear from Sartre's examples, shame and fear, as well as from his exposition of the being of the Other and from his cryptic metaphysical remarks at the conclusion of the chapter. But he has listed three basic passions through which the Other is revealed. The third, pride, he expounds briefly, but does not illustrate. Perhaps before we go further we should ask abouts its nature too. Shame, we have seen, is my being as I live it in the Other's look which degrades me to an object in his world. Fear, too, is my being as I live it in the Other's look, as the look exposes me to his power. He has not yet torn me from myself, but on principle he can, through humiliation or even death. Thus in either shame or fear the Other is the permanent possibility of my destruction. But in pride, on the contrary, I seem to assert myself. I rise up over against Others and glory in my Being. This too may come as a sudden upsurge; out of absorption in the world, accompanied by non-thetic awareness of myself, suddenly I become aware of the Others as spectators, not of my humiliation, but of my prowess, of my success. The runner running a mile is (thetically) intent on getting to the goal; non-thetically he is living his own effort, he is that effort; nothing else in all the world is there. He wins —and the commending, acclaiming Others appear. He grasps the coveted cup, holds it aloft, is himself held aloft on Others' shoulders; proudly he acknowledges his own being as Winner before the grateful crowd. This sounds straightforward; but is it? If our Winner really objectifies the Others, they have lost their Otherness and become merely objects in his world; so they have not revealed themselves as Others acclaiming him, but as the tools of his own aggrandisement. This is surely not pride, but vanity. And in fact in Sartre's own terms, vanity is the use of my objectivity for this purpose: my beauty or prowess, what the Other finds objectively in me, I use to objectify him. But where in all this is pride?

Let us reflect again. I fear the Other's look, on principle, as the possibility of my fall. When the Other, this one Other, does in fact look at me, I fall into shame. But pride, it seems, arises as the converse of shame: it is my superior look against the falling Other, my self-assertion which responds to his by threatening him. And Sartre does indeed insist that pride arises on the foundation of "fundamental shame." It is the attempted reaction to it, turning the force of my free existence against the Other's freedom. But pride is also transitional and unstable, for in fact

I must either defeat the Other and so become wholly my own freedom, or succumb to shame and alienation before him, abandoning freedom for thinghood. Moreover, for Sartre, pride, like vanity, is necessarily in bad faith. It is in bad faith because it has allowed the illusion of objectification to creep into my self-consciousness. My consciousness, formerly absorbed in the effort to reach the goal, is now somehow made focal, taken as a being I can put before Others and "be proud of." But that is to make my freedom thing-like, to flee the dreadful self-making, the nihilation of the in-itself that is the for-itself. The runner running has winning-the-race before him as a not-yet-being whose non-being he has to nihilate. Winning, he becomes the one who has won. The others acclaim him, in his pride he seems to lift himself above them; but this thing-like being-the-winner is nevertheless a betrayal of his pure freedom. Moreover, it is a relation to anonymous Others, to the crowd, not to the Other. Only a non-denumerable, generalized Other can be before me in this fashion. To one Other I can be only victim or destroyer. Pride, in short, is the fleeting resurgence of the For-Itself against the Other-in-general, unstable, and, in its delusive use of self-objectification for self-assertion, necessarily in bad faith. In its revelation of the Other, therefore, it seems to be secondary to the basic emotions of shame and fear. It is ephemeral, abstract (directed to Others, not the Other), and self-deceptive. Basically, it is shame and fear that reveal the Other. Pride is an attempted, but impotent, alternate to shame.

For-Itself and For-Others:
An Ontological Excursion

Sartre has discovered, then, a second *cogito* which supplements the first and defeats solipsism. As Descartes moved from reverent inspection of his own innate idea of God to the revelation of the Divine Other who founds his—and all—being, so Sartre has moved through the experience of shame to the discovery of a Satanic Other who, by his existence, threatens to undermine and subvert the being of the for-itself that has discovered him. This is not so much the "refutation of solipsism" as it is the discovery that though I have to be myself alone, there is, against me, an Other who will not let me be— because *he* would be instead. Such, for Sartre, is the ground of all community: language becomes a form of seduction, love becomes an alternation between sadism and masochism, solidarity becomes class struggle. Although much in his account is subtly and convincingly observed, and although his argument, on his own premises —on the foundation, as he proudly acclaims, of the *cogito* alone—is irresistible, one wants nevertheless to question it.

What grounds have we for doing so? We may of course simply invoke the testimony of experience: the rare but still indubitable experience of mutual understanding, of the reciprocal look of peers; or the look of mother and infant, where the one protects and the other is protected. In its immediate appearance there seems no internecine warfare here. Or we may rely on an empirical generalization as counter-example: the fact that human infants deprived of a family setting develop more slowly, and deprived of some simulation at least of an affectionate initiation by Others into the human world, become retarded perhaps beyond recall. But counter-examples, though useful, are not sufficient to answer philosophical questions. We may still ask, in general, what philosophical objections we can raise to Sartre's position and to what alternative they lead us. There are, I believe, three different junctures in his argument, all interrelated, at which he clearly goes astray, and his phenomenological or empirical narrowness, his failure to *see* the counter-examples that invalidate his "solution," stems, philosophically, from the wrong turnings he has taken along the way.

The first and most fundamental error we have already noted: it is the confinement of the pre-reflective *cogito* to consciousness (of) self. Piaget's example of children who can do arithmetic but can't say how they do it illustrates, as we have seen, not in fact Sartre's consciousness (of) self, but a non-thetic consciousness that carries us away from self to the world. The usual thrust of non-thetic (or as Polanyi calls it, subsidiary) awareness is *from* clues within myself *to* something out there, for the understanding or performance of which I am relying on those inner clues. For Sartre, the for-itself develops as the negation of the in-itself, but this uncompromising negativity obscures the positive relation that binds me to the world. All that I appropriate from it, all that becomes part of me—like the child's skill in arithmetic—becomes at the same time a repertoire of attitudes, of incipient actions, through which I attend to my present concerns out there in the hope of achieving my future goals. There is a flowing reciprocity here of inner and outer, non-thetic and thetic, past and future. If Polanyi, with his distinction between focal and subsidiary awareness, has best described the epistemological core of this situation, Heidegger in *Being and Time* has best described the fundamental character of human being which makes this relation possible. Being-in-the-world is prior to "consciousness" and shapes it. Human being from the first is out there with things, just as the things are from the first "there" as stuff (*Zeug*) of interest or of use to human being. There is no cut between a consciousness (of) self and an external world which it denies and by whose denial it is. On the contrary, there is a primary and pervasive tension from "self" to world and back again—a tension through which, and through which alone, "consciousness" develops. Husserl has christened the forward and backward aspects of temporal consciousness "protension" and "retention." I suggest that the term "tension," with its connotation of tautness, of a stretch from—to—, would best characterize in general the concern-for, the being-out-there-with-, that founds the relation of man to world, and so the being of man himself.

Now if, as Heidegger and Polanyi have jointly shown, we are, in all the varieties of from-to awareness, out there with things, we are also always—perhaps first of all—already out there with other people. Being-with-others is an essential aspect of being oneself. Sartre, of course, resists this Heideggerian insight, which does, indeed, beg the question of solipsism. But it begs the question precisely because at long last we are not starting from the *cogito* but from a very different beginning: the everyday existence of human being before methodological doubt. And when we look carefully, without Cartesian prejudice, at the structures of this everyday existence, at the way in which human being is in the world, with things and other human beings, we find no reef of solipsism. We find, on the contrary, structures which eliminate the very question of solipsism. To put the question at all in these circumstances is to join Russell's correspondent, who wrote to him, "I am a solipsist; why isn't everybody?" In a refined and reflective intellectual posture, one can indeed wonder about our "knowledge of other minds." But in its fundamental way of being, human being becomes what it is in and out of its being-with-others. It is being-with that is primary and being-alone, being against the world and others, that is a negation, through philosophical contrivance, of that primary being.

One passage in the chapter on the Other shows clearly how, at this juncture too, Sartre has taken a fatal misstep—a step necessitated, indeed, by his initial misreading of non-thetic consciousness. Specifying a number of ontological theses suggested by the phenomenology of the Look, he declares: "being-for-others is not an ontological structure of the For-itself. We can not think of deriving being-for-others from a being-for-itself as one would derive a consequence from a principle, nor conversely can we think of deriving being-for-itself from being-for-others." [4] Now of course it is true that the for-others cannot be *deduced* from the for-itself nor the for-itself from the for-others. But what Sartre fails to see—and, given his Cartesian starting point, could not see—is that both the for-itself and the for-others depend for their very possibility on what we may call the among-others (to adopt for the moment his Hegelian style). For-itself and for-others are both expressions, and developments, of the fundamental structure of being-with-others-in-the world. To put it in ordinary language, the human individual is, in his humanity and in his individuality, necessarily and essentially an expression of a social world. Were he not among-others, in a world made by others, he could not become, and so could not be, himself. A human individual acquires humanity, not just by being born a member of *homo sapiens,* but by learning to participate in a given social world, which in turn, however he may rebel against it, he expresses in his very existence. Without being-among-others there is no human reality of any kind at all.

To admit this, however, would be to abandon, not only the primacy of the *cogito,* with its threat of solipsism or alternatively of annihilation by the Other, but also its corollaries: the ideal of the instant and the conception of freedom as pure activity. I mentioned earlier, in the discussion of Sartre's predecessors, his adherence to the Cartesian concepts of time and freedom. But let us consider here, very briefly, how his account of situation is affected by these preconceptions.

A situation, Sartre says, is wholly out there in the world and is the situation it is in view of my way of being in it. The watcher at the keyhole is "beside himself" in the scene he is watching and yet the scene is the scene it is because he casts himself into it. I throw myself into a situation, and so make it one. Looked at this way, the situation has two contradictory aspects: it is all in the world and at the same time all in my (non-reflective) consciousness. How can this to-and-fro be stabilized? Only by the appearance of the Other, who objectifies it. Only the Other, and my relation to the Other, Sartre recognizes, create a public world of objective space and time. Yet in terms of the for-itself, which is primary, the giving of myself to these organized totalities is always flight from myself. To act now, in here, this instant, would be freedom. To move out there, by means of the "character" I have "for others," from the situation into which I have been cast toward the future situation I envisage: all this can happen only in bad faith, as the flight of consciousness from itself. Only the present could be authentic, and thus free, if anything could.

Yet Pierre has not been dropped from heaven to watch and listen at the keyhole. His past, Thérèse's past, indeed the past of Gallic sexuality, combine to constitute his present preoccupation and reverberate in it. Besides, to watch or listen is to anticipate what may be happening on the other side of the door. The past into which I have been cast, the future possibilities to which I am attending, these make my present, make the spatiality that surrounds me. The present is a precipitation of the past through its direction to the future. Its spatial dimensions, however ample or however narrow, express, in the mode of simultaneity, the stretch toward the future that is mediated by the past. And that past is social. True, it is my past, as the future is my future. But it is "mine" in a perspectival sense: as the narrowing to one sector of a constant stream of interactions. Moreover, the future, too, will be not only mine but ours and theirs: the stream that founds the past of future projects, both my own and others'. Only out of this interplay of future and past, temporality and spatialization, can the present situation of this individual emerge as such. Social time and social space are already presupposed as necessary conditions for the existence of the for-itself. Thus the concept of a pure detached instant as the model for the existence of consciousness is illusory. On the contrary, human being is social precisely because it is historical. I have come "to myself" in and out of the tradition of some particular social world into which I happen to have been born. Human time is built out of historical stretches, not instants of pure consciousness.

If the moment is illusory, however, the moment of pure freedom, *a fortiori,* is illusory also. Human freedom is never instantaneous and complete. It entails the interiorization of standards, themselves socially—that is, historically—developed, standards in free submission to which I have learned to act responsibly, even if I often fail to do so. Indeed, the very concepts of "success" or "failure" imply submission to standards by which achievement or its denial can be judged. And again, however idiosyncratic one's standards may become, they must be communal, and thus historical, in three senses. First, they must have grown out of a social world. Secondly, as standards they must claim universality: they entail what Polanyi calls "universal intent." They express, not just my "subjective" preferences, but rules by which I judge my own performance and judge that any other person in my circumstances should judge his. Thus the very concept of free action demands a relation to others; I as a free agent am this unique center of action and choice that has developed through participation in, as well as expresses, the standards of this culture, accepted by me with universal intent. Acting as free agent, in other words, I act not only as myself, but as he-who-would-do-so-and-so-in-such-and-such-circumstances. It is this possibility of *de*tachment that makes an action free. For it is characteristic of a human person, as Helmuth Plessner has emphasized, to be able to put himself in another's place and another in his. Thus the human present, too, the moment of action itself, has a social extensiveness. In this sense roleplaying is not as such a betrayal of freedom as it is with Sartre's waiter, who does not exist as waiter but only plays the part; it is rather—the instantiation of freedom.

Finally, if freedom arises out of a social past and exists through generalization (spatialization?) of the present, its primary thrust is to the future, but a future which reverberates beyond my own possibilities; it will be the stuff of others' actions as well as of my own. Now admittedly, Sartre himself, like Heidegger, stresses the futurity of human existence: I am my possibilities. But his all-or-none dialectic, combined with his Cartesianism, leads him to interpret this being as a non-being: a possibility is what is not (yet), and so to be a possibility is to be what is not—and thus to not-be, to be only in the mode of nihilation. To be in the mode of possibility, however, is also to be: to be as a protension, a stretch to the future; to follow Merleau-Ponty's metaphor, a "fold in being" rather than a "hole." The present situation, once more, becomes what it is through the *prospecting* of possibilities founded on, and limited by, the development of a retrospected past. The introspection of a for-itself is the condensation into a relatively instantaneous stretch of consciousness of these primary temporal relations. But those relations, too, as I have been trying to suggest, also entail sociality. The history out of which I act is the history of a culture; the future into which I act is social both as the stuff of history for future actions, whether of myself or others, and as demanding, in its character of responsible action, reference to standards that are socially derived, and universal in their intent—applicable to myself at other times and to others as well as to myself.

The Body

In all this "beating about the neighboring fields" I have been commenting on Sartre's statement that the for-Others is not an ontological structure of the for-itself. I have been arguing that, on the contrary, the for-itself (and *a fortiori* the for-others) is an expression of the among-others, the primary relation which Sartre, in his commitment to the *cogito* and associated concepts, fails to see. This was the second misstep I wanted to point out. The third, equally apparent in a number of passages in the same chapter, is equally fundamental, perhaps even the most fundamental of all. For it concerns that most basic Cartesian error: the division of consciousness from the body.

In the text explaining his first Rule for the Direction of the Mind Descartes distinguishes between the unity of mind and the plurality of bodily skills. Thus his method from the very start rests on the separation of a pure and self-contained consciousness from the extensiveness of bodily existence. In the Third *Meditation* also—which corresponds, as we have noticed, to the place Sartre has reached in his argument in the chapter on the Other—Descartes is still operating wholly within the sphere of consciousness; the body in its real existence only reappears in the last Meditation. Sartre, it is true, has already admitted the in-itself as the target of intentionality, that plenitude from which the for-itself rises up as nihilation. The Other, however, we have seen, far from being the passive exteriority of the in-itself, is, menacingly and paradoxically, an-other *consciousness*. It is not, Sartre insists, the Other's eyes that look at me, but the gaze "behind" them, the consciousness that threatens to organize me into its world. So, through an-other consciousness, I fall from being for-myself toward the inertia of mere corporeality; thus it is that through the Other's look I discover my body. That discovery, however, is founded, Sartre insists, on the for-Others as an upsurge *in* consciousness. Even my relation to the Other is a relation between consciousnesses, in which the objective fact of his looking at me is "a pure *monition*," [5] the occasion of my *feeling* of being looked-at. Indeed, I can be aware of the Other even when "in fact" he is not there. Thus, in the keyhole scene, Pierre may suspect someone is watching him watching and experience that watching as (or in) shame, and even though he finds himself mistaken—it was only someone leaving by the street door, there is no one there at all—his shame may linger.

Now of course it is indeed true that I may be aware of my presence to others even when in fact no Other is at hand. But is this experience therefore disembodied? Is it pure consciousness-of-peril-as-for-itself-before-the-

Other's-possible-gaze? Sartre's own description betrays the untenability of this view. My shame, he says, "is my red face as I bend over the keyhole." [6] In other words, the emotion through which I find myself before the Other is at the same time a state of bodily being. My shame *is* my red face. . . . Similarly, Sartre has described earlier the fear that reveals the Other to a reconnoitering soldier. He hears crackling over there in the undergrowth—and becomes vulnerable, a body that could become another's target. What happens here? In Sartre's terms, I fall from thetic consciousness of the surrounding territory, sustained by non-thetic consciousness (of) self (I am curious, interested, alert), to thetic consciousness of my body as an object in another's world, carried by the special non-thetic consciousness (of) self that is called fear. Now what is correct in this account, it seems to me, is that I do, in shame or in some kinds of fear, become aware of my body in a new way. But that is not to say that I was not in any way aware of it before. My shame *is* my red face as I bend over the keyhole. But my jealousy, too, my intentness in watching, was, not just non-thetic consciousness (of) self as such; it was non-thetic consciousness of my embodied self, it was the stealthiness of my posture, the quiet with which I breathed, the way I strained to see what was going on on the other side of the door. I exist as embodied being-in-the-world, and in no other way. Of course Sartre knows this; he is no believer in a Cartesian *res cogitans* or disembodied soul. Then how, on the one hand, does he see my relation to my body prior to the Other's degradation of me to an object in his world, and, on the other hand, what really is the bodily aspect of my being that the Other reveals to me?

To answer these questions we need to examine the next chapter, on "The Body," and we can then return to the question, how Sartre's view of the body / consciousness relation has helped to mislead him in his view of the Other.

In general, we have seen, Sartre's philosophical method in *Being and Nothingness* is one of flights and perches. He passes by dialectical moves and countermoves from one phenomenological description to another. But sometimes he also adopts the Heideggerian habit of piling up oracular pronouncements, so that the argument all but vanishes beneath their weight. This holds especially of the discussion of the body, and most of all of its first part. Thus the argument is difficult to disentangle; but let me try to summarize its main theses and, as I see it, its major difficulty.

Sartre expounds in turn three aspects of the body: the body for-itself, the body for-others, and the body for-itself as known by the Other. In all three sections he is reworking themes we have already met. Thus the body for-itself is the concrete expression of my facticity, of the necessity that I be born *some* where, *some* how. It is the necessity of my contingency, the condition for all possible action on the world. In other words, it is simply the necessity that there be *a choice*. It is the choice that I am. As for-itself, however, the body is consciousness. It is the non-thetic consciousness through which, thetically, I act out and into the world. And at the same time that consciousness is wholly body. For it is, again, precisely the necessity of my contingent existence, born thus and so into a world, that body for-itself is. Secondly, the body for-others is what results when the Other consciousness, emergent into my consciousness as alien transcendence, is in turn transcended. What enters my consciousness first, to be sure, is not the Other's body, but the Other as transcendence, as Other-consciousness and threat; but in responding to this threat I can in turn transcend his transcendence and so make him—flesh. That is how I live the Other's body for-himself, through my demotion of him to the protoplasmic quivering of mere life. Not, mind you, to the in-itself: that would be to know the Other's body just as I know inanimate things, to know him as a corpse. No, the degradation to flesh is the transcendence of his transcendence, which still entails reference to his transcendence in my very conquest of it. It is the means by which I reduce to the level of mere living the spontaneity by which the Other organizes his world, his world including myself in it as transcendence to be transcended. "Out, out, vile jelly!" Gloucester's eyes are not pieces of gelatinous matter, but the instruments of another's gaze, the accusing gaze of a wronged father and friend. It is that sort of transcendence that torture aims to transcend. Thirdly, I live my body, not only as for-myself, but as known to the Other. I live my body as alienated, as slipping from me into a place in the Other's world. This is the root meaning of alienation for Sartre, on which his social theory will be built. All these aspects of bodily being, finally, Sartre sums up in a final phrase: "The body is the instrument which I am." [7] This summarizing statement, he holds, lays to rest once and for all any problems that the body, appearing to the for-itself, might have evoked.

Yet it also summarizes, in my opinion, both the impasse to which Sartre's approach to the body has brought him and the way out he is, thanks to his own premises, unable to take. What is it to *be* an instrument? It is to be a means, but to what end? The end is the for-itself's project, the nihilation of what is in favor of what is not, the nihilation that I am. But how can I be at the same time my possibility and the means to that possibility? And how can I know that I am so?

The answer to both questions is a single one. Sartre has been operating all along, we have seen, in terms of a strict dichotomy between knowing and being, or knowing and living. Knowing is a thetic confrontation with the object of thought; contrasted with it is the non-thetic awareness of the fashion in which, the passion by which, I relate myself to that object. The Other looms up not as the object of knowledge, but as lived by me as threat to my own being. Similarly, the body, for myself, is lived and not known. Sartre makes this crystal clear in a brilliant analysis of the traditional philosophy of sensation, in which he moves from the will-of-the-wisp "sensation" (or sense-data), to sense and sensible objects, and then to action as the necessary correlate of sense. His argument leads him to the insight that our sense-mediated interaction with the world, and therefore all our information about the world, is necessarily tied to its point of origin, the point of view that is my bodily being. The cup is not just on the table, it is to my right, from where I sit, beyond the pencil, and so on. If I remove from such relations all perspectival reference, I remove their content. Thus my body is the instrument that I am, the instrument of instruments, because it is my point of view. The body, Sartre says again, is the neglected, the surpassed. Precisely. It is the surpassed because in and through it I act out onto the world and am acted on by things (and people) in the world. It is also, and for that reason, the indispensable ground of knowledge and of action. Without it knowledge would vanish into contentless relations. For suppose the body, instead of being a non-thetic ground of action, were itself known. Such knowledge would be empty. Sartre writes:

> In this case . . . the fundamental tool becomes a relative center of reference which itself supposes other tools to utilize it. By the same stroke the instrumentality of the world disappears, for in order to be revealed it needs a reference to an absolute center of instrumentality; the world of action becomes the world acted upon of classical science; consciousness surveys a universe of exteriority and can no longer in any way enter into the world.[8]

Alternatively, therefore, for Sartre the body must be lived and not known. Thus, secondly, he continues:

> . . . the body is given concretely and fully as the very arrangement of things in so far as the For-itself surpasses it towards a new arrangement. In this case the body is present in every action although invisible, for the act reveals the hammer and the nails, the brake and the change of speed, not the foot which brakes or the hand which hammers. The body is lived and not known.[9]

And these two possibilities, he insists, are wholly disparate and mutually exclusive. Living is never and cannot be knowing; knowing is never lived.

Yet if the first alternative is empty and for us impossible of achievement, and the second full of all the concrete content of experience and, for us, necessary, why must we keep up the pretense that there is a dichotomy here? In fact, there is none—or rather, there is the duality of subsidiary and focal awareness, a duality inherent in all knowing and all action. But this is not the irreconcilable duality of living against knowing. It is the unity-in-plurality of lived bodily being as it bears on knowing and, indeed, on all rational action. Thus the body is present though invisible in the hammer and the nails just because it is through my subsidiary awareness of hammer, nails, hand, arm, that I am focally aware of placing the picture the way

I want it on the wall. All reasonable action on the world, all knowledge of the world, from perception to the grasp of the most abstract theories, shares this same structure. Read in terms of the concepts of focal and subsidiary awareness, then, Sartre's dicta on the body take on a different meaning. Thus, for example, he writes:

> My body is everywhere: the bomb which destroys my house also damages my body in so far as the house was already an indication of my body. This is why my body always extends across the tool which it utilizes: it is at the end of the cane on which I lean and against the earth; it is at the end of the telescope which shows me the stars; it is on the chair, in the whole house; for it is my adaptation to these tools.[10]

This is true. But it is not a description of living as against knowing; it is a description of the structure of knowledge itself.

Once more, however, this simple move is one Sartre cannot make. The pure act of consciousness and the tension of living must be for him wholly and ineradicably opposed. He declares early in the chapter, for example, that touching and being touched, the one purely active and the other purely passive and external, are entirely opposed to one another. At the close of the chapter he insists again: my hand as touched is a mere external object, my hand as touching is my consciousness in act. Two hands, both mine, belong to two worlds, and are forever separated by the total gap that isolates for-itself from in-itself, nihilation from reality, consciousness from the external world. It is, I believe, with the exposition of this chapter in particular that Merleau-Ponty was wrestling from *The Phenomenology of Perception*—which begins with a theory of the body—to *The Visible and the Invisible*, where he was still struggling with the mystery of the touching-touched, the seer-seen. And it is, in my view, Polanyi's distinction between focal and subsidiary awareness, and the theory of tacit knowing elaborated on the basis of that distinction, that provides the solution for the problem. Merleau-Ponty comes very close to it in *The Phenomenology of Perception* and, as we have seen, even Sartre himself comes close to it in many passages, especially in this chapter. But, as always, his Cartesianism continues to hold him in thrall. The step to enfranchisement of lived bodily existence as the vehicle of knowledge and of rational action he is unable to take.

But the crucial question for our present discussion still remains. I have been considering the account of the body as, in my view, the third place where Sartre goes astray in his approach to the Other. It seems clear to the point of truism that history and with it sociality are prerequisites to an understanding of our being with others, as distinct from Cartesian instantaneity and the isolation of the single for-itself. What has bodily being to do with this?

The answer is given, by implication, in Sartre's own argument. The Other for me, he makes it clear, is in fact the Other as embodied. Consider my perception of the Other. Suppose I see Pierre raise his arm. This is not, Sartre says, the perception of an arm raised beside a motionless body; what I see is Pierre-raising-his-hand. Thus, he concludes, Pierre's body is *in no wise* to be distinguished from Pierre-for-me: "The Other's body with its various meanings exists only for me: to be an object-for-others or to-be-a-body are two ontological modalities which are strictly equivalent expressions of the being-for-others on the part of the for-itself." [11]

Yet if this is correct, what has happened to the Other as Consciousness? Other as body, Sartre has insisted, is posterior to that first, hemorrhagic starting into being of the Other which threatens to organize the world around him and so drains me away from myself. The Other as body is secondary to this experience, just as my own living of my body for me is secondary to my being, the same being, but in a wholly other ontological dimension, as nihilating for-itself. But isn't Pierre-for-me Pierre in his *original* way of being in my world? Is it not bodily being-with that comes first, ontologically as well as empirically?

Sartre comes very close here to saying this himself —for instance, in his discussion of expression. In those phenomena mistakenly called "expressive," he insists, there is no hidden spiritual something behind what appears. The expressions are the phenomena: "These frowns, this redness, this stammering, this slight trembling of the hands, these downcast looks which seem at once timid and threatening—these do not express anger; they are the anger." [12]

Yet this is not behaviorism. The Other's expression and in it his very being are not given me as the inkwell is, as an inert piece of matter. What I see is *an angry man;* his mood is in his looks as their meaning. It is Pierre acting on the world through anger that is before me, directly and all at once. But this is just the bodily being of others through which, and in interaction with which, the for-itself develops. In the family, in social groups, in the workaday world, it is the bodily being-there-with-me of the others that enables me to become, among them, the person I am. Now for Sartre, of course, this being with others is always being against others. To perceive the Other in his bodily being is to perceive him as a transcendence transcended, as a center of meanings which I try to apprehend, and overcome, out of my own for-itself. It is to see his bodily presence as derived from that first clash of consciousnesses which is the original emergence of the Other. I make him a body in order to defeat him, to put him *out* of action.

Yet if we take the phenomena of expression as primary, and forget the compulsion of the *cogito,* the story is very different. For the Other's expression, and mine, may embody solidarity as well as conflict. Even in Sartre's example of anger, there may be mutuality—if, for instance, I share Pierre's indignation. And there are expressions which by their very nature exemplify, not transcendence transcended, but encounter. F. J. J. Buytendijk has analyzed in this sense, for example, the child's first smile, and Plessner the expression of the smile as such. Starting from the for-itself as solipsistic consciousness (of) self, such expressions can appear only as strategies in the internecine war of each against each. If, on the contrary, we start from bodily human being in the child's first year of life, we find the human person emerging in and through, not conflict, but love. It is affection, as the ground of encounter, and encounter itself, that shape the space in which the for-itself can grow, in which it can develop its own consciousness and its own freedom. But affection as much as anger is the bodily being-there of another with me. Thus if Pierre as a body and Pierre for me are correlative ontological indices of the same reality, I being-with-Pierre am also equally myself as body and myself for Pierre—and I myself-for-myself, in turn, am the inward resonance of those outward relations. I argued earlier that both the for-itself and the for-Others are expressions, and developments, of the among-others. We can now add the further thesis: that the among-others, like the for-itself and the for-others, is indistinguishable, in its root nature, from the bodily being—in this case the being together—of persons. The space I live in is the space created, however indirectly, by such bodily being-with. It is created in the first instance by maternal affection; it is developed and deepened, cramped or cut off, by the human presences, whether directly given, or mediated by cultural artifacts, that mark each personal history. The Other is there, as Sartre, too, notes, even in solitude. It is only with the others that I can have the breathing space to be myself. Thus, however inward and immediate its feelings, the for-itself is not a pure, self-dependent negation of an alien in-itself, but a bodily sedimentation, subjectively experienced, of the among-others.

Finally, if, as I have been arguing, the phenomena of expression illustrate the principle just stated, its best instantiation is the most institutionalized, as well as the most comprehensive, form of expression: language. For language is not only the primary medium in which we dwell together; it is perspicuously *both* mental and physical at once. "Man of words" though he is, Sartre's philosophical account of language is minimal and, indeed, absurd. True, language can be used as a "form of seduction"; in terms of Sartrean sociality that may well be its only use. But an adequate philosophical account of language must have at its disposal both a concept of human community that transcends Cartesian solipsism and a concept of a psychophysical unity that transcends Cartesian dualism. On the one hand, language demands for its possibility speaker *and* hearer; and on the other hand, language *is* the mediation of thought through a physical medium. Speech is indeed the primary vehicle of reason; yet it exists only in utterance. It is sounds or marks on paper with meanings *in* them. In this context, Merleau-Ponty's chapter, "The Body as Expression, and Speech," is the culmination of his dialogue with Sartre in *The Phenomenology of Perception*. Reference to it here must suffice to indicate where Sartre's view of bodily being-for-others has received its most definitive refutation.[13]

The Emotions

Sartre's account of the Other depends largely on his account of the passions of shame, fear, and pride. And the passions, for him, exemplify the non-thetic consciousness (of) self which is the under side, so to speak, of the thetic awareness by which the for-itself intends, and negates, the world, and so, by its nihilating activity, constitutes its own fundamental project—to be what it is not and to not be what it is. As I noted at the start of this chapter, this account of the emotions, and of the pre-reflective consciousness in general, carries over from Sartre's early essay on the same subject. Although worked up differently, at first sight, it continues in essence the analysis of consciousness initiated there. The example he had used in the early sketch was the way, in a puzzle-picture, I look for the figure (say, a gun) which the superscription says is there. It is the gun (which I do not yet see) that I am searching for; I'm not thinking about my searching, but sideways or underneath, so to speak, I am aware of what I am about. Emotions, then, are intensifications of this generic non-thetic consciousness. And in *Being and Nothingness*, as we have seen, starting from the cigarette example, the non-thetic consciousness (of) self, christened the pre-reflective *cogito*, stands firmly at the head of the whole argument.

It is worth looking briefly, in conclusion, at the fate of this theory in Part IV of *Being and Nothingness*, for we see there, that it is, paradoxically, not so much the irrationalism of which he has often been accused that prevents Sartre from breaking out of the impasse to which his argument has led him, as it is his thoroughgoing and incurable rationalism.

In the last part of *Being and Nothingness* Sartre is trying to found ontologically the structures which he has so far discovered phenomenologically. He is trying to establish the kind of reality that I have (or am) in and against the world, my body and the Other. But of course he is still working within the Cartesian distinction between human freedom, the unfettered choice of myself as my own project, and a passive, non-free, determined nature. Thus for him man must be either wholly free or wholly determined: for-itself and freedom, or in-itself and utter passivity— those are the alternatives. But what then of the passions —literally "sufferings": surely if I run away from danger, let alone fainting at the sight of it, it is because I am *overcome* by fear? No, says Sartre, I choose myself as fearing. I choose to exorcise the fearful magically, by running or fainting, instead of coping with it instrumentally and rationally; I make myself that kind of person and my world that kind of world. This is the same disjunction established in the *Sketch:* rationality or magic. Yet even when I act "rationally," I do have "subjective" "motives" as well as "objective" "reasons" for what I do. I have a goal which can be accounted for in both ways. Suppose my end is to help minority groups. Why? Because our society is divided and must be healed. But why do I want to help overcome this division? Because I am indignant at the unfairness with which minorities have been treated. Which is the real reason: the objective situation I want to see changed, or my feeling about it? Evidently, Sartre says, we are dealing with two radically distinct layers of meaning. How, he asks, are we to compare them; how can we determine the part played by each of them in the decision under consideration? This difficulty, he insists, has never been resolved; indeed, few have so much as glimpsed it. Thus historians, he points out, assign an objective reason where they can and where that fails point to an "irrational" motive as an alternative. If Clovis became converted to Catholicism, he points out, the explanation could be "objective"; we would say that since many barbarian kings were Arians, Clovis saw an opportunity of getting into the good graces of the episcopate which was all-powerful in Gaul. Here, then, the objective "reason" for his decision is characterized as a rational account of the historical situation. The reason for Clovis' conversion, in short, is the political and religious condition of Gaul, including the relative strengths of the Christian episcopate, the landowners, and the people. But for Constantine's conversion, on the other hand, one historian can find no such objective reason and so says: "he yielded to a sudden impulse." [14] If this were a correct analysis, Sartre suggests: "the ideal rational act would . . . be the one for which the motives be practically nil and which would be uniquely inspired by an objective appreciation of the situation. The irrational or passionate act will be characterized by the reverse proportion." [15] This dichotomy seems on the face of it to correspond so far to his own theory of emotion. Rationality and rational techniques or irrationality equivalent to magic: take your choice—and it's you who take it.

Now, however, Sartre wants to build this dichotomy into his account of freedom, and since both kinds of action, rational and magical, are after all action, he needs freedom on both sides. Let us look again at the reason: it is objective, but it is so only as "revealed to a consciousness" and in particular to the project of that consciousness as positing through the world what it—and the world —are not. Thus, it is *objective,* he tells us, that the Roman plebians and aristocracy were corrupted in the time of Constantine; it is objective that the Catholic Church was ready to favor a monarch who at the time of Clovis would help it defeat Arianism. Yet this state of affairs could be revealed only to a for-itself—"since in general the for-itself is the being by which 'there is' a world." Indeed, it can be revealed only to "a for-itself which chooses itself in this or that particular way—that is, to a for-itself which has made its own individuality." [16] For it is the for-itself, in its particular choice, that makes, not only itself, but the world of instrumental things as instrumental things. Thus, Sartre suggests, a knife is objectively an instrument to cut with; but if I had no hammer, I could just as well take up the knife and use its handle to hammer with. This apprehension of the knife would be no less objective than the view of it as a thing with a blade and handle, a thing to slice with. The same situation obtains for Clovis and the Church. That a certain group of bishops should assist him is merely probable; what is objective is what any for-itself could establish: the power of the Church over the people and its worry about Arianism. But what makes these particular "facts" a "reason"? Only their isolation by Clovis himself and their transcendence toward the possibility of his kingship. In short, Sartre concludes, "the world gives counsel only if one questions it, and one can question it only for a well determined end." [17] Reasons, therefore, are relative to ends. But the ends are made such by the project of the individual consciousness, and the very same project, as subjective, as felt, is a "motive." Clovis was ambitious. How shall we interpret that statement? "Ambition," Sartre says, has here the role of filling, giving its peculiar tone, to the non-thetic consciousness which carries inwardly, sideways so to speak, the outward thrust of consciousness. We are dealing here, he tells us, with one particular case of being-in-the-world. And just as it is the upsurge of the for-itself which causes there to be a world, rather than the meaningless exteriority of the in-itself, so here too it is the being of the for-itself itself as a pure project toward an end which causes there to be "a certain objective structure of the world, one which deserves the name of reason in the light of this end." [18] The for-itself therefore appears now as *the consciousness of this reason.* That is the positional side of consciousness. At the same time, however, this positional consciousness of the reason is also a *non-thetic consciousness of itself as a project toward an end.* It is in this sense that it is a motive. It lives itself non-thetically, as a project toward an end, a project, Sartre asserts, "more or less keen, more or less passionate," and this non-thetic, impassioned consciousness occurs, of course, at the same instant at which the for-itself is constituted "as a revealing consciousness of the organization of the world into reasons." [19] Thus through the recognition of the pre-reflective *cogito,* the apparent dichotomy of reasons and motives, or rationality and magic, has been assimilated to what seems to be a single theory of free action: reason and motive are correlative, exactly as the non-thetic consciousness (of) self is the ontological correlate of the thetic consciousness *of* the object. Just as the consciousness of something is consciousness (of) self, so the motive is nothing other than the apprehension of the reason in so far as this apprehension is consciousness (of) self. It follows, then, that the reason, the motive, and the end are "three indissoluble terms of the thrust of a free and living consciousness which projects itself toward its possibilities and makes itself defined by these possibilities." [20] So "reason" and "motives," rationality and magic, appear to be united as the single, yet double, upsurge of one consciousness in the apprehension of a determinable end.

How then does it happen that psychologists (and historians) can separate out "motives" and assign them as pre-existent determinants of action? It happens because of the nature of temporal consciousness. I make myself each moment out of nothing. But what I *had* made before takes on in memory a pseudo-thinghood: this is the illusory "circuit of selfness," in which, through a flight from ourselves, we make ourselves into things. It is in fact the production and the expression, not of original freedom, but of bad faith. Clovis sought the help of the Catholic bishops; that is the objective fact. What more is involved in saying he was ambitious? One may either be referring to an illusory "self" with properties, a pseudo-thing precipitated by the flight of time; or, more truly, to speak of the affectivity that accompanied his action, his "ambition," is simply to describe the feeling tone, the unreflective consciousness (of) self that carried his objective behavior on and in the world. It is still that pure moment of choice, the positing of a given end—in Clovis' case, the choice of conversion for the sake of possible kingship—that in the last analysis made the action what it was. Thus emotion is really the irrational converse of reason, which appears as a force of its own only through the illusion created by history. At the instant of choice, however, it is the reason that matters; the irrational "motive" is only its non-thetic other side. We have an objective end, a thetic positing of it which is a reason, and a non-thetic awareness (of) ourselves as so doing, which is a motive.

Two consequences seem to follow from this account. On the one hand: reason is primary. If passion is emancipated from its non-thetic role, if it moves on its own, it can be seen in two ways, either of them self-deceptive. It is either sheer magic, a surrogate for impotence—Sartre still accepts this formulation. Or it is a delusive hypostasisation into thinghood of what can, by its very nature as a kind of consciousness, deserve no such ontological stability. On the other hand, however, the reason itself which Sartre here elevates to primacy in the for-itself's existence—that reason has been emptied of all content. For "determinate ends" cannot after all stand on their own; it is simply the act of pure freedom that *makes* them ends. Thus if Clovis must isolate the facts from their context in order to aim at them, he can only do this—as any for-itself can only do—by nihilation. The possibility he aims at, the possibility that the church will support a Christian king, can be revealed to him only if the facts as they now are are transcended toward a state of things that now is not: he must surpass the present situation *toward a nothingness.* He must imagine himself crowned king, but to imagine is to posit what is not. He must see his lack as subject, that is, as non-monarch, and seek the lacking, kingship, and the bishops' support. Only in that nihilating choice does his reason assert itself as free. Thus we have at bottom either choice as subjective and irrational but illusory, or choice as rational and objective but empty. Determinate ends, seen as positive, would again issue in bad faith. The demand of reason, the primacy of positional consciousness, is absolute. But its content is— nothingness. If Sartre has banned Cartesian substance, if he has reduced extended things to the mere spread of a meaningless exteriority and "mind" to the moment of thought, positional or non-positional, he has also reduced Cartesian reason to Cartesian will, drained it of positive content for the sake of its autonomy. In the last analysis, it is the demand for total rationality in the instant of total freedom that forces him to turn the non-thetic, the less than luminous, mode of consciousness back into itself. It cannot, for him, give itself to the world, it cannot guide its possessor to the world, because to permit this would be to contaminate pure reason with feeling. Sartre, like his master Descartes, seeks a state "free of all cares and disturbed by no passions." He has not found, and cannot find it: for him, man is a useless passion, who tries to become God and fails. Only a radical rethinking of the concept of rationality could overcome this impasse. If passion is to be more than useless, it must be seen to have an end that is less than the pure reason of a *causa sui,* an end that is both known and lived, that is founded in history and fellowship, and in the embodied being out of which it takes its growth.

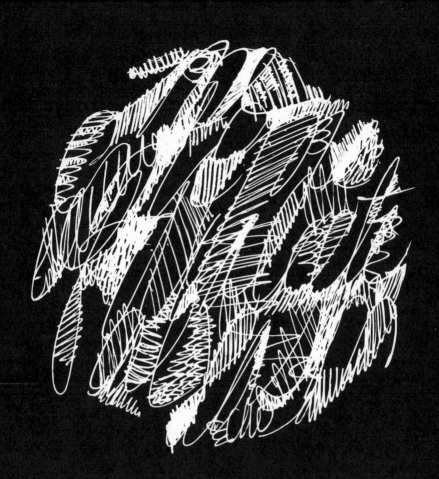

chapter six: the critique of dialectical reason

I. the development of sartrean dialectic

the critique: volume one, 1960

Being and Nothingness
was published in 1943. Sartre's
second major philosophical work, Volume One of the *Critique of Dialectical Reason,* appeared in 1960. Although I have referred
in passing to the *Critique,* my exposition so far has
been chiefly concerned with the sources of *Being and*

Nothingness, its argument, and some of its special problems. For many, however, including Sartre himself, the *Critique* marked a definitive step forward from his earlier work. Even an introductory essay, therefore—which makes no claim to giving a comprehensive analysis even of Sartre's philosophical work—must take account of the *Critique,* and especially of the question, whether and how Sartre's basic views have altered.

Although at this writing the *Critique* is not yet available in translation, its argument has been summarized for English readers in a number of places, notably by Wilfrid Desan in his *Marxism of Jean-Paul Sartre,* by R. D. Laing and D. G. Cooper in their *Reason and Violence,* and by Joseph MacMahon in his recent detailed study of Sartre, which is chiefly concerned with his literary work. Although I am not entirely happy with any of these summaries, I hesitate to embark on yet another. For one thing, the reason one feels one ought to present a summary of the *Critique* is relatively trivial. Seven hundred and fifty-five badly printed, scantily paragraphed, and altogether headache-inducing pages are furnished with the following guide:

Table des Matières	Pages
Questions de Méthode	13
Critique de la Raison Dialectique	113
Libre I	163
Libre II	379

That is all! So after one has laboriously made one's own table of contents, one would like to make it available to other readers (Laing and Cooper and MacMahon have done so, though MacMahon has failed to catch Section C4 of Book One!). This egocentrism on the part of Sartre and his publisher, Gallimard, doubtless will be rectified in the forthcoming English translation. Besides, on the one hand, the overall structure of the argument is perspicuous, and, in representing it one can only repeat what others have already said; and on the other hand, the contents, and even the method in its details, burst out, so to speak, in a number of directions, so that every reader seems to have his own *Critique* and his own perspective for the comparison of this work with the earlier one. Thus any attempt to recapitulate beyond the barest outline is bound to seem idiosyncratic, and had better be presented as criticism rather than mere summary. I shall offer here, therefore, only the sketchiest outline of the work's structure, and go on to look at some facets of it in the context of the question of Sartre's philosophical development— giving due warning that I am focusing on those puzzles that happen especially to fascinate me. To others, other problems and other concepts may seem of overriding interest.

The *Critique,* Volume One, is preceded by the essay "Questions of Method," published separately in English as *Search for a Method.* Here Sartre makes two major methodological points. First, he acclaims the exclusive, and victorious, candidacy of Marxism for the title of *"the* philosophy of the twentieth century," and claims for existentialism the ancillary task of reinstating the individual existent within an ossified pseudo-Marxist dogma. I have already discussed briefly Sartre's relation to Marx and Marxism, and can only echo here Aron's remark that in this connection Sartre behaves very much like the *poursoi* of his own analysis: he seems to be a "Marxist" in the spirit of being-what-he-is-not and not-being-what-he-is.[1] In all his professions of faith, and despite the care with which he expounds or takes issue with some classical

Marxist texts (notably with Engels) in the *Critique* itself, Sartre's "Marxism" appears as somehow strained and artificial. I must leave it to better connoisseurs than I am to explain in detail why this is so. Secondly, Sartre outlines in this introductory essay what he calls the "regressive-progressive" method, in effect a rewriting of his theory of existential psychoanalysis, but with a more explicit emphasis on the role of social factors in providing the conditions for individual self-choice. Existential psychoanalysis was the method introduced in *Being and Nothingness* for studying the way a person makes, and has already made, himself. In the new version, based on a formulation of Georges Lefèbvre, one goes back, it appears, to the individual's beginning and then seeks to build up his history, progressively, from the origin thus understood. As he has approached his hero, Genet, in these terms, in *Saint Genet,* so now Sartre suggests the same method for the study of his favorite anti-hero, Flaubert, to whom, indeed, he has since devoted the first two volumes of a projected four-volume analysis under the title *The Idiot of the Family.* In the *Critique* itself, however, it will be society—and ultimately human history as a whole—that will be dealt with by this dual method of retrospective analysis and prospective reconstruction.

The groundwork for this vast project—to make the whole of history intelligible—is prepared in Volume One (all that exists to date). Book One of this volume moves from individual *praxis,* the act of what Sartre here calls "the practical organism," to the *practico-inert,* the movement, generated by human response to human need, which perpetuates itself as inhuman and anti-human. Sartre analyzes in detail two cases: the drain of gold from sixteenth-century Spain and the deforestation of China. In the latter instance, for example, the need for timber has let loose a chain of physical events from which an even more urgent need, the need for water, arises. The consequences of human action turn inhuman, and demand, in self-defense, new actions—which will again bring in their train new threatening results. This is in effect the for-itself, translated into "praxis," in interaction with the in-itself, now conceived, not as sheer exteriority, but as the network of material events and entities which both delimit and negate the agent's intent. Activity, in itself free—for, whatever befalls, man is still sovereign—is contradicted by passivity, or, better, by a kind of passive activity that runs away with it and threatens it with extinction.

It is out of this fall of *praxis* into its inertial consequences that Sartre sees arising what he calls "collectivities." These are mere "inorganic" collections of practical organisms, organized from outside by the demands of material needs and the scarcity of means to supply them. We depend on "worked matter," and it in turn sums us up, through its presence and its power, into additive totalities. The simplest case of this effect is the series, which Sartre illustrates with the (by-now famous) example of the queue at the bus stop at St. Germain des Près. There is not room for all—who will get a place? Only the limited dimensions of this material object serve to unite the would-be passengers, each of whom has *his* destination and *his* reason for going there. In terms of the abstract dialectic of the *practico-inert,* moreover, class too belongs to this category of collectives. In industrial society, for example, it is obvious that the machine, external to the worker, organizes him from outside himself. And, in general, the materials we work up to satisfy our needs revenge themselves by imposing a mechanical quality, a non-human organizing principle, which by its nature undermines our freedom. It is this external relation which determines class, as it does other "serialities."

This first major move, from *praxis* to the *practico-inert,* establishes an abstract and negative dialectic. Book Two of the *Critique,* "From the Group to History," is supposed to move toward the concrete and so to lead us to history itself—although at page 500, Sartre announces that we are still at the abstract stage! The first step, moreover, is not *from* the group, as the title suggests, but *to* the group, for we have not yet seen how there can be a *positive* dialectic of social reality or social action. Sartre looks first, therefore, at the "group in fusion," from which, if from anywhere, such a reality can be seen to rise. The case he studies is—almost *a priori*—the storming of the Bastille. Out of this classic instance of spontaneous action there comes in its dialectical turn the oath, which binds the joint actors into a brotherhood where each is "third man" to all the others. In the group that results there is thus a genuine, if mediated, reciprocity between each and among all. So far, so good. But the *practico-inert* must not be forgotten: as groups solidify and become traditional they become institutions. These, however, generate their own inertia, so that the threat to freedom, the self-denying consequence of action, returns to plague us. The constituting dialectic of group-formation gives way, thanks to the *practico-inert,* to a *constituted* dialectic, which is, not pure *praxis* but a mixture of *praxis* and *processus.* "Taylorism," a forerunner of time-and-motion studies, is an example Sartre analyzes at length in this connection. One expects at this stage a recurrence to the tragic to-and-fro of *Being and Nothingness;* true, man here tries to become man, not God, but here too he fails. Yet Sartre's conclusion is optimistic: he has laid the ground for a "structural anthropology," he declares at the close of his long and labored argument, and, on that foundation, for an account of history as intelligible: intelligible in the sense that free men understand it as the meaning of their own free actions. This would indeed seem to be a new message, written in the language of a new, and more hopeful, vision.

Reason, Analytical and Dialectical

With this sketchiest of sketches behind us, let us look now at some aspects of the *Critique* with the question in mind of whether, and how, Sartre has changed his position since *Being and Nothingness,* and first, the question, how he has changed his method. Here there is, at least in the first movement of the *Critique,* a striking innovation, and at the same time a development—or, to use a favorite term of Sartre's, a "totalization"—of the dialectic already characteristic of *Being and Nothingness.*

The novelty concerns the method of physics, or of the exact sciences in general, as Sartre understands it. Dialectic paired with phenomenology gives way to the "hypothetico-deductive method" with "dialectical reason" first as its explanation and finally as its source.

From his Cartesian beginning, we have seen, Sartre first discovered phenomenology, and applied it, according to his lights, in the *Emotions,* the *Imaginary,* and the *Transcendence of the Ego.* In *Being and Nothingness,* while he is fundamentally loyal to Cartesian method— and even, in some basic respects, to Cartesian metaphysics—he has set phenomenological description into the frame of a dialectical movement from which the power and direction of his argument derive. In the *Critique,* however, phenomenology has all but disappeared. There are, indeed, immensely detailed descriptions of historical events, and lengthy analyses of historical phenomena. An example of the latter (to which I shall return later) is the role of the radio in modern (chiefly pre-television) society. But these are either empirical accounts, subsumed under Sartrean dialectical categories —as with the Bastille—or abstract social analyses, again constructed with dialectical tools. One may indeed conjecture that, since phenomenology deals with the solitary consciousness, the turn to social themes was bound to involve a turn to other methods. Yet if one recalls the work of Alfred Schutz and his school, one must admit that phenomenology has in fact proved especially fruitful for the description of social worlds and the rereading of sociological problems. To turn phenomenology to this purpose one may of course have to abandon the transcendental ego—the ultimate I, still lonely in its sovereign power, that "constitutes" the whole panorama of "reduced" experience. But the transcendental ego was what Sartre had firmly exorcised in his earliest work: the "ego" is empty; indeed, it doesn't exist. Yet, at the same time, as we have seen, Sartre's phenomenology, like Husserl's, was still Cartesian, and therefore, as I have argued, still impotent to conquer solipsism. A Cartesian, and therefore a Sartrean, social phenomenology is inconceivable. Hence in Sartre's case it is reasonable that a deeper concern with the problem of social reality should entail a diminished interest in phenomenology as a philosophical method.

What is striking in the *Critique,* however, is not the absence of phenomenological description, but Sartre's new relation to a very orthodox conception of "scientific method." In *Being and Nothingness* the positivist conception of science and of the method of science is entirely marginal to Sartre's concerns. In that work he had argued tersely—and convincingly—for the meaninglessness of a pure "objectivity" which would be equivalent to pure exteriority—a Cartesian pure extension without its substantial base. The for-itself, though always out there with the in-itself, bestows on the in-itself whatever meaning that indifferent plenitude of being may acquire. "The world is human." Neither the in-itself in itself, nor the "objective" methods by which physicists study it, are of interest in the context of this ontology. Now it is otherwise. For one thing, a major model for understanding social life is drawn from physics: human action generates its own inertia, the *practico-inert.* Tariffs, or a price index, for example, "lived individually as impotence," constitute as an external "common material object" a *social* reality, a force which is "the practico-inert power of hundreds of thousands of men as *potential energy.*" [2] Thus social reality is conceived on the analogy of physical reality, as distinct from the *praxis* of the individual. Sartre's use of this analogy, and its relation to the earlier conflicts of for-itself and in-itself, would be worth a detailed study. In the previous work the social world appeared as a vast network of techniques for my own aggrandisement (or for my fall into bad faith). Here, however, physics, not engineering, serves as the source for Sartre's explanatory model, at least of one major and recurrent aspect of social reality.

What I want to stress here, however, is another side of Sartre's new reliance on physics: his actual use of what he conceives to be the style of scientific reasoning, the so-called hypothetico-deductive method. In *Being and Nothingness,* as a phenomenologist aiming at ontology, Sartre is sucked into dialectic despite himself. In the latter work his attitude is critical: hence the title. Far from plunging into dialectic at the start, he relies on analytical reason to inquire whether dialectical reason exists. That is what he does not yet know. He asserts it as a hypothesis, then (as scientists have traditionally been thought to do) deduces consequences from his hypothesis and tests them empirically. Over and over he reminds us (and reminds himself; dialectical thinker that he is by nature and second nature, it is hard for him to remember) that we have not yet ascertained, are still trying to ascertain, whether in fact there *is* "dialectical reason" at all.

The hypothesis, of course, is vindicated, and in the end we see clearly, or so Sartre believes we should, that indeed our critical method is but one consequence of the all-inclusive power of dialectical thinking. Once established, therefore, the thesis first hypothetically entertained explains the very method by which it is discovered. But the tentative and experimental nature of our approach to its assertion is emphasized again and again. The whole argument is explicitly presented as one vast experiment.

Two brief comparisons may help to illuminate this Sartrean methodology. This work is a *Critique,* as massive and as ambitious as the *Critique of Pure Reason* itself —indeed, in a sense more ambitious than Kant's *Critique.* But Sartre's method differs radically from Kant's. First, he begins as an empiricist. He is trying to confirm a conjecture. He is experimenting, not moving among *a prioris*—a procedure Kant would radically reject. Clearly, then, he ought, moreover, to claim for his conclusions no such apodeicticity as Kant insists upon. Admittedly the dialectic will turn out, as we shall see presently, to be both "necessary" and "intelligible," but this will be an ontological, not a logical necessity—not even a necessity of "material logic," as Kant calls it. We are moving from the *a posteriori,* the realm of experimental investigation, to some other plane. Finally, when we arrive there, we stay there:

dialect takes over. If we can enter into the self-understanding process of history as an intelligible whole—not a totality, indeed, but a "totalization," a whole process made of *praxeis* which understands itself from within— we shall see our initial method of analysis and experiment as one tiny, and pitifully abstract, offshoot of the concrete immensity within which we have found our intellectual home. True, the method is circular, in so far as its last stage founds its first; and Kant's method is circular, too.[3] But the first stage in Sartre's argument appears at its later stage to have been a taking-off place only, a springboard into a deep sea of significances. Kant's transcendental method, on the other hand, is much more modest in its circularity: for the justifying principles discovered by it and the experience, or the objects, they justify are precisely coterminous as well as interdependent. If there is no informed matter of experience, neither is there any form except as the form *of* the experience (or object of experience) whose form it is. The circle, though not vicious, is serenely static. Sartre's argument, by contrast—the reader will have seen it coming—is a rapidly expanding Hegelian spiral. If we follow Kant we rest secure in the knowledge of why things are as they were already. If we follow Sartre—or better, if we *could* follow him—nothing would ever be the same again.

Before we look at Sartre's Hegelianism as developed in the *Critique,* however, we might well compare his analytical method and its scope with another familiar theory of the method, not of science in general, but of social science. Since the turn of the century numerous philosophers and social scientists, accepting the positivist ideal of pure objectivity for the exact sciences, have argued that the study of man, in contrast to that of nature, demands "understanding" (*Verstehen*). In the first instance the purpose of history was said to be not the formulation of general laws but insight into unique events, and then the social sciences too were said to demand this kind of insight. Such "understanding" was usually presented, if not as a kind of empathy, at least as somehow more direct, more immediate than the highly abstract and impersonal scientific knowledge with which it was contrasted. Now Sartre, too, in the *Critique,* speaks of "comprehension," which appears to be the equivalent of *Verstehen.* Yet in the main, "comprehension" or understanding seems to be, for him, a highly reflective attitude, to be achieved after the labors of analytical reason, and even of the dialectic, and on a new logical level. True, in "Questions of Method" he equates understanding with "existence itself." Thus he seems to be taking it as direct and, as such, contrasting it, as existentialism's offering, with the impersonal, objectifying attitude of an ossified Marxism. Existentialism, we are told, will inject human self-understanding into the bloodstream of Marxist social and historical theory. When the life-giving elixir has done its work, it will disappear; Marxism, revivified, will reign alone. Yet even in this very passage, where understanding, acting, and the project are identified, understanding is nevertheless described, not as immediate or intuitive, but as an "indirect non-knowledge" which must found the immediate knowledge of the intellect.[4] We seem to be offered, in other words, knowledge as a purely intellectual operation of immediate apprehension, and understanding as its reflective, non-cognitive, but nevertheless "rational" supplement. As physics has treated nature wholly "objectively," so, Sartre tells us, anthropology, too, has treated man as object. That was wrong. Yet this error is not to be corrected by turning aside to some more immediate awareness of man by man. It is to be corrected by a more complicated process. First we have the field of "knowledge" which is equated with the scientific or "analytic," yet "immediate," apprehension of a subject-matter: still the Cartesian ideal of totally explicit self-generating truth. Then, hypothetically, we embark upon the labor of the dialectic which will ultimately [5] bring us to the stage where we see as a "permanent possibility" the reflective understanding of human organizations by human agents who observe them. Only by this devious route can we move from the single agent—if re-christened, still in effect the isolated for-itself, rising up as negation against the in-itself—to a social organization understood as such by a social observer who is himself an agent. The task of the social scientist—and even of the member of a social group—seems hard indeed.

Totalization

Hard, too, it appears, is the task of the dialectician who, taking over from the experimental reasoner, must prepare the ground for such social understanding. Nothing less than the total sweep of human history will do as his domain, and he must exhibit that vast totalization, Sartre insists, as both "necessary" and "intelligible." Such, he argues, is the indispensable prolegomenon to history—or to a critique of history?—itself. But if, as I have already suggested, Sartre's relation to dialectic here is more reflective, and, at the start at least, allegedly hypothetical, still the power of the Hegelian method over his thought, already evident in *Being and Nothingness,* is ready to display itself again—and more vigorously than ever. However wordy the text, however abstract its analyses, the Dialectic, once initiated, will carry us like a torrent, over any intervening rocks and boulders, to its inevitable close.

Again, I shall not venture to attempt here anything even approximating an exhaustive analysis of Sartre's dialectic as exhibited in the *Critique*. But an enumeration of some of the chief counters out of which it is constructed should sufficiently indicate its scope and style, and its difference, as well as its likeness, to the earlier dialectic of *Being and Nothingness*. I shall focus on three concepts: totalization, necessity, and intelligibility.

First, "totalization." The for-itself comes to be, and exists, as nihilation; it seeks to realize its own instant of action as pure freedom. Sartre has never abandoned this ideal; in the *Critique,* for example, he baldly denies that there is a "problem" of sovereignty. Man—each man—is sovereign; there can be no problem. But in contrast to the total independence of each individual-in-action, his social world is not only the wholly other, it is the whole of the wholly other. The world as worked up by others' actions, a humanized-dehumanized in-itself, must be seen as total in order to be denied as total, in order to serve as ground for the expression of *my* values—that is, of *my* lacking what I lack, and thus of myself as lack. If Sartre looks at society, therefore, starting, as he must do, from the for-itself, he can only "totalize." He *must* swing over from the pole of empty inwardness toward the other pole of indefinitely extended, totalized outwardness. True, he cannot reach it *as* totality, any more than Sartrean man could in fact achieve the glorious instant of his own free act. But if totality is unattainable, *totalization* is the only process by which what is other than instantaneous, free self-choosing can ever be understood. Granted, also, that, in the *Critique,* the concept of "lack" is abandoned for that of "need," with its more explicit (and allegedly Marxist) foundation in material situations and material wants. Still the skeleton is the same: for-itself / in-itself or individual *praxis*/totalization. If the trend toward the broader, almost all-engulfing category is more pronounced, the ingredients of the dialectic are analogous to, if not identical with, their earlier counterparts.

Moreover, that trend is already foreshadowed, I should like to suggest, in some puzzling passages in *Being and Nothingness.* The concept of truth is not one of Sartre's explicit concerns in either of his major works; but when he does touch on it in *Being and Nothingness,* he sets it in contrast to "reality," almost as "universal" is traditionally contrasted with "particular." The truth of being Jean-Paul Sartre, it seems, is being a Parisian, the truth of being a Parisian, is being a Frenchman, the truth of being a Frenchman is being a European, and so on. Or, to take Sartre's other example: here is a man doing a particular skiing figure. He does it Norwegian style—that is the truth of his performance; and the truth of *that,* in turn, is skiing as such. For reality, however, the series goes just the other way: the reality of being a European is being a Frenchman, and so on; or the reality of skiing is skiing Norwegian style, until in each series we come to this particular event here-now, Jean-Paul Sartre as *pour-soi* choosing, say, to reject the Nobel prize; this skier executing a christiana just here on this particular slope. For essence and existence the same inversion holds: Jean-Paul Sartre exists, his essence is to be Parisian, the essence of being Parisian is being French, and so on. Thus it seems that step-by-step impoverishment is the process by which, from the real or the existent, truth or essence are obtained.

But is "truth" really obtained by starting with the real and subtracting successive properties? Are even "essences"—*un*real though they may seem—to be discovered simply by stripping the existent, one by one, of its particularizing attributes? Man, we are told, has no essence; he exists first, and must make himself what he is (not). Does he achieve that goal simply by this sort of abstractive generalizing? Ultimately, along this line of reasoning, both the "truth" and the "essence" of anything at all will be—Being, which, existentially speaking, is as good as nothing. What is Sartre after here? One might suppose that, in his emphasis on existence and the concrete reality of this nihilating *pour-soi* here and now fleeing *its* past into *its* future, he is intentionally draining "essence" or "truth" of *any* content. But existentialism began with the cry, "Subjectivity is Truth." Is that not still its clarion call? To read individual existence into Marxism, not to generalize it into universal "truths" and "essences," is supposed to be Sartre's mission in the *Critique.* Yet, as we saw in the last chapter, there is an indefeasible impulse to rationalism in Sartre's thinking which runs the other way. The individual real, the existent, has its truth, its essence in the general—and even, it seems, in the most general. Remember that in the First *Meditation* it is the most general things of all—*generalissima et universalissima*—that Descartes finds it hardest to doubt! But an apter comparison here is Spinoza's third kind of knowledge: only when we have grasped its roots in the all-encompassing can we understand the particular a right. Only in full, independent, total Being-itself does the truth of *this* finite mode reside.

Is this Spinozism, latent in *Being and Nothingness,* given free rein in the *Critique?* Yes and no. Totalization does indeed take over: it is the context through which alone the individual's *praxis* becomes intelligible—and therefore true?—to the historian, to the social scientist, or even to himself. But the totalization Sartre envisages, of course, is human, not divine. It is a pan-humanism, one might say, that Sartre is after. Man, the nihilator of Being, the being whose very being is to say no, can find himself only if he nevertheless places his nay-saying, dialectically, within the context of Being itself.

Yet that is precisely what Sartre had not succeeded in doing in his earlier work—it is even what he proclaimed could not be done. *Causa sui* is impossible, the for-itself cannot become for-itself-in-itself; man tries to become God and fails. Thus, in the Hegelian terms already characteristic of *Being and Nothingness,* let alone of the *Critique,* the dialectic of existence appears to be one of pure contradiction, repeated thesis and antithesis lacking a synthesis to put the two contradictions to rest. What has happened to Sartre's negative dialectic in the *Critique?* Again, the role of "synthesis" in that work merits a special study; there are complex relations to Kantian as well as Hegelian synthesis which the historian of philosophy finds tantalizing, but which neither space, time, nor the reader's patience allows one to embark on here. But, crudely and as a first approximation, I think we may hazard the statement that the *Critique* differs from *Being and Nothingness* in permitting, and even in conclusion stressing, the possibility of synthesis: hence the optimistic, even triumphant, coda at its close. And we may see this new outcome either as a development of Sartrean dialectic, or as a change. To borrow another Hegelian slogan, quantity has turned into quality: more dialectic has turned into a different dialectic after all.

Or nearly so; even this statement I hesitate to make dogmatically. Let me qualify it a little. *Praxis* vs. the *practico-inert,* the group in fusion followed by the oath vs. the group institutionalized, itself becoming *practico-inert;* these are the poles of a dialectic which seems, either on the "constituting" or the "constituted" side, to reach no resting point. And, indeed, the Hegelian issue in an "organic" state Sartre emphatically and repeatedly rejects. The only organism is the practical organism, the individual agent. Otherwise there are organizations, which are made by men and, as material centers of resistance, come, negatively, to control men. But the possibility of any hyper-organism is decidedly rejected, over and over again; that is one of Sartre's major polemical themes. Yet both for the constitutive dialectic of the group in process of formation and for the constituted dialectic of a social organization, once formed, Sartre opens the way for synthesis. Thus, in discussing the role of "thought"—of controversy on the current issues—in the formation of subgroups, he writes:

> It is a question of a dialectical transcendence, by a practical project: that in turn supposes *a synthetic grasp* of all the contradictions, in brief, the living reunification of the group by the third man, taking the dissensions themselves as the instrument of reunification.[6]

In that sentence there is, after all, hope for mankind. Admittedly, the "living synthesis" [7] of a new community will always regenerate its own contrary, its seriality, its practico-inert. Yet even in the "constituted dialectic" that results Sartre sees not only contradiction, but also synthesis. True, the members of every generation are cast, willy-nilly, into groups already formed, which press on them from without and so limit, even deny, the upsurge of their freedom. Nevertheless here, too, where *praxis* has become enmeshed in *processus,* where truly communal action has relapsed into institutional compulsion, Sartre speaks of a "totalizing synthesis of diverse circumstances." [8] "This plurality of temporalizations," he writes: "and this temporal unification (*a synthetic unification* of the antecedent by the consequent, an actual reunification of the novel multiplicity through [*à travers de*] the older *cadres*) constitutes in fact the evolution of humanity as the *praxis* of a diachronic group, that is, as the temporal aspect of the constituted dialectic." [9]

Both diachronically and synchronically, indeed, there is alienation in such "objectivized" *praxis*—in the action of the individual within an extant tradition and within an organized society. But now, it seems, there is not only the to-and-fro of for-itself / in-itself, freedom / bad faith. From the perspective of dialectical reason, it now appears, a broader vision is possible. There is an "evolution of humanity" which embraces the double alienation of the individual—in the factual history of his nation and in the levelling seriality of his institution or his class— within the grandeur of a synthesizing whole. There are no Hegelian states, no hyper-organisms; yet the synthesis of History is in sight. Thus totalization appears no longer as an empty ideal, but as a concrete possibility: the concrete issue which the huge abstract "experiment" of the *Critique* has all along had as its aim.

Necessity

So far I have been talking about "totalization" as an intensification and expansion of Sartre's Hegelian method. Since his express goal is to understand history, and since he believes that a "totalizing" view of human action is the necessary forerunner to such understanding, totalization is the overarching dialectical conception that controls the work. But his other conceptual tools, too, are characteristic of dialectical thinking from Hegel onward —in particular, his use of modal concepts and their cognates, and especially of the concept of *necessity*.

Analytical reason atomizes, dialectical reason total-izes. Sartre sees this contrast—as we noticed earlier—politically: he equates positivism, liberalism, and fascism, and opposes to them all the all-inclusive truth of Marxism (as he understands it, and of course with the injection of an existentialist core). But back of this contrast there is also a contrast in philosophical method, a contrast between "logic" as traditionally understood and dialectic as its alternative. "Analytical reason" appears as the method of positive science understood in the sense of positiv*ism.* It appears to rest, in the last analysis, as most empiricist philosophy has done, on the occurrence of actual individuals. Its operations are indeed those of deductive logic, and hence necessary. But logic in its canonic form is conceived as purely extensional; it is truth-value logic. Although it tells us nothing about the real world, its connectives depend entirely on what there is or is not. It works with atomic particulars, a, b, c, or their variables, x, y, z, or with statements of atomic facts, p, q, r, related solely in terms of their truth or falsity. Even if it takes the leap from "x Phi's" to "(For all x) (x Phi's)," an indefinite aggregate of "facts-that" is still what it refers to. "Formal implication," as Whitehead and Russell called it, is no more "totalizing" than "material." It still rests on indigestible, itemizable, unintelligible particu-lars. Thus the contingent "that" or "that not" appears to be the ultimate foundation on which the calculations of analytical reason rest. But surely logic provides rules of *necessary* reasoning? So it does; given its contingent premises, it does of course trace deductive relations among them. Indeed, the "analysis" of "analytical rea-son" consists precisely in finding such relations: rela-tions that are necessary just because they consist in con-nections already given among the items to which they refer. Given that p.q, or ~ p. ~ q, or ~ p.q, then necessarily p ⊃ q, because ~ (p. ~ q) is all that p ⊃ q says. Thus what follows by logical necessity doesn't really "follow" at all; given what is given, it just is. Logic necessitates emptily. It provides analytical connections between meaningless givens. It is a mere content-less skeleton of thought. So we have indeed the dichotomy Hume gave us: bits of mere givens which are contingent, never necessary, and necessary statements which are empty, necessitating not what they say but only how they say it.

How can thought overcome this disability? The answer of the dialectical philosopher, as we have already seen, is to get thought moving. Far from resting content with given counters tautologically connected, the dialectician ruminates upon his concepts so that they themselves change their shape and nature as his reflection proceeds. Thought is not a game with fixed pieces, but a process of development, of growth. And in particular, dialectical philosophers have felt the need to overcome the dichotomy between contingency and necessity. Our experience makes sense only if on the one hand "mere" facts are somehow assimilated to reasons, and if on the other the connections between data are shown to be demanded on some real and rational ground, not only tautologically. Thus the modal concepts, possibility, actuality (or contingent givenness), and necessity need to be reflected on and reassessed in relation to one another. The contingent must be absorbed into the rational core of reality, not left dangling as *mere* given, yet its necessitation must be neither external compulsion nor the *petitio principii* of deductive argument—it must be a *reason,* a principle that makes sense in some comprehensive way of the whole process of which all contingencies are now seen to form parts.

All this, admittedly, is a highly speculative piece of non-history. The thesis of extensionality in logic is a modern one, and by now may even be said (*pace* Quine) to belong to a phase only of the development of that discipline. But taking off from a particular philosophy of logic—or even from a caricature of it—I have been trying to suggest a context for—what *is* historically the case—dialectical philosophers' concern with modal concepts. Textually, the tradition goes back, I suppose, to Kant, where the three modalities, possibility, actuality, necessity, appear as the final three in the table of categories, and represent in the Dialectic the fourth antinomy—the attempt to prove a necessary Being. This impasse, like the others Kant had presented, Hegel must then evade by working into the destiny of his Absolute Spirit the necessary transition from the possible to the actual, and to the actual as necessary—in some grander sense of "necessary" than the humdrum one of formal logic.

In the case of Sartrean dialectic, modal concepts already figured prominently in *Being and Nothingness*. The for-itself *is* its possibilities; it is as its possibility—its not-yet-actual—that it is what it is not and is not what it is. My body, on the other hand, is "the necessity of my contingency": the sheer facticity that absurdly underlies my freedom. As making myself, I *am* my possibility, but as situated, as this body in this fashion at this time, I am necessarily, not what I may be, but what I happen to have become. The two-pronged dialectic of nothingness and being is at the same time a two-pronged dialectic of possibility and actuality-as-necessity. There is no escaping *either* the burden of freedom, the whole future as my possible, the *un*making of the present which is the very quintessence of the upsurge of consciousness, *or* the irresoluble facticity of what has been.

As we have already seen, however, *Being and Nothingness* offers no synthesis of its dominant contraries. I am always free, yet the die is always cast; there is no way out. But in the *Critique* we are offered, in the concluding movement of the argument at least, some hope of an all-embracing resolution. And this new outcome is mediated by the concept of necessity, which now plays a new and dominant role in making the dialectic work. Let us see, again very schematically, how this comes about.

The *Critique,* we noted, is an experiment. Starting from analytical reason, we are asking whether dialectical reason exists. The two givens we observe at the outset are: on the one hand, individual *praxis,* which here replaces the free act of the for-itself, and on the other hand, the fact of scarcity, the limited supply of goods on which and with which to perform our acts. The stage-set is different: we have, not consciousness as for-itself and the target of its intentionality, the in-itself, but the "practical organism" and the material it needs—but can find only in scarce supply—for the fulfillment of its wants. We shall have to consider later how deep an innovation this change of concepts constitutes. Clearly, if only out of respect for Marxist truth as he conceives it, Sartre *has* to locate the human condition more concretely in the material world than he had earlier seemed to do. And clearly he is here concerned with the generation of social structures, not of the individual's destiny as such. But for our present purpose—of tracing the argument in terms of modal concepts—we can still (as we did above) take *praxis* and the *practico-inert,* the human agency and the anti-human inertia it has generated, as the analogues of the familiar contraries of *Being and Nothingness*. On the one hand, there was already in the earlier work an attempt to make the for-itself "material." In other words, consciousness, in the chapter on the body, was already seen as "all body," although at the same time body was said to be "all consciousness." So now, similarly, the practical organism's *praxis* is man as sovereign, the individual's free act, but in the material world. And on the other side, scarcity, which generates the *practico-inert,* seems here to take the place of the individual contingency, the facticity, of *Being and Nothingness.* Scarcity, one could say, is the social body: it is the contingent necessity, or the necessary contingency, on which and against which, the individual, cast among others, has to work. Sartre seems to recognize this analogue when he writes:

> The contingency of scarcity (that is, the fact that immediate relations of abundance between other practical organisms and other environments are not *a priori* inconceivable) is reinteriorized in the contingency of our reality as men (*la contingence de notre realité d'homme*).[10]

Indeed, this is not so much an analogue as an identity. He continues: "A man is a practical organism living with a multiplicity of similar (organisms) in a field of scarcity." [11] Scarcity is the contingency, the facticity of the given, identified in *Being and Nothingness* as the body, but now seen, across the fact of social multiplicity, as the contingent limitation of the materials on which the satisfaction of bodily needs depends.

The starting place of the experiment, then, is, though in a social and more explicitly material setting, still possibility (free action) versus contingency (limited givenness, facticity). We see the human generate the anti-human—cutting down trees makes drought. Further we see the multiplicity of human agencies generating—in relation to worked matter—*human* inhumanities, the passive collectivities of series or class. Being a worker, being a member of the idle rich: these are external impositions, as passive in relation to my action as a lack of water. But this, Sartre tells us, is an anti-dialectic. What is needed for dialectical reason is not just this to-and-fro. What is needed to generate a proper dialectic is a movement of totalization, but, further, a totalization seen as the movement of *necessity*.

That the concept of necessity plays a crucial role in the discovery, and vindication, of dialectical reason is clear from a brief but pivotal section in Sartre's argument. He has first considered individual *praxis,* in relation to need, as totalization: my environment becomes a total field in relation to the needs I exteriorize in it (Book I, A). Next he has shown how it is that human relations arise as mediation between various segments of matter (Book I, B); in other words, it is matter, related to their respective needs, that mediates between individuals and so generates their social relations. (Consider, for instance, the postal system, or the "delivery" of health services.) Now (Book I, C), we have to derive from our view of matter as "totalized totality" a first constatation of the *necessity* of the movement we are considering. This section of the argument has four parts. First (C, 1), Sartre studies "scarcity and the method of production" [12] then (C, 2) "worked matter as alienated objectification of individual and collective 'Praxis,' " and in particular the phenomenon of interest.[13] Then, before he comes to the description of "social being as matter" (C, 4)—that is as the expression of the *practico-inert*—"and particularly the being of class" [14] and, further, to (Book I, D) the study of "The Collectives," [15] that is, of serialities in general, the passive externalities generated as constraining aggregates by human activity itself, he injects (C, 3) the concept of necessity "as a new structure of the dialectical experiment."

What does this mean? We have discovered the dialectic, or the anti-dialectic, generated by the "behavior" of worked matter over against the needy individual. This totalizing relation is "intelligible," [16] that is, it is transparent: like the *cogito*. My action simply *is* a totalizing movement, by which I constitute my environment as a whole-for-my-action; in terms of *Being and Nothingness,* I make my world a world. This is a clear self-referring act and therefore, Sartre points out, indubitable. But the indubitability of self-evidence is not "necessity" in the sense in which dialectic demands it. Dialectical necessity must be, not intelligible with the pure translucent self-identity of an immediate intuition, but in movement: it must be *the external interiorized and made necessary by means of such interiorization.* But this does not mean that necessity is compulsion simply from without. It is compulsion *made* mine and felt as such. It is the internal necessity of external action. Sartre's argument is carried here by the ambiguity of the French *"expérience":* the dialectical experiment becomes dialectical experience, or both in one. What we have so far seen, via analytical reason, in the anti-dialectic of man and matter is now made dialectical by the experience of man himself, who discovers *within* himself the necessity of his action *out there.* And it is this experience of necessity that confirms the hypothesis of the dialectical experiment. For the necessity so discovered is neither external constraint as such, nor the static "necessity" of the logically evident: it is *destiny.* When Oedipus takes into himself the need to have fulfilled the oracle, what had appeared as arbitrary compulsion becomes *his fate.* It is that awareness of an overriding necessity, which is nevertheless my own, an awareness which must be learned—and learned through suffering —that confirms the existence of dialectical reason and at the same time makes the dialectic real. It both confirms the experiment and embodies it in a real development.

Dialectical necessity, then, is destiny. Or, conversely, as Sartre puts it, necessity is *the destiny of freedom in exteriority.*[17] It is the necessity *that I act out there.* Note that this is not, as in *Being and Nothingness,* the necessity of my contingency—to recognize that is to recognize ineluctable constraint, the inevitable contrary of freedom, unalterably opposed to freedom itself. Nor is it, again, the self-containment of the indubitable: that would be logical truth, self-evident because self-referring, but incapable of development. No, dialectical necessity is neither the stubborn resistance to freedom by the contingent and unintelligible, nor is it the quiescent self-evidence of the intellectually indubitable. Dialectical necessity is the necessity of freedom itself: it is freedom destined to act out there in the world, and understanding its own nature as destined so to do.

The perspective of *Being and Nothingness* is different. There it is the factual that is necessary, and that is the total other of freedom. If I *am* my red face at the keyhole, it remains absurd that this should be so. Moreover, that it is the factual, or the contingent, that is necessary is itself absurd; for the "contingent" is precisely the non-necessary; in revealing itself as necessary it contradicts itself. On the other hand there is in a sense a necessity of freedom, but again a self-contradictory necessity. I *have* to be free: indeed, I am "condemned" to be so. But the condemned prisoner is precisely the person *without* a destiny: society has misjudged him, robbed him of the destiny a free agent ought to have. Thus freedom as what we are condemned to is the contradiction of freedom. *Being and Nothingness* presents us, therefore, with a double contradiction: the non-necessary—that is, the contingent—is what is necessary; the free, which should not be necessary either, is compelled, and so unfree, a necessity imposed from without.

But now, in the *Critique,* necessity appears neither as constraint nor condemnation: it is the successful interiorization of the external action that embodies freedom. Man really does act freely out there in the world and recognizes as his destiny that this should be so. It almost seems that role playing has become authentic, that the waiter can serve us with a waiter-like flourish without thereby falling into bad faith. Perhaps he really *is* a waiter, and freely so.

This issue of Sartre's argument will become clear in Book Two, where "freedom as necessity" and "necessity as freedom" will emerge as the vehicles of the group-information, that triumphant we-subject, evanescent but glorious, in which each must act freely with each other, so that out of this mutality they do for once act as one. What makes them do so? Again, the dialectic of modalities instructs us. *The impossibility of the impossibility of freedom:* that is the common need from which their common action flows. The populace is starving, it is impossible for each to live—that is, as practical organisms, to act. But each is a human agent, for whom such an impossibility is impossible; therefore, each uniting the others as their mediating third, they together storm the fortress that represents their oppressors, the agents of that impossible impossibility. They take the Bastille. For the Faubourg St. Antoine, indeed for the French nation, that was destiny.

But of course this is Sartre, and the solution is not quite that simple. The Bastille gave way to the Terror, the Directory—the *practico-inert* took over again. Still the new place given to necessity in the *Critique,* to necessity as *belonging* to freedom, not as *denying* it: this is certainly a crucial step on the path to Sartre's new synthesis, if such it be. For only if freedom is vindicated as truly necessary will the totalizing process of history prove *historical:* a pattern of human action in the world, not just of human suffering or of the fall into inertia and absurdity.

Intelligibility

Totalization and necessity are two of the concepts which function in the *Critique* to give Sartre's method new scope. But a third is needed to effect the synthesis he appears to have in view. He introduces "necessity," we have just noticed, as the supplement to the "intelligibility" of the anti-dialectic that was his first experimental discovery; but this intelligibility seems to be a first and abstract surrogate for the dialectical intelligibility which crowns the whole. Indeed, each necessary step in the dialectic demands its matching intelligibility. Necessity as destiny may be obscure to those it overwhelms. It must become intelligible, at each stage of the dialectic, to the agent himself. The "become" of that statement, of course, is "abstract": we have not yet reached history. But with the conceptual movement of dialectic it must be shown that each phase of social development ultimately has its own mode of being, not only in the *praxeis* of individuals, but in their consciousness. Each member of the crowd storming the Bastille not only adds to the number. He acts *as* one of the crowd and thus as other to all the others. He is mediating third to every other pair; if there are a hundred, it is he who, as the hundredth, makes it so, and so does every other. The group-in-formation comes to be, therefore, not only from the impossibility of the impossibility posed by the enemy or the oppressor; it comes to be from the joint action of agents who express the impossibility of that impossible, not only in their movement as crowd-storming-the-Bastille, but in their intent—in their mutual, interlocking awareness that they *are* a group-in-the-making. As such, indeed, Sartre declares, they may even be called a "We-Subject," [18] an example of that social reality whose existence in *Being and Nothingness* he had emphatically denied. The second dialectical development Sartre traces, the oath, again clearly binds the members of the emergent group in solemn awareness of its meaning. Performative utterances entail knowing what one is saying and therefore knowing what one is doing, as well as, by saying, doing it.

But what of the group once stabilized, the institutional group, with its impulsion back to seriality and the *practico-inert?* The industrial worker is alienated by definition from himself and his work; how can his action and his consciousness be identified? The answer is complicated. On the one hand, Sartre discovers, in an analysis of rights and duties, an intelligibility of social *function,* and even, for organization as such, an intelligibility of *structure* (*à la* Claude Levi-Strauss).[19] In such rituals as baptisms, for example, members of an organized group perform a "second oath" which marks their acknowledgment of "the necessity of freedom." [20] Now this necessity, Sartre tells us, is the inverse of the practico-inert. The *practico-inert* was characterized as *passive activity:* the consequences of our acts take off and run away with us, despite ourselves. But organization, as "exteriority structuring interiority," has precisely the character of *active passivity*. This category characterizes, in fact, the performance of social functions [21] as well as the ritual occasions of the passage just quoted. Thus it seems that in general through my commitment to a social structure and through my institutionalized action in it, I give myself to it. I seem to acknowledge its goals as my norms,

to accept it—that is, to accept the *praxis* of its members
—as the ubiquitous medium of my existence.

This appears indeed to be an astonishing transformation of the Sartre of *Being and Nothingness*. There, activity was activity, passivity passivity, and that was it.
What metamorphosis has the dialectic wrought? It has
been suggested by one of Sartre's commentators that his
earlier dialectic advisedly dealt with the single for-itself
only, and that he is here filling in the social framework
whose existence—and whose power—he would all
along have acknowledged. In other words, he might be
read as using, like Kant, a method of "isolation," in which
strands of a synthetic whole are sorted out for reflection,
but no claim is ever made that they exist apart from that
synthetic unity.[22] But this explanation really will not do.
The author of *Being and Nothingness* clearly believed
that all social role playing is in effect bad faith, that there
is no We-subject, that the act, to be free, must be totally
active. The very idea of active passivity is, in Sartre's earlier terms, inconceivable. The notion that a human being
can *ever* freely and without self-deception give himself to
anything but his own freedom is for him truly a discovery.
Had this not been so, indeed, the road to this point in the
Critique would not have been as long and devious as it
has been. For some one who had all along acknowledged
the social being of man, the rootedness of freedom in society, there would have been no need to invoke the immense apparatus of these five-hundred pages to demonstrate its possibility.

Besides, the victory of a socialized freedom is far
from complete. For one thing the "second oath" of ritual-
ized commitment belongs, it appears, to the "constituted
dialectic" only, to the institutionalized dialectic which is
always ready to degenerate once more into the *practico-*

inert. This dialectic must be held subordinate to the "full intelligibility of the constituting dialectic" [23]—that is, to the generation of the truly "common individual" in the group-in-formation and then in the original oath. Apart from these unique situations, then, we are almost back with the old alternatives—the impossible wholly free act or else the fall into bad faith. Thus norms, for example, result from an "ossification" of the group, such that the agent "loses" [24] his comprehension of his own action and that of others. Only the resultant gap between act and understanding gives them their "normative" character. So the individual's concrete self-giving slips after all into the abstract recognition of an external apparatus; he is alienated and betrayed.

Yet the change is there; active passivity, as characteristic at least of the constituted dialectic, is a phase of dialectical reason, abstractly considered. It has even its concrete reality in the exercise of social function or on the occasion of the "second oath." Moreover, the intelligibility of each stage of the dialectic—the emergent group, its solidification in the oath, and even, to a degree, the exercise of a function in the organized group, or the re-enactment of its birth in social ritual—marks a "synthesis" impossible in terms of *Being and Nothingness:* a synthesis of *being* and *knowing.* Indeed, to mark this synthesis at each appropriate stage along the way is, it appears, the chief function of the concept of intelligibility in the discovery and development of dialectical reason.

At key places in the argument of *Being and Nothingness,* on the other hand—as we saw in tracing its course —"knowing" and "being" or "knowing" and "living" are sharply and irreconcilably contrasted. The pre-reflective *cogito* is the for-itself as lived, but only on the detached intellectual level of reflection can there be knowing, which is neither lived nor of the living: it is instantaneous intuition of its purely external object, the in-itself. (Even when we "know" ourselves it is our quasi-objective "selves," our "characters," that we know, not the non-thetic "conscience (de) soi" that underlies such, and all, knowing as its real being.) In Sartre's view of emotion ("passion"), moreover, the affects are the irrational alternative to reasons, the hidden under side of action. Even though, as Cartesian wills, we do in a sense choose passion, choose to find the grapes sour, or the enemy unconquerable, we do so unknowingly, excusing our own failure by the resort to magic. To understand our own self-surrender, and yet by that very act of understanding to give ourselves freely —that is, for Sartrean man, a radical innovation. It springs, if you like, from an intensification of the rationalism and the idealism already present in the earlier work. There, however, these motifs were kept in check by the radical dualism of Sartre's starting point. Despite the dialectical structure of its argument, the reason of *Being and Nothingness* remained analytical: knowledge was pure inspection, the static contemplation of the self-evident, being was its Other, the object of intuition, never at one with it. Only the demonstration (by analytical reason!) that dialectical reason exists can give us the perspective from which this duality can be seen as one. Only if we see that human reality does in some typical circumstances necessarily—yet freely—act in the service of something more than the act itself, can we bring together consciousness and its object into a viable whole. That "something more," of course, must be human—that is, social. There is neither Deity nor substance on which we could rely for its source. The world is still human. But neither is it, despite the Hegelianism of Sartre's method, Hegelian "objective mind" or "world mind" that provides the new synthesis. There is no hyper-organism; it is always individual *praxis* to which we return—but individual *praxis* intelligible, in the appropriate context, in its bearing on, and meaning for, a social whole. Now even the material—the social matter of the *practico-inert*—comes to mean something *to* the individual; and in that awareness knowing and being *can* be reconciled.

His *Critique,* Sartre says, is meant to introduce an existentialist foundation into Marxist philosophy. The reiterated return to intelligibility shows us what he means by this—for it is, as we have seen, the intelligibility of his own action to the individual agent that he has in mind. The dialectic, however totalizing, will develop only in and through the individual "practical organisms" who, apart from "matter," are all there really is. So we read the individual existent into the social, and eventually historical, dialectic of the whole. That is how, on Sartre's own account, his message should be read. Yet on the whole—and in view, too, of his own confession—we may also, and better, read the story the other way around. Sartrean existentialism was a brilliant exegesis of the failure of humanity; only the Marxist dialectic of history, as Sartre conceives of it, can rescue us from that "tragic finale." Not existentialism supplementing Marxism is the heart of the story, but Marxism giving a social-historical frame that makes possible a more fruitful issue than Sartre's existentialism in its own terms could have allowed. The old ingredients are still there, but they have been literally translated, and in their translated form and place, there may be some hope, sometimes, of escape from what had been previously ineluctable catastrophe.

History: Sartre and Kierkegaard

It is "the place of history" that Sartre has been seeking in Volume One of the *Critique.* All *praxis,* he has argued, is *totalizing,* at least in relation to the "passive activity" of the *practico-inert* which it initiates. To become the locus of history, however, such totalization must in addition prove both *necessary* (in the sense of "destined") and *intelligible* (in the sense that the agent's action is assimilated to his own awareness of that destiny.) These are the conditions for history which dialectical reason both institutes and discovers. But this conception of history stands in sharp contrast to another dialectical view, that of Søren Kierkegaard as presented in the "Interlude" of the *Philosophical Bits.*[25] Before we leave our reflections on Sartre's dialectic, therefore, we may put it into perspective by comparing it briefly with Kierkegaard's argument in the "Interlude."

On two points, to be sure, they agree. Both follow the Hegelian method, yet deny Hegelian "absolute mind" in favor of the concrete human individual. And, of course, both make heavy use of modal concepts in their reasoning. But to how different a purpose! For one thing, "totalization" is not a Kierkegaardian concept at all. Starting, like Sartre, with individual existence, he needs to arrive, not at social reality (which does not concern him), but at the confrontation of the finite individual with the Infinite Being who made him—in this case at the still more vexing paradox of the historical Christ, that is, of God in history. So his whole dialectic is one of individuals, finite and infinite, temporal and eternal. The other two Sartrean concepts we have been looking at, however, are dealt with in the "Interlude," the first explicitly, the second by implication. For his two major questions are these: is the past

necessary? (and, as a corollary of this, what is the historical?), and what is the sense of the past? (how can we
"know" history?). The first exactly parallels Sartre's speculations on necessity, and the second certainly bears on
the problem of the intelligibility of human action seen in
a historical context.

For Sartre, action, to be matter for history, must be,
not only indubitable or factually undeniable, but necessary. For Kierkegaard, the historical can never be necessary. True, what has happened has happened, one cannot
deny it; but—and Sartre would agree—that is not a sufficient condition for necessity. But here the ways part.
Sartre seeks the ground for a historical dialectic, and this
means to him that there must be an inner necessity to the
structure and the consequences of human action—otherwise there would be only a fragmented, meaningless
aggregation of mere facts, and no dialectic at all. To
Kierkegaard, however, such reasoning would simply repeat the Hegelian error of confusing essence and existence, the abstract and the concrete. There may be, in
the "System," some "ideal movement" of concepts, which
is necessary. But this has simply nothing at all to do
with what really comes about in the real world. Necessity was alleged to be the union of possibility with actuality. Nonsense! Necessity is, if you like, the actuality
of the possible *qua* possible; it is Leibniz's possible
worlds, the world of pure logic and mathematics, whose
only being is that it doesn't contradict itself. But once
something *comes into being*—instead of something else
—it could have been otherwise. That is actuality, precisely the non-necessary. And in this respect, Kierkegaard
insists, the future and the past are perfectly symmetrical.
The one happened as it happened, that cannot be denied,

and the other has not yet happened; but neither is necessary. That is why it is correct to describe the historian
as a backwards prophet.

What, then, is the historical, the subject matter of
history? Here Kierkegaard follows Hegel in distinguishing the merely spatial dialectic of nature from the truly
temporal dialectic of history. Natural events simply happen, over and over, and proliferate spatially. But human
events introduce true novelty: they create a second dialectic within time. And within that re-creation there is always the marvel that it happened this way and not otherwise. This is never necessity; it is the marvel of the
coming-to-be of what might not have been. For Kierkegaard, in other words, the locus of history is time, not
clock time, indeed, but time as the mysteriously experienced medium of the individual's life. Now Sartre, too, follows Hegel in dividing nature from history. He stoutly
combats Engels' view that nature is dialectical, only
human action is so. But for him time is, so to speak, a late
comer. In *Being and Nothingness* "temporalization" was
flight, the fall from the perspicuous instant of action into
bad faith. In the *Critique* he is indeed seeking to vindicate
the "temporalization" of action as the work of dialectical
reason. The action of the group in fusion has its temporal
reality (July 14, 1789) and its temporal consequences
(ever since). Were that not so, history could not result. Yet
these events can be seen as historical, Sartre still insists,
only if the total flow of temporal development is assimilated to an inner pattern of necessity—and so *"aufge-
hoben,"* sublimated and wiped out in its sheer temporal
contingency. But that is, from Kierkegaard's point of view
—and indeed, I believe, truly—precisely to deny the historical. Human existence *is* temporalization, first, last,
and foremost. Time, existential time, the time of becom-

ing, is its proper medium: the medium in which our acts succeed or fail, prove right or wrong. The United States went into Vietnam not because of the necessary development of capitalist imperialism, but because it had made a series of stupid, immoral, and, indeed, horrible mistakes.

How, secondly, can we "know" history? Kierkegaard seems to agree with Sartre in insisting that knowledge, which must be certain, must therefore be immediate. It is presence-to, whether to intellect or to sense. But obviously the past is never present. Moreover, even the contemporary who "sees" the event happening, only sees it as there—he cannot see it *coming* to be. There is *always,* in the sense for what comes to be, a wrenching loose from sheer presence, and thus from the indubitability of knowledge. Indeed, the past carries with it, when we seek to grasp it, its own uncertainty. To face it is not, and cannot be, to know it, but to face the question: was it, how was it, why was it so and not otherwise, and so to face the alternative: doubt or belief. Time and existence are the place of faith or skepticism, eternity and essence alone are the media for knowledge. Thus from a Kierkegaardian point of view the search for "intelligibility" as the unity of knowing and being, the search for the kind of human action that knows what it is and why it is there where it is: that search results from a category mistake. There may be historical faith; strictly speaking, there can be no historical knowledge—whether in the self-knowledge of the agent or the hindsight of the historian.

Can we apply this Kierkegaardian criticism also to Sartre's view of history? Yes and no. If knowledge must be certain, if to know is to know that one knows, then history is beyond its range. If belief and knowledge are totally different human attitudes, then history belongs to the former, not the latter. Kierkegaard of course stresses the dichotomy because it is faith in the supernatural—in the historical foundation of Christianity—that he is after. But if, as I believe it is, all knowledge is belief—"justified true belief," in the modern phrase, but still belief—then historical belief should not be singled out as different in kind from the beliefs induced in other contexts, whether by our intellects or our senses. And in that case there is no absolutely special problem about the "intelligibility" of historical actions. We act within a human world, as well as on objects mediated by human actions. Sometimes we know what we are doing; sometimes we are swept along by currents we fail to understand; sometimes we think we know what we are doing and are mistaken. In science we act, in a more limited way, by putting to nature questions to which we may or may not get significant answers. Sometimes our questions are the wrong ones to ask; sometimes we misinterpret the answers. Yet sometimes we do pretty well. Since in history men are both agents, objects of inquiry, and questioners about those objects, the situation is more complicated. But it is not essentially different. We are trying to make sense of something in the world around us: sometimes we fail or partly fail: sometimes we succeed or partly succeed; we can never be sure. Still, we needn't stop trying. For Sartre, however, such a modest and compromising aim would never do (indeed, it smacks of liberalism!). On the contrary, his extreme rationalism, his demand for Cartesian clarity combined with Hegelian scope, forces him into the difficult course of the search for a Dialectical Reason which shall have a Total Intelligibility of the whole panorama of historical action as its outcome.

chapter seven: new concepts in the critique

the practical organism

Sartre's move from a
phenomenological dialectic of the
individual consciousness to a critical
dialectic of society demanded substantive
as well as methodological innovations. I want to
examine these innovations, or apparent innovations,
in three areas, all of which were neglected if not altogether

overlooked in *Being and Nothingness*. First, there is the problem of the biological nature of man, the relation of consciousness to the living organism that "has" consciousness. Secondly, there is the theme of individual development: the treatment of childhood—a theme that Sartre broods over in incredible detail in his recent work on Flaubert, but hinted at also in the *Critique*. Finally, there are concepts introduced by Sartre with the explicit purpose of explaining social reality, on the material side the concept of *scarcity* (which I have already dealt with to some extent in comparing Sartre's earlier and later dialectic), and on the human side *reciprocity,* the symmetrical relation between man and man. Be it said again, however, I am by no means trying here to expound all the major concepts of the *Critique,* nor even to look at those I am concerned with in their precise articulation in the argument. But I want to ask in each case: is there a substantive new development? Why or why not?

In an interview published in *The New Left Review* (and in abbreviated form in *The New York Review*) Sartre distinguished three stages in his philosophical growth.[1] In the early work—where Roquentin, Orestes, and, I would suggest, Mathieu, are the literary surrogates for his philosophical problem—it was the for-itself that was central. He was seeking an ontology of individual consciousness as pure activity in a purely passive world. With the turn to a social ("Marxist") perspective, he substituted for the for-itself the concept of the *practical organism.* In the last decade, however, from the *Critique* to *The Idiot of the Family,* he has been concerned with yet a new dimension, *le vécu, the lived.* This sequence suggests at first sight that Sartre has been moving away from his Cartesian point of origin—where pure consciousness is what concerns him—to a more biologically rooted view of man. It suggests, indeed, a rapprochement with the thought of his friend and enemy Maurice Merleau-Ponty. For Merleau-Ponty the "lived body" is a central conception: a human person is an embodied being, inescapably psychophysical, inextricably natural *and* cultural, an organism which achieves self-consciousness within the natural and human worlds, rather than a moment of consciousness rising up *against* the world as nihilation and as lack. Is this in fact the view toward which Sartre has been developing? This and the concluding chapter should provide us with an answer, at least from the perspective of the present, if not with a prognosis for the future. It will be, in effect, "Yes" and "No," but, for the *Critique* at least, more "No" than "Yes."

That the "practical organism" has replaced the for-itself as the central *persona* in the realm of dialectical reason already suggests a turn to a new emphasis on man as animal—a unique sort of animal, who makes himself by his *praxis*—but still an animal. This is a dimension of human existence, as we saw earlier, almost wholly missing from the Sartrean man of the earlier period. If I *am* my red face as I bend over the keyhole, this "being" expresses the flat contradiction of inner and outer, not the ambiguity of an animal life which, while remaining animal, has yet achieved humanity. As for Spinoza, so for Sartre, body and consciousness, as the two parallel aspects of one existent, remain utterly disparate, even though they express, in their disparate ways, one single nature. In Spinoza's view, I, as a finite mode, can approach the understanding of God or Nature, and therefore indirectly of myself, under the attribute of thought *or* of extension, but never both at once. So it is for the self-understanding of the for-itself in *Being and Nothingness*. Consciousness and body are still Cartesian contraries, deprived of substantial status, but intelligible only as strict alternates to one another. True, "consciousness is wholly body, body wholly consciousness," yet an entwinement, an entanglement, of the two is inconceivable—or conceivable only through confusion.

Can an "organism" be understood at all in these terms? I think not. An "organism" is not just a body, and certainly not just a consciousness. If it is an organism sufficiently advanced on the evolutionary scale to be called "sentient," it is both together, body and sentience, sentient body, or bodily sentience, both in one, and reverberating to one another. It is neither unequivocally, but inalienably both together. Moreover, a *human* organism, a "practical organism," capable of action in and upon a world that is both human and material, both cultural and natural, such an organism is still body-and-sentience, but able also to take a stand within its natural-cultural setting and self-consciously to appraise, and even, within limits, to alter that environment. To express such a situation the parallelism of Spinoza, or of Sartre in *Being and Nothingness,* is utterly inadequate.

In the context of *Being and Nothingness,* of course, this may not matter, since Sartre expressly excuses himself there from any claim to found an "anthropology." Yet one may surely feel uneasy about a phenomenology, or an ontology, of human agency—and this the tale of the for-itself must be admitted to be—which leaves out of account the biological, and for that matter also the social, foundation of human life. Now the *Critique* does claim to have founded an "anthropology"—that is, a general theory of man—and it claims to do so in terms of a general concept, "practical organism," which seems to refer to our animal as well as to our social nature. Has Sartre, in turning more explicitly to a social perspective, also given more weight to the biological basis of human action? Merleau-Ponty, in *The Structure of Behavior,* distinguished three types of order—"physical," "vital," and "mental" (or human)—in terms of which behavior must be interpreted. Sartre, in the *Critique,* is working, as we have seen, between the physical or quasi-physical (the material and the *practico-inert*) and the human, or the social as the product of the human, notably the group in formation and the oath ("institutions" are indeed "social," but not wholly human, since they tend to fall back into the quasi-physical sphere of the *practico-inert*). If he sees men as "organisms," however, he appears at least to be giving recognition also to the mediating level of the *living,* as distinct from the sphere of physical inertia on the one hand or conscious *praxis* on the other.

To ferret out the reality behind the appearance, however, is extremely difficult. As I have tried to indicate in the previous chapter, the general tenor of the argument in the *Critique* is clear; the overall movement, from the question put by analytical reason, through the genesis of the dialectic, to its hoped-for issue, is plain to see. When one searches the text, however, with the aim of discovering whether and to what extent Sartre is treating the practical organism as an *organism,* one feels almost hopelessly at sea. Sometimes he seems to do so; sometimes his "practical organism" is indeed made of flesh and blood. But sometimes, on the other hand, it seems to shrink back into the abstract moment-of-action of the for-itself. Once more, as Iris Murdoch puts it, "The agent, thin as a needle, appears in the quick flash of the choosing will." [2] Let me try, if I can—though I am by no means sanguine of the issue—to sort out some of Sartre's references in the *Critique* to biology and to the biological nature of man, and see what conclusion we can reach.

In the *Critique,* as we have seen earlier, Sartre substitutes the concept of *need* for the more abstract *lack* of *Being and Nothingness.* What is "lacked" or "lacking" can be thought of in terms of a relation to consciousness alone, whether to the intentionality of consciousness or to the non-thetic consciousness (of) self that accompanies it. Indeed, "lack," "lacking," "lacked" form a trio that Sartre plays with almost as if the game were one of pure logic. But "need" suggests a relation more directly rooted in the real world. Hunger, thirst, sexual appetite are drives of living human beings, felt in and through their bodies, and assuaged only by bodily satisfaction. And in some passages Sartre does indeed stress the bodily nature of need[3] or the biological character of his "practical organism." [4]

Yet somehow the category of the biological hinted at from time to time is never wholly assimilated into the theory of social relations that the dialectic is to give us. This is clear from the first section of Book One, "On Individual 'Praxis' as Totalization," where Sartre gives his basic exposition of "need" and faces the question of its relation to its biological foundation. It is true, he admits, that if we consider "the body as function, function as need, and need as praxis," we obtain a first view of human work in which we see "the lived revelation of a goal to be reached as nothing but the restoration of the organism." [5] But this, he insists, is not a fundamental view. What matters in the last analysis is human *work*—that is, the organization by human agency of a field that lies outside the human agent himself. If I go hunting or fishing, if I gather fruit, I thereby organize my environment in virtue of my aims. It is in this sense that *praxis* totalizes. It not only ne-gates the in-itself (it is still man who introduces negativity into the world), but makes of it a whole. The river or the forest with its game, the orchard with its fruit, are made the organized unities they are by the human intent that seeks in and through them the satisfaction of its needs. True, Sartre admits later, *praxis* takes place "within the general milieu of animal life." [6] But that is a mere contin-gent fact which lies outside the dialectic and remains ob-stinately opaque. Even if biology should succeed in "solv-ing" the "problem" of the origin of life, he argues in the section now before us, this would be, like any scientific success, a purely analytical achievement, unassimilated and unassimilable by dialectical thought.[7] Life, once given, must be understood dialectically, in terms of the oppositions of freedom and necessity (or need?), exter-nal and internal, organic (that is, organized, or, better, or-ganizing) and inorganic (that is, material and inertial). It is these fundamental contrarieties that will generate the whole series of interactions between *praxis* and the *prac-tico-inert* and will thus provide the totalizing view which alone, Sartre believes, can serve as framework for his-tory. Needy being that, by some unintelligible chance, I am, I act freely to satisfy my needs. In this way I interiorize the external world, and organize the inorganic. Some-times, indeed, Sartre talks as though he admitted degrees of organization, rather than simply the organic and its ab-sence. Thus, for example, need is understood, he says, in relation to "the unorganized or the less organized." [8] Thus also in one passage at least, in discussing the ques-tion of the permanence of the group, he remarks that so far we have found two kinds of permanence: that of the or-ganic and that of biological integration (although it is not clear just where he has noted these two as distinct varieties).[9] For the most part, however, I think it is fair to say, "biological integration" is relegated to a purely background status. Life in the sense of animal life, it has been emphatically decreed at the very start of the argument— and in the context of the exposition of "need," the seemingly biological concept from which the whole movement of the dialectic will arise—life as animal life is merely the brute given which lies outside the reach of dialectical intelligibility. As against that indigestible and irrational fact, it is *praxis* as organized, and organizing, action, over against an "inorganic plurality" that is of primary interest. It is from the pair organic/inorganic, in the sense of organized/inertial, that the dialectic flows. Between action and inertia, organizing activity and the passive flow of the material, there is no mediating third. True, life cannot be understood mechanically. Given that it exists, we have to go dialectically about making intelligible what we can understand about it. What we can understand, however, is the interaction of human action as organizing principle and the inertial force of materiality, or of the quasi-material which action itself produces. As in *Being and Nothingness,* so here, the living as such is not a basic category of Sartrean thought.

This interpretation is confirmed, not only by the section on need, but by two passages in which Sartre refers, in passing, to the theory of evolution. In the first, a footnote to the discussion of Engels' "dialectic of nature"—whose "dogmatism" Sartre decidedly rejects—he remarks that biology in its present state is still "analytic and positivistic," and will not be able to provide a proper theory of the origin of life unless it moves to a "totalizing" view, which would envisage biological facts "in their interiority."[10] In this connection, he notes, it is strange that Marxists, allegedly dialecticians of Nature, tax with idealism those like Kurt Goldstein who try ("rightly or wrongly," says Sartre) to see organized beings as wholes. For what this amounts to, he remarks, is precisely to demonstrate, or to attempt to demonstrate, "the dialectical irreducibility of that 'state of matter,' life, to that other state—inorganized matter—which has nevertheless produced it."[11] Sartre's cautious reference to Goldstein is commendable; his position is indeed obscure. But what is remarkable about this note, it seems to me, is that it indicates how very peripheral to Sartre's own thinking is the whole question of biological theory and the philosophical issues it raises. Engels must be dealt with at length; but the biological problem of the (ir)reducibility of the living is worth only a sidelong glance. But how can one seriously attempt to develop a theory of human action on the Sartrean scale while ignoring almost entirely its basis in animal behavior and the biological nature of man? And what is this "practical organism" whose organismic character can be so blithely ignored?

The other reference is at least as peripheral to Sartre's argument, but revealing for his attitude to biology. In the section on interest (part of the section on "Worked matter as alienated objectification of individual and collective 'Praxis' ") he refers to the Darwinian struggle for life as equivalent to the so-called law of interest. Now he is clearly equating Darwinian theory here with social Darwinism, and hence with the utilitarian theory which, he argues, makes "human relations a priori antagonistic." He finds it strange, moreover, that even some Marxists should hesitate "between the law of interest and the Marxist conception of history, that is, between a sort of biological materialism and historical materialism." [12] Two points may be made about this very incidental reference. First, the equation of "Darwinian" with "utilitarian," etc., betrays an almost total want of interest in biological theory as such. And secondly, from the reference to the Marxists in question it is clear that Sartre's own materialist, and allegedly Marxist, theory of society is "historical" *as against* a "biological" view. Again, one wonders what a "practical organism" can be whose *"praxis"* can generate history in abstraction from its biological development. Is it, not in fact a new *persona* of Sartrean philosophy, but the for-itself rechristened?

Indeed, Sartre reaffirms in the *Critique* his earlier thesis: *there is no human nature*.[13] And in a sense, of course, he is right. Normal infants of our species are born, not human, but potentially so. To become a person is an *achievement* of a human organism, not a fact given from birth as such. And that achievement can be accomplished only through the infant's participation in a human social world. A person develops through learning to express his culture, the culture of his family, his neighborhood, his language, ultimately the subcultures of the interests he develops and that make him the person he is. As Sartre puts it in his reflections on Flaubert, it is through the human that the baby becomes human.[14] There is no simply given nature that he has, by genetic endowment alone, and which his history cannot shape in one direction or another. But on the other hand the development of a human being is not a springing into existence of a pure consciousness. A developed human being becomes so only through participation in a human world, in a network of human worlds, but in so developing he *embodies* that world or those worlds. And by that process, conversely, he *personalizes* nature. Thus a human person, one can say, is at one and the same time an *embodiment* of culture and a *personalization* of nature. True, there is no new "essence," no new stuff, added to the human neonate over and above, say, his simian cousins, that automatically makes him human. He has, for himself and uniquely, to make himself. But, on the one hand, as Adolf Portmann has demonstrated, his very biological nature prepares him for this self-making.[15] In his first year, in which he learns to speak, to stand upright and to perform responsible actions—that is, in what Portmann calls the year of the social uterus—the child takes into himself, into his very bodily being, the world offered him by maternal affection (or, if Sartre is right, in Flaubert's case, by the lack of it). Man is not *without* a nature; rather, as Helmuth Plessner puts it, he is *naturally artificial:* it is his nature to need culture, to need the sedimentation into a human world of the actions of those who have preceded him.[16] It is this need, the need for human meaning, built into our very ontogeny, which unites, in every human history, the organic with the social, the artificial with the biologically given.

For Sartre, however, the relation between these three—need, nature, and culture—is very different. He introduces biological needs, with the contingent fact of the scarcity of goods for their fulfillment, as the starting point of his dialectic. But this is simply animal need, not the need for meaning, which is uniquely human, and as we have seen it serves as the *unintelligible* base on which and beyond which the dialectic will take place. That dialectic, however, results solely from the interaction of *action* with *inert matter.* "Man," Sartre says, "is that material reality by which matter receives its human functions." [17] Action comes first; [18] through the inertial consequences of action, the "passive activity" of the *practico-inert,* alienation follows. But it is man "who has put into the thing his own action, his own knowledge." [19] This is no dualism, Sartre insists, but a monism, a monism not indeed of substantive matter, but of "materiality." Matter as such, he holds, could exist, only for "God or a pebble." [20] What we have instead is "worked matter," matter viewed, and handled, through the medium of human action. Thus ". . . worked matter, with the contradictions it contains, becomes *for* and *by* men the fundamental engine of History." [21] But this is still, I submit, the sharply dualistic "monism" of *Being and Nothingness:* first action, the for-itself (*now praxis*) springing up as the Other of the In-Itself, and then the In-Itself as its Other, as what by its very upsurge it nihilates; but yet, the other way around, the In-Itself (now the inertial) as the whole locus, the factual reality, in which and against which the For-itself tries to assert itself. Bereft of substantiality, these are still the Cartesian realities of the pure interior and the pure exterior, the *cogitans* and the *extensa,* only no *res.* The embodied human being in whom the dialectic is to operate is represented only as the contingent fact of need and scarcity, or in the reference to the "general milieu of animal life." Everything is material or everything is human—or (*contra* Descartes) both at once: hence the dialectic. But between these two there is still no place for life.

Granted, there are numerous passages in which Sartre does stress the biological reality of the human organism.[22] Indeed, in general, he seems to be playing on an ambiguity in the concept of organization itself. "Organization" may be understood as the ordering principle of any material aggregate, or for that matter of any collection of actions. Thus a corporation, a club, a school, is characterized by the way it is organized. But "organization" may also be used to characterize the structure—and the functioning—of certain natural wholes. It is the latter meaning which seems to be entailed in the concept of an organism, and sometimes Sartre acknowledges the existence of his "practical organism" in this sense. But more fundamental, for him, it seems to me, is the conception of the "practical organism" as the center of organization of action. As material, Sartre argues, we are infected with inertia, but as agents we also "lend to matter our power of transcendence toward organized action." [23] It is this power of organiz*ing* that Sartre is often—and misleadingly—referring to, I believe, when he contrasts the "organic" with the "inorganic," or with an "inorganic plurality." Thus he compares *praxis,* not with any animal behavior, but with a seal which imposes its figure on a receptive wax.[24] Pure agency shaping the purely passive, the revenge of passivity on agency through the *practico-inert:* that is his basic model. So for example the whole range of "collectives," the merely serial togetherness of human individuals, is described as "inorganic" in contrast to the organic unity of the individual agent, who really acts.

But there is a further complication here. As we noticed in the preceding chapter, one of the recurrent themes in Sartre's argument is a firm opposition to "organicism" as a theory of society. There is no such thing as a "hyper-organism" generated by the formation of social structures.[25] Social "organizations" are the creatures of *constituted* dialectic only,[26] the *constituting* dialectic stems from the *praxeis* of individuals alone. Only individuals can produce, by their mediating but individual actions, a group in fusion, only individuals can swear a solemn oath to be true to the group so formed. And constituted dialectic, as we have already seen, must be produced, and understood, under the guidance of the constituting, active, and fundamental phase. So, after all, Sartre has to insist, all *praxis* is founded on "man as *bio-*

logical unity." [27] "Organizations" are after all the product of "organisms" in the ordinary biological meaning of the term. Only this dictum can save Sartre's dialectic from a full Hegelian or idealist issue in some supersociety or superstate. The "intelligibility" of the dialectic also, we have already noted, consists, not in the self-containment of "objective" or "absolute" mind, but in the perspicuity to the individual, active consciousness, of the social, and ultimately historical, context of his act. But the individual agent, in this situation here and now, is the embodied human being, and no one else. Sartre has to fall back on the individual *life* as the locus of history. If there is history, it is individual human beings, "biological unities," who make it. Is not the biological then after all a fundamental category for his view of social action?

Not quite—perhaps even not at all. In his introductory argument ("Introduction B: Critique of Critical Experience"), Sartre stresses *life* as the object of his investigation, but this is "life" in the biographical, not the biological, sense. Referring back to "Questions of Method," he writes: "the epistemological starting point must always be *consciousness* as apodeictic certainty (of) itself and as consciousness *of* such and such an object" [28] —still the position of *Being and Nothingness.* And he continues:

> But it is not a matter of questioning consciousness about itself: the object it must give itself is precisely *life,* that is, the objective being of the investigator, in the world of Others, in so far as this being has been totalizing itself since birth and will totalize itself till death.[29]

The question is still: how can the *cogito,* non-thetic or thetic, pre-reflective or reflective, with its instantaneous upsurge out of nothing and as nothingness: how can this strange yet most familiar being grow? How can I, how can Sartre, how can any agent, totally free, imprint its project by its freedom on inert matter, and yet develop? How can totalization happen over time? Sartre seems to glimpse, at the close of the *Critique,* a vision of history as universally totalizing; yet the power of any one individual to "totalize," to shape his environment into a human life, remains a mystery. If anything is to be intelligible, Sartre seems to hold, the larger totalization, the totalization of *all* history, must reverberate in the individual life, the totalization of each practical organism, "no matter who." [30] And conversely, the individual life must totalize the universe: it must rise up into being as this unique expression of all history, of all humanity: for there is only each for-itself against *the* in-itself, as exteriority, as being as such and in totality. And all this must really happen, from birth to death, not in abstraction, but in the concrete reality of human hopes and frustrations, decisions and disappointments.

From the point of view of *Being and Nothingness,* all temporalization is flight. If that is so, there is no history, neither of individuals, nor of societies, let alone of humanity as such. That is Sartre's most fundamental problem, the problem with which, in *The Idiot of the Family,* he is still wrestling: how, out of the contradictory, and abstract, to-and-fro of for-itself/in-itself, or action/inertia, can a life—any single human life—develop? In the *Critique* he hoped, it seems, that the social perspective of Marxism, hopefully materialist and hopefully totalizing, would enable him to break out of his initial quandary and see the individual life as growing with the dialectical growth of a greater whole. The tortured reflections on Flaubert which have replaced, or at least anticipated, Volume Two of the

Critique, suggest that his hope was vain. It was so, I believe, in part at least because of his failure to assimilate the living in the biological sense to his conception of life as individual history, because he sees man still primarily in terms of thought *versus* being, consciousness *versus* the merely inertial. Granted, history, whether individual or social, is not to be identified with organic growth. But human development is nevertheless an extrapolation of growth, a diversion of the natural into new channels, not its denial. Man has to make himself within a human world, not only, like other animals, within a biological environment. But that development is the history of the human *organism* becoming human. Temporality originates, not in the stream of consciousness, but in the life-span of the embodied individual, who is born, learns to walk and talk and love and hate, grows old, and dies. Engels or no Engels, if nature were not dialectical, neither would we be so. Real human development is rooted in the real biological development of members of this species on this planet. That there are living things, that there are these hominoid living things, is, to be sure, a contingent fact: it might not have happened, it might soon be no more. But it is not a *mere,* unintelligible contingency. It contains, in the hierarchically organized functions and structures of life as it has evolved, the frame for all intelligibility.

Childhood

The passage I have just been considering—as well as the whole tenor of "Questions of Method"—suggests, secondly, a concern with biography, with individual development, which was conspicuously absent from Sartre's early philosophical work. Has he changed fundamentally since then in his attitude to childhood?

It is worth considering in this connection one of the

few explicit parallels Sartre himself draws between *Being and Nothingness* and the *Critique.* In a note at the conclusion of the section on necessity, he first reminds us that, in his present terms, and referring to the practico-inert, "the foundation of necessity is practical." [31] This means, he says, that "it is the for-itself, as agent, discovering itself first as inert, or, better, as practico-inert in the medium of the in-itself." Indeed, the very structure of action as "organization of the unorganized" first exhibits to the for-itself its own alienated being as in-itself: in other words, action generates the "circuit of selfness," the flight from freedom to objectivity or pseudo-objectivity. Thus Sartre can easily put the basic theme of his earlier work in the new terms: "This inert materiality of man as foundation of all knowledge of oneself by oneself is nevertheless an alienation of knowledge at the same time that it is a knowledge of alienation." [32]

But what about the pre-reflective *cogito?* It is still there: *"praxis . . .* is always consciousness (of) self," yet that consciousness is impotent against "the practical affirmation that I am what I have done"—or "made." As in *Being and Nothingness,* so here, the ambiguity of *"fait"* in this context is important, since it is by my action that I have made myself, and by making myself that I act on and in the world. What is crucial here, however, is the recognition that this *I* which I am as what I have done-or-made always escapes me, and does so "by constituting me immediately as *another.*" [33] It was this relation, Sartre continues, that made it possible to understand "why man *projects himself* in the medium of the In-Itself-For-Itself." But the fundamental alienation flowing from such self-projection does not come, he insists, "as *Being and Nothingness* might mistakenly lead one to believe, from a prenatal choice: it comes from the universal relation of interiority which unites man as practical organism to his environment." [34]

Has Sartre changed his view in this respect? Aron seems to think that he has done so.[35] That is, he seems to take Sartre as confessing here an error of his earlier position. Previously he had thought of a "pre-natal choice." I make myself, yet wherever I stand, the die is already cast. Now he gives more weight to environment and its "interiorization" by the individual—presumably, as in the case of Genet or Flaubert or the young Jean-Paul himself, the developing individual at some crucial moment in his childhood. Yet basically, it seems to me, the paradox of the Sartrean free act remains the premise for both arguments. On the one hand, *Being and Nothingness* did not literally predicate of the for-itself a "pre-natal choice"; only one might mistakenly have thought that it did. And on the other hand, the very emphasis on social and material environment in the *Critique* makes a "pre-natal choice" inevitable: the child born into a class, into an institutionalized social niche, "is its victim before birth." [36] He cannot choose himself except as what he has already been made to be.

True, Sartre has acquired an interest in the decisive moment of a child's history which he formerly lacked. This is plain from *Saint-Genet,* with its detailed study of the moment in which the young Genet made himself the thief he was accused of being. It is plain from *Words,* with its slogan "Childhood decides." It is plain to the point of supersaturation from the new study of Flaubert. Of course, there is little said of childhood in the *Critique* itself, since its subject is the dialectic of social life in general; but "Questions of Method," which, Sartre has alleged, should really have followed, not preceded, the main text of that work, clearly foreshadows this type of interest. As I suggested earlier, the regressive-progressive method is especially well suited to the study of individual histories, rather than of "History" itself. And in the period of *Being and Nothingness,* on the other hand, a concern for such analysis and synthesis in depth of the individual life was certainly missing. Oddly enough, Sartre remarks in "Questions of Method," "Marxists care only for adults," [37] but so in the main do "existentialists" from Kierkegaard to Heidegger and, in the period of *Being and Nothingness,* Sartre himself. Even his "existential psychoanalysis," it seems to me, deals rather with the expression of my choice of myself in my present preferences than with the emergence in childhood of a process of self-making. That is one of the ways in which Sartre "corrects" Freud. All is consciousness, and consciousness is *now.* True, my hatred of viscosity, for instance, may stem from what my mother did to me in infancy; but what interests Sartre is the analysis of adult consciousness as self-projection and as the flight to bad faith, not its emergence out of the shadows of childhood in the individual life history. Even in Sartre's literary corpus of the earlier period childhood is conspicuously absent. The one striking exception, so far as I know, is the central figure in the story "The Childhood of a Leader," in which the child portrayed is a sort of empty shell and the point of the story is the speculative one made more directly and convincingly in Sartre's essay on anti-Semitism. Lucien's decisive act, moreover, the refusal to shake hands with a Jew, is that of a young man, not a child. *No* project had been initiated in that empty childhood; for this emptiness the young adult substitutes a typical pseudo-act, an identification of himself with a stereotype: I am a Jew-hater, therefore I am somebody. The interest in concrete individual life and its early development, therefore, seem on the whole to be an innovation, at least of emphasis.

At the same time, however, as I noted earlier for the *Critique* in general, the ingredients of the human condition are still the same: total freedom, yet total facticity. The I by its very nature as agent in the world *must* alienate itself from itself; cast into the world by Others, it makes even itself an Other when it acts, as it must do, in and upon that radical Other, the in-itself, whether the purely material or the dehumanized human, the *practico-inert*. If childhood has come to interest Sartre as it used not to do, that is because he is fascinated by the terrible—perhaps the insoluble—puzzle, how a Sartrean for-itself can in fact *come to be*. The for-itself *ought* to be instantaneous; temporalization is flight. Yet people *do* develop; how is this possible? What Sartre wants to know principally in the *Critique,* of course, is: how does humanity develop. But since humanity is an aggregate of individual *praxeis* —there is no social superorganism—that question leaves at its base the question of individual genesis. Mankind can develop only if men can do so; no overarching dialectic, however sweeping, can evade that truth. There is only one *Madame Bovary;* yet in a sense the problem of Gustave—the "idiot" as genius—is the problem of us all. To that problem we must yet return, as Sartre has done.

Scarcity

Meantime, however, the *Critique* was centrally concerned, not with individual biography, but with the social developments that make a history of humanity possible. For, as I suggested in the previous chapter, Sartre seems to have seen in Marxism, or in his own interpretation of

Marxism, an escape from the solipsism of *Being and Nothingness,* and the ground for a rational theory of society and social history. Here he explicitly claims to have introduced new concepts, which are meant to alleviate the bleakness of his existentialism—or, in his own view, to place it at the human center of a larger and therefore truer scheme. Two concepts in particular mediate this new development: *scarcity* as the basis for the interaction of man with matter and indirectly of man with man, and the *reciprocity* of I-Other relations, whether mediated by a third man or by matter, or (perhaps) immediate. Both these concepts are employed, it seems, to alter fundamentally the I-Other relation as set forth in Sartre's earlier argument.

First, scarcity. In *Being and Nothingness* the Other looms up as threat or victim. Logically or ontologically, there is no other possibility. Thus, it seems, every consciousness wants, *a priori,* the death of another, or wants, at least, the victimization of the Other, or, alternatively, of itself. This principle the Sartre of the *Critique* emphatically denies. True, the practical organism is threatened by the Other, but not directly—and not, it seems, in virtue of the very appearance of the Other as such. The practical organism, we have seen, is needy: it needs to be replenished by the inorganic. But, alas, the materials to satisfy its needs are *scarce.* That contingent fact generates the chain of events that will produce social structures: serialities, to begin with, in which each becomes himself part of an inertial aggregate, then groups and institutions, with the exploitation consequent upon them. Scarcity, however, might be defeated; so the ills of organized society are non-necessary. We can hope for a utopia.

There are a number of difficulties in this alleged "solution," even apart from the abstractness of the dream it offers. To begin with (as I noted earlier), scarcity when interiorized is simply the sense of contingency characteristic of the for-itself: it is the awareness that I am—and must be—just so and not otherwise, just here now and not there then. It is simply facticity all over again. Were it overcome, this would be, Sartre announces, the overcoming of man himself. Such, of course, is dialectic: self-devouring contradiction. But as a vision of humanity to replace the concept of the for-itself as "useless passion," it is cold comfort. The human condition rests on scarcity; some day there may be abundance and so no humanity!

Besides, why scarcity and only scarcity? Suppose there were room in the bus? The British, for example, would queue up in any case: they *like* to be orderly. The self-alienation, Sartre could answer, of members of the oldest industrial society! They have made themselves serial. There is something in it. But the point is: if you change the image, you see, not a crowd pushing for places, but a small number of people each using a material object for his own ends. It *serves* each of them; they are not (not necessarily or not always) enslaved by it. Things in the world, as Heidegger tells us, are "ready to hand" for our use. They can also be maddeningly *unready;* they can also be in short supply. But why must that be the basic fact? Because scarcity shows me the Other as competitor, and shows me to myself too in my Otherness than him. That is, for Sartre, what is most striking in the fact that there are Others at all. But suppose, as Rousseau suggested, we find in facing nature the need to cooperate rather than to compete? Think of a barn-raising in the homesteading days of the Midwest. Think of a dam, produced, not by the struggle for scarce goods, but by cooperation for plenty. Granted that the quest for power or profit may, and usually does, enter into all such projects; but that is no reason to make such motives exclusive—unless one is, as Sartre appears to be, already so Hobbesian in one's view of man that no other alternative seems possible.

This seems a strange analogy. Sartre rails against "liberalism" and "positivism," against the atomizing view of man and society taken by utilitarian thinkers. They are mechanical, anti-dialectical, unable to "totalize." Hobbes is the arch example of this kind of thinking. But why, unless he himself shares this atomistic style of thought, must Sartre find competition for scarce goods *the* source of social organization? The truth is, I suspect, that when he thinks about society he really *is* a Hobbesian. There are three passions, Hobbes told us, that necessitate the social contract: fear, gain, and glory. The upsurge of the Other, in *Being and Nothingness,* was also carried by three passions: fear, shame, and pride. Now pride, we saw, is the obverse of shame; shame, then, is pride (= glory) facing the other way: it is my humiliation before, rather than my triumph over, the threatening Other. So in the basic relation of any individual to any other we already had, in effect, two of the Hobbesian three. Now Sartre looks more directly than he had done at men as "material agents" and finds them, whether in want of bread or bus seats, vying with one another for the scarce goods available to satisfy their needs. They compete, not only out of fear or pride (and shame), they compete for gain as well. This vision of human interaction arises inevitably out of—and only out of—a thoroughly molecular conception of the individual. Like particles in a container full of heated gas (to speak anachronistically), or like self-impelled billiard balls, we go off each in his own direction, each pushed by his own appetites—and we collide. That blind inertial consequence necessitates society. And society is alienation: I give myself away to others, simply because otherwise I could not live at all. Society is necessitated by the impossibility of an impossibility. Not, of course, that Sartre would recognize the authority of the Hobbesian sovereign; shades of Rousseau, as of Descartes, forbid! Each man is sovereign. Yet all men can survive only through mutual alienation, only through the self-denying ordinances that institute society.

What most strikingly differentiates Sartrean from Hobbesian man, however, is Sartre's preoccupation, both before and after the *Critique*—though minimally in it— with the inwardness of the individual. Consciousness, and in particular the unhappy consciousness, is his true medium. Hobbes good-humoredly admitted human beastliness, content to engineer an obsequious survival in the face of the worse evil of violent death. Sartre, shut up in phantasms, suffers the alternate agonies of dread before his lonely freedom and remorse at its self-alienation in the world out there. "It's never fun to be a man," he says.[38] Dialectical reason, in its laborious course, offered, perhaps, hope to transcend that pain, or at least its temporary assuagement. In *The Idiot of the Family,* however, it has been, if anything, intensified.

But for the moment we are still with the *Critique* and its construction on the ground of scarcity. Scarcity is not, I have suggested, so exclusively the mediator of social action as Sartre would make it. Let me mention, finally, an example offered by Sartre himself which bears this out: his account of the social structure of a radio audience. To produce a series the member of the bus queue must be there. Those who stay home or go by Métro have no part in the constitution of the series. A radio audience, however, is defined by *absence.* There is a voice speaking; there is the *praxis* of language as its foundation. But the voice by its presence to me and to him and him and him . . . by that very presence indifferently to each makes impossible a common *praxis* for us all. Not only is it an object—a radio—that mediates the disembodied voice; that voice, received, dehumanizes. Indeed, it uses the original reciprocity of discourse *in order* to dehumanize. For it makes of its hearers "inert objects, subjected as inorganic material to the human work of the voice." [39] Of course I can turn the radio off. But that very action, Sartre argues, exhibits "the series defined by absence" constituted by the broadcaster's voice. For my exit from the listening audience makes no difference to its structure: the voice "will continue to sound in thousands of rooms before millions of hearers. It is I who precipitate myself into the ineffective and abstract solitude of private life without changing anything in the objectivity [of the broadcast]. I have not denied the voice; I have denied myself as a member of the crowd (*rassemblement*)." [40] Sartre analyzes the situation further for a political broadcast. Either I am convinced by the government's message (and they have constituted me as their Other), or I am skeptical (and every relation of doubt is one of Otherness), or I am already convinced of the falsity of their rhetoric, and then I either envisage Others as those I could relieve of their deception, or rely for my conviction on the authority of some Others who have persuaded me. But in any of these cases, here I am, listening in absence from the speaker, in absence from the indefinite Others objectified by his address. My powerlessness in this situation, my powerlessness to act on the Other listeners, Sartre declares, "makes of those Others my destiny." [41] Even if the speaker is introduced by name, the reciprocity of language has been destroyed—and it is *no one* speaking.

There is no need to fill in the voices—or, for television, the faces—to illustrate what Sartre is saying. His description strikes home. But does it justify his theory about scarcity as the origin of seriality and seriality as the origin of social relations? This seems to me more questionable, for several reasons. Sartre is arguing at least four points: (1) it is the scarcity of material objects that throws men into serial relations; (2) series are ordinal relations; (3) they are (as in the bus queue) irrelevant in any direct way to mutual *praxis* and so easily relegate human agents into the medium of the *practico-inert;* and (4) the group in fusion and so ultimately the group itself, Sartre will try to demonstrate, originates from the denial of seriality. In the case of the radio audience, (3) is clearly apposite. Mass media do objectify by means of an inertially organized multiplicity-in-absence. Sartre's account is apt, and aptly terrifying. But what of the other points? What has the radio to do with scarcity? Granted, each listener, or someone in his neighborhood, must have money to buy a set. But even if Big Brother endowed each infant at birth with his own set, the situation Sartre describes would hold. Scarcity, it seems to me, is not the definitive factor in the case. Unless of course power originates from competition for scarce goods—and so Big Brother was the product of scarcity. But that is too far-fetched. The point is: here is a characteristic structure of the practico-inert, of the dehumanized human, which in a world of plenty might still exist, might even be exacerbated. The very indefinite possibility of extending such anonymous audiences of disembodied voices—the potential globalization of the media—renders the vision *more* annihilating.

Nor can I see here any clearly *ordinal* character of the aggregate involved. The indefinite set of Others-absent-from-one-another appears rather to be a cardinal collective. Sartre tries to anticipate this objection. If I protest, he says, against a broadcast, and, for instance, write to the newspapers, thus making a public statement of my view, nevertheless each reader in turn must read what I have to say. But surely the contrary is the case. Newspaper readers read—as radio listeners listen—at one time. It is precisely a false network of pseudo-contemporaneity that the mass media constitute. We are together, now, in virtue of our very separation, each at his set, each in his armchair, but all at once. Why is Sartre so confident that not only this one, but all human collectivities, are generated from ordinal relations? Possibly his insistence that social relations are generated only by the plunge into series is related to his concept of temporality. It is still the bead-like moment of a single consciousness that is for him the fundamental reality; a mutual presence-to of one such consciousness and another would be impossible. So if we are to relate consciousnesses, as we must do in order to build society, we have to start by taking one such moment after another, and putting one consciousness after the other. But such an act is wrong, since *every* man is sovereign; society is based on an original fall. Were there a mutuality of human presences, however, this move would be unnecessary. Series exist, indeed, but they need not be *the* foundation of society.

Finally, the notion that groups arise only as the denial of seriality appears even more arbitrary. *If* scarcity were the sole mediating ground of human relations, and *if* seriality, with its transformation of agents into objects, were the sole response to scarcity, then, indeed, groups could emerge only as contradicting, in their turn, the serialized denial of individual *praxis*. But are there no other human relations, more direct than the mediating influence of scarce matter, through which society might originate? Taken at face value, Sartre's own example of language and its degradation through the mass media seems to suggest that there might be such. To speak, must not you and I be present to one another? To answer this question, or at least to suggest some reflections related to a possible answer, we must look, however, in conclusion, at Sartre's other chief innovating—or apparently innovating—social concept: the concept of *reciprocity*.

Reciprocity

By means of a "second *cogito*," the Other looms up as threat to my existence. *He* organizes the world, and so my world, which my for-itself makes mine, bleeds away into his, and—since I *am* that making—I bleed away too. The Other's appearance engenders a hemorrhage of my world toward his. I can reclaim my freedom, therefore, only by denying his. Simone de Beauvoir recalls in her memoirs how she and Sartre worried in their youth about "the problem of the Other." They used to invent life histories for strangers observed in cafés—never mind whether those stories were true. That is one way to put the Other out of action, by fictionalizing him. Then he, too, becomes my creature, powerless to harm me. But of course between myself and the Other there is, within this framework, no reciprocity. He and I, I and Thou, can never be *really* together. We may be united, indirectly, against a common Other, but we are never, as two freedoms, face to face. There can be no respect. Though Sartre did make one effort, in his popular essay "Existentialism and Humanism," to infer the freedom of all from that of one, and hence to provide a basis for human mutuality, his argument there is palpably sophistical and, so far as I know, he has never repeated it in that form. At this stage of his philosophical development at least, the only relation he could validly acknowledge between one human being and another was that of torturer and victim.

As he has turned to social and political concerns, however, he had had to seek, philosophically also, for some more adequate conceptual foundation for social life. If the whole human world of artifacts, the café, the Métro, the newspaper, the radio, is *my* set of instruments, and mine alone, and if this obtains, as it must do, for each for-itself making its world, how can this highly organized system have come about? There must be, there must have been, some actual cooperation in effecting some shared ends that has produced the institutions and artifacts I use. Besides, if one is truly concerned, as Sartre has been, with the oppression of others, one does respect those whose part one takes. One loathes injustice, not simply out of negativity, but out of respect for those who deserve justice and fail to get it. Somewhere, somehow there must be, not only mutual threat, but mutual respect.

It is in this context that Sartre believes he has found in "Marxism" the "true philosophy" into which his existentialism can be harmoniously assimilated. On the one hand, as we have seen, Marxism offered him a platform for revolution into which the concept of class struggle adumbrated in *Being and Nothingness* could be easily integrated. And it also offered the kind of "totalizing" perspective which the turn from individual consciousness to the world seemed to demand. Neither of these relations, however, bears on the fundamental social problem: how can one for-itself be positively and reciprocally related to another? How can there be, not only oppression, but brotherhood? How, except destructively—by the direction of each one's hatred to the common exploiters of all—*can* the workers of the world unite? It is in "historical materialism," as he understands it, that Sartre finds his answer. Each man acts to shape his own world: that is the existentialist insight which must be retained in any true account even of social action. But men act, and have acted, together to generate history: the rise and fall of societies, governments, institutions in general. And they are able to do this because their relations to one another are *mediated by matter.* The mutuality of men, their ability to respect one another so as to act together, *is made possible by the relation of each to material objects.* The dialectic of history is generated by the interaction of man with matter. Hence "historical materialism."

The first example of this process that Sartre presents is that of language. Language, he says, *is* matter: words must bombard my ear; it is through their material presence that they unite speaker and hearer. A phrase is "a totalizing in act where each word is defined by relation to the others, to the situation and to the whole language as an integrating part of the whole." [42] The language itself, then, is an indefinite network of such connecting links, a complex object through which particular subjectivities can relate to one another. But language cannot connect, Sartre argues, unless individual men use it. A necessary condition for the existence of language is that there be *particular* subjectivities to connect and who do the connecting. It is for that reason, he holds, that reciprocity fails in the case of the radio audience. Telephone conversations are another matter; here I speak, via audible sounds, to *you:* two for-itselves are in fact mediated by materiality. But in the case of radio or television it is no one subject that is addressed; therefore reciprocity fails, and the speaker too vanishes into objectivity. Hence the "vertiginous" character of the experience. In their proper functioning, words flow from one *praxis* to another.

Now this is clearly an advance on *Being and Nothingness,* where language was "a form of seduction." Not that it may not, but it need not, be so. On the other hand, there is still something forced about this account too. "The word is matter"? [43] It is true, of course, that language is necessarily embodied. It has always seemed to me rather a joke on Descartes that he makes so much of the uniqueness of language as the mark of man's possessing a disembodiable mind. For speech is perspicuously mental-*and*-bodily, all in one. Words are meanings and *are* only *as* meanings, but as meanings potentially heard or (in writing) seen. They *are* not matter; the same word repeated is not the same matter, but it is the same word. They could not exist apart from matter, and neither could the thoughts they carry. But neither can words be matter as such. They are classes of sounds, or marks, that signify—and signification cannot be reduced to any finite or specifiable series of particular objects. Sartre recognizes, to be sure, the necessary component of "signification" in language; but this comes, in his view, from the particular legislative enactment of each *praxis* (= each for-itself), who gives meaning to each word he uses as he uses it. Thus he adds to the dialectic of his individual action—making the world and being made by it— a dialectic of inter-individual relations: "a moving and indefinite dispersion of reciprocities." [44] It is upon the foundation of such "dispersed reciprocities" that Sartre will construct (or discover?) the dialectic of social organization which develops from them. Thanks to the mediation of material bits—words—there can after all be reciprocal relations between individual consciousnesses, there can be society.

But is language as the foundation of social life, is social life itself, as additive as this? Man lives *in* language, and therefore in a world; he is *in* a world, and therefore in language. Sartre is still hamstrung by his solipsistic starting point—and, clearly, in his exposition of language, by his nominalism, his conviction that only particulars are real. In *The Idiot of the Family* he suggests a more global view of the child's relation to his mother tongue, a view very close to Merleau-Ponty's, in fact; but that's another story. In the *Critique* there are still only active individuals, centers of sense-giving, and the purely inertial matter—phonemes—that can link these otherwise isolated centers to one another.

Hence the importance for Sartre of "the third man." Two individuals may work the same matter—for instance, speak the same language or dig the same ditch—but each is "interiorizing" what is out there in terms of his own project. How can they have a common project? How can there be shared *praxis*? Two workmen sharing a task —regulating a chronometer, Sartre suggests—each interiorize the same imperative; but for each it is assimilated as quasi-material. Each relates to it as an object which he either uses as the technique for his self-projection, or (and this is the usual case) submits to as the Other that has robbed him of his freedom. The dyadic relation of man to man, therefore, remains rooted in matter, in the *inhuman*.

It can become human only when it is mediated, not by matter, but by a third *praxis:* by an agent who assimilates to his action the acts of the Other Two. Here Sartre envisages a situation in which he looks from a window at two country workmen invisible to one another: one a gardener, the other one working on the road. Each has organized his world around his work. But the urban intellectual looking at them both unites them: they are both workers and both rural. Though separated in space—that is, external to one another, as all practical organisms are—they are related internally through their relation to the spectator, and through this dialectical transformation he also relates, internally, to them. Thus the relation of two men through matter, "dispersed" and fleeting in its dyadic form, can become the foundation for a richer dialectical development through the injection of a third *praxis* who assimilates to his activity the matter-mediated relations of the other two. The dyad, realized by a third subjectivity: that is the "Trinity" from which social structures can develop. Of course there is always the danger that one of the Three will dehumanize the other-two-in-their-reciprocal-relation: hence the "anti-dialectic" of the *practico-inert,* from which history has (so far) never escaped. But hence also the possibility of the group-infusion, the possibility, even the necessity, of the constituting dialectic at the heart of social reality, and even the hope, in the long run, of an ultimate synthesis.

The question is: has this move to the dialectic of *praxeis* mediated by matter in fact enabled Sartre to overcome his initial solipsism? Is he able to move on, as he has promised to do, to the concrete reality of men in societies created by history? He has seen much: the *Critique* for all its deviousness and repetitiousness and for all its abstract Hegelian language contains a number of brilliant analyses, as for example in the account of the mass media or in the examples used to introduce the *practico-inert.* But something is wrong still. The net of abstractions by which Sartre would catch history never gets woven tight enough. The human reality slips through. I cannot specify in detail all the evidence for this statement, but several points of varying degrees of vagueness should suffice to indicate that this is indeed what has happened. Consider for one thing the strangely contrived character of the example by which Sartre introduces the "third," on whose *praxis* as assimilating consciousness depend both the development of society itself and of the social scientist who is to understand it. Two utterly separated laborers and an even more utterly detached observer: is that the sort of situation out of which social life is generated? True, human individuals are always, except pre-natally, external to one another in space (and presumably the un-born child can be ignored here, since it is not a "practical organism"). Moreover, that in consciousness also, not only in his spatiality, every man is an island, the Sartre of *Being and Nothingness,* and of the literary corpus of that period, has amply demonstrated. Starting from there, however, is exactly the way *not* to demonstrate the con-trary. If one is to mediate successfully between the for-itself and the for-Others, as I have argued earlier, one must start from the among-Others—where we all start. And that is just where Sartre, looking out his country win-dow, like his childhood forerunner looking out, I rue de Goff, over the roofs of Paris, is *not.* The indwelling of man in the human world, once exiled in favor of the sovereign Cartesian moment of self-contained clarity, cannot be drawn back into existence by any weaving of material links between a mulitiplicity of such isolated units.

Corresponding to the artificiality of this beginning, moreover, is the recurrent uneasiness of the reader (at least of this reader) throughout the *Critique* about the conceptual foundation of mediated reciprocity on which the whole dialectic rests. Relations between two *praxeis* are mediated by matter, then by a third *praxis* mediating the matter-mediated dyad, and so on. But Sartre's insis-tence on such mediation in social structures suggests, by contrast, an *immediate* reciprocity which, in the *praxeis-processus* that generate society, has been dialectically transformed. Is there such a thing? Late in the text there is at least one explicit reference to it—at least as an ab-straction.[45] Moreover, the initial account of "human relations as mediation between different sectors of materiality"—the section in which the basic unit for the dialectic is laid down—suggests that there may be. At least an element in reciprocity is that "I acknowledge the Other *praxis* . . . at the same time that I assimilate him as object into my totalizing project." [46] The two "totalizations," Sartre says, "respect one another." [47] True, this mutuality never comes to rest in unity, for there are *two,* each of which still "integrates the whole universe." [48] But unstable though this mutual recognition is—and who can deny its instability?—it must exist if the whole superstructure is to develop. Yet if, on the other hand, as Sartre also insists they are, all human relations are solely mediated by matter—if it is a question of the for-itself, as a pure subjectivity, linked to other subjectivities by the intervention of the purely inertial, whether of the literally material and inhuman or the quasi-material inhumanity of institutions—then the foundation in mutual respect is missing. Even on Bastille Day the fleeting "we-subject" is an abstraction: triadic relations in which each dyad is indirect cannot themselves achieve concrete reality. Despite the brilliance of many of Sartre's historical descriptions, in short, Merleau-Ponty was right in insisting that he is too much concerned with "totalizing" to acknowledge the very limited, concrete realities on which in fact human history rests. Subjectivity, materiality, totalization: these three counters, so separated, cannot by any dialectical ingenuity reconstitute the human situation. Subjectivity is always already embodied, and our bodily being is always already embedded in a concrete whole, in a natural environment which is at the same time a human world—as (in Whitehead's term) a *concretion* of the universe, not the universe itself. And in this kind of wholeness there is always already some mutuality, however fleeting and however imperiled. Again language is the best example. If there could be no human understanding without speech, the converse also holds. Without mutual understanding there could be no speech, for there would be nothing to mediate, and no medium in which to mediate it.

That Sartre himself recognizes this difficulty in the *Critique,* finally, seems clear from the very fact that he has taken a long detour in his proposed path from the foundation of history to history itself and is trying in his study of Flaubert to reconstruct somehow a single life—a single life, to be sure, within a highly complicated network of institutions already mediated by countless thousands of past *praxeis* and countless movements of the practico-inert—but still a single life in which the immediate reciprocities underlying all these abstract complexities are somehow to become evident. Most tellingly, Sartre even envisages here the founding relation for a human life of a mother's affection for her child. That was what Flaubert lacked, he is sure, and what few infants, he is equally sure, have ever had. But nevertheless love between mother and child exists, and where it exists there is an unquestioning reciprocity between two subjectivities in which individual development can be rooted as in no other ground. So he seems to suggest, even more surprisingly, does sexual love, as distinct from the sado-masochism of *Being and Nothingness.* Whether, so late in the day, Sartre can really assimilate to his philosophy the astonishing phenomenon of love, and hence of a concrete, immediate reciprocity as the coping-stone of human relations, is another question. But its introduction in *The Idiot of the Family* brings into focus once more its absence in all his earlier work, in the dialectic of the practical organism as well as in the ontology of the for-itself and the for-others.

On the whole, then, the answer to our question:

whether in the *Critique* Sartre has succeeded in introducing subjective innovations in his view of man is, as predicted, "Yes" and "No," but more "No" than "Yes." His "practical organism" is still a subjective center of action, not an organism of flesh and blood. It has not been born and grown to human stature in a concrete human world, carried by human affection (as well as hate, which, Sartre admits, by the way, is "a recognition" [*"une reconnaissance"*]).[48] "A man," it has turned out,[49] is "a practical organism living with a multiplicity of similar [organisms] in a field of scarcity." [50] The "with" is still inadequate, and so the "man" in the case is not quite man. Too much is absent from Sartre's original premises; not even so laborious a reconstruction can restore what the initial vision had overlooked.

We have still to ask, in conclusion, whether the most laborious reconstruction of all will succeed where both earlier efforts have failed—and finally, how, as far as Sartre has gone till now, we are to see his philosophical work as a whole in the context, not of a "totalizing" history, but at least in the context of the history of philosophy in the West.

chapter eight: postscript

on first reading the idiot of the family

"Every great philosopher
has only one thought." Does this
Heideggerian tag apply to Sartre? Philosophy is a conversation about fundamental problems, a conversation going back to Thales, in
which, generation after generation, each person takes
his special place. Thus each great thinker, it seems, repre-

of substance and of content, and had become simply the negation of the external world; and on the other hand the external world, shrunken to a subjective series of impressions, was re-objectified in a fashion by taking our special "form of life" as if it were an unquestionable and objective given. Doubtless this is an unfair view of Wittgenstein, both in his early and late phases, but if so, it is scarcely unfair to the practice, some years ago, of many of his alleged disciples. If philosophy in the one demi-tradition was anguished, in the other sector it was trivial.

But things have changed. In its slow and gentlemanly way, even British philosophy has gained a little broader perspective. And, in its more dramatic style, so has the philosophy of the Continent. On both sides, the change has come through attention to the problem that defeated Hume, the problem of the person. Descartes *said* the "mind" was housed in the body more intimately than a pilot in a ship, but, starting where he did, there was little he or his successors could do to explain this mystery. It is here, in the philosophical description and understanding of human beings as embodied persons, that conceptual reform must take, and indeed has taken, its start.

The thinkers and the arguments that have started us on this new course need not concern us here. Our final question is: where does Sartre come into this story? Is it correct to set his philosophy as a whole, with its Cartesian provenance and its Cartesian foundations, in the historical place we have so far assigned to it? Retrospectively from *Being and Nothingness* and, on the whole from the *Critique,* it seems to be so. *Being and Nothingness* does indeed express paradigmatically the agony of twentieth-century thought; the *Critique* does embody in its strained and abstract reasoning the terrible effort of the Cartesian ghost to get out of the machine. But a philosopher may not only present in his *magna opera a* position or *a* crisis in the dialogue that is philosophy; he is a person too, and persons develop. Sartre is still twenty years younger than Plato was when he wrote the *Laws*. Where his whole work as philosopher will stand in the history of thought depends on where he is going now and where he will go from now on. So far the evidence is mixed; one can only hazard a guess.

The view Sartre himself takes of his own development, I have already mentioned in discussing the *Critique.* He has worked, he says, with three concepts: the for-itself, the practical organism, the lived. Basically, we found, however, the second of these did not represent a clear-cut advance on the first. The *Critique* could be translated without significant residue into the dialectic of for-itself/in-itself. There was, indeed, a hint of an "active passivity" inconceivable in the earlier mode; but this was unstable, relapsing, almost instantaneously into the "passive activities" of the practico-inert. Is there now a significant advance in the third stage: in the use of "the lived" as central concept?

The material which could—perhaps—supply us with an answer is massive: the first two of a projected four-volume work in which Sartre undertakes to reconstruct as *lived* the reality of one individual, Gustave Flaubert. It is of course a work of biography (though in part of extremely speculative biography), of psychoanalysis, of literary criticism, and not in the first instance a work of philosophy. But it contains, recurrently, glimpses of Sartrean philosophy—some familiar, some, on the contrary, surprisingly novel. What will issue from all this in the way of a developed new position is, it seems to me, still hard to say. The evidence, if I read it aright, is confusing and contradictory. Let me hazard some brief general remarks about it, and then substantiate my general impression by reference to three particular passages, one illustrating the constancy of Sartre's position, one its ambiguity, and one its novelty.

Sartre's aim in *The Idiot of the Family* is to reconstruct a single life as lived. Is the lived here really a new category? Looking at its usage throughout the two volumes one is inclined, on the whole, to think that it is not. If Sartre in the *Critique* had to march by the most ingenious dialectical detours toward the plain fact of human sociality, here he is straining even more ingeniously and exhaustingly to show how one consciousness can know another in its experienced conscious quality. For of course there *are* only individuals and we cannot pretend to know social action really unless we can demonstrate how one of these existents can somehow enter into the consciousness of another. Moreover, the conceptual units out of which Sartre's reconstruction is effected are the old familiar ones, a combination in fact of the two sets of earlier concepts. "Being" and "Nothingness" are fundamental, perhaps because they suit Flaubert—whose mode of existence is "irrealization"—but also, clearly, because they suit Sartre. The old Sartrean view of imagination is fundamental—again for the same twin reasons. Further, just as emphatically as in the earlier work, man is ideally action, action is *praxis:* acting upon passive matter, and *praxis* is rational. What ails Flaubert is that, first by the *fiat* of his father, who "made" a doomed younger son, then (in Sartre's "fable") by his mother's minute but unloving care, he has been constituted as *passive activity*. In other words, he *is* chiefly through Others and therefore also as Other than himself. We are to learn in a later volume how, in and beyond the seizure of '44, Flaubert freely made himself what he had been made: we are to know his liberty as well as his enslavement—for of course every man *is* freedom, however others may have enslaved him. But the point here is that in the framework of these all too familiar concepts, "the lived" beckons us like the light at the end of a long tunnel. It is something we have to try to get at with deviousness and difficulty as the underside of a life's rationale, the inwardness of an alien consciousness. It is still, I think, that consciousness (of) self which, however we assimilate ourselves to ourselves, escapes the reflective level and looms as emotion, as the magical aspect of our being-in-the-world. "Rational thought," says Sartre, "forges itself in action, or rather *it is action* itself producing its own illumination (*lumières*)." [1] To act, to give reasons, to be free—and therefore to be properly a man—all these are one. From this vantage point I, as free agent, order my world. When rationality breaks down, on the other hand (and in Flaubert's case it had broken down *a priori:* father, mother, elder brother all had made it so), action collapses too (since they are identical). Things happen to me, chance reigns, and I suffer it. "Chance," writes Sartre, "the course of the world interiorized in passion." [2] In other words, it is when I fail to make sense of things, and thus to act on them, that I fall back on feeling: why did this have to happen to me? Feeling is failure, the assimilation to my own consciousness of the horrid fact, the ultimate fact, that I am not my own foundation. In this context "the lived" appears as surrogate for the emotion of the early essay and of *Being and Nothingness.* In this context Sartre still appears as the arch-rationalist in fascinated pursuit of the irrational.

Persisting also, moreover, in the case-study of Flaubert, is the quasi-Marxist slant of Sartre's social philosophy. Not only Flaubert's father and mother made him, but the Family, with its solid bourgeois status founded on the nearly feudal sovereignty of his self-made father. The fact that Flaubert is a member of the bourgeoisie, committed through his father's decree to fealty to his class, loathing it yet inalienably one with it—and thus alienated from himself—all this, again, gives Sartre a theme on which he rings endless, and wholly familiar, changes. From *Being and Nothingness* on, it could have been foreseen, and it is illimitably boring.

Yet throughout the long discursive course of Sartre's reconstruction of Flaubert there are hints here and there of something different. There are hints that a man *might* be not only a mask—*"un personnage"*—but also a living person—*"une personne"*—that if the wretched Gustave was a "useless passion," [3] in search of an illusory and impossible in-itself-for-itself,[4] *man* is not necessarily so. In *Being and Nothingness,* for example, the instant, as moment of lucid self-knowledge and independent action, both in one, haunted the argument as the ideal from which all temporalization is flight. Now Flaubert is accused of allowing temporality (understood as Husserl's "inner time consciousness") to collapse into a succession of instants.[5] He is said to flee temporality toward the instant, not, as in the earlier work we all appeared to do, the instant in the direction of temporality. He cannot really grasp the future, he cannot live it really, but only in dream. Is there then after all in contrast to Flaubert's case, free action in the world that *really* makes sense?

To this reader, moreover, there is a tantalizing though wholly implicit suggestion of philosophic innovation in Sartre's references, throughout the text, to the work of Merleau-Ponty. I have elsewhere described the relation of Sartre's philosophy to that of his former fellow-student as a "dialogue"; but I had thought of the term as only half-applicable, or as metaphorical.[6] Much of Merleau-Ponty's philosophizing, both in his major work and elsewhere, is indeed "dialogue" with Sartre: he wanted, not only to transcend Cartesianism, but particularly to transcend the Cartesianism of Sartre. Over and over, all the way to the notes for the unfinished *Visible and Invisible,* it is an argument of Sartre to which he is seeking to reply, or a Sartrean concept he is seeking to modify. But never before, so far as I know, has Sartre (at least in his published writing) in turn listened and replied. Not only their quarrel, but even Sartre's tribute in *Les Temps Modernes* after Merleau-Ponty's death, suggest this want of response.[7] When they were first reconciled, Sartre reports there, Merleau-Ponty told him he was working on a project inspired by Whitehead's saying: "Nature is in tatters" (*"La nature est en haillons"*). Far from seeing the philosophical implications of this remark, Sartre interprets it in psychoanalytic terms as referring to the death of Merleau-Ponty's mother! Merleau-Ponty's struggle, the post-Cartesian struggle, to found a new image of nature, and of man in nature, seemed to elude him altogether. The "dialogue" of Sartre and Merleau-Ponty was a dialogue between two positions, not between two men. Merleau-Ponty was indeed replying to Sartre, but the reply was unheard. Ten years after his death, the case has altered. True, Sartre still does not reply to Merleau-Ponty's reflections; in *The Idiot of the Family* he is not in any case explicitly writing philosophy. But he quotes him recurrently, tacitly accepting his phrases as if Merleau-Ponty were a writer whose thinking he had wholly assimilated to his own. They are quotations very much by the way; not much is made of them. But that is just the point. Merleau-Ponty's turns of phrase are quoted as one quotes a writer to whom one is very close indeed, a writer whose language one uses because one thinks his thoughts. Yet at the same time Sartre is still speaking his own old language, whose over-abstraction, whose hopeless "totalization," Merleau-Ponty had, in the view of many of us, so tellingly criticized. What will become of this strange assimilation? After putting aside the *Critique* to embark on a four-volume Flaubert, will Sartre put aside the Flaubert to give us a new philosophical work? Will he himself change from the last great Cartesian to one of the pioneering post-Cartesians? Will he give us, what Merleau-Ponty never succeeded in achieving, a fully developed philosophy that will transcend the nihilism in which the Cartesian tradition necessarily issued and which he himself has most fully and rigorously stated? As of this writing, I think it is too soon to say.

Meantime, however, let me close this inconclusive postscript by pointing to three passages in the new Flaubert which illustrate the Janus-faced nature of the philosophical views it implicitly contains.

The first is an analysis of the comic, which takes off from Bergson and adds what Sartre says Bergson missed: the social function of comedy. Bergson was right, he holds, in seeing in the comic the demotion, in relatively harmless circumstances, of the vital to the merely mechanical. The individual who appears as funny is thereby reduced from agency to the level of the inorganic. The social effect of this, moreover, he believes, is to reduce the group to seriality. The comic is indeed "social" in that it is contagious; but it spreads, serially, from one laugher to another, and thus it loosens or even negates the unity of the group in action. This negation, however, is not skeptical in its import; it serves in fact to strengthen "the spirit of seriousness." This would-be eloquent politician stumbles on the platform; how amusing. But the social structure we each believe in is strengthened, not weakened, by his lapse. Dignity is confirmed by this small indignity. But what of the comedian himself? The comic *actor,* Sartre believes, is always felt as less than human. If you pass him on the street surrounded by his family, you get a shock. Can that funny man nevertheless be a serious person, like you or me? Surely not! For the comic, Sartre holds, works essentially by the twin means of *derealization,* from the reality of *praxis* to the imagined level of a pseudo-praxis that fails of its purpose: the conspirators overheard by their enemies or the clown who jumps into the river to get out of the rain; and *dehumanization*—the reduction of the practical agent to puppetry, of the vital to the mechanical, and at the same time of the group to the series (that is, to the practico-inert).[8] Or where, as in Chaplin's films, there is patently humanity in humor, Sartre remarks in a note, it is not pure comedy! Moreover, this one-sidedness of comedy can only be corrected, he says later, by the whole apparatus of dialectical reason.[9]

What is wrong with this picture? It is, I find, an excellent analysis of farce—which is what in fact Sartre will need later on in his reconstruction for the interpretation of Flaubert's "Garçon"—but it misses humor, and misses indeed something essential to the nature of laughter as such: the *ambiguity* of the human situation from which it springs. (I am relying heavily here on Helmuth Plessner's *Laughing and Crying;* if I do not give chapter and verse it is not for want of recognizing my indebtedness to his work.) [10] Sartre does, in connection with the young Flaubert's relation to the comic, mention "ambiguity," but what he is referring to is the ambiguity of what he calls the "tourniquet": the back and forth of a turnstile from which there is no exit. Both sides, the vital and the mechanical, the rational and the absurd, *praxis* and its failure, are undeniable and inescapable; there is "ambiguity" in so far as one swings, in comedy, from one aspect to the other. But in the comic as Sartre sees it they never reverberate together. The ambiguity of two-in-one, which is precisely the duplicity of the eccentric position of man—I *am* the body I take a stand to—this organic ambiguity eludes altogether the scope of Sartre's analysis. But it is just this kind of ambiguity—an ambiguous ambiguity—that characterizes the comic. In puns, for example, other than the crudest word plays, one does not *just* swing back and forth from one meaning to another. One has them both together; as in "a little more than kin and less than kind." What sustains comedy, moreover, as distinct from farce, is not the unequivocal casting down of dignity into indignity, but an ambiguity that casts its spell on both sides, on action *and* its failure, and holds them both together. Even comedies as lighthearted as Shaw's *Arms and the Man* or *You Never Can Tell* illustrate this difference.

The sociality of humor, further, is not, or is not solely, what Sartre declares it to be. It is true, of course, that laughter breaks out when action breaks down, and breaks down in relatively harmless circumstances. But what laughter releases is not merely the contagion of the practico-inert. On the contrary, laughing *together* is one of the most characteristic forms of bona-fide reciprocity. The necessary indirectness of language breaks down in laughter, sometimes indeed because communication fails, but sometimes also because it is too powerful for speech. The laughter of two people in love excludes the rest of the world, but it very much unites the lovers. Or again, the laughter of children—whose verbal competence is still inadequate effectively to support their sociability—is not, I should think, as such separative and serializing. Finally, it seems to me, the clown as a person is not necessarily sub-human: he is lovable and indeed loved, just because he is funny and we see ourselves as funny with him. For *contra* Sartre, it is sometimes, and in some ways always, funny to be human.

Sartre's analysis of the comic, in other words, has just the kind of abstraction, of literalness, of strict rationality, that we might have expected from the author of his two major philosophical works. It "totalizes" too soon and too drastically and thus misses the half-lights that make comedy at its best both so elusive for theory and so satisfying a representation of the ultimate ambiguity of the human state.

Yet there are passages in *The Idiot of the Family* which seem to pre-figure a different Sartre. He uses, as I have already pointed out, his old vocabularies, and indeed fuses them effectively into one vocabulary: Nothing and *praxis,* Being and seriality, here live happily together. And in one place at least he presents, with surprising condensation for so rambling a text, a statement in little of his whole philosophic position—but (and here is the surprise) with overtones, or undertones, that seem to be new. Doubtless there are other passages too in these more than two thousand pages that might convey a similar message; but let me take this one as especially telling, since it happened to strike this particular reader so.

Sartre is again discussing the comic in connection with the emergence of the schoolboy Flaubert's grotesque creation "Le Garçon"; he introduces the topic of *"farces attrapes,"* the paraphernalia of the crude practical joke. These work, he says, on a simple principle: a small collective selects a dupe whom it proceeds to mystify "for a laugh." By so doing it "wishes to conjure away the anguish of being-in-the-world." [11] This anguish, he tells us, "specification of a fundamental anguish which is nothing else but freedom, is born of an inescapable contradiction of our *praxis."* [12] No one, he thinks, in fact lacks the knowledge that "appearances are deceptive," yet, however vigilant we may be in remembering this truth, "the necessities of action—for instance lack of time —oblige us to consider the 'appearances' as manifestations of being." [13]

This is all straight Sartrean doctrine—although it should perhaps be noted in passing: if time is part of scarcity, as indeed it is for any living being, the hope of transcending scarcity and the *practico-inert,* of stabilizing freedom and the "active passivity" of shared action, is exposed as the utopian dream, which, on Sartre's original premises, it is. We are back with the purely negational revolution of the earlier Sartre. That is by the way. Meantime, he tell us here, we do for convenience, and because it conforms to "an original relation of adhesion to the world," and especially if, preoccupied with our pursuits, "we have no time to spare," take the appearances for the reality. But, he continues, "this adhesion, always contestable and silently contested, is not lived without anguish, if not in the particular case, at least as a global feeling of our insertion in the world. It is not a question here of a doubt —explicit and methodic doubt is reassuring at least to a degree—but of a more or less actualized " 'estrangement.' " [14] Usually, he tells us further, we mask this fundamental anguish "by remaining at the surface of ourselves and attaching ourselves to security-inducing constants displayed in external sequences." Thus the basic estrangement which is always there is "hidden by habits or purely and simply *beaten back."* Moreover, he goes on, it should also be considered that "I come to myself 'from horizons,' the world is what separates me from myself and announces me to myself, so that there is in every 'worldly' ('*mondaine*') appearance a disquieting menace and a still more suspect promise which address themselves to me in the depths of my existence." [15] And now comes the theme of the *Critique:* daily labor through the mediation of the material we use and through our tools reveals to us "the coefficient of adversity" in things. This, Sartre reminds us, varies with the mode of production which defines it, and so with the society, "whose type of integration is extrapolated and projected in view of objective unification on the entire aggregate of facts in the world." Thus with Marxist loyalty, he assures us: "nature" is defined in every case as "the material and the limit of current techniques." And finally, in this situation, "the environment announces me as coming to myself *also* through others, that is, as alienation and destiny." [16]

Vintage Sartre, it seems, except that as against the *Critique* destiny is equivalent to alienation: it does not appear here as a destiny *of* freedom, but of its loss. But now Sartre moves on to his present theme, the theme of *one* individual's development:

> In particular the relation-to-the-world has been lived from birth starting from our relation to our surroundings: *the text of the world* is the sense of the familial setting, itself conditioned by institutions; we are not *at ease* in the world except to the degree to which we are *at ease* in our own family—and that "ease", in truth, is nothing but a lesser uneasiness. For that reason, every being which reveals itself as appearance and every appearance which confesses its non-being are in danger of denouncing us as *pure seeming* or of revealing our "abysmal being" as ignominious or terrifying.[17]

And so to the interpretation of the practical joke:

> Thus when an object in the world appears to us awry, it
> is the whole world, ourselves and our relation to the
> world which become suspect: what formerly went without
> saying no longer holds of itself; compromised to the se-
> cret depths of existence, we glimpse a monstrous *other-
> ness of being* which would be the truth of the cosmos
> and of our person.[18]

Here, it seems to me, is the heart of Sartre's philosophy in a paragraph. He goes on then to describe at length
how this fall into uncanniness takes place when he puts
into his coffee a seeming lump of sugar that is in fact mar-
ble (and sinks) or celluloid (and floats). This particular analysis need not concern us; nor need we linger over the
phenomenon of so prolix a writer's putting so pithily what
he has taken volumes, and years, to say. What is sugges-
tive about this passage in view of our present question is
something rather slight, a shadow, somehow, of a different sense of being-in-the-world, a more rooted sense of
existence than had been typical of Sartre's thinking in the
past. True, my "ease" in the world must be "only a lesser
uneasiness"; true, the abyss is always there. But some
phrases are new. "From horizons," which he puts in
quotes, is not, I believe, a usual Sartrean concept. Taken
the other way, *to* a horizon, it is characteristic of Merleau-
Ponty's adaptation of Husserl in the theory of perception.
Admittedly, Sartre uses it here to show that I come to myself "from elsewhere"; he refers in a note to "the menac-
ing promise" of discovering to myself at a distance what I
am, since every object "can put in question the world as a
totality and in consequence myself insofar as I come to
myself from horizons." [19] Yet, I submit, the "horizonal" relation to things is less absolute, less uncompromising,
than the utter negation of the in-itself by the for-itself and
of the for-itself by the in-itself characteristic of *Being and*

Nothingness. True, the for-itself is said to be, as to content, wholly out there; but the relation is one of emptiness to fullness, not of center to horizon: a very different relation. Indeed, it was precisely the sense of being in a landscape, at the center of a perspective, that was missing from the earlier account. The for-itself was over against the world rather than in it. Being in the world as a relation to horizons from which we come suggests, at least to the reader of Merleau-Ponty, a more promising direction for the description of human rootedness in being, which is as ineradicable a part of our condition as is the "estrangement" Sartre has so far preferred to see. More striking, perhaps, further, is the expression "text of the world," reminiscent of the title of Merleau-Ponty's unpublished fragment "The Prose of the World." (This will soon become, in relation to Flaubert and the Garçon, "the farce of the world," but that is another story.) If the world is a text to be read, then, again, the explicit Otherness of reader and read, of consciousness and matter, may yet be overcome. In short, if we put this together with Sartre's very Merleau-Pontyian account of "being in language" earlier in this work, we may hope at least that he is moving to something like a theory of interpretation as the model for being-in-the-world, a theory in which the *implicit* grasp of sense underlying all *explicit* reading is necessarily included. Such a theory, in other words, in which not "negation of being" but "understanding of being" is fundamental, would alter the self-directedness of the non-thetic consciousness (of) self and admit that our way of "living" the world—and ourselves—is directed primarily *from* clues within ourselves, in our inescapably bodily-and-mental being, *to* processes in the world, of which, through these clues, we are constantly striving to make sense. To ignore this vector in non-thetic consciousness, we noticed much earlier, was Sartre's first misstep at the very start of *Being and Nothingness*. But there are, I would suggest, hints in *The Idiot of the Family* that he may yet set his course in a different direction and so evade after all the catastrophic issue of his earlier premises. I may be making too much, in connection with the passage just quoted, of very slight shadows indeed; but there is something about his way of putting things that has changed. For one who is habituated to the analysis of arguments rather than of style the difference is hard to specify; if the reader fails to feel it, especially in paraphrase and translation, I can only say: Sorry; I do. And through these two long volumes there are recurrent places where despite the constancy of the main conceptual framework the same impression of novelty comes through.

Sometimes, indeed, though rarely, the change is very explicit. One case is the passage on language already referred to. I have also referred already to what appears to be Sartre's altered view of love, which seems in turn to be related to a (possibly) altered concept of the person—or rather to *a* concept of the person. Previously, in common with other modern philosophers, that is just what he lacked.

Sometimes, indeed, it still appears that there are only "personnages," not persons. This was in effect the theme of *The Transcendence of the Ego,* and of the doctrine of "the circuit of selfness" in *Being and Nothingness*. It is still with us, conspicuously in the case of Flaubert himself, the very fabric of whose being, Sartre argues, is insincerity. The gap between authentic action, if it were possible (as for Flaubert it is not), and the construct of himself that he presents to others as well as to himself: this gap is forever unbridgeable. But is the doom of Flaubert the doom of Everyman? Is bad faith after all *the* human condition? In the *Critique,* we noticed, one seeks uneasily for information about the *immediate* reciprocity which Sartre obscurely hints at as the alternative to those mediated relations of men to one another on which society is built. In *The Idiot of the Family,* similarly, the philosophical reader is bound to wonder about the hints occurring here and there which suggest that not every man need be a mask. The two problems, of reciprocity and of personal authenticity, of course, are intimately related, since bodily being with others in a social world is the necessary condition of becoming myself. It was this dimension of human existence, we found in *Being and Nothingness,* that Sartre had most grievously misread. What does he make of it here? What does he make, in particular, of the two cases of bodily being together that most conspicuously characterize the development of a human person: maternity (or its reciprocal: infancy) and sex? As to the first, his interpretation is ambiguous. In constructing his legend of Mme. Flaubert and little Gustave, Sartre suggests at least a happier alternative. Flaubert's dislike of himself, he holds, issues from his mother's loveless care of an unwanted infant. Some few babies, he says, *are* wanted by their mothers, and they will be able to *act.* So existence as a free agent seems to be constituted, or enabled, by maternal affection. But sometimes he characterizes this enviable state in other terms: he speaks of the inordinate *vanity* of the wanted child, who is unquestioningly the center of the universe, as for example Flaubert's elder brother doubtless was: a mediocre nonentity made Somebody by the position his father gave him, the very quintessence of the stuffed man, the hollow man. So the situation may be still in Sartre's view as hopeless as ever; the upshot is not clear. There is, however, at least one passage on sexual love that quite unambiguously contradicts the sado-masochistic thesis of *Being and Nothingness.* Sartre is talking about Flaubert's talk with Louise Colet before she seduced him (*sic;* Sartre emphasizes the way in which Flaubert's passivity demanded that women possess him rather than he them). He writes:

> The absurdity of Chamfort is to use the word "contact," which applies to caresses—and not even to all of them —when the essential of love is that a man, *enters, wholly complete* (*tout entier*), a woman who receives him, herself *wholly complete* (*tout entière*), which supposes that, in receiving him, she closes herself on him, contains him and penetrates him in her turn with what Doña Prouhèze calls "the taste I have." Love is not mute, especially when it is silent: through the flesh, its "taste," its smells, its elasticity, its colors and its forms, through the grain of a skin, the distribution of hair, the total but ineffable sense of the person is transmitted to the other person; from one side and the other, this sense becomes a material and silent condensation of all language, of all the phrases said and to be said, of all the actions done and to be done. The two naked bodies, in the present instant, are the equivalent of an infinite discourse which they promise, transcend and instantly make useless.[20]

Is this the man for whom language was a form of seduction, for whom the Other was doomed to be either torturer or victim? Sartre himself has said that he has changed, chiefly, by his own account, because he found politics. It was the Spanish Civil War, then Hitler, that took him out of his preoccupation with the single for-itself, that made him loathe *Nausea* and *The Flies* with their self-centered heroes. And it is Algeria and Vietnam that have kept him there. But, alas, the Sartre of political philosophy, the Marxist Sartre, remains an abstraction, and he remains an abstraction because, believing in the rootedness of all social life in individual *praxis,* he has nevertheless no theory of such *praxis* that can found society on any concrete immediacy of human beings existing with one another, in fellowship rather than in mutual isolation. Not that such fellowship is frequent or permanent; I am not suggesting some rosy idealism as the corrective of Sartrean gloom. We *do* live mostly and most of the time in alienation from ourselves and others; we *are* swept along by the dialectic of the *practico-inert*. Yet if there were no other possibility, no moments, however rare, of a true and more immediate communion, there would be no humanity, not even an unattainable ideal from which we might inevitably fall. In shame and fear, we saw, the Other looms up immediately, demoting me from maker of the world to object in his world. These are the passions which confirm loneliness, which underline the truth that each man is fated both to try to make himself and to fail to do so. But there are also passions which grow out of mutuality: out of a space in which two persons exist together, and in which each becomes himself out of and in that coexistence. The love of mother and infant, when it exists—not always, indeed, but not perhaps as rarely as Sartre suggests—is one such passion, the one which founds, or ought to found, the lived spatiality of each of us. Another is the mature coming together of two individuals in sexual love. Even hatred, the contrary of love, acknowledges, as shame and fear do not, the existence together, if in mutual rejection, of two persons: true enemies can respect one another as true lovers do. (I noted earlier that Sartre himself acknowledges the latter point in a passing remark in the *Critique*.) [21] What is essential in all such cases is the social space—the *Mitwelt*—which I and Thou together have cleared for each of us. Only in such a space is human temporality, and therefore history, personal or social, possible. If Sartre has come to see this, and if he is yet to give philosophical expression to this insight, then the Cartesian Sartre will have been indeed transcended, and the man of words will have become something he was not, or did not earlier know he was to be. He will have conquered his own rationalism, he will have discovered in earnest, and expressed philosophically, the *active passivity* mentioned, indeed, but scarcely used, in the *Critique*.[22] The place of Sartre in the history of philosophy is at least that of the last great Cartesian; for that alone his philosophical work is worth reading, again and again. What his place in intellectual history will finally be, however, is a question still to be answered. On first reading *The Idiot of the Family* one is moved to puzzlement and to patience: we must wait and see.

BIBLIOGRAPHY

Recent works on Sartre have provided detailed bibliographies which I could not hope to match, and which in any case would be out of place at the conclusion of this introductory volume. I am therefore listing only (1) philosophical works of Sartre available in English; (2) a few nonphilosophical works, also translated, on which I have drawn fairly heavily; (3) untranslated works that I have been dealing with in some detail; and (4) a very small selection of the many English titles on Sartre, some to which (as indicated in the text) I am myself indebted, and some that I think might help the English-speaking reader in search of some other introductory approach to supplement or correct my own. For those in search of more, and more exact, information, the definitive bibliography to 1970 is:

Contat, Michel, and Rybalka, Michel. *Les Ecrits de Sartre*. Paris: Gallimard, 1970. In English there is a very careful list of books and articles by and on Sartre at the close of Joseph H. MacMahon's *Humans Being,* which, despite the scandalous title, is a very useful work.

Philosophical Works of Sartre Available in English (as of August 1971)

Being and Nothingness. Translated by Hazel Barnes. New York: Philosophical Library, 1956.

The Emotions: Outline of a Theory. Translated by Bernard Frechtman. New York: Philosophical Library, 1948. (A very unreliable translation; there was a better one by P. Mairet, which is out of print.)

Imagination. Translated by Forrest Williams. Ann Arbor: University of Michigan Press, 1962. (This is the historical portion of Sartre's work on imagination; for his own view see *The Psychology of Imagination,* below.)

Literary and Philosophical Essays. Translated by Annette Michelson. New York: Criterion Books, 1955.

The Philosophy of Jean-Paul Sartre. Edited by R. D. Cumming. New York: Random House, 1965. (Contains passages from the *Critique* not yet available in English elsewhere.)

The Psychology of Imagination. Translated by Bernard Frechtman. London: Rider, 1950.

Search for a Method. Translated by Hazel Barnes. New York: Knopf, 1963. (Translation of *Question de méthode*.)

The Transcendence of the Ego. Translated by Forrest Williams and Robert Kirkpatrick. New York: Farrar, Straus, and Giroux, 1957.

Some Other Works (in Translation)

The Flies. Translated by Stuart Gilbert. New York: Knopf, 1947.

Nausea. Translated by Lloyd Alexander. Norfolk, Conn.: New Directions, 1950.

Saint Genet, Actor and Martyr. Translated by Bernard Frechtman. New York: Braziller, 1963.

What is Literature? Translated by Bernard Frechtman. New York: Philosophical Library, 1949.

The Words. Translated by Bernard Frechtman. New York: Braziller, 1964.

Works Discussed in Some Detail, Available in English

Critique de la raison dialectique. Paris: Gallimard, 1960.

L'Idiot de la Famille. Volumes I and II. Paris: Gallimard, 1971. Volume III, 1972.

"L'Ecrivain et sa Langue," *Revue d'Esthétique,* XVIII (1965), 306–334.

Selected Works on the Philosophy of Sartre

Aron, Raymond. "Sartre's Marxism," in *Marxism and the Existentialists.* New York: Harper & Row, 1969, pp. 164–176.

Cranston, Maurice. *Jean-Paul Sartre.* New York: Grove Press, 1962.

Cumming, R. D. Introduction to *The Philosophy of Jean-Paul Sartre.* (See above.)

Desan, Wilfrid. *The Tragic Finale: An Essay on the Philosophy of Jean-Paul Sartre.* Cambridge, Mass.: Harvard University Press, 1954.

Desan, Wilfrid. *The Marxism of Jean-Paul Sartre.* Garden City, N.Y.: Doubleday, 1965.

Laing, R. D., and Cooper, D. G. *Reason and Violence: A Decade of Sartre's Philosophy, 1950–60.* New York: Humanities Press, 1964. (Summaries of Sartre's work: little exegesis.)

MacMahon, Joseph H. *Humans Being, The World of Jean-Paul Sartre.* Chicago: University of Chicago Press, 1971. (Chiefly literary, but also dealing with the philosophy.)

Murdoch, Iris. *Sartre, Romantic Rationalist.* New Haven: Yale University Press, 1953.

Thody, Philip. *Sartre.* London: Studio Vista, 1971. (A biographical introduction.)

NOTES

Chapter One

[1] J. P. Sartre, *The Words,* trans. Bernard Frechtman (Green-wich, Conn., 1964), p. 25 (paperback edition). The title should have been rendered *Words,* but the translation of the text is neverthe-less reliable—though no English could adequately render the style of the original.

[2] *Loc. cit.*

[3] *Ibid.,* p. 30.

[4] *Ibid.,* p. 38.

[5] *Ibid.,* p. 30.

[6] *Ibid.,* p. 114.

[7] *Loc. cit.*

[8] *Loc. cit.*

[9] J. P. Sartre, *What is Literature?,* trans. Bernard Frechtman (London, 1950), p. 5.

[10] J. P. Sartre, *What is Literature?*, trans. Bernard Frechtman (London, 1950), p. 5.

[11] *Ibid.*, p. 6.

[12] *Loc. cit.*

[13] *Loc. cit.*

[14] *Loc. cit.*

[15] *The Words*, p. 31.

[16] *What is Literature?*, p. 6.

[17] *The Words*, p. 159.

[18] *Ibid.*, p. 21.

[19] Simone de Beauvoir, *The Prime of Life*, trans. Peter Green (London, 1962), p. 16.

[20] *The Words*, p. 38.

[21] J. P. Sartre, "L'Ecrivain et sa Langue," *Revue d'Esthétique*, XVIII (1965), 306–334.

[22] *Ibid.*, 333.

[23] J. P. Sartre, *The Transcendence of the Ego*, trans. Forrest Williams and Robert Kirkpatrick (New York, 1957).

[24] J. P. Sartre, *The Psychology of Imagination* (New York, 1948).

[25] J. P. Sartre, Introduction to Jean Genet, *Our Lady of the Flowers* (London, 1964), p. 53.

[26] J. P. Sartre, *Situations*, trans. Benita Eisler (Greenwich, Conn., 1965), p. 125.

[27] J. P. Sartre, *Sketch of a Theory of the Emotions*, trans. P. Mairet (London, 1962), p. 125.

[28] *Ibid.*, pp. 61–62.

[29] *Ibid.*, pp. 62–63.

[30] *Ibid.*, p. 83.

[31] *The Words*, p. 38. *"Ludion,"* "bottle imp," is synonymous with *"litote,"* which can be rendered "Cartesian diver"! The following chapters should make clear the rich implications of this epithet for Sartrean philosophy.

Chapter Two

[1] Cf. J. P. Sartre, "Cartesian Freedom," in *Literary and Philosophical Essays*, trans. Annette Michelson (New York, 1955), pp. 180–197.

[2] J. P. Sartre, *Being and Nothingness*, trans. Hazel Barnes (New York, 1956), p. 254.

[3] *Loc. cit.*

[4] *Loc. cit.*

[5] *Loc. cit.*

[6] *Ibid.,* pp. 110 ff.

Chapter Three

[1] G. W. F. Hegel, *Die Phänomenologie des Geistes,* Philosophische Bibliothek (Leipzig, 1928), p. 50.

[2] J. P. Sartre, *Being and Nothingness,* p. 239.

[3] Louis Mackay, "The Poetry of Inwardness," in G. A. Schrader, Jr. (ed.), *Existential Philosophers: Kierkegaard to Merleau-Ponty* (New York, 1967), pp. 45–107.

[4] Søren Kierkegaard, "The Sickness unto Death," in *Fear and Trembling; The Sickness unto Death,* trans. Walter Lowrie (Garden City, N.Y., 1954), p. 146.

[5] J. P. Sartre, *Being and Nothingness,* p. 78.

[6] Søren Kierkegaard, *Loc. cit.*

[7] J. P. Sartre, *Being and Nothingness,* p. 89.

[8] Søren Kierkegaard, *Sickness unto Death,* p. 147.

[9] J. P. Sartre, *Being and Nothingness,* p. 87.

[10] *Ibid.,* p. 597.

[11] J. P. Sartre, *Critique de la Raison Dialectique* (Paris, 1960), p. 22.

[12] *Ibid.,* p. 23.

[13] *Loc. cit.*

[14] *Loc. cit.*

Chapter Four

[1] J. P. Sartre, *Being and Nothingness,* p. lvii.

[2] *Ibid.,* p. xlvii.

[3] *Ibid.*

[4] *Ibid.*

[5] *Loc. cit.*

[6] *Loc. cit.*

[7] *Loc. cit.*

[8] *Ibid.,* p. xlix.

[9] *Loc. cit.*

[10] *Loc. cit.* My italics.

[11] *Ibid.,* p. 1.

[12] *Loc. cit.*

[13] *Ibid.,* p. li.

14 J. P. Sartre, *Being and Nothingness*, p. lii. My italics.

15 *Loc. cit.*

16 *Ibid.*, p. liii.

17 *Ibid.*, p. lv.

18 *Ibid.*, p. lvi.

19 *Ibid.*, p. lxvii.

20 *Ibid.*, p. 38.

21 *Ibid.*, p. 45.

22 *Ibid.*, p. 77. My italics.

23 *Ibid.*, p. 90.

24 *Ibid.*, p. 129.

25 *Ibid.*, p. 93.

26 *Ibid.*, p. 102.

27 *Ibid.*, p. 149.

28 *Ibid.*, p. 142.

29 *Ibid.*, p. 218.

30 *Ibid.*, p. 194.

Chapter Five

1 J. P. Sartre, *Being and Nothingness*, trans. Hazel Barnes (New York, 1956), p. 221.

2 *Ibid.*, p. 223.

3 *Ibid.*, p. 273.

4 *Ibid.*, p. 282.

5 *Ibid.*, p. 277.

6 *Loc. cit.*

7 *Ibid.*, p. 359.

8 *Ibid.*, p. 324.

9 *Loc. cit.*

10 *Ibid.*, p. 325.

11 *Ibid.*, p. 346.

12 *Loc. cit.*

13 M. Merleau-Ponty, *The Phenomenology of Perception*, Part One, Ch. Six.

14 J. P. Sartre, *Being and Nothingness*, trans. Hazel Barnes (New York, 1956), p. 446.

15 *Ibid.*, p. 447.

16 *Loc. cit.*

17 *Ibid.*, pp. 447–448.

18 *Ibid.*, p. 449.

[19] *Loc. cit.*

[20] *Loc. cit.*

Chapter Six

[1] Raymond Aron, "Sartre's Marxism," in *Marxism and the Existentialists* (New York: Harper & Row, 1969), Dialogue Three.

[2] J. P. Sartre, *Critique de la Raison Dialectique,* p. 339. My italics.

[3] Cf. (at a different level) Sartre's comparison of his own method with Kant's in *L'Idiot de la Famille* (Paris, 1971), Vol. I, pp. 653–654.

[4] J. P. Sartre, *Critique,* p. 107.

[5] E.g., *ibid.,* p. 509, and then pp. 658–659.

[6] *Ibid.,* pp. 525–526 (My italics); cf., e.g., pp. 281, 411.

[7] *Ibid.,* p. 635.

[8] *Ibid.,* p. 634.

[9] *Loc. cit.* My italics.

[10] *Ibid.,* p. 688.

[11] *Loc. cit.*

[12] *Ibid.,* pp. 200–225.

[13] *Ibid.,* pp. 225–279.

[14] *Ibid.,* pp. 286–305.

[15] *Ibid.,* pp. 306–377.

[16] *Ibid.,* pp. 279–280.

[17] *Ibid.,* p. 285.

[18] *Ibid.,* p. 420.

[19] Cf. *ibid.,* pp. 487–488; earlier also, Sartre's treatment of the dyad turning triad (see below, Ch. VII) is taken explicitly from Lévy-Strauss.

[20] *Ibid.,* p. 494.

[21] *Ibid.,* p. 462.

[22] C. Audry, *Sartre et la réalité humaine* (Paris, 1966).

[23] J. P. Sartre, *Critique,* p. 533.

[24] *Ibid.,* p. 560.

[25] In S. Kierkegaard, *Philosophical Fragments,* trans. David F. Swenson, revised by Howard V. Hong (Princeton, 1962).

Chapter Seven

[1] "Sartre: An Interview," *New York Review of Books,* XIV (6), March 26, 1970.

[2] Iris Murdoch, "Of God and Good," in *The Anatomy of Knowledge* (Amherst, Mass.: University of Massachusetts Press, 1969), p. 239.

[3] See e.g., J. P. Sartre, *Critique de la Raison Dialectique,* pp. 166, 174.

[4] *Ibid.,* p. 535.

[5] *Ibid.,* p. 168.

[6] *Ibid.,* p. 248.

[7] *Ibid.,* p. 175.

[8] *Ibid.,* p. 166. My italics.

[9] *Ibid.,* p. 435.

[10] *Ibid.,* p. 130n.

[11] *Loc. cit.*

[12] *Ibid.,* p. 277. My italics.

[13] *Ibid.,* p. 206.

[14] J. P. Sartre, *L'Idiot de la Famille* (Paris, 1971), Vol. I, p. 141.

[15] See my account of Portmann's work in M. Grene, *Approaches to a Philosophical Biology* (New York, 1969), Chapter One.

[16] See *ibid.,* Chapter Two.

[17] J. P. Sartre, *Critique,* p. 249.

[18] *Ibid.,* p. 248.

[19] *Loc. cit.*

[20] *Loc. cit.*

[21] *Ibid.,* p. 250.

[22] See e.g., *ibid.,* pp. 261, 361, 369, 435, 507, 535.

[23] *Ibid.,* p. 281.

[24] *Ibid.,* pp. 231–232, 250.

[25] *Ibid.,* p. 431.

[26] *Ibid.,* p. 433.

[27] *Ibid.,* p. 431.

[28] *Ibid.,* p. 142.

[29] *Loc. cit.*

[30] *Ibid.,* p. 141.

[31] *Ibid.,* p. 286n.

[32] *Loc. cit.*

[33] *Loc. cit.* My italics.

[34] *Loc. cit.*

[35] R. Aron, "Sartre's Marxism."

36 J. P. Sartre, *Critique,* p. 585.

37 *Ibid.,* p. 47.

38 J. P. Sartre, *L'Idiot de la Famille,* Vol. I, p. 142n.

39 J. P. Sartre, *Critique,* p. 321.

40 *Loc. cit.*

41 *Ibid.,* p. 323.

42 *Ibid.,* p. 181.

43 *Ibid.,* p. 180.

44 *Ibid.,* p. 182.

45 *Ibid.,* p. 688.

46 *Ibid.,* p. 192.

47 *Ibid.,* p. 193.

48 *Loc. cit.*

49 *Ibid.,* p. 192.

50 *Ibid.,* p. 688.

Chapter Eight

1 J. P. Sartre, *L'Idiot de la Famille,* Vol. II, p. 1372.

2 *Ibid.,* p. 1692.

3 *Ibid.,* p. 1591.

4 *Ibid.,* p. 1376.

5 *Ibid.,* pp. 1645 ff.

6 Cf. M. Grene, "The Aesthetic Dialogue of Sartre and Merleau-Ponty," *Journal of the British Society for Phenomenology,* I (2), May 1970.

7 J. P. Sartre, "Merleau-Ponty vivant," *Les Temps Modernes,* 1961, 17n, 184–185, 304–376.

8 J. P. Sartre, *L'Idiot,* Vol. I, pp. 811–824.

9 *Ibid.,* Vol. II, p. 1440.

10 H. Plessner, *Laughing and Crying,* trans. J. Churchill and M. Grene, Evanston, Ill., 1970.

11 J. P. Sartre, *L'Idiot,* Vol. II, pp. 1311–1312.

12 *Ibid.,* p. 1312.

13 *Loc. cit.*

14 *Loc. cit.*

15 *Loc. cit.*

16 *Loc. cit.*

17 Loc. cit., "the text of the world." My italics.

18 *Ibid.,* p. 1313.

19 *Ibid.,* p. 1312n.

[20] J. P. Sartre, *L'Idiot,* Vol. II, pp. 1274.

[21] I am grateful to Professor Donald Lowe of San Francisco State College for a conversation on this matter.

[22] The phrase in fact recurs in *The Idiot of the Family* in connection with Flaubert's own assimilation of his own neurosis (1742 ff). We are promised further interpretation of this event in a future volume.

ABOUT THE AUTHOR

Marjorie Grene is Professor of Philosophy at the University of California, Davis. She studied in Germany in 1931–1933, took her Ph.D. at Radcliffe in 1935, and has taught at the universities of Chicago, Leeds, Belfast, and Texas, and at Boston University. Her earlier books include *Dreadful Freedom* (reissued as *Introduction to Existentialism*), *Heidegger, A Portrait of Aristotle, The Knower and the Known,* and *Approaches to a Philosophical Biology.*